# BodyMAGIC!

the comprehensive guide to end
compulsive, emotional eating **forever** with

*health, healing and happiness*

by
**Chinmayi Dore**

# Welcome to BodyMAGIC!

One important thing to do before you get started...

This is not just a book for reading. The MAGIC! is in the completion of the exercises. You may be happy to write in the book itself. It is yours after all!

Alternatively, I have prepared an Exercise Workbook which you can keep separate to the book if you prefer.

Just put the following link in your browser to download and print it off. It's printer-friendly so it won't use up too much ink and condensed into around 25 pages. If you need more space for completing the exercises, you can always use the back of the pages.

*chinmayi.leadpages.net/workbook-opt-in/*

When you enter this link, scroll down and find out why this workbook is fundamental to your success. I want you to have the absolute best chance of success with this programme. The exercises should be completed fully before moving on to the next chapters.

### *I'm ready when you are!*

In peace, Chinmayi x

## Disclaimer

The information in this book is designed to provide helpful information on overcoming emotional overeating. This book is not meant to be used, nor should it be used, to diagnose or treat any medical condition. For diagnosis or treatment of any medical problem, you should consult your doctor. The author is not responsible for any specific health or allergy needs that may require medical supervision and is not liable for any damages or negative consequences from any treatment, action, application or preparation, to any person reading or following the information in this book. References and Resources are provided for informational purposes only and do not constitute endorsement of any of their content. Readers should be aware that the reference and resource information listed in this book may change.

*To my mothers*

Janet whose living and passing inspired me so much and
Mother Earth or M.E. - always connected but not always aware

# How BodyMAGIC! is transforming lives

*How often have you started a new 'diet' and realised that you have spent your whole adult life doing this? How often have you wondered if this behaviour, this over and over and over again battle with your weight will go on? How often have you thought there will be a miraculous 'cure' just around the corner and that you will live the rest of your life as that skinnier 'sorted' person? If you are like me then you will understand where I am coming from...*

*I read this book with an open mind and the usual scepticism that I approach all potential life changes, only to find that the advice in these pages has allowed me to let go of the way that I have always thought about food and life in general. Quite simply, I just don't think about eating in the same way, there is no panic, no guilt, no anger and no disappointment whenever I eat. And my body is slowly beginning to listen and let go of the weight that I have carried since childhood.*

*Please read this book and please take on this advice. It comes from a real person with the same issues as you and I. It is not a quick fix and it is not a fad, you will have to do a lot of thinking for yourself but it can, and does, change your outlook dramatically for the best.*

*This might just be the one thing that changes your life.*

*- Mary Patterson*

*BodyMAGIC! takes the stigma out of emotional eating and gives you a new approach to healing. Reading BodyMAGIC! I realised for the first time, I'm not alone and no longer have to be ashamed about being an emotional eater. This is a beautifully written book with a revolutionary approach to healing. It is honest, inspiring and it works!*

*- Angie Parsons*

*Even though I don't really know Chinmayi it is clear to me that she has poured so much of herself into writing this book. I can feel how difficult and painful some of her experiences have been while she was travelling this self-same journey. She's one brave lady! This isn't just a book or programme of practical strategies, it has been written from her deepest heart and soul, and she's there, with you on every single page. That's what makes it so powerful.*

*This book is iconoclastic! - it challenges the beliefs, customs and opinions that most people in society accept. Chinmayi herself is not afraid to challenge the widely held views about dieting and weight loss.*

*- Laura Hancock*

*Something has happened to me since I have been reading BodyMAGIC! and talking to Chinmayi regularly. I have not 'started' a diet or thought constantly about what I want to eat. Instead I am thinking about how I am living and how it affects my environment - shopping at the market to avoid so much packaging, the fruit and vegetables are fresher, and cheaper too! I have always enjoyed cooking but now I feel a bit more creative as I make meals out of all the produce I have bought. I'm trying to shop locally wherever possible, which might be a bit more expensive, but I don't buy as much now. I feel free of guilt, of greed, of lethargy. I feel energetic and focused. I have actually lost seven pounds in six weeks, without even trying. I have done it honestly. But I also feel healthier and happier too! I have found answers to questions that I didn't think were relevant. Like why do we buy all those strange chocolate bars and salty snacks at a diet club and munch away with lots of other people and then talk about 'making healthy choices'? And then we pay to be weighed and applauded or not! BodyMAGIC! is changing the way I look at lots of different aspects of my life, not just food. Thank you.*

*- Brigit Smythe*

*This book and its calm, reflective approach has deeply altered the way I feel about food. Its methodical application of carefully considered exercises gave me permission to let go of some long held negative beliefs about food, myself and the way I ate.*

*- Layla Carter*

# Contents

Acknowledgements ........................................................ 19

Foreword ................................................................ 21

Introduction ............................................................ 23

**Emotions Explained** .................................................. 29

    Exercise ........................................................ 31

    How Emotions Manifested ......................................... 32

    The BodyMAGIC! Emotion Elevator ................................. 34

    "Why did I do it?" .............................................. 36

    Ideal ........................................................... 39

**The 7 Spells of BodyMAGIC!** ......................................... 41

    The Nine Reminders .............................................. 43

    Exercise ........................................................ 47

**Discipline and Willpower** ........................................... 49

    The first time we need Discipline is when we are challenged ...... 49

    So what is your investment? ..................................... 52

    Exercise ........................................................ 53

    Make a Vision Board! ............................................ 53

**Journaling for Joy!** ................................................ 55

    1. Gratitude Diary .............................................. 56

    2. Your Journal ................................................. 56

    Creative Solutions .............................................. 57

    Exercise ........................................................ 58

    Get Journaling! ................................................. 58

**MeditationMAGIC!** ................................................... 59

    The Science and the Stigma ...................................... 59

    How it has worked for me ........................................ 60

    So What is Meditation? .......................................... 62

    Benefits of Meditation .......................................... 62

Methods of Meditation ........................................................63

Anapanasati ....................................................................63

Exercise .........................................................................65

**Support or Solitude?** .....................................................**69**

The People Who Might Help ..............................................69

The Lucky Ones ..............................................................72

Exercise .........................................................................74

**Food Facts** ..................................................................**75**

Knowledge for MAGIC! .....................................................75

Protein Principles ............................................................77

Carbohydrates Credentials ...............................................78

Fat Facts .......................................................................80

Vitamins ........................................................................83

Minerals ........................................................................85

Fibre - Friend or Foe? ......................................................86

My N-eat Nineteen ...........................................................87

Water ............................................................................89

**YogaMAGIC!** ...............................................................**91**

History and Philosophy in Brief ..........................................91

What will it do for me? ......................................................94

Notes on Practice ............................................................96

Tips on Breathing in Yoga ..................................................97

Simple Yet Profound Yoga Practices ....................................97

**Nature Calls!** ...............................................................**105**

Exercise .........................................................................107

Sami Chakuay ..................................................................107

The Elements ..................................................................108

Natural Food, Natural Health .............................................110

Exercise .........................................................................114

Natural Water, Natural Hydration ........................................115

Natural Air, Natural Breath .................................................116

Exercise .........................................................................117

Natural Exercise, Natural Fitness ........................................118

Natural Sleep, Natural Relaxation ........................................121

Natural Medicine, Natural Healing ........................................ 123
Natural Cleaning, Natural Waste ......................................... 128
Natural Beauty, Natural Skin ............................................... 131

**Eating Habits and Addictions** ............................................. **135**

What is an addiction? ........................................................ 135
Exercise 1 ......................................................................... 138
Other Addictions ............................................................... 138
Addiction to Food .............................................................. 138
Hope for the Overeater ...................................................... 140
Exercise 2 ......................................................................... 141
Eating Habits ..................................................................... 141
Exercise 3 ......................................................................... 143
Reasons for Overeating ..................................................... 143

**Intuitive Eating and Mindful Munching** ............................... **147**

Awareness of the Diet Trap ............................................... 147
Understanding your Appetite ............................................. 148
Friendship with Food ......................................................... 148
Respect for Cravings ......................................................... 148
Peace in the Present .......................................................... 148
Knowledge of Hunger ........................................................ 149
Learning to Leave ............................................................. 149
Nature's Way ..................................................................... 149
Emotional Healing ............................................................. 149
Exercise ............................................................................ 151
How to Munch Mindfully ..................................................... 151

**Fads and Fallacies - Myths and Truths** ............................... **153**

Research ........................................................................... 156
The Famine Response ....................................................... 157
The Novelty Factor ............................................................ 158
The Latest Offerings .......................................................... 159
My Time for Change .......................................................... 159
The world of pure energy and bliss .................................... 160
My weight stabilised! ......................................................... 161
The 10 Principal Understandings of BodyMAGIC! ............... 163

Exercise ............................................................. 164

Affirming Energy ................................................. 164

## Stress and the Mind ...................................... 165

Recognising Stress ............................................. 165

Types and Causes .............................................. 165

What Happens When You Stress ......................... 166

Causes of Stress ................................................ 167

Stress and Eating ............................................... 167

Back to the Old Ways? ....................................... 168

Mind over Matters .............................................. 168

1. The Conscious Mind ....................................... 169

2. The Unconscious Mind .................................... 169

3. The Subconscious Mind .................................. 170

Exercises .......................................................... 172

## A Review - Time for Reflection ....................... 175

Exercises .......................................................... 178

## Traditional Medicine ...................................... 187

Relaxation mode ................................................ 188

Yoga Therapy .................................................... 188

Aromatherapy .................................................... 189

Crystal/Chakra Therapy ..................................... 190

Massage ........................................................... 192

Kinesiology ....................................................... 193

Reiki ................................................................. 193

Shamanic Healing .............................................. 193

## Emotional Freedom Technique (EFT) ............... 197

Some Benefits of Tapping for Health ................... 199

How to Tap! ....................................................... 200

EFT Points Map ................................................. 201

Getting to the Real Reason ................................. 202

Wise Words ....................................................... 203

Integrating EFT .................................................. 204

**The Enneagram** .................................................................................**205**

    My Enneagram Experience .........................................................206

    Basic Observations of the Nine Enneagram Types ....................206

    Delving into Discovery ...............................................................208

    Incorporating the Enneagram ....................................................208

    Exercise .....................................................................................209

**The Seven Seldom Sins** ....................................................**211**

    Personal Power .........................................................................212

    Never Say Never! ......................................................................212

    Seven Sins (because none of us are perfect!) ...........................213

**See it! Say it! Give it! Get it!** ...........................................**225**

    Defining Health Healing and Happiness ....................................225

    Be careful what you wish for! .....................................................230

    Exercise .....................................................................................231

    How to Affirm to Attract .............................................................231

    You Gotta Give To Get ..............................................................232

**The Gremlins in your Gut** ..................................................**235**

    Gut Instincts ..............................................................................235

    1.   Candida Albicans ...............................................................236

    2.   Parasites ............................................................................238

    Exercise .....................................................................................239

    Recommended Treatments .......................................................239

    Going Deeper ............................................................................239

    Exercise .....................................................................................241

    Letting go ..................................................................................241

**Going Hungry** ....................................................................**243**

    Fear of Hunger of the Overeater ...............................................243

    Hungry, Starving or Peckish? ....................................................243

    The Hunger Scale ......................................................................244

    Hungry or Angry? ......................................................................245

    Exercise .....................................................................................246

    Fantasy Feelings .......................................................................246

Water and Hunger ................................................................ 247

The Famine Response .......................................................... 248

## Ritual for the Soul ................................................................ 249

Ritual Revival ...................................................................... 249

Exercise .............................................................................. 251

1. How to Build an Altar ...................................................... 251

2. Smudging ........................................................................ 252

3. Gratitude for an Attitude ................................................. 253

## Energy and the Chakras ........................................................ 255

Energy in Essence .............................................................. 255

Map of the Chakras and Nadis ........................................... 257

Chakras and Overeating ..................................................... 260

Exercises ............................................................................ 263

Chakra Cleansing ............................................................... 263

Chakra Mantras .................................................................. 264

## A MAGIC! menu for Emergency Emotions ............................ 267

Help for Hunger .................................................................. 267

Help for Stress .................................................................... 268

## Kick Ass in the Kitchen! ...................................................... 271

Working Day Menu .............................................................. 272

Weekend Day Menu ............................................................ 273

## Health, Healing and Happiness - the Daily Recipe ............ 275

The BodyMAGIC! approach ................................................ 275

Health ................................................................................. 275

Healing ............................................................................... 275

Happiness ........................................................................... 275

Knowing Myself .................................................................. 276

Knowing My Worth .............................................................. 276

Ingredients ......................................................................... 277

Method ................................................................................ 278

Eating Practices ................................................................. 279

More on Mornings ............................................................... 280

Lunchtime ........................................................................... 281

Evening Endings ........................................................281

Daily Discipline........................................................282

A Rhyme for Life ......................................................283


**BodyMAGIC! for life** ...............................................**285**

Affirming Improvement...........................................285

Remember and Review, Recall and Revisit!.............286

The Daily Recipe....................................................295

**I Care About What You Think!**...............................**297**

**References** ..........................................................**301**

**About the Author**................................................**307**

**Resources** ..........................................................**309**

# Acknowledgements

To Mother Earth Spirit for your divine intervention. When I read back what I've written, I know you helped me to help others on this challenging journey to health, healing and happiness. I pray for yours. I pray that readers of this and other books will be inspired to reconnect and to protect you in whatever and however little way then can.

Leonie - my beautiful daughter, who was due to follow the diet trap in my tracks. Erase all you know about dieting darling and reload the new programme! I want only for you to be happy EVERY day, no exceptions! I thank you for your acceptance of the massive changes you watched me go through becoming "all spiritual." I only hope that it inspires you to be the person you want to be, without worry or fear of anyone else's views.

Myron - my gorgeous husband and the greatest influence and support on the huge change I've gone through in the last decade or so. We have drifted together and grown stronger beyond my dreams. You were able to find words of support and encouragement when words failed me in the writing of this book and my confidence and self-worth waned. You have always been "Good for Me my baby."

Mum - whose living built my A and whose passing designed my B. What a journey you have left me! I miss your unconditional love and concise way of telling me that I can achieve whatever I want. I just have to get on with it! But I feel your loving spirit around me all of the time.

Dad - for always helping me to do my very best and dismissing my lame excuses. For putting up with my eccentricities and loving me regardless.

Sue - my aunt, my 'sister' in all things healthy and my friend. You planted some seeds very early in my life which have without a doubt driven me in delivering this message. You have inspired me to travel and to follow my dreams.

Chandler Bolt, Chelsea Miller and all the amazing authors in your Self-Publishing School - you have all, in US English, kicked my butt to get this book done and out into the world, turning a daunting task into a breeze. I feel empowered and motivated to do this again, soon! You make book-writing fun!

Elaine Scanlan - my super copy editor, you have saved me the kind of criticism that (!) I would not have had since my English classes at school!

My amazing yoga and meditation teachers:

Janet Dobbie - my first yoga teacher. You have no idea how your classes shaped my future.

Layah Davis - my first teacher trainer. One of the most passionate and sensitive teachers I know.

Ervin Menyhart - for showing what the human body can do in asana and some amazing adjusts!

Yogrishi Vishvketu and the Akhanda Family for gifting me the most holistic practice in the world.

Dr. A.L.V Kumar and his teachers - for his scientific approach to health, healing and happiness.

When I'm teaching and I open my mouth, a bit of all of you comes out!

Kailash Mistry - a fellow yoga teacher, Capricorn and thought leader for sure. We meet but twice a year and yet, in a lunch hour catch up, you can blow me away with your wisdom, love and support. You are a special soul sister to me. A divine messenger!

Carrie Mitchell - for your loving healing. I don't exactly know what you do, but it works every time!

Eliana Harvey, Seersha O'Sullivan and all of my Shamanka teachers and sisters - for the exquisite, thorough shamanic journey around the traditions of the world, I am enriched and very grateful.

Wendy Salter for your nurturing guidance, encouragement and friendship. They were truly magical gatherings when I experienced healing way beyond my expectations.

I have met many other yoga, meditation and shamanic teachers on my travels. Whilst I didn't always resonate with them or agree with their methods, I thank them too, for they taught me some of the most powerful lessons of all.

The beautiful souls who test-drove this book when it was just a draft - typos and all! I'm ever grateful to you for your constructive criticism, your words of gratitude and of encouragement. But moreover, I'm honoured that you should open your hearts and share your journeys with me. I know it has been a challenge for you all and I'm in awe of your tenacity and strength of spirit. You have taught me so much. It has deepened my knowledge of emotional overeating and offered even more different perspectives for healing.

Shahara - my dear sweet soul sister, my mentor and my friend. Together we have been through so much. Always understanding, always caring and always there, despite our physical distance. The only person who can tell me when I'm being a total idiot with such colourful vocabulary and yet with so much love. You are one in a million.

Angie - my friend from the very beginning of this journey of change. You taught me that change is not only OK, but necessary for lasting happiness. And you were there through some pretty major changes that's for sure! You showed me the true value of friendship and helped me to break down my walls of doubt and delay.

Lisa - one of the best friends of my life and one of the most positive and non-judgemental people I know. I adore you for your sensitive spirit, your love and devotion to the people who matter most to you and your open heart. Together we always have such brilliant fun, belly-busting laughter and playful times. I'm always truly me when I'm with you.

I have taught yoga in many different places over the last decade. My students and my student teachers have also been *my* greatest teachers. Every class has been a joy to teach and I want to thank you for smiling with me :-).

I am blessed to have so many beautiful dear friends all over the world and I want you all to know that you have all taught me something special and profound for which I thank you dearly.

My trance family. It's hard for many people to believe that I could meet so many awesome souls on the dance floor! But it proves that music not only lifts a soul and opens a heart but can really unite them, regardless of background or walk of life.

I acknowledge, thank and love all of you from the depths of my heart.

# Foreword

Food is one of the most powerful drugs on the planet. It has the ability to alter our physiology through our biochemistry. Which, in turn, has the ability to affect our emotions, energy, health and ultimately our outlook on life. If we discover that we have a compulsive, obsessive, unhealthy relationship with food, unlike other drugs we cannot just cut it out of our lives "cold-turkey". Food touches every part of our lives: personal, social, cultural, traditional, religious, etc. We need food to survive. Not only is it the building blocks of our body but the common thread that weaves many of our cultural and social fabrics together. If you're holding this book in your hands, then you are very aware of this.

There are thousands of books on dieting and weight loss. Each promising some sort of result if you follow their restrictive, unappetising menus, follow a certain set of "rules". We power through the difficult days without ever realizing that THIS way of eating and relating to food is unhealthy, unstable and unsustainable. What many of these books do not address is the underlying emotions that surround our experiences with food and body image. We are constantly bombarded with images that tell us how we should look while simultaneously being bombarded with images of food and food information. We end up feeling confused and hopeless. We are consistently stimulated by external information that influences our thoughts, feelings and consequently, our behavior regarding our relationships with our bodies and with food.

What makes BodyMAGIC! different is the examination of the internal information that is influencing our relationship with food and our bodies. You see, without knowing the internal experience we become a "victim" to our obsessive and oppressive experience with food. This constant external influence and unexamined internal reaction creates a perpetual cycle of suffering. Food and eating becomes a point of contention. And despite our heartfelt efforts to diet and eat well, we inevitably find ourselves the victim of overeating again and again.

Within BodyMAGIC! you will bravely and courageously discover this internal landscape of your psyche, your emotions and with tools and exercises come to know yourself better than you ever have. It is from this place of awareness of self that the underlying emotions beneath the overeating and self-loathing behavior will surface and can be truly transformed. THIS IS THE MAGIC. Taking the time to do the inner work and discovering the emotions that drive our behavior, empowers us to be able to choose a different experience. In this very important body of work, BodyMAGIC! will help you to uncover the possibilities of a new, healthy and loving relationship with food and your body, starting from the inside out.

I have been privileged to watch Chinmayi discover the healing magic of the BodyMAGIC! philosophy and practice in her own life. We met in 2006 at our first yoga teacher training in Mexico. I was impressed by her vast knowledge and study of several healing modalities and was drawn immediately to her candid yet very compassionate nature. We became fast friends, soul sisters really, and met again in India in 2009 for our advanced yoga teacher training. Through the intense and vigorous study, many of our deep emotions, attachments and beliefs about ourselves and the world began to surface and together we worked through them. As a result, we have transformed our lives through the magic of learning to meet ourselves where we are, accept and love ourselves and believe that change and transformation is possible when we understand our inner processes and our driving emotions behind behavior.

Chinmayi is one of the most deeply committed, passionate, hardworking people I know and has dedicated her life to discovering how excavation of our emotions combined with the reconnection to the Earth and body/mind practices can transform our lives fully and completely. She is living proof of total transformation. I am truly honored to introduce her important work in this world. The BodyMAGIC! process takes work and at times will be challenging, but I assure you, you have the most compassionate, knowledgeable woman holding your hand on this journey. She has been exactly where you are and knows what it means to walk a mile in your shoes. If you are ready, Chinmayi will guide you from the eternal darkness of compulsive, emotional overeating and into the light of learning to love and truly nurture yourself.

Shahara K. Mattingly, CHHC, TCM, CYT
CEO and Founder of Compassionate Carrot,
*"Empowering women to transform their health, confidence and claim their magnificence; growing their glow from the inside out."*
Transformational Health Coach and Yoga Teacher
Golden, Colorado, USA

# Introduction

*"There is a part of me that wants to write, a part that wants to theorize, a part that wants to sculpt, a part that wants to teach…. To force myself into a single role, to decide to be just one thing in life, would kill off large parts of me."*
*~ H. Prather*

Sitting down to finally write this book feels like an incredible release!

After around 35 years of being obsessed with my weight, my thighs, my stomach, my calorie intake and expenditure, diet plans, fitness plans, dress sizes and so much more, and finally working towards a place where I am at last *really* happy, I am overjoyed to get my message out to you!

I feel as though this book has been in the writing for most of my life. However, as an emotional overeater, my lack of self-esteem would allow me to think only:

*'Who would want to buy my book?'*
*'Surely all this has been written before!'*
*'Am I not just writing about the obvious?'*
*'I'm not good enough, creative enough, disciplined enough, slim enough, intelligent enough, qualified enough' – blah, blah, blah!*

However, despite the initial criticism of myself, my body and my eating habits, sharing the ideas and the message in this book turned out to be a massive journey of very positive learning for me. What's between the covers of this book is *that* learning, *that* knowledge, which I dearly hope will serve you and save you the trouble of years of painstakingly searching for a solution to your emotion-related body image issues. For this is such wasted time!

Think about it for a moment.

How many of your daily thoughts are about the food you have eaten, are eating, or the food you are planning/going to eat?
Do you consume food or does it consume you most of the time?
Do you feel in control around food?

Although food is an absolutely necessary part of life, it is just that, a part. If you need a nudge to get you started on answering these questions, think about what *you* want to remember about your relationship with food at the end of your life.

Is it all the diets you tried and failed at?
The constant battle you had to eat the 'right' thing?
Will you remember any fun in dieting, counting calories or the hesitation every time you stepped on the scales?
Or do you want to remember those special occasions where you had a meal you enjoyed with your partner, your friends or your family? And in remembering a few of those times right now, were you counting calories, GIs, carbohydrates, sugars, additives or salt?

Of course not! You remember these occasions not for the diet, but for the positive sensual experiences and the fun you had. The letting go of the struggle and the time off from 'diet duty', overruled by the joy of being with people you love, eating the food you love, in surroundings you love, on a day you will love to remember forever.

An experience full of love!

Of course, what follows the next day might be totally different – recollection, analysis, realisation and guilt. A glance in the mirror showing where every morsel of what you now see as bad food has gone (for me it was usually on the thighs!).

What a shame!
Where did all the love go?
That perfect occasion has turned into huge, self-loathing regret.

So to deal with this negativity, we find ways to punish ourselves with abstinence from food and promise ourselves to do better next time. What a sad, sad situation!

I have probably thought about my weight and the food that determines it, all of my life. For more years than I want to remember, food was the first thing I thought about when I got up in the morning and the last thing I planned before I went to bed. My daily mood was totally determined by what I saw on the scales each morning. Often, I knew what my weight would be before I even stepped onto them, based on what I'd eaten the day before. But I'd still get on them anyway. Rarely did that step bring me much joy.

This book is for you if you can identify with some, or even all of the following:

*Does it feel that you spend some or most of your days making decisions about food?*
*Have you started a day with great intentions of what you are going to eat/not eat, only to find yourself on a slippery slope to failure by early evening?*
*Does your inability to control your diet make you depressed?*
*Does your depression make you want to go and eat?*
*Do you eat for comfort?*
*Do you eat when you are full?*
*Do you feel you have to eat everything on your plate?*
*Do you eat fast and wonder where it all went, wishing you could have it again, a little slower this time?*
*Do you have cravings for foods that you know aren't good for you?*
*Do you know what's in your food, where it comes from and what it can do for your body?*
*Do you spend far too long in the supermarket, questioning whether the foods you love are the foods that love you? Do you pick up things and put them back while you have a battle with yourself? Do you grab things at the checkout without thinking, when they weren't on your list?*
*Do you have any other dependencies – drugs, alcohol, sugar, chocolate, coffee?*
*Do you turn to simple, refined carbohydrates such as white bread when you feel worried, angry, sad, guilty or frustrated?*
*Do you ever take/steal food (have more than your share in secret, sneak food between meals, eat before a food function, store food when there is plenty available, eat while you are cooking)?*
*Do you use excuses to overeat – "I have my period, I ran 10 miles today, I had a bad day at work, it's cold, it's the weekend, I need a day off dieting, I'm on holiday, I deserve it, I've already had x today so therefore what does it matter? I need a break, I'm hungry, I've been good all week"?*

I realise now that I had an eating disorder and food addiction for most of my life, but that I'm finally feeling freedom. This freedom is here to stay. It is permanent and everlasting. It has come about from looking within myself, not from any diet, pill, supplement, detox, fast, herb, spice, or fitness programme. I'm no longer battling with food as my enemy but loving food as the friend I couldn't live without! We love, cherish, honour and respect each other. And it feels good. I have broken the chains of dietary confinement and I am me, myself, I, total, whole, and perfect as I am!

This freedom is the essence of the message I have to share with you now.

Is this your time to find your personal power and make friends with the food you eat?

When most people consider an eating disorder, they usually think of anorexia or bulimia. These are extremely destructive and serious conditions that affect long-term health and relationships. I by no means intend to belittle these conditions. But this book is not specifically about either of those. I have no personal experience of either and won't pretend to have, although some of the solutions offered within this book, I'm sure, could be useful. I am writing about an eating disorder that is often unseen and rarely spoken about, at least by anyone who has suffered from and/or recognises it. To give it a name, it is often called **emotional** or **compulsive overeating**. You may be surprised at how common a problem it is.

For most of my life, no-one would ever have known that I was suffering. Neither did I really. I was sometimes a little heavier than others, but there's nothing wrong with that, right? I would obsess over which restaurant to eat at. Again, not really anything major to pick up on there. I would think about the food constantly during meals, would struggle to be really present in conversations, but again, as I notice, many people aren't present in conversations, especially when you mix in social circles involving food! And I wasn't rushing to the toilet to throw up, so all was well in the world around me. The problem was on the inside. It was like a dark shameful secret that explained why I was not the skinny bean I wanted to be. It was the reason I was nearly always on a diet or in a fitness regime, yet never seemed to lose weight for long. It was the reason why I was not obese, yet I seemed to be able to eat so much. It was why seemingly nearly everyone I met said, "I don't know where you put it all!"

The relentless internal obsession went something like this:

"*what to order? will I miss out if I order the wrong thing? they don't have many vegetarian choices? has he got more than me? can I try theirs? can I have their leftovers? how could she leave that much food? why doesn't anyone else want a dessert? can I ask the waiter if I can have ice cream instead of cream? why do I feel so full? what did she say about her new job? I wonder how many points that was altogether, I won't eat for the rest of the day, I'll do a detox tomorrow, next time I eat there I'll have salad instead, why do I always choose the wrong thing? I'll skip slimming club tomorrow because I'm sure to have put on three pounds and I'll work hard this week to lose some weight, I won't weigh myself for a couple of days and I'll eat only fruit tomorrow*".............. and on and on it went.

This was the reality and perhaps the extreme of *this* eating disorder. It was the only way of life around food for me, for too long. As I look back at it now, it's mental torture! When I *did* tell people I was dieting, they would say, "You don't need to lose weight! You're fine!" I would then convince myself that I *was* actually fine and very often go and binge to celebrate that I was fine!

But of course I wasn't fine on the inside.

If you recognise any of these thoughts or traits around your intentions to lose weight, then the BodyMAGIC! message will help you enormously.

This book includes my own experience of the diet revolution, from all its failings through to finding real solutions. However, it is not an autobiography. I will refer to my experience for the benefit of real-life illustration. I already know, from talking to my audience, that listening to someone else's experience is very helpful. It's why people all over the world go to slimming clubs each week – either to share their success or to be motivated by the success of others. I shall be discussing some diets, clubs and plans and some of their methods; the good features about them and in my experience, why, in the end, most of them are fundamentally flawed. I shall be recommending those methods that *do* help and I hope you will investigate these for yourself. One of the benefits of this book will be that you won't have to keep spending your time and money trying out different methods that, at the outset, you really believe will help you to lose weight – only to be bitterly disappointed and feel like *you* have failed. I will teach you why *they* fail *you* and why you wasted your money.

I used to be signed up to many different food, diet and fitness 'gurus'. Just a few years ago the reason was to try out what I thought was the latest diet trend. I now realise, of course, that most of these 'new' techniques were just fads or a variation of something someone somewhere made a fortune from previously. I'm still signed up to most of them, for research and analysis for this book and for my programmes and coaching clients, so that I know what's around. I get emails, at least three per week, leading me to PowerPoint presentations, long e-mails promising free information about the best foods to eat, the best ways to eat foods and the best times to eat them, the latest miracle combination of herbs, seeds and exotic fruits. These are all questionable, not just for their effectiveness but also for whether they are ethically sourced and fairly traded. It seems we will stop at nothing to lose weight. And businesses will stop at nothing to make lots of money from it. The marketing techniques used are very clever. But when you have researched as many as I have, you know the pattern. They fill you with so much fear, then hope, that you really do believe that their product or programme is your last and *only* real chance:

"*It's not your fault that you are overweight. It's your hormones, the sugar industry, the pharmaceutical industry, your parents, your school teachers, your genes, your attitude, your metabolism, the lack of X chemical in your body.*"

This may be true to some extent. Then you will feel like a fool when they talk about how you have been spending all your hard-earned cash on other diets and products.

"*But never mind, you are saved, as long as you act today,*"

because they will be giving you some apparent huge discount off their (already hugely-inflated) normal price!

The obesity crisis is feeding a multi-million dollar diet and exercise industry that, I have to say, has had very little success in actually addressing obesity. There are many beneficiaries from this development, and sadly, not one of them is you, the dieter. We know that the main reasons for the rise in obesity, heart disease, type II diabetes, early osteoporosis and so much more have to do with eating too much unhealthy stuff (I hesitate to call *all* of it food), not eating enough healthy, real food and not taking a decent level of exercise. Add to that the stress of modern life, the constant pursuit of wanting more success, more money, more holidays, more gadgets. It's no wonder we become dis-eased. The problem is increasing so fast that for the first time in history, as adults, at the time of writing, we are likely to live to an older age than our children.

Brendon Brazier noted in *Thrive Fitness* that over 910,000 people in North America alone die from heart disease every year. That is the equivalent death toll of a 9/11 disaster every 27 hours! Do statistics like this reach the newspapers? Very rarely. The press seem to be more concerned about pushing the message of which model, actor or singer we should look like, rather than how to be healthy and how to stay that way. One of the saddest realities of our time is that we believe that skinny means healthy. Again, this is not the case. Reports show that being underweight can have repercussions on health, especially in old age. It is a paradox that those same newspapers, on the one hand, receive good money from food manufacturers to advertise processed 'foods' full of sugar, salt and other harmful synthetic substances, and on the other hand, they advertise diet programmes, diet organisations and diet foods, that claim to help us to lose lots of weight very quickly.

I thought crash diets were a thing of the 1980s, but they are still out there in their plenty. I never have understood even my *own* obsession with losing lots of weight in just a few days. Time and again, in our desperation, we buy into quick-fix schemes, when we already know that they are unsustainable. Research also shows that rapid weight loss can be harmful to health, contributing to muscular and cardiac dysfunctions (1). If nutritional needs are not met, immunity can be compromised.

How many times have you heard, when someone comes down with a cold, 'Are you eating properly?' We need our vitamins on a *daily* basis to stay healthy. The body is great at adapting, but it can only do it so much, for so long. Then immunity suffers and we become ill.

Do we know why it has come to this? What changed in our evolution that made us turn away from the healthy stuff of life? I believe it had to do with a huge detachment from everything truly natural and the increasing powers of persuasion of the processed/junk/fast food industry. Yes, reducing obesity and its many effects involves exercise within the individual's abilities, healthful whole food containing nutrients for the individual's needs, ample clean water and sufficient rest. But most important of all, balanced mental and emotional health is what keeps a healthy weight, fitness and overall wellbeing in place, so that we no longer need to be obsessed with food and life can be the joyful experience it was meant to be. This emotional drive to overeat cannot be managed through a food plan alone.

There is one more huge reason why this current system is failing you in the long term. It may be a new discovery for you, as it was for me, but this knowledge has been around this planet for thousands of years. It is reconnecting with the wisdom of nature and our ancestors. I have been exposed to many traditional cultures and philosophies on my path. I have a collection of knowledge nuggets to share with you in the pages of this book.

We know in our hearts that diets don't work in the long term, and there is seemingly someone new with every email wanting to call them something else – switches, plans, methods, solutions, a way, a club, a world! Some of them are extremely well-researched and even scientifically-backed. And judging by the testimonials, seemingly very successful. However, most of them haven't been around long enough to prove their permanent, life-long success. Even the long-standing ones seem to boast very little in the way of long-term statistics. In this book I shall explain why this is so.

I am not a scientist or a dietitian, nor do I have a Degree in Nutrition or any Degree that's relevant to this topic. I have a Diploma in Nutritional Guidance and another Diploma in Drug and Alcohol Addiction Studies. What I *do* know about nutrition is enough and completely up-to-date at the time of writing. Nutritional research is developing so fast that even some of the websites you will visit are out-of-date with the facts. Current knowledge is far more important than, say, a 10-year-old qualification. All too many diet leaders go to great lengths to tell you about their qualifications. Are you really interested? If so, you can skip to the end of this book and read more about me. I have a folder full of certificates in relevant subjects! This book is about looking at food *and life* from a higher perspective. I will explain why this is necessary to really heal your relationship with food, and I'll give you some practices to help this to happen. I teach yoga, complementary therapies and shamanic healing. However, I believe my greatest qualification for guiding you in overcoming overeating is my personal experience of that journey, and in-depth knowledge of the practices *you* need to effectively heal yourself forever.

Why is this book called BodyMAGIC!? Surely I'm not going to wave a wand at you so you will instantly feel great and be slim? I wish I could, I really do!

No, you do have to do some work! But it won't be hard work. I don't want to replace one dieting struggle with another one of *any* kind. It involves looking after yourself. It doesn't mean setting new goals down at the gym, new target distances on your rowing machine or treadmill. It doesn't mean shakes, cereal bars or even piles of salad and bowlfuls of fruit. It means some gentle self-care, and adjustment to a way that is kind to all aspects of your body, mind and soul. I'm going to show you a very different kind of beauty, one that will open your heart and mind to a more joyful life.

In these pages, I will be laying out knowledge and concepts for you to take on board, and I'll be giving you actual practices and exercises for overcoming emotional overeating that are crucial to your success. The key principles will be highlighted in **bold** to keep bringing you back to them throughout the book and to affirm their importance.

You will find it at least enlightening to learn about yourself at this deep level, but at best it will be a whole lot of fun! You *will* need to be a little self-centred. You have to put your happiness first. To give of yourself happily – to your job, your family, your hobbies – you have to have happy energy stores in the first place. Stores of happy energies, like self-esteem, courage, compassion, enthusiasm – but most importantly, **love**. To give love, as with all of these traits, you have to have love in the first place. That's

LOVE FOR YOURSELF!

With a little time, patience, nurturing and love for yourself, I promise you will *feel* the MAGIC!

MAGIC! is the word I use to include its energetic, spiritual and metaphysical nature. That's how it feels to me. Once we connect with ourselves again, with the energy given to us by nature (through food, air, water etc.), specifically Mother Earth, we can *feel* the magic working through us. You will realise that when you allow yourself to be connected, you feel totally supported by all that you are connected to. And decisions about what you put in your body come naturally and with wisdom. You have always had this ability. It just needs uncovering, reworking and remastering. This mastery will empower you in all aspects of your life, and it will rub off on your friends, your family and most importantly on your descendants.

This book will show you what needs to shift, why, when and how to do it.

If that seems a little 'out there' for you, then for now, just be curious. I will not suggest that you make any drastic life changes before you are ready. You may already have a good knowledge of the healing arts, but maybe much of this will be new to you. I want you to keep both of your feet on the ground. Introduce these practices at your own pace and with close attention to your body *and* mind.

At the same time, make this fun! You have nothing to lose. I am tempted to say 'except pounds!' but I know that's been said in some cheesy diet commercial somewhere in my distant past!

## Chapter One
# Emotions Explained

*"If you don't think your anxiety, depression, sadness and stress impact your physical health, think again. All of these emotions trigger chemical reactions in your body, which can lead to inflammation and a weakened immune system. Learn how to cope, sweet friend.*
*There will always be dark days."*
*~ Kris Carr*

According to the National Centre for Eating Disorders in the UK, the definition of compulsive or binge eating is when:

**"someone feels compelled to eat when they are not hungry and who cannot stop when they have had enough."**

Emotional overeating affects more people than anorexia and bulimia added together. One of every two people, who seek help with weight loss, eats compulsively. And 12 million people in the UK alone suffer from compulsive eating to some extent. Personally, I feel that it is far more common than anyone realises. I was 44 before I realised I had an eating disorder that had a name and symptoms and offered any reason to consider what my healing should look like. We can't take steps to heal ourselves if we don't know we are ill in the first place. There is something going on in the world's emotions, because over half of all American women also eat compulsively.

There is absolutely no doubt that the driving force behind uncontrolled eating is emotion. There are probably hundreds of emotions that fuel our desire to eat compulsively. Whatever feeling, impulse or craving that takes us to the refrigerator when we are not hungry, is an emotion.

It is e-motion. It is energy in motion.

So what is the energetic force behind emotional eating? Can we take that eating emotion away so that we don't overeat? This book will show you that you can break the link between the emotion and eating. Everywhere there are diets, plans and methods to help you to not overeat or eat the 'wrong' foods. But it's the *reason* why you are compelled to eat that these pages address, and the ways that you can change the emotional power behind the hand that feeds you.

For years you may have been numbing your emotions with food. This book asks you to look at another way of living. One that feeds your health, healing and happiness. To cease numbing these emotions will mean that they are going to surface. They may hurt, and you may be quite surprised that they can still be so strong, even years later. Not only are you going to let them come up, you are going to be encouraged to dig them out, to recognise them as outdated behaviours, to heal them with love and to create space for new beginnings.

The whole process really boils down to two very important aspects to master. These are the two **Keys to Freedom.** Write them down in the first person, as if the keys are already yours; stick them around the house, on your computer, your phone and your bathroom mirror. Check in with them daily, for they are the fuel that lights your healing fire:

**I Know Myself**
and
**I Know My Worth**

*The Keys to Freedom:*

- ☐ **To Know Yourself** – looking at your behaviours and going deeply into why you overeat.

- ☐ **To Know Your Worth** – what you deserve, i.e. the time and energy to do the personal growth work for radical change, so that you can enjoy lasting happiness. You will know that overeating affects your body, your mind and your spirit in all aspects of your life. It controls your thoughts and your actions day after day, in so many ways. This does nothing for your self-worth. **Knowing yourself**, your true essence, by pulling back the curtains concealing all the traits of the overeating nightmare, you will see your true self and you will come to know and fully appreciate **your worth** in this world.

You will continue to see these words repeated in **bold** throughout this book, to remind you of these very important keys.

I had years of internal dis-order.

In my mind, for most of the time, I was full of self-loathing and self-criticism. In my poor body, I experienced years of what I can only call self-abuse. We now know the effects that long-term yo-yo dieting and feast-to-famine food habits have on our bodies and minds. Consuming diet pills, laxatives, processed diet foods with artificial everything, low-fat/high-sugar diets and so much more, plays absolute havoc on the hormones, the nervous system and the digestive system, particularly the liver, kidneys and bowel.

And then we tie them together. The body-mind connection. Think for one moment how the digestive system responds when we are stressed: irritable bowel syndrome, diarrhoea, constipation, colitis, acid reflux, heartburn, bloating, stomach ulcers and more. And this is not just work and life stress. This is the stress caused by ingesting too many toxins (we'll cover these later). Notice how the mind reacts when we have too much coffee, or how our sleep can be disturbed when we eat too late. They are irrevocably linked.

> *"When the mind, body, and spirit work together I believe anything is possible."*
> ~ Criss Angel

Consider this simple concept. Is it possible that perhaps we wouldn't take in so many toxins if we were happier in ourselves? And is it therefore conceivable that if we were happier in ourselves, we wouldn't want to eat food that doesn't serve any aspect of our health – body or mind?

The fact is, if you are reading this book you will likely agree that in the last three decades or so, there has been a fundamental shift in our body and mind connection when it comes to food. We seem to be almost literally 'out of our mind' when we eat. Most of us don't go straight for the healthy fruit bowl when we are hurting emotionally. In my emotionally-charged state, I would go for the wine and cheese, chocolate cake and coffee, beer and pizza, fish and chips, or my mum's puddings and cakes. This is what we call *comfort* food.

But we are becoming ill. Digestive-related disorders are on a massive increase. Crohn's disease and ulcerative colitis are now the most common inflammatory bowel conditions, and they are serious problems. They don't just affect the overweight and overeaters either: they can affect anyone. There are thousands of seemingly healthy, slim young people taking prescription and non-prescription medicines for dietary-related or stress-related conditions, all over the developed world. They are diseases waiting to happen.

*What* we eat *is* important. Any diet that tells you to go and eat what you want is not only destined to fail, it is not concerned with your health, your healing or your happiness. I have tried many of them, from meal replacement shakes to diet pills, eating at specific times, calorie counting, carb counting and more. These diets are not serving your wellbeing. Until you *feel* better (permanently), you will never have the emotional driving force you need to eat healthily, lose weight and keep weight off. We have been too preoccupied with how we look and *not* how we feel. Happiness is not what you *see* in the mirror, it's how you *feel* when you see what you see. It is a feeling, not a physical thing.

It's time to try and find out when and where the change happened for us as individuals and how we have been steered to change through our culture. Our world is full of junk food-eating opportunities. By junk, I mean food that has very little nutritional value. Our bodies don't need it and if our digestive system is so weak that it can't process it properly, it will store it as fat. The food marketing giants are very clever. They know the exact science behind getting people to buy junk food. It still takes a great deal of strength for me to walk through my home town without stopping for some kind of food or drink as a treat. But what seems like a treat is torture to my body, and you are no different. My torture is all but over now, because I have knowledge of both myself and what I'm worth. I know what I *truly* deserve.

We are going to get straight into the emotions here and now, in this first chapter. This may seem tough. And it is. Emotions are delicate things and they can hurt. But it is the intention to change something that gives you your power back. The power of your **health**, your **healing** and your **happiness**. It is the knowledge of your habitual emotions, resulting eating patterns and lack of self-care that will lead you to realise and **Know Your Worth**.

When you know your potential value then you can be potentially invaluable to others.

To understand our emotions, we need to be prepared to look very deeply at ourselves. And we may not necessarily like what we see. This makes sense, because if we didn't mind this self-enquiry of our emotions, we would maybe not resort to food to numb them.

It isn't easy! But you CAN do it NOW!

There are essential and valuable exercises in each chapter. I haven't recommended any that I haven't tried and tested myself. You can integrate some of them into your daily personal practices, and some of them may be one-offs, like these first ones.

## Exercise

You are going to take a huge step towards **Knowing Yourself** right now.

Give yourself the gifts of self-enquiry and honesty. It is your time for this.

There really are no wrong answers, and usually your first thoughts are the best ones, so write them down. When you get stuck or feel resistance, take a break, meditate, walk the dog (or yourself) or sleep on it and then come back.

Be brave dear friend. It is time.

1.) In the table below, or on a separate piece of paper, give an example of a time where you experienced these emotions. It may be related to something that is happening in your life at the moment and is ongoing, or something that happened in the past. It doesn't necessarily have to have resulted in periods of struggle with your eating. You are just bringing emotionally-driven events to the present time, for self-analysis. What in your life comes to mind when you read each word? Don't think too much, just write the first thing you recall.

## How Emotions Manifested

Add any other emotions you can think of:

*People crossing into my Personal SPACE - boundary*

| Emotion | What/How this has manifested in me (just briefly). |
|---------|---------------------------------------------------|
| **Anger** | People taking advantage - unfair situations. Pool chairs |
| **Boredom** | When I don't take "next step" |
| **Cruelty** | Kids at school - mean to others - Reading horrific news |
| **Disappointment** | Wanting things for my kids - recognition, parts in play |
| **Disgust** | At my body after a binge - gaze at bloated stomach |
| **Doubt** | When faced w/ new situations, jobs, trip planning + |
| **Fear** | Of "what ifs" when positive new opportunities arose |
| **Greed** | My binge foods - leads to shame |
| **Hate** | People who do "wrong things" |
| **Hurt** | When I feel unseen and unheard by loved ones |
| **Loss** | My father, Rhonda |
| **Overwhelm** | New situations, not knowing how to do something |
| **Panic** | When something "bad" happens, juggling all |
| **Shame** | Over bingeing / lies about it |
| **Sorrow** | Rhonda's illness |
| **Worry** | Parents safety - obsess |
| *Other* | |

2a.) Pick three emotions that you wish you could resolve in your heart, because they would make the **biggest difference** to your level of happiness

Anger
Hurt
Doubt

2b.) Which one of these three emotions would, if resolved, bring you the **biggest increase** in your happiness?

DOUBT

2c.) Which one of these three emotions would involve the **most effort**/pain/discomfort for you at the present time?

*HURT - unseen, unheard stirs ANGER too*
*Don't understand why → Angry = the feeling that comes when I'm asked ??*
*about my day, my kids from my mother*

2d.) Which one of these three emotions which, if resolved, might also resolve one or more of the others, or at least take away some of their intensity? *HURT*

2e.) Taking all of the answers of question 2 so far (a-d) into account, which one would you like to you work on at this point in time?

*HURT*

2f.) What other feelings and emotions do you feel about your chosen one and the event or situation?

*I want my own self-love to be enough. When I'm not*
*seen by my mother - I want to be able to move on - I'm bl. When I'm*
*not heard by Ricky, I want to be able to build myself, lose the anger towards him.*

Every chapter in this book is written to help you to recognise what's holding you back or what you are holding on to emotionally. This is **Knowing Yourself**. Once you agree that you are ready to release it and therefore **Know Your Worth**, you will also find the tools to do so.

3.) It's also a great idea to take a look at where the other emotions are. Let's take a snapshot of how you feel right now.

Take your time and be honest with yourself. This is your practice. It is extremely important to complete this exercise now, and before moving on with this book.

Mark down the current month and year, where you feel on the scale between the opposites. For example, if you feel lots more sorrow than joy right now, you will mark, say 03/16 (if it's March 2016 now), somewhere along the line between the two, but closer to the sorrow side.

I promise you that this is going to me a great source of motivation for you as you travel through this programme.

*Sorrow* ———————————————————— *JOY*

# The BodyMAGIC! Emotion Elevator

| Unhelpful | Where I see myself at the start of working through BodyMAGIC! (how I feel most of the time). Mark with the date (MM/YY) on the scale between the two polar opposites. | Helpful |
|---|---|---|
| | ⟶ | |
| Anger | 6-23 | Gratitude |
| Boredom | 6-23 | Spontaneity |
| Cruelty | 6-23 | Compassion |
| Disappointment | 6-23 | Contentment |
| Disgust | 6-23 | Admiration |
| Doubt | 6-23 | Faith |
| Fear | 6-23 | Hope |
| Greed | 6-23 | Generosity |
| Hate | 6-23 | Love |
| Hurt | 6-23 | Relief |
| Loss | 6-23 | Gain |
| Overwhelm | 6-23 | Serenity |
| Panic | 6-23 | Knowing |
| Shame | 6-23 | Pride |
| Sorrow | (e.g.) 03/18 ... 6-23 | Joy |
| Worry | 6-23 | Peace |
| Other | | Other |

I assure you that when you have worked through the exercises in this book you will see how far you have moved away from emotions that don't serve you towards those that do. This may seem like a difficult start to the book, because it's highlighting and delving in to your difficulties head first.

Take your time with these exercises. It's the one major time in this book where you will be looking into the past. You need to know what it is you are holding on to before you can let it go. The honesty you afford yourself with this exercise is the wisdom, from your past, that you are taking into the future. Dig deep and find the nuggets of knowledge of and for yourself. From this exercise, you will hopefully be starting to define the emotions that can lead to emotional eating for *you*. There will be one or two common trends. There are many different types of emotions. I have just listed those related to emotional overeating *in my experience*.

*"Happy is the man who has broken the chains which hurt the mind and has given up worrying once and for all."*
~ Ovid

4.) After the first three exercises, and taking everything into account, how well do you think you Know Yourself? Give yourself a figure between 1 (not very well) and 10 (extremely well) if you like. Make some notes too, if it helps you. Think of your emotions, reactions and personality.

I feel like I "know myself" (7) but that doesn't mean I know what to do when I feel the uncomfortable, unhelpful feelings that simmer & brew and lead to subsequent binges.

I over-react to things that "aren't my problem" working to separate myself and my insides when I feel that uncomfortableness stirring. Let people be who they are — guess I feel threatened by that. Don't want their ways/thoughts to enter my space.

5a.) First column - Looking at yourself as you are now, how much importance, on a scale of 1 (no importance) to 10 (extremely important) do you put on each of the following aspects of yourself. For example, if your weight is not hugely important, you might give it a 6 but if your clothing size is really important, you might give it a 9 or 10.

5b.) Second column - Please now take your answers from 5a.) and list them in order. For example; if the highest score you gave was your diet, you will list c) first next to number 1). If your sleep was awarded the lowest score, then you will enter e) next to number 8). There may be a few with equal scores. And that's fine!

| | | rating (1-10) | | | order of importance |
|---|---|---|---|---|---|
| a) | your weight | 10 | | 1) | a, d, f |
| b) | your clothing size | 9 | now list them in order of importance here > > > > > > > | 2) | b, c, e |
| c) | your diet | 9 | | 3) | g, h |
| d) | your exercise | 10 | | 4) | |
| e) | your sleep | 9 | 1) = most important | 5) | |
| f) | your health | 10 | | 6) | |
| g) | your healing | 7 | 8) = least important | 7) | |
| h) | your happiness | 7 | | 8) | |

Try not to judge yourself here. Please don't worry about what you *should* think but note what you *actually* believe about yourself.

Now we shall take a look back at eating habits for a while…

## "Why did I do it?"

If I had a penny for every time I said that, I'd be a rich woman! In the thick of the next day's guilt and self-hatred, the failure syndrome, I really didn't know why I overate. However, the guilt would nearly always stem from a combination of two things:
- ☐ eating too much food and
- ☐ eating the foods that I knew would not help me

Here's an example of my typical thoughts following an episode of overeating. In this illustration, I have separated the two for clarity.

## Eating Too Much

Here are some of the conscious reasons why I would eat until I could hardly move:

- ☐ I wanted to get my money's worth
- ☐ There are people starving in the world
- ☐ It's such a waste
- ☐ I don't need to lose weight, I'm fine as I am
- ☐ I can burn it off tomorrow
- ☐ I may not get such lovely food again

and then I go deeper into my unconscious mind (obviously not at the time) and I realise *this* is what was really going on...

- ☐ I shall eat my stress and it may go away — to numb pain
- ☑ I have a void I need to fill — heal loss and regain power
- ☐ I'll be a better person if I eat the leftovers — needing approval
- ☐ Food is energy. It's what I need to survive — fear of scarcity
- ☐ I'm so stressed! I need comfort food — a quick fix, denial
- ☐ No-one loves me enough to notice — lack of love and power
- ☑ I feel useless, hopeless/helpless — desperate for love, help, care
- ☐ I can eat, no-one knows how bad I feel — wanting a break from struggle

## Eating the Wrong Things

And here's why I would eat the things that do not nourish me: I hesitate to use the word 'wrong' too much. However, we have to realise that there are many foods that do not serve us. This book is about why we eat them when we have emotional drivers asking us to do so:

- ☐ I can't be bothered to cook
- ☐ It's not fair that other people should be able to eat that
- ☐ I don't have the right ingredients to prepare what I'd planned
- ☐ I am going to be eating too late
- ☐ It's Friday night, the weekend, and I need to relax
- ☐ I deserve to be cooked for
- ☐ I fancy a take-away (not what I planned)
- ☐ I deserve a treat; one take-away won't do me any harm

And then I go deeper......

- ☑ Why can't I eat like everyone else? — feeling inadequate
- ☐ Why me? Why do *I* have this weight problem? — isolation, victim
- ☐ What does anyone care if I'm overweight anyway? — anger at self/others
- ☐ If I can't beat them, then I may as well join them — lack of will, anger
- ☑ F**k it!! (sorry but the truth has to be said) — surrender, giving up
- ☑ I'm sick and tired of dieting so I'll eat what I like — betrayal, sadness
- ☐ It's so hard when everyone else can eat whatever — lack of support, envy

Sound familiar?

Ok, it's your turn.

Don't hesitate for a minute. Don't come back to this later. Do this right NOW!
Have a look back at the previous page, where I consider times when I ate too much and ate the 'wrong' things.

6.) List some of the reasons why you *think* you are compelled to overeat. Just generally. Note anything that comes to mind, without thinking too much about it or analysing. Leave a space between each reason that comes to mind.
e.g. *I overeat because I...when I'm...if I...at times when I...*

1 - unsettled feeling - doubting myself, insecure, self-critical

2 - uncertain - feeling weak & ineffectual, helpless

3 - lonely, sad - emotions unexpressed, misunderstood, overwhelmed w/ mixed emotions towards R

7.) Read each reason, in turn, closing your eyes and taking a deep breath. Go deep inside your heart with this reason and see what else is there. You will probably find some of the same underlying feelings as my example, but don't be surprised to be surprised. Make a short note underneath each reason. Take your time and write what you find, without judgement.

8.) Now list all the reasons why you think you sometimes eat the 'wrong' foods. Foods that, as far as you know, are not serving your health. Leave a space between each reason.
e.g. *I would eat ice cream rather than fruit salad in times when.......because I....if I feel...*

1 - CHOOSE chips to binge because I can keep shoving one after another. (quantity)
nuts
crackers
- with each "piece" I bury myself deeper from the surface of what's really bothering me
I binge when I don't want to be with myself, don't want to feel what I'm feeling. After - I feel bad about binge - distanced from what really was bothering me. That empty angst.

9.) Read each reason in turn, as before. Close your eyes and take a deep breath. Go deep inside your heart with this reason and see what else is there. You may find there's a lot of overlap, and that's ok. Add notes to the list above or make new ones here.

10.) Now go back over the answers in 7.) and 9.) and try and go deeper. Breathe deep, go into your heart and find the truth. What is it you are really feeling? What are you really craving? What are you lacking in your life? Make some notes here. Be selfish. Continue in the back of the book if necessary, or on a separate piece of paper you can staple in here. Use my examples to help to guide you to go deeper. Just a few words will be fine. Take a break here if you need to.

*"Holding on to anger is like grasping a hot coal with the intent of throwing it at someone else; you are the one who gets burned."*
*~ Buddha*

11.) Time to dream! There is little point in starting any journey if you don't know what desires are really in your heart. Every journey needs a destination, or it's like walking off into the desert without a compass. But with this book, the goal is not a set of vital statistics, a number on the scales or getting into a certain size of jeans. It's a feeling. A feeling of bliss. A feeling of joy. A feeling of acceptance and peace. Write a few random words for what comes into your mind, how you feel when you imagine your:

**Ideal Health** - e.g. energy levels, your skin, your sleep etc

Positive
Clean
Pure

**Ideal Healing** - e.g. recovery from emotional overeating, illness, disability, fitness, other addictions

Recovery, Free, No inner turmoil,
No churning or Aprehension
Feel love w/o angst + fear of people taking my
stuff away!
Feel strong, confident of my ideals

**Ideal Happiness** - e.g. your relationships, your work, your family, your social life

Back + forth in relationships - satisfying
Feel love, give love
Don't have to defend myself - don't feel anything
by others' differences
Live + let live

12.) Take a moment to visualise your ideal health, healing and happiness. Lie down or sit back and relax for a few minutes for each ideal. Close your eyes and imagine each ideal situation. What is happening when you are nearing these ideals? Who is there with you? When in the future is this happening? Where is it? Create your ideals in your heart. Then, when you open your eyes, for each one add some words here that come from these ideals to 'colour' your pictures.

*Live and let live. Keep myself from bleeding into others and v.v. Make breaths a dividing space.*

Whatever words you have written above are your **visions**. They are the feelings that will replace the emotions that motivate you to overeat. As a dieter, you have had your fair share of targets and goals. There have probably been many times when you have been waiting to achieve something or for something to happen before you can really enjoy yourself, live your best hour, day, week or month. I don't know how many times I have said that I have to be X weight before I can do Y. I have said I will buy a pair of shoes as a reward when I lose seven pounds!

Dieting puts living on hold, and it's so cruel:

- ☐ "I'll starve myself if I have to, just to get into that dress."
- ☐ "I refuse to buy a size bigger."
- ☐ "I'm not wearing that bikini on holiday unless I lose another three pounds."

Be reasonable with yourself and your visions. If you have just had a baby and are still breastfeeding, for example, now is not the time to start training for a marathon! But maybe you will want to set goals to feel better, look healthier, be calmer. The marathon can wait until next year! Be careful not to put too many numbers and dates in. This is a vision, not a target. If you feel that you would like to lose ten pounds, that's great. There may be all sorts of reasons why you don't or can't at this time. But you might find yourself feeling happier in your skin than you have for years. If you are an emotional overeater, your weight will drop eventually anyway, because you will gradually let go of the emotions causing you to overeat in the first place. That, in essence, is the message of this book. You will crave foods that enhance your health, and you will have more energy than you ever thought was possible.

This is joyful, meaningful living! We all want that.

> *"Our plans miscarry because they have no aim.*
> *When you don't know what harbour you're aiming for, no wind is the right wind."*
> *~ Seneca*

### Chapter Two
# The 7 Spells of BodyMAGIC!

*"Nobody grows old merely by living a number of years. We grow old by deserting our ideals. Years may wrinkle the skin, but to give up enthusiasm wrinkles the soul."*
*~ Samuel Ullman*

I am going to introduce a framework, a process that you can work with. This work, the practice and all of the changes you are going to see, feel and know, need a little organising. The key is to work through the book from front to back, but there are some traits you can learn, adopt and embrace as you move through this shift. It's pretty methodical and it helps you understand what is necessary to reach your goals, and it helps you to **Know Yourself**.

It doesn't have to be the goal of health either – it can be any goal that you have for yourself and your life, assuming it is for your highest good. I have called them spells because each part of the work magically transforms into a new trait! I have written them in bold here and in the rest of the book, to illustrate their importance and remind you of their MAGIC!

### The **7 Spells of BodyMAGIC!**

1. **Idea** which transforms into an **Intention** leads to
2. **Focus** which transforms into **Understanding** leads to
3. **Confidence** which transforms into **Enthusiasm** leads to
4. **Determination** which transforms into **Commitment** leads to
5. **Discipline** which transforms into **Willpower** leads to
6. **Self-Knowledge** which transforms into **Patience** leads to
7. **Tenacity** which transforms into **Success** leads to

Lasting, lifelong **health**, **healing** and **happiness!**

The first thing to consider here isn't the **Idea**, it's the **happiness** you will enjoy when you achieve some **Success**. That is the most powerful driving force you can imagine. You can go and eat pizza and it will make you happy. You can drink a bottle of wine with your best buddies and that will make you very happy! But you know that is not the kind of happiness I mean. Those moments might create great memories, but as we discussed, if they divert you, even temporarily, from your healthy **Intention**, then that memory will always come tainted with a sense of regret or failure.

The happiness I'm talking about here is the kind of happiness, peace, contentment and joy that comes from knowing what you want in the long term and knowing that you really do deserve it. Like putting a dish on the side of your house to get more channels on your TV, the **7 Spells of BodyMAGIC!** will open up all the necessary channels for you to receive your deserved **health**, **healing** and **happiness**.

There will be no need to overeat. This doesn't mean that you will never overeat again or that you will never enjoy foods that don't particularly serve your health. But when you do, it will not be emotionally charged either before, during or afterwards.

## Spell Number One:
### *Idea which transforms into an Intention*

The good news with the **7 Spells** is that you already have one of them in the bag.
Your **Idea** was that if you bought this book you might be able to overcome your emotional eating disorder. Your ideals, you have listed above. They are your visions. If you have jumped past them, GO BACK! They are a fundamental part of your life and this process.

Your **Intention** started as soon as you completed the exercises above. You now have a cast-iron intention to do something about your emotional eating.


## Spell Number Two:
### *Focus which transforms into Understanding*

Your **Focus** is also happening already. This is the information gathering. I hope that you will agree that I have made this part easy for you. You do not have to research emotional overeating by reading several books, following programmes or seeing a therapist. Everything you need for your path to BodyMAGIC! is right here. I have piled a whole lot of personal experience, knowledge and research into this book for you, so you have your focus right here in your hands! All you have to do is keep reading and this will evolve into **Understanding.** Knowledge is power, and this power will drive you onto the next stage, your confidence.


## Spell Number Three:
### *Confidence which transforms into Enthusiasm*

**Confidence** is what will help you to enjoy this path. You will want confidence in this work and what I'm teaching you, but most of all, you will need confidence in yourself. I make no apologies for repeating that this work can be really easy, especially if it's fun. Your confidence will manifest **Enthusiasm** for the whole process.


*"Success is knowing what your values are and living in a way consistent with your values."* – ~ Danny Cox


**Quick Fun Exercise – Now!**
Observe your body language. If you want instant confidence, stand up straight with your chin level and your shoulders back and say out loud, "I know what I want and I'm going to have so much fun getting it!" or any other affirmation you want. How do you feel now? Even if you feel silly, I bet you're smiling. We'll cover affirmations in another chapter, because they are so important!


## Spell Number Four:
### *Determination which transforms into Commitment*

Next comes your **Determination.** With bold enthusiasm comes a force that helps you to really believe that you can do it. Maybe it's not as difficult as you thought. Maybe this book is, or will be, making a positive difference in other aspects of your life, like your job, for example. But at some point you will find the power to move from enthusiasm to determination, because that's where your **Commitment** comes from.

You may have already committed several thousand pounds to faddy diets, programmes and groups. You have likely committed many hours of your time to going to slimming clubs, shopping for recipes, preparing food that you thought would help you to lose weight. I cannot blame you if you falter here. But you just have to keep going and see it through. This work is extremely powerful, not just with a focus of losing weight but with a real commitment to living a life of **health, healing** and **happiness**, every minute of every day.

So with that **Commitment** you start putting time aside for yourself for your practices and you work page by page through this book. You're ticking along nicely, learning lots of new strategies for enhancing your health and you find that you are feeling a little more in control of your overeating.

Then BANG! The buffet table at your friend's wedding is incredible! It has all of your favourite foods on it and more. With a couple of glasses of champagne inside you, you think "what the hell, one day won't matter!" Enter **Discipline.**

Here, I have given you **Nine Reminders** that are powerful shifts in that brief moment, when you decide to have some time off from your practices. In reality, it's not really that much different to having a day off a diet, and we all know what happens there! Your practice, like taking a shower, is an essential part of your daily routine, so it's important to your success.

## The Nine Reminders

– to keep BodyMAGIC! *in* your life *for* life!

1. Have I ever had the opportunity to focus so intently on my emotions related to eating before?
2. How many diets have asked me to get to **Know Myself** or **Know my Worth**? How cool is that?
3. How much money have I actually spent so far on this book, compared with other programmes?
4. When have I ever had the opportunity to find out what really goes on in my mind around food?
5. How hard can it be to see it through? What do I have to lose? What is my commitment?
6. How will I ever know if I don't try?
7. Look at my ideals for **health, healing** and **happiness**. They have MAGIC! powers!
8. I really can live the rest of my life exactly the way I want to, guaranteed! I have that much personal power now and in the future if I keep up my practice.
9. I am more likely to regret *not* doing this programme than doing it.

*"Some days are just bad days, that's all. You have to experience sadness to know happiness, and I remind myself that not every day is going to be a good day, that's just the way it is!"*
*~ Dita Von Teese*

Spell Number Five:
*Discipline which transforms into Willpower*

**Discipline** is the most difficult spell of them all!

Let me explain. This is one of the most enlightening things I learned about myself, that helped me turn a corner in my relationship with everyone and everything, including food. It was one of those huge 'Aha!'

moments that have filled my heart with joy every day as I have followed this path. You may now be getting excited!

All of the other spells are conscious thoughts about other conscious thoughts. You are aware of them most of the time and are able to influence their success. For example, if you don't understand something, you will find it is because your focus is on the wrong aspect of your goal, or that you haven't got all of the information you need just yet. So you find a *way* to understand. It is methodical **action** and you are totally in control of it.

However, discipline, whilst it can be very strong, is the one spell that has the hardest job to do. The reason is because it is called upon when you are challenged by a **reaction** rather than a thought. And those reactions travel very fast. We need fast reactions every day, from stepping back onto the pavement when you see a car coming and realising that it's better to go back than run over the road, to catching a china plate as it falls off the shelf. These are quick reactions. They are there for our safety and protection, or to protect someone or something. It is the fight, flight or freeze reflex that all of the animal kingdom has. Whilst we no longer need to run away from dinosaurs, we still need to react quickly to more modern dangers! One of those dangers, for an emotional overeater, is the temptation to overeat.

Inside that **unconscious mind** are all of the other reactions you have learned, based on your experiences so far in life. Some of them can be very useful, like knowing how to react when someone offers us a gift. We know, based on our experience, to say "thank you". Manners are an example of social reactions. Unfortunately, almost everyone will have the potential within their unconscious mind to react inappropriately. As a compulsive overeater, there are challenging reactions to offers of food. This, again, is based on your experience.

Then there are other habitual patterns that you have established in your **subconscious mind**. If, nearly every time you walk down the High Street you stop at Starbucks for coffee and a doughnut, it's going to be hard for you to walk past without imagining the taste of coffee and doughnut in your mouth. If, every week, you go to the same cinema and you have nachos or popcorn and a diet cola, your subconscious mind is going to remind you that's exactly what you usually do. And your unconscious mind may be thinking that if you don't have them, you are going to suffer in some way or you will be lacking. We are creatures of habit, and those habits are programmes that kick in very fast indeed. You are reacting because of a habit or a bit of programming that may be preventing change. It is at this stage where you can feel like you have no control. We can blame the food marketeers, the flashy images, the subliminal messages and the overwhelming advertising, but that makes us a victim. We need to find, take and step into our natural power again. As in the serenity prayer of Overeaters Anonymous:

*God grant me the serenity*
*to accept the things I cannot change;*
*courage to change the things I can;*
*and the wisdom to know the difference.*

I'm not a religious person, but I do believe in a Higher Power. God is the name that some people give to this power. This Higher Power is the spirit, that is around you, within you and in everyone and everything else you make contact with. Everyone has a different path, but we are all driven by the same force. It is that very force that will serve you in your **health, healing** and **happiness**. Flow with it!

The reality is that we cannot tear down all of the enticing food posters in our town, take ads off the TV, out of newspapers and magazines. But we can change the way we look at them and see them for what they are – well-researched techniques designed to get you to overeat and therefore buy more and more!

You'll read more about the different levels of mind in *Chapter Thirteen* - Stress and the Mind. It really is life-changing, fascinating stuff, just watching and knowing your mind.

So, back to the buffet table...........
There will be lots of reactions going on based on your past experiences. Your unconscious mind will probably be saying some or all of the following:

- ☐ *Look! My favourite foods – I know how delicious they really actually are!*
- ☐ *It's as if someone knew exactly what I wanted and has done this especially for me!*
- ☐ *I'm starving, I really should eat now, the photographs took forever!*
- ☐ *I deserve to eat lots now because I'm starving!*
- ☐ *If I don't take one of those vol-au-vents now, they might all be gone later*
- ☐ *It would be better to fill my plate now than have to come back for seconds*
- ☐ *I should grab mine now, before there's a queue!*

What unhelpful emotions are coming out here? Well at first, you may think greed, or maybe fear. But you *are* hungry. The overriding emotion here is usually PANIC! It's a fast reaction associated with fight or flight and it comes at you so fast, it is hard to recognise it, let alone rationalise it. But remember, knowledge is your power and sooner or later, you will see it coming and the opposite will happen. You will have a KNOWING. To get there, you need **Discipline**.

If you are aware of the panic, you will rationalise these thoughts and you might feel this:

- ☐ *Some of these are my favourite foods and I'm going to choose mainly the ones that I know serve me best.*
- ☐ *How lovely that I should have such good food to choose from!*
- ☐ *I'm hungry because the photographs took a long time, but I won't starve!*
- ☐ *Just because I'm really hungry doesn't mean that I need any more food than normal.*
- ☐ *Those vol-au-vents look amazing, maybe if there's one left, I'll have one.*
- ☐ *I'll take a little now, eat as consciously as I can and then, if I'm still not satisfied, I'll come back for more.*
- ☐ *If there's a queue, I'll get to talk to some more people before I start eating and I know I won't starve if I do have to wait a while. There will be plenty for everyone.*

How about that for a different way of programming! This is the way the unconscious mind of a non-overeater *might* work. And remember, these are unconscious thoughts at the time. Notice your reaction to the second set of thoughts, for a moment. Write down *those* reactive thoughts if you like. With practice in **Discipline**, you *can* intercept the unconscious thoughts, long before the first vol-au-vent hits the back of your tongue!

*"It's not the mountain we conquer, but ourselves."*
*~ Sir Edmund Hillary*

When you work through this book and you begin your regular practices, you *will* see a change. You will start to notice that although the emotions are there, you are not affected by them so much. So you haven't switched off, you are actually more turned *on* to your emotions than ever before. But they are not overwhelming you; you are not reacting adversely to them. You are maintaining your balance, your joy *and* your happiness.

It doesn't happen overnight. Rome wasn't built in a day, but it was built to last. Your work here will have long-lasting effects on your health, and probably your longevity.

The whole of the next chapter is dedicated to **Discipline**, because it is the most challenging aspect of anything you want to achieve. However, let's finish our journey through the 7 Spells...

Once you learn **Discipline**, then you will magically find that you have **Willpower**. Again, I'll talk more about Willpower in the next few pages. This Willpower is a result of mastering your unconscious mind's reactions to food (in particular foods that may not serve you, in quantities that are inappropriate for your needs), when they are presented to you.

The **powerful** force of **will** is pretty awesome. It reinforces all of the Spells you have worked through so far:

Your **Intention** – it strengthens your resolve
Your **Understanding** – you learn so much about yourself and about tools for the future
Your **Enthusiasm** – you feel elated that you really *can* do it and keep up the practice with gusto
Your **Commitment** – you really believe in your goals and start to trust yourself around food more

## Spell Number Six:
### *Self-Knowledge* which transforms into *Patience*

This leads to new comprehension of yourself. **Self-Knowledge** is the essence of the two Keys to Freedom – to **Know Yourself** and to **Know Your Worth**. The gift you receive from this **Self-Knowledge** is **Patience**. As refugees from commercial diets, we bring with us a huge amount of knowledge and wisdom, but we are also cynical. We are almost literally fed up with the promises of weight loss and sick of the time, money and heartache we have wasted on our false hopes. So we have to take a step away from that process and think about a lifestyle adjustment, a mind switch and a change of heart, to allow this work to do its **MAGIC!** Do not let yourself or your past get in the way of your dream.

You are worthy of **health, healing** and **happiness**. Let it come and let it flow. You didn't become an overeater overnight, and you won't heal overnight. But you WILL heal and you will feel better sooner than you probably think.

## Spell Number Seven:
### *Tenacity* which transforms into *Success*

This patience with the process will give you the **Tenacity** or staying power you need to go on living your best life with joy and without struggle and in that space will come the **Success** you so rightly deserve.

You will look at your vision one day and you will *realise* that you have *realised* your vision. You may look at it and feel it isn't exactly as you hoped, but you will also understand *why*. Perhaps it's to set you up for the next part of your vision, or maybe it's more suited to your highest good. But you will **Know Yourself** and what you are **Worth,** enough to really 'get it'.

*"Your intellect may be confused, but your emotions will never lie to you."*
~ *Roger Ebert*

Now for some more self-analysis. Please resist the temptation to move on without completing these exercises to the best of *your* ability *right* now. Take a break regularly to look out of the window, or step outside and just breathe deeply if necessary. Notice and move through any resistance that comes up.

Just write something. Remember <u>you are digging out some previously pushed-down emotions</u> in order to <u>create room for new foundations</u> on which to build a new life,

*free* of emotional eating and

*full* of health healing and happiness

# Exercise

1. Set a diary note to review the **7 Spells of BodyMAGIC!** regularly (weekly is great).

2. Now - look back at the **7 Spells** and check where you feel you are in the process towards success in **BodyMAGIC!** Whether you may have skipped a step and whether you have got to the point where you can move on to the next stage. This is a cycle that will repeat itself over and over again in almost everything you want in your life, provided it is for your highest good. But each step and where it leads is important. Like pieces of a jigsaw puzzle – the bigger picture is incomplete without one piece. Make some notes here if you like

   *I am in "the understanding" mode - need to stick with it to regain confidence. Need to see the emotions as fleeting, but tangible not powerful, not permanent.*

3. Photocopy the **Nine Reminders** a few times. Put a copy in places where you might need them, e.g. in your desk drawer, on your dashboard, on your refrigerator, in your purse. Read them to give your **Enthusiasm** a boost every day or so.

4. Write a little on your thoughts on the **7 Spells** process with regard to your most recent dieting (intention to lose weight) experience. Where in the process did you encounter challenges?

   *My challenge is to stop and sit with emotions that drive a binge.*

5. Think about one of your goals that is not food or diet-related. Write down how you could use each of the **7 Spells of BodyMAGIC!** to manifest your vision.

   *Letting others' differences be theirs not feel like it touches mine.*

6. What regular eating patterns do you have? Reflect on how you feel when those patterns are disturbed for any reason. Are there set times that you 'treat' yourself?

Know my patterns — Yes they are somewhat "set" but I have learned to "be okay". Harder if I can't exercise.

7. Think about when your regular lifestyle changes, e.g. holidays, birthdays, weddings, business trips. How much discipline do you feel that you have at those times? How do your unconscious and subconscious minds influence your reactions?

These are harder — try to allow variation. Some times I am okay with it — sometimes these times have led me to binge. Feel already "out of sorts" so I just lose it!

### Chapter Three
# Discipline and Willpower

*It was character that got us out of bed, commitment that moved us into action, and discipline that enabled us to follow through. I have learned that I really do have discipline, self-control and patience. But they were given to me as a seed, and it's up to me to choose to develop them.*
*~ Joyce Meyer*

Even just a few years ago, when I was trying to lose weight and failing miserably, the very idea of **Discipline,** to me, spelled a big struggle, strife and having to sacrifice everything I loved in order to gain what I thought I deserved in the first place! Of all of the **7 Spells of BodyMAGIC!**, **Discipline** is probably the toughest nut to crack. As we discussed in the previous chapter, this is because it comes from the unconscious or subconscious part of your mind. I will share even more of this with you later.

I have written a whole chapter on **Discipline**, not because I want to tell you that you will need to struggle to achieve peace with your body. That would be a paradox. Struggle and peace couldn't possibly exist in the same person! It is simply that you have to have some emotional input to take you from where you are now to where you want to be, and to help you from slipping back to where you have come from. Whether your goal is finding your BodyMAGIC!, running a marathon, setting up a business, keeping in touch with a distant friend, learning a new language or finding MAGIC! in everyday life, that energy-in-motion is **Discipline**!

The hard truth is that goals don't just happen; the **Idea** or dream has to have lots of power behind it to thrive. Sometimes, especially at the start, the difficulty is with really and truly believing that it can manifest what we want. As we discussed in the last chapter, from the dream or **Idea**, we need an **Intention**, **Focus** to learn more about the **Idea** and give us **Understanding**, so that we can then find **Confidence** in ourselves to allow our **Enthusiasm** to flow into **Determination** where we start to take our vision really seriously into the **Commitment** phase (whilst still having fun of course!).

## The first time we need Discipline is when we are challenged.

Please remember that, if you remember nothing else from this chapter. The first time you are tempted to eat more than you need of something you don't need, you will need your **Discipline**.

I did run a marathon in May 2014. When I signed up for it in July 2013, I felt very nervous indeed. It was just a dream. I remember saying to myself, "What the hell have I just done? I've just handed over some money to run 26.2 miles!" I'd only ever run a half marathon before. And that was in 2011. At that time, I was just ticking over with my running, on average three miles, three times a week, probably less in fact. I'd go through phases of not running at all, and then have to start from scratch all over again, with just a mile or maybe two. A marathon seemed like the challenge of climbing Mount Everest.

Enter MAGIC! – I'd done a vision board in May 2013, just two months before, and had found a picture of a beautiful blonde woman stretching, with a caption below that read "Your debut 26.2". I was mesmerised. I cut out the picture and stuck it on my board without hesitation. These vision boards really do work!

How did I do it? How did I make myself get out there and do the training? It was **Discipline**. My **Focus** developed from gathering as much information as I could about training for a marathon, and I really enjoyed the research, which increased my **Confidence**. I took several experts' training plans and moulded them into one that suited *my* body, *my* time and *my* lifestyle. That bit was easy because I *love* planning and that fed my **Enthusiasm** beautifully! I knew somewhere deep in my soul that if I could do it, just once, I would prove to myself that **anything humanly possible is possible for me.** This was my **Determination** phase, which led me to my **Commitment** and to the necessary training.

The **Discipline** came about when it was icy cold outside, and many other times besides. Like when I had, in my plan, to go out on Christmas morning and run seven miles. There were outside forces challenging my vision, such as opening presents, making a great breakfast, staying in bed a little longer! It was my **Discipline** that faced the challenge and my **Willpower** that got me out into the cold. And here's the MAGIC! – it actually was never as bad as my mind thought it would be. After a mile or two, the hat was off, the gloves were off, I was warm and enjoying the freshest air and the most beautiful scenery on one of the most tranquil days of the year. I felt privileged!

Most of the time, I believe, when it's needed, **Discipline** has to come fast and strong. It's not as if you have to find it *all* the time. It's like an unexpected kick up the bum. It's needed to face a reaction to something you didn't plan on, factor in or expect. And that challenging aspect comes from your unconscious mind. Yes, it's a big effort to find **Discipline** sometimes. You have to remind yourself why you want this, what you are committed to. Once you push through that, then it's downhill from there. You get to **Know Yourself** on a deeper level, and that **Self-knowledge** shows you **Patience** and **Tenacity**, so that you can succeed in anything you want.

**Discipline** gets easier, I promise you. If for any reason it doesn't, then you are either:

- ☐ Doing the wrong thing for yourself, your health and/or your wellbeing at that time,
- ☐ Not enjoying what you're doing (very important) or
- ☐ You have lost sight of what it is that you truly want

You then need to have a rethink.

*Character contributes to beauty. It fortifies a woman as her youth fades. A mode of conduct, a standard of courage, discipline, fortitude, and integrity can do a great deal to make a woman beautiful.*
*~ Jacqueline Bisset*

For years I believed I had no **Willpower**. Looking back, did I think willpower was genetic or something? And because I wasn't born with willpower, then it was never going to be mine? It makes me smile now. It was one of those excuses for giving up and overeating. And like all of the other excuses, it felt like a rebellion. Against who though? No-one else was going to feel it, and I certainly wasn't getting any love or attention from my bingeing. So sadly, the only person I was really hurting was myself. I understand this clearly now. Where and when I felt that I lacked willpower, I tried to gain back power from rebelling against my goals to lose weight, by overeating.

It was a hopeless and worthless cycle.

When I learned the value of **Discipline**, the **Willpower** grew stronger. It was all the power I needed. The bingeing stopped, because, in my new wisdom, I saw the power of will as stronger than the power of rebellion. This rebellion had probably come from my angry past. It doesn't even matter what part of my past. Eventually, with a little insight, and various practices (that I'm sharing with you in this book) I chose to let go of the need to rebel, because I realised that it was a cycle of victimhood. I over-ate because I was feeling low and I was feeling low because I over-ate. When I was down, I would justify why I had a right to feel like that. The negative stuff that had happened to me was mostly long since passed, but I held on to the pain to justify my overeating. Then I could overeat to escape my pain.

Complicated self-sabotage, I know!

This was all internal. I shared this only with a few counsellors and therapists who helped me on my path to healing. But none of them really understood or could help me, either because I didn't know this stuff about myself, or because they didn't have the experience to ask me, or because they focused all of their work with me on healing my past. All of the healing I have had has been helpful and you should not hesitate to find other help and healing with past trauma. But this book is specific to overcoming emotional eating, and it is working on the present time – that is NOW.

That is why this chapter is so important. You have to find a way to draw a huge line under your previously perceived failings at losing weight and know that EVERY moment NOW is a HUGE opportunity for change, growth and happiness. You don't have to wait until the new year, your birthday, next Monday, the new moon or even tomorrow. The BodyMAGIC! can – and should – start today, in the next few minutes. You deserve *so* much! We are all influenced by our past, of course. Most of us have had a fair share of pain through trauma, grief, worry, sadness, anger, even shock. We can't change a single bit of the past, but we can change the way we look at it *and* choose how to feel about it.

When my mother passed away from cancer in 2006, it totally changed my world. It hurt so much, all of the time, for about two years. It still really hurts sometimes. But I look back at my life since she went. Her passing shifted everything in me. My life and values changed beyond anything I could've ever imagined, and all for the better. I would give up everything to have her back, but the reality is not that she's gone, but that her essence is still here. The lessons she taught me vibrate around me all of the time. When I speak, I hear her voice in mine. She continues to guide, nurture and inspire me with her spirit. So you see, the most stressful events that can happen in anyone's life can hold the greatest opportunities for growth, learning and even joy. You *too* have a choice. You can either hold on to the pain of the past or you can take whatever wisdom, knowledge and experience it gave you and get the hell out of there! Every second of your life you have the chance to do this, so do it when you are ready. But DO IT, and SOON! And in that shift, you will find all the positive **Intention**, **Discipline** and **Willpower** you need to succeed with *anything* in your life.

*With faith, discipline and selfless devotion to duty, there is nothing worthwhile that you cannot achieve.*
*~ Muhammad Ali Jinnah*

There will still be times when you feel short on **Discipline** and your **Willpower** fades. There is always a good reason for this. And it's just life. We are not robots. We have variables! Maybe your energy stores are low. There could be something lacking in your food intake, maybe you didn't get a great night's sleep, or you have been ill/unsettled/stressed. It's usually a bit of all of these. For example, if you are ill, you perhaps haven't adjusted your diet according to its current needs, and your sleep may be disturbed. If you aren't getting a good night's rest, there is usually a reason – maybe you ate late before bed or you are stressed about something. In the next chapter, I'll be discussing the benefits of journaling. But suffice to say that journaling about how you feel really helps you to identify 'low' days and accept them as part of the flow of life, rather than reacting with food as a comforter. The practices in this book will provide that acceptance, giving you the **Discipline** you need to exercise your **Willpower**.

This book is a tool to help and guide you to move gracefully to that place of balance, at least most of the time. The MAGIC! of a fulfilling life is that everything comes in cycles. Just like the seasons, there are times when we feel great and times when we don't. It is possible to accept that all of it is perfectly timed, and then you can, and will, feel peace.

*Winners embrace hard work They love the discipline of it, the trade-off they're making to win. Losers, on the other hand, see it as punishment. And that's the difference.*
*~ Lou Holtz*

## So what is your investment?

Well, you have already bought this book, so you've made a financial investment in your body's future. There may be a few things you choose to buy, as tools to help support you on your path to lifelong BodyMAGIC! At the time of writing, I'm not selling any of these things. Maybe I will in the future, so check the BodyMAGIC! website if you like. Just about everything is available online these days. I will list them in the Resources section so you can get hold of them yourself if you wish. Think about what you already have that you can use, buy from a charity/thrift store or from a friend having a clear-out (reuse), or recycle something you already have. This is another step to reducing your individual impact on the very planet that serves your health with the food you eat, the water you drink and the air you breathe. More information on these essential connections, later.

Your investment of time is the most important aspect of this book. Allow a *minimum* of half to one hour in the morning, a half hour at lunchtime (optional) and a half hour in the evening to work on yourself. This will be for your **daily practices**. This is the minimum you deserve. You have work to do, and you will need time to do it. It will not be hard work. In fact, I hope that you will really enjoy it. You clean your teeth morning and evening, and you probably miss this rarely. It is my hope that you will feel this way about your daily practice time. You may have to ask for support from your partner or family, especially if you have young children. But it can be done, and it must be done. Do you know the average American spends four non-working hours in front of the TV or computer every day? That's thirteen years of the average lifetime. But did you also know that twenty minutes of focused meditation is equivalent to two hours' sleep? What choice is there to make?

Take your time with this book. Obviously, you will want to know what to do with this time as soon as possible. If you haven't got so far in the book that you know what the practices actually are, take the time anyway. Just to sit, contemplate or write. You will be amazed how your body and mind react to the fact that you are allowing time for them. You are showing yourself some love and attention. This alone will calm your nervous and cardiovascular system, overcome stress, allow your digestive system to function better and strengthen your immunity *and* your resolve to overcome your emotional eating.

After a maximum of two weeks' continual practice, you *will* feel different. After three to four weeks you will have a habit. You will be considering life-long lifestyle changes. But take it slow. For most of us, it takes 21 days to change a habit, and that's one habit at a time. It is better to take a year to fully integrate some of the material from this book and feel the benefits, than to try and do it all at once and be totally overwhelmed and give up. And then you would never know what could have been. I have put 35 years of experience into these pages, and I have tried to make them as easy as possible. But healing and health take time. You may have understood from this book so far that this is not a crash course in perfect health and wellbeing. It is a life-changer, yes, but please be patient. Find *your* **Focus, Discipline, Enthusiasm,** *your* **Commitment**, and above all *your* **Patience**. How many years have you wasted already trying to lose weight, get fit and feel healthy? Allow time for this process, and I promise you, you will succeed!

See it as a pleasure, not a chore. When you do see the change, don't stop. This is another common mistake. We feel better, so we think we can have a break from our practices. You are not a machine, but a creature of habit. These habits are to stay with you, to be integrated into your life, whether you are at home, in a hotel or staying with friends. When you are ill, when you are happy and when you are sad. Like brushing your teeth, you take whatever tools you need with you. This commitment to your daily practice, however brief it might be on some days, will have an everlasting impact on the whole of your life. That, my friend, is the MAGIC!

# Exercise

*In order to carry a positive action we must develop here a positive vision.*
*~ Dalai Lama*


## Make a Vision Board!


Get a large piece of card or thick paper. It will need to go on a wall, somewhere where you will see it every day. So make sure you have a space on the wall in mind before you start. I have heard of families doing this exercise together and posting on a bathroom wall where all can see it when nature calls! I have mine next to my bed, and I take a look at it when I'm getting dressed and waking up.

Find some paper, scissors and glue and make yourself a cup of tea (not with the glue obviously!).

Grab at least six (the more the merrier) magazines, brochures, catalogues etc., that interest you. Start flicking through and cutting out any pictures you are drawn to. Don't consider the possibilities, your goals, or how you might reach them. Don't stop to think, just cut out the pictures. This is a creative exercise, not a logistical one. So just allow that energy to flow. Have fun, dream and play with your imagination! Your pictures can be related to food or not. When you feel you have enough, arrange them on your board. They can overlap or you can leave space between them. It's up to you entirely. Stick the pictures down when you are happy with the positioning of them. Don't put any aside because you have had second thoughts about them. Stick them ALL on.

You may find that you spill over onto another board. Just go with it, until you feel you are done. Sometimes your second board is for the future, the long term, and you can come back to it and complete it later. If you want to, draw, doodle and decorate around your pictures.

This is a great exercise to do with friends over a morning or afternoon, and even as a family. It's a great way to connect and have fun. Maybe set a loose timescale, e.g. 2-3 hours, with a break from the cutting table for tea. When everyone is finished, each person presents their board(s) to the group. This is an incredibly powerful moment. It's like an affirmation. You are telling them what you are doing in each picture as if it has already happened. *That* is the MAGIC!

Maybe you have a vision board already. If it's not on the wall, get it out and take a long hard look at it. Why did you post what you did? Was it a reflection of your aspirations at the time, and does it reflect what you dream of in your life now? If yes, keep looking at it! If not, get out your glue and scissors and dream big!


*Confidence comes from discipline and training.*
*~ Robert Kiyosaki*

## Chapter Four

# Journaling for Joy!

*The starting point of discovering who you are, your gifts, your talents, your dreams, is being comfortable with yourself. Spend time alone. Write in a journal. Take long walks in the woods.*
*~ Robin S. Sharma*

This is a book. As an object it belongs to you because you paid out cash for it. But the content of it is mine. It's my story. It's a collection of facts and fallacies, methods, experiences and ideas that I have wanted to share with you. But I don't know you personally. Much of what you are reading will make absolute sense to you; some of it could seem a little strange to you. It may bring up some resistance because of your own personal story. All of this is normal and it is good. I already know that the details of my journey with food, body image and emotional eating are very common. I've done my research. But the truth is that no-one will have exactly the same challenges as I have had, or the same experiences as me, or explored the same solutions. No-one else has exactly the same tastes, ideas, habits, lifestyle. No-one has my body or my mind.

In an ideal world, I would be by your side, helping you as an individual, teaching you, guiding you, coaching you, giving you healing, praising you and picking you up when you feel like falling down. But, as much as I would love to, unfortunately I cannot personally coach all of you at the same time. In the spirit of my own **7 Spells of BodyMAGIC!** it is my **Determination** that, as this book is published in print, I have the **Commitment** to you to produce courses, seminars, webinars and even more support for you on your journey. But unless I coach you personally, I'll never exactly match your needs with my message and methods.

At the time of writing you are able to visit www.BodyMAGIC.website and request a FREE 30-minute coaching session with either myself or one of my team of experts. I strongly suggest that you take this offer, as the coaching will be in line with the principles of this book. You could also visit a therapist to support you on this path. Maybe they have similar concepts for your journey as this book, but I doubt if they are the same. However, the more support you can get, the better.
Whether you do or you don't have a coach I'm going to suggest that you start one very important practice now:

## Writing!!

There are **two** practices that I recommend. Neither take much time but the results are simply amazing. I suggest that you write a gratitude diary at the end of each day (why not start today?) so that you can unravel and contemplate the day that has just passed and look forward with maximum happiness to the following day. Then, secondly, a journal practice first thing in the mornings to release whatever is on your mind, maybe from your dreams (your unconscious problem processor), even if you don't remember them, any reservations you have about the day and any emotions that are not serving you (you can refer to your **Emotion Elevator**).

# 1. Gratitude Diary

The first practice requires that you write *something* at the end of every day about the MAGIC! you have experienced. It may be something you did, or something that happened to you. And it may not necessarily be particularly good at the time either. But when you reflect, try to write a little about the MAGIC! in each event. You can write about one thing or several things. If you write about only one thing, let it be the thing that had the greatest impact on you that day, good or bad. Don't write as a bragger or a victim. Be humble. Write with gratitude in your heart. It might be about a lesson you learned, an 'Aha!' moment, a rush of joy, the release of an emotion. Write from a place of positivity and thanks. Even if you had the worst day ever, write about some glimmer of hope, joy or love that you felt or saw in someone's eyes. You will take some extremely good energy to bed with you, and the following day will *feel* like a new beginning, as it should be.

*A pessimist sees the difficulty in every opportunity; an optimist sees the opportunity in every difficulty."*
*~ Winston Churchill*

## Shut-eye

A gratitude diary is a way of ensuring that you sleep easy too. Can you even begin to guess how many hours of sleep we miss because we take our unresolved thoughts, challenges and problems to bed with us? Sleep is not only necessary, it's essential to your success. Remember the **7 Spells** and their related emotions. If we want to continue to **Focus**, have **Confidence**, **Determination**, **Discipline**, **Self-Knowledge** and **Tenacity**, we need energy. If we are to feel **Understanding**, **Commitment**, **Enthusiasm**, **Willpower**, **Patience** and **Success**, we need a positive view of the world, and we need to be well-rested. Sleep is food for your mind and healing for your body. Do you know that your body renews itself every seven years? This is an average. To get above average you need a healthful diet of course, but it is useless without proper rest. Most of your body's rejuvenation takes place when you are asleep.

# 2. Your Journal

A journal can be anything from several pages a day to one sentence. There is something very magical indeed about journaling. After reading only the first few pages of Julia Cameron's book, *The Artist's Way*, I starting getting up a half hour earlier every morning and writing three full pages of anything that was in my head. I discovered that a piece of paper can be a therapist! And if you are an artist, a writer or facing a block in your creativity, I strongly recommend this book. My learning from it is that when you write stuff down, your consciousness shifts. It's as if you really can read between the lines. Ideas, solutions and healing seem to leap invisibly from the page.

Yes! Just like MAGIC!

I'm not asking you to get up another half hour earlier than you already are, for your other practices. This is a slightly different exercise. But if you have the time, or there is something major going on in your life, you may like to try it on those days. It's undoubtedly the shift that gave me the **Tenacity** to finish this book!

BodyMAGIC! requires that you simply write *something* at the beginning of every day. At some point in the first part of your morning, spend at least five minutes, of your allocated thirty, writing about anything and everything that's on your mind. Sit somewhere quiet for a moment to contemplate on your life and emotions at this time.

- ☐ What do you really want to say? Don't be afraid to moan! This is *not* being negative, it's detoxing your heart and mind, healing your emotions and therefore your soul, *and* hence, your relationship with food.
- ☐ What is having the greatest impact on you and why?
- ☐ What, if anything, is shifting?
- ☐ What have you learned?
- ☐ What would you like to do differently in the future because of it?

Refer to **The 7 Spells of BodyMAGIC!** for guidance and remember it all starts with an **Idea**. Ideas only come from positive thoughts about the future. To get them we need to evacuate the stuff that holds us back.

Your journal can be a summary of your previous day, your feelings about what happened in the day, the people you met with and any challenges you faced. Maybe write about your dreams if you remember them. This journal is for expressing your emotions. It can also be the learnings you are getting, the brilliant stuff that's happening in your life right now. However you feel – good, bad or ugly; Let it flow! Get it out! The paper is your therapist.

## Creative Solutions

When we write, we use the right side of our brain. We let go of logic, constraints, rules and methods. We just write. We write from our hearts. Like anything creative, it can be limitless. And it is like a meditation in itself. Notice how children playing will go into their own world. Things are happening all around them, but they don't notice, they just keep playing. They don't care about time or rules or whether dinner is ready or not, they just keep playing until they *have* to stop. This is the right brain. Through our rule-driven society, as we grow up, we become very left-brain oriented. We learn rules from everywhere – our parents, our friends, our schools, our workplace. Rules are for the masses; creativity is for the individual. Journaling will help you to activate your right brain, your creative side. And when you do, you will find that you will have your own creative solutions to life's problems, but particularly to your challenges with eating.

*"This pouring thoughts out on paper has relieved me. I feel better and full of confidence and resolution."*
*~ Diet Eman*

$$\mathsf{E}\text{xercise}$$

## Get Journaling!

Buy yourself **two** books. You need a small diary with room for a couple of sentences of **Gratitude**. No more. You can keep it in your purse or bag and look at it when you feel low on energy and enthusiasm, but make sure it's next to your bed to fill in daily, just before you go to sleep.

Also, get yourself a blank book that you are happy with for your **Journal**. Make sure it has lots of pages. A little purse-size notebook will not allow you much room for writing. I know you can spend a small fortune on beautiful journals and if you want to do that, do it! You can buy journals like diaries, that have a space for each day. If that suits you, then go for it. The only downside to that is that you are limited by the amount of space you have each day. If you feel like a waffle about how brilliant, or a rant about how awful your day was, then you are going to struggle. Remember it's not good for a creator to have limits. When that moment of creativity comes, you want to have room for it to express itself! I use a simple A4 lined pad. Sometimes I fill three pages, but I almost always finish a page if I start one. They are not really for reflection at a later date, unless you particularly want them for some reason. When I fill a pad, I put it away. I may destroy them one day. They can be compared to a bucket collecting stuff that you don't want. Like today's newspaper, each page is important at the time, but not afterwards. Unless you have a use for the pages, such as that you intend to write a book or something with them, then let them go periodically, along with your past.

How about a more earth-conscious alternative? Maybe you can find a blank notebook you have lying around your home somewhere. My daughter went through a phase in her teens when she loved to have notebooks with the latest fashionable style or craze on the cover. She hardly used more than a few pages before a new design became more attractive. I've probably seized every discarded one from the back of her cupboards over the years! Write your name on the cover and personalise it with pictures, cut-outs, doodles, drawings, quotes, affirmations and the like, if that makes it more fun for you. Do what you want. It's yours, and there are no limits and definitely no rules. These are just suggestions for you to consider.

Many of the practices you will be learning in this book will help you tremendously, but none will impact your behaviours as much as meditation. And that's what we'll be discussing in the next chapter. I hope you are still excited. This is truly MAGIC!

*"Writing is the only way I have to explain my own life to myself."*
*~ Pat Conroy*

## Chapter Five

# MeditationMAGIC!

*"Remember, happiness doesn't depend upon who you are or what you have; it depends solely on what you think."*
*~ Dale Carnegie*

Of all the concepts, options and practices in this book, this is the most important. It has already been proven to get results, and I will stand by it and shoot its benefits like fireworks from the rooftops for as long I live! So if the idea of sitting with your eyes closed, without thinking about your task list horrifies you then take a deep breath, make yourself a hot drink (without caffeine!), and open your mind. This will be a game-changer for you. It will break the circuit of suffering you have trudged around time and time again, trying to live in the body you dream of. It's time to figure out exactly what goes on in your mind, whether it's real and whether you really need to feel the pain of what is in it. Meditation is the key to the door of peace and self-knowledge. In **The 7 Spells of BodyMAGIC!** meditation is the **Focus** and **Self-knowledge** is the **Understanding**. It *will* help you, which is why meditation is the most important part of your daily practice.

## The Science and the Stigma

This is not a cult, but it is a culture of peace. Meditation is not brain-washing either, although it will cleanse your mind of all the dross that has probably been holding you back for years. You don't need to buy beads, bells or a tambourine! And for the record, no-one is going to knock on your door and ask you to sacrifice yourself to a commune, or ask you for your salary, your soul, your kids or to repent your wrongdoings (at least not from my office!). Meditation is not a religion: there is no dogma. Meditation is a science. Each session is an experiment. Every time you close your eyes in meditation, you are changing your physical, mental and emotional energies.

Modern science has proven what tradition has always known. Meditation really helps with *all* stress, including eating-related stress. Dr. Peter Malinowski is founder of the Meditation and Mindfulness Research Group at John Moore's University in Liverpool, UK. In the video 'Mindfulness research at LJMU', on his website and on YouTube, he explores the physiological and psychological effects of mindfulness practice, with reference to cognitive ageing and healthy eating. The results so far are based on people practising mindfulness compared with those who don't. The results are exciting and leave no doubt about the benefits of meditation for those struggling with food addiction, emotional eating or life stress in general:

- ☐ Once we reach the age of 30, cognitive skills start to deteriorate slowly. Although research is in the early stages and will continue over a long period of time yet to come; early signs indicate that mindfulness helps to slow down this cognitive decline.

- ☐ Eating behaviour is psychologically motivated. Researchers understand the emotional process in eating and are aware that increasing mindfulness, through the regular practice of meditation, changes emotional drives and will help us to have more control when we choose what we eat, how much and how often. It will help us to stick to our plans for losing weight. What a result!

Mindfulness is one style (of many) of meditation that has really increased in popularity over the last few years. It has a clear structure, framework and practice, and because of this has been very popular in the corporate setting. However, it is a structure that is based on a very traditional practice that has been around for many centuries. Meditation has been transmuted into many of the modern alternative and complementary health practices that exist today. Techniques such as hypnosis, Neuro-Linguistic Programming (NLP), even simple affirmation practices are derived from traditional meditation techniques. I have studied many of them and have had guidance from teachers who have dedicated their lives to studying meditation.

There is a new and increasing demand for meditation in the workplace, particularly the office environment. Over many years now, meditation has become a new age buzz-word in many stressful settings. Practising meditation has been shown to improve performance and output, enhance relationships between workers, reduce absenteeism by boosting health, and also develop the ability to find creative solutions to problems.

## How it has worked for me

But it hasn't always been this way. If we go back to the turn of the century, when I was a people manager, in an office setting, the idea of helping staff to be more mindful and enhance their lives with practices based in eastern mysticism would've have been on another planet. There's no doubt that it would've helped me and my staff in the bank where I worked. But it just never entered our heads as a concept, let alone a solution to our sub-par holistic health. Absenteeism was a given. People 'just got' flu, stomach bugs, migraines, backache, long-term stress. As long as our department's absenteeism statistics were below the organisation's average then no questions were asked. I may have been good at my job, but I was pretty bloody-minded about most things I didn't understand. Even if anyone could actually have asked a stressed-out banker like me, living life continually on the edge of burn-out (as I was), to start sitting in meditation, at best you might have received a smirk in return. It used to have such stigma around it for me and the people I worked with. My route to finding meditation as a healing really happened through yoga. And it took years.

> *"If fear is cultivated it will become stronger, if faith is cultivated it will achieve mastery"*
> ~ John Paul Jones

I was at the top of my game as far as a corporate career was concerned. I felt that I had really 'made it'. Even as a single mum, I had a loving and supportive family who were proud of me, a great house, a fast sports car, an enviable circle of friends and an amazing social life, fancy clothes and memorable holidays, and I never had to check my bank account before I spent any money. But there was still something missing. I looked for it blindly. I realised any more promotions at my job would mean that I would probably have to relocate and work even longer hours, and the work/life balance would have tipped way out of my favour. So I was happy with my career. I was earning a good income and had time to enjoy it. I was never short of company, with something planned every day of the week. There were always holidays to look forward to. I was never short of enthusiasm for a diary full of tickets for shows, festivals and gatherings to celebrate with friends.

My life was full of fun, but there was still a void there for something I couldn't buy or even touch, but that I sensed I really needed. I was perceptive enough to realise that I needed knowledge, but the only way I could see to get it was to study for a Degree in Business and Finance. I don't know how I got through those years of study, juggling being a mum, working stupid hours, managing a home and my social life. Yes, I had a lot of help, but I wasn't as fit or healthy as I am now, writing this book. My body was in an elevated state of stress the whole time. For some years, I found my happiness in alcohol, drugs (including anti-depressants and sleeping tablets), cigarettes, but mainly food. My immune system was so weak that I fell prey to flu several times each winter practically every time anyone sneezed in my direction. What I needed was to learn how to be really happy, in my **body** *and* **mind**. I leave out the **spirit** or **soul** word deliberately here, because I didn't have a clue what that was back then!

A friend and I noticed that a local college was offering yoga classes one evening a week, for beginners and improvers. I had heard that yoga was good for health, but to be honest, I didn't know what yoga was. I probably chose it over going to the gym because I thought it would be a good stretch! We did the first class and I remember feeling completely out of place. Everyone was so relaxed. The teacher spoke very softly and it all seemed so slow. I had been used to aerobics and circuit training, with loud pumping music and someone screaming at me! I found myself holding back a combination of giggles of embarrassment and yawns of exhaustion. I was like a fish out of water. Yet by complete contrast, I felt that I had come home. Everything about that first class nudged me into a change of perspective. I remember thinking, I wonder if I could ever teach this? How arrogant that might've seemed back then! But part of me just knew. I went back, week after week, and something started to shift. It didn't happen overnight, but was a gradual, gentle introduction to a world where I would eventually find peace. It was this peace that had been missing from my life. I hadn't found it anywhere, no matter where I looked, what I owned or how successful I was.

> *"All man's miseries derive from not being able to sit quietly in a room alone."*
> ~ Blaise Pascal

For a few years more, I hung on to my old paradigm. I realise that many of us are just brought up that way – with the fear of scarcity. It was essential to have the biggest house I could afford, a pension, a secure job, a future. So I held on. And then the bomb dropped - my mum passing away from cancer. I knew it was stress that caused the dis-ease that eventually killed her. She had to find her peace in another world. I didn't want to follow in her emotional footsteps, or have my daughter follow in mine.

In those dark grief-filled days, I started to ask some pretty harsh questions:

- ☐ was I partly to blame? She worried about me and my siblings constantly
- ☐ was she happy? She often expressed that she wished things were different
- ☐ did she eat well, exercise well? She was bought up in a meat-and-two-veg culture with puddings and cakes, *every* day. She considered housework to be her exercise
- ☐ did she rest well? She was always saying she was tired
- ☐ did she have a personal practice? She always said she never had enough time for herself
- ☐ did she have any hobbies, creative avenues? She never had interests of her own, even when we kids left home, preferring to do stuff with my dad, who *did* have his own interests but not what she particularly liked. She liked the garden, knitting and reading historical romance
- ☐ did she have a spiritual practice? Although she married into the Catholic church, she never really embraced *any* faith or spirituality

Can you see a pattern here? It hurts me to write it and see it for myself. She *did* have a choice, as we all do. We need to understand our energy resources and their limits. The hard truth is that if we don't take gentle care of ourselves, we will get sick – either mentally or physically. The mind and body are absolutely and irrevocably linked. What happens in one instantly affects the other. The good news is that both mind and body are pretty awesome. They can take a huge amount of abuse over many years before they become really ill. One of the most profound things we can do to redress the balance and turn a monumental corner in our **health, healing** and **happiness**, is to meditate.

## So What is Meditation?

Here is the Cambridge Dictionary definition:

***"The act of giving your attention to only one thing, either as a religious activity or as a way of becoming calm and relaxed."***

In the yogic tradition, meditation is known as a state. It is part of yoga, not separate from it. It is not a religion. Many people believe that yoga is Buddhist or Hindu. It is neither. Yoga, as the practice of meditation, has probably been around for 5,000 years.

The Yoga Sutras are 196 pieces of information about meditation. Within them, meditation is referred to as one stage on the path to enlightenment. If you want to go deeper into traditional practices, now or in the future, the Sutras are worth studying. They were written in the ancient language of Sanskrit but there are many good translations. I have recommended a couple of them, that I have studied, in the Resources section of this book.

It is a practice that helps us not to react to the things that can cause stress within the mind and body. It helps us to see the bigger picture, and learn that most of our negative thoughts are not real. It is always these reactions that cause us to overeat.

*"Rather than being your thoughts and emotions, be the awareness behind them."*
*~ Eckhart Tolle*

It is not a particularly relaxing practice, although one can feel more relaxed afterwards, and with regular practice more relaxed in general. But actually practising meditation can feel like the opposite to relaxation. It can feel quite challenging at times. But guess what? These are likely to be the times when you need it the most.

A relaxation practice is usually quite different. Meditation is usually working on the mind. Relaxation is usually focused on relaxing the body. However, remember that both are connected.

## Benefits of Meditation

I really do believe that meditation can have an effect on just about every aspect of the mind and body, but here's a taster to whet your appetite. Meditation:

- Relaxes the nervous system - calms stress and creates a relaxation response in the body
- Reduces negative thinking - allows us to see the bigger picture

- Balances hormones - especially those involved in stress, such as reducing adrenaline and increasing serotonin
- Improves immunity - by bringing all of the body's systems back into balance
- A reduction in stress reduces the risk of heart disease, high blood pressure and other cardiovascular conditions
- A reduction in stress reduces the risk of digestive disorders such as Crohn's disease, irritable bowel syndrome and other conditions related to acidity
- Slows down the ageing process
- Helps with chronic pain management

We are not really sure of the extent of the effects of stress on the body. But many believe (as do I) that *all* illness and disease evolves from stress, whether this is from what we put into our body (e.g. eating, breathing, medicating), where we live (e.g. air, water, light, noise pollution) or the emotional/mental challenges we have with the demands we face in modern life. We shall be discussing this in more detail later in *Chapter Thirteen* - Stress and the Mind.

## Methods of Meditation

There are many methods to meditation, from visualisations of being somewhere tranquil to chanting a mantra. All of these meditations do have one thing in common – they are training the unconscious mind. Their objective is to focus the attention on one thing and therefore to train the mind to be still.

These methods are extremely useful. Most of us find it difficult to stop the 'monkey mind' by trying to think of nothing, and we need some *thing* or some *concept* to redirect the thoughts when we meditate. Details of the many different styles of meditation are beyond the scope of this book.

I have produced a set of 6xCDs:

### MeditationMAGIC! - The Collection

that are put together to give you a thorough introduction to meditation and some of its practices. I have studied with many masters over the years and pulled the knowledge together from those I have found to be the most effective. It is highly experiential. If you are signed up for mailings on www.BodyMAGIC.website I'll let you know when they are released and how to get a 10% discount off the retail price!

> *"Throughout the years I have tried to hone my skills to gain mastery over the music in my head."*
> ~ Kip Winger

There are just two meditation practices given in this book. They are very simple to understand and you will not have to think too much about the practice. It may be challenging though, especially if you haven't practised meditation before, or for a while.

Stick with it! Within a week or two, you will start to feel subtle, but quite profound benefits.

**Anapanasati** meditation focuses on the breath in one place - at the entrance to the nose. The breath has the essential qualities of being neutral and of being present. Whilst no two breaths are ever the same, there is also no judgement about the breath. If we are focusing on the breath in this way, we are completely in the present moment. All stress, no matter how slight, is related to judgement and reaction about something that happened in the past or worry (based on experience in the past) about something in the future.

This practice serves to decondition the unconscious (reaction) mind and has been proven to deliver much deeper and longer term results in removing negative mental habitual patterns and emotions such as anxiety, anger, hatred and fear. We are working on the reactions of the unconscious mind, deconditioning them to behave differently, and changing those reactions.

So if your reaction to receiving a box of chocolates for your birthday is to devour them to get rid of them as soon as you can, then one of the benefits of this meditation, in time, may be that you don't react that way when you are given chocolates in the future. Maybe you give them away, maybe you open and share them when you have guests, or maybe you even take one a day until they are gone. Who knows what regular practice over time will do for your **discipline** and **willpower** levels!

What you *will* find is that you will have an opportunity to consider your options before you act. Often, as emotional eaters, we have eaten all of the chocolates before we have even thought about the emotional or physical consequences!

**Anapana** refers to the inhalation and exhalation, **sati** means mindfulness. Therefore, this practice is mindfulness on the breath. Although a simple practice to learn the practice itself is a challenge, and the mind is more likely to wander off than during many other meditation practices. Awareness of the breath in this practice is in just one place, the tip of the nose.

I will offer some ways to keep awareness on the breath throughout. With regular practice and commitment, you will not need these variations and will be able to focus more easily on the breath at the tip of the nose. The mind will wander less as you train the unconscious mind to remain with the breath. I love the analogy often given, of training a new puppy. You will pull the lead to bring the puppy to heel many many times before it stays there. It is only with repetition and practice that this can happen. But it can when you practice regularly, and then magical things will start to happen.

The **Discipline** is only to practice regularly, as that is the *only* way to feel the benefits of meditation. It is important to let the need to control the mind go once you are meditating, for the need to control may only bring about more stress.

# Exercise

**Let's go meditate!**

The first practice below is a script for you to record, so that you can close your eyes and meditate. If you really can't cope with the sound of your own voice, get a well-spoken friend or relative to record it for you. I have even included pauses so you can get into the flow. Choose a time to record the script when you won't be disturbed. Any background noise is likely to cause a distraction.

When you have your recording, you may also like to check out my videos on preparing for meditation. They are available on YouTube for FREE!:

**MeditationMAGIC!**
Part 1. Exercises for sitting magically
Part 2. Poses for sitting magically

Apart from these guidelines, you will also want to choose a time and place where you will not be disturbed, by other people *or* other creatures, by the cold, by sleep, indigestion, hunger or thirst. Turn your phone off, put it on airplane mode, or on silent in the next room. Get used to making the most of your sacred space and your special time. Give it the reverence it deserves. Here is the script. It is part of just one of the meditations taken from my programme. If you don't fancy recording it yourself, I'm giving you private access to it on Soundcloud for FREE! by following this link:  https://goo.gl/KSA6KI

## Meditation Practice

**Practice 1 - about 25 minutes.**

Find a comfortable seated position with some contact with the ground. This can be on a chair or seated on the floor, perhaps on a cushion. Lengthen your spine so that you can breathe fully and comfortably. This will also help you to not feel sleepy during the practice. Your shoulders are back and relaxed, with your hands in a comfortable position. Your legs are in a position that supports your back and your neck.

Set your intention to be still during the practice, as you close your eyes.

Take some deep breaths into your chest. *Pause.* Now relax your breath so that it is silent as it moves in and out of your nose. Concentration is on the breath in and out of the body but only at the tip of the nose. You are watching your breath pass this position, not following it into your body. Think of a saw moving through a log. You do not follow the movement of the saw back and forth, but you keep your eyes on the position of the log that the saw is cutting. Watch your breath moving past the end of your nose in this way.
*Pause - 2 minutes*

When you become aware of a thought or even a train of thoughts, bring your attention back to the breath. Don't analyse the distraction from the breath or purpose of the meditation. Move back to the breath with gentle awareness and without judgement.
*Pause - 3 minutes*

Staying with the breath, notice the temperature of the breath as you breathe. Is the inhale cool or warm? And is the exhale cool or warm?
*Pause - 2 minutes*

Notice the subtle difference in temperature between the inhale and the exhale as you breathe.
*Pause - 2 minutes*

Keep your attention on the breath. Begin to count the cycles of the breath. One cycle is one inhale and one exhale. Count from 1 to 5 and then begin again. If you lose your count, don't analyse or judge, just start again.
*Pause - 2 minutes*

Remember every time you become aware of a thought you are training your consciousness. This is very important. Just count your breaths for as long as you can now, at this point in your learning and discovery.
*Pause - 2 minutes*

With your attention on your breath in the nose, notice which of your nostrils your breath is moving in and out of mostly. It is rarely moving evenly between the nostrils. Be curious. Is the inhale AND exhale primarily moving out of the right nostril or the left nostril? Or is the inhale moving mainly in through the right and the exhale out of the left nostril? Or is the breath moving in mainly through the left nostril and out of the right side? Or do they seem even in your experience right now?
*Pause - 2 minutes*

Still holding your attention on the breath in the nose, and without following the breath, notice its speed and length. How fast does each inhale and exhale move past your focus point? Notice the speed of each inhale and of each exhale, and how the speed changes during breathing.
*Pause - 2 minutes or more until there are 2 minutes to go*

Now, bring your awareness back to breathing in and out of your nose. Keeping your eyes closed, bring your awareness back to the room by visualising its walls. Make some small movements in the fingers and toes. Rub your palms together and then cover your eyes. When you are ready to, let your hands fall from your face, letting the light in through your fingers.

Bring your hands into Prayer Pose and bow your head…Namaste.

I would recommend that you practice this meditation with your recording for about 21 days. It can be either in the morning, at lunchtime, or as part of your evening practice. But try to make it the same time every day. In my experience and in that of the groups I have worked with, it seems that we love a routine. Meditation becomes easier with a regular practice routine.

# Practice 2

After 21 days, you will start to feel that it's getting a little easier.
You can then stop the guided meditation and practice without it.
You do not have to count the breaths or be aware of the nostrils.
You will have to remember just one thing, to focus on the breath at the tip of the nose.
You will not have a voice to bring you back from your thoughts, but you will be strengthening your mind when you do.
You will find that you are able to focus for increasingly longer periods of time, with practice.

There are several apps you can get for your phone, that have a chime to let you know when your time is up. This is great, as it saves you worrying about time. When we really get into our meditation, time can pass quite quickly! Some of the apps will chime at your chosen intervals, which I really like. It's like a little voice checking that you haven't wandered off somewhere! Don't forget to set the phone to airplane mode. You can also use an alarm. Just check it's not too alarming! You don't want the kind of out-of-body experience you get by jumping out of your skin!

Be curious as you explore the practices and benefits of meditation, but most of all, be patient. My greatest wish is that you will value your meditation time, as you see huge improvements in your life. You will look forward to practising it, not because you are developing another addiction, but because every cell in your body and every impulse in your mind knows how good it is for you.

*"Curiosity is one of the permanent and certain characteristics of a vigorous mind."*
*~Unknown*

## Chapter Six
# Support or Solitude?

*"Those who look for the laws of Nature as a support for their new works, collaborate with the creator."*
*~ Antoni Gaudí*

Before, during and after *any* challenging goal we need support. The work in this book, this journey, is no exception. The book alone and the work suggested in its contents may be all the support you need. You can take it with you almost everywhere you go and refer to it for support when you need it. You can also visit www.bodymagic.website, another website, read a blog, get some inspiration from other books and articles for support. You may go on a meditation retreat or a workshop to help you go deeper into the practices introduced in this book. You could also feel that you receive a lot of support from being in nature, or spending reflective time in a sacred space. And then there is the support that you can't see. You may get support from your faith in the form of prayer or perhaps from a healer. However, there will come a point in this journey where you will strongly consider the help and support of a human being, face-to-face, in real time.

## The People Who Might Help

### Family and Friends

It's in our make-up to need support. We are tribal by our very nature and this support structure, traditionally, would have been mainly our other family members. There are many reasons why the family may no longer be the support mechanism it once was:

- Nowadays, families divide and flee to all corners of the globe. So the traditional support structure has been lost within many families who don't spend so much time together as before.

- Parents are more likely to separate than ever before in our history, which has also contributed to a weakening in the strength of a family's cohesion.

- Furthermore, in the last two generations (about 50 years), the pace of life has accelerated. Ethics and values have changed and more often than not, the elders in our families do not understand the challenges we face now.

- When it is something as personal and delicate as our body challenges we need someone with experience. Our elders just didn't have the body image pressures and weight control issues that we face today.

- Another important factor is that the way we communicate is changing. We are exchanging more information, more often, with more people than ever before, using mobile devices and social media. But it is usually the stuff that we don't mind the world and its neighbour hearing or knowing. We have learned not to open up in social situations. The really important stuff for our growth and real happiness, the intimate fabric of our being, needs someone very close to us, who can listen without judgement and can show compassion. And we need to re-learn how to share it!

- The compulsive and emotional overeater has other, added challenges. Even if we know that we have the support of a loving family and loyal, trusted friends, it is still hard for us to confide. Compulsive overeating doesn't always show up physically. It doesn't mean we are obese or even overweight. Most people can't see our emotions. Even our closest family, living down the street, don't pick up on our feelings around food and how it seems to own our lives. This recently recognised eating disorder (like others) is often a secret one where we don't want anyone to know. There are a ton of reasons why. For example:

  a) if my friends know that I binge, they'll watch how much I eat
  b) if I go up for seconds, they'll know I'm an overeater
  c) they'll think I'm greedy
  d) they'll label me
  e) they won't understand this; I don't understand it!
  f) they'll think they know what's wrong and give me advice
  g) they'll tell me I'm not fat, so what's my problem?
  h) they'll give me advice that I really don't need
  i) they'll assume I'm bulimic or anorexic
  j) they'll tell someone else
  k) I will be judged if I eat cake
  l) they'll worry about me
  m) they'll gossip about me
  n) they'll embarrass me

Our overeater already knows how to lose weight. She doesn't need anyone telling her how to do it, what to eat, when to eat and how to exercise. She knows more than most of her relatives and friends. It's been going on so long now that she is an expert! So why does she need anyone's help?

> "People who keep stiff upper lips find that it's damn hard to smile."
> ~ Judith Quest

I do believe that a lack of valid, helpful support actually perpetuates our need for food. If we are lacking in something, anything, in our life, then surely it is understandable that, in feeling that void and lack, we will probably want to fill it with food. To an emotional overeater, food is nearly always the answer, even if it is a quick fix. In essence, we would rather fill the void with food than ask for support from our friends and relatives.

## Anonymous Support

There are addiction groups that offer support from like-minded people and from a structure specifically dedicated to serving that need. Overeaters Anonymous, for example, offers a structured approach to their meetings, with the opportunity for everyone to speak and share their experiences of overcoming and/or struggling with overeating. It works for many people, provided you agree with its principles. Even if you don't agree with everything said, just being with and hearing from like-minded people can really offer you a great deal of comfort, confidence and strength.

**Weight-loss meetings**

The dieting industry has jumped into that vacant spot that once would have been filled by traditional family support. There are slimming clubs in every neighbourhood of the developed world, and the need for support for slimmers has been the main reason for their survival. Even in the age of online programmes, slimmers still like to get together with other people with the same goal – losing weight. But that is the only thing they really have in common.

My experience of slimming clubs has been very mixed. Whilst they offer a support resource, they offer very little information or practical help for the emotional overeater. My memory of attending meetings was the same as my daily visit to the bathroom scales. It mattered very little what was said at the meetings, or what was going on in my life. My emotions were a slave to how much I weighed in at every week, not how healthy or happy I was. It also mattered what the group leader said to me personally when I went. It would make me feel either like a superstar slimmer or a total waste of space. All based on what those blessed digits said on the day. On leaving the weekly meeting hall, I would either feel elated that I'd lost a pound or in despair if I'd gained half. And in the darkness of my despair, as a compulsive overeater, what would I do?

You got it!

I would go and eat lots of all the things I was told I shouldn't.

What's healthy about that way of thinking?

You got it again!

Nothing!

It certainly didn't support me, my feelings, or my chances of success. Because, at the end of the day (or week), the problem is not what you eat, or how much of it you eat. It's *why* you eat what you do and *why* you eat so much of it! There is a reason for emotional overeating *every* time. Once we can see what those reasons are, we can do some work that strengthens our resolve to take good care of ourselves.

To understand *that* is the work of this book:

*Remember the Keys to Freedom?*

1. **Knowing Yourself** - looking at your behaviours and going deeply into why you overeat

2. **Knowing Your Worth** - what you deserve i.e. the time and energy to do the personal growth work for radical change, so that you can enjoy lasting happiness

It would seem, therefore, that we do need support in any challenging process, but it has to be helpful of course! So we need:

*the right kind of help,*
*at the right time*
*from a neutral source.*

*"You can do anything as long as you have the passion, the drive, the focus, and the support."*
*~ Sabrina Bryan*

## The Lucky Ones

There are many people who know that diets don't work. Some of those people are ex-dieters who have sacrificed their souls one too many times. They have finally put their foot down about trying anything else. However, the rest of these people have probably never dieted, and never felt that they needed to. Yep! I call them 'The lucky ones!' In a good way, they are able to see the huge con of the majority of the diet industry. Some of them will point out that we are wasting our money. They have watched us for years, like fattened lambs to the slaughter, blindly led into another trending scam promising a body like Jamie Lee Curtis. However, be warned that some of these wise people, who can see the diet crazes for what they are, will also come out with some pretty ridiculous and unhelpful comments like:

- □ *"eat less, move more"*
- □ *"cut out the crap"*
- □ *"if you haven't been cheating you should have lost weight"*
- □ *"get yourself down to the gym"*
- □ *"buy a dog"*
- □ *"stop eating muffins for breakfast"*
- □ *"you just need more willpower"*

How useful is this? What they really want to say in the midst of their ignorance is,

- □ *"you're a liar and you're greedy"*

You will find this everywhere. It really hurts! Be kind to yourself. These people can never know about your personal challenges, so their comments are never personal. Some believe they are trying to help you. You are unique and you shall **Know Your Worth!** Then there are folks who don't know you and don't love you, who will write this, and worse, on every single comments page of every single article about health and weight loss all over the internet. They are cowards who get a kick out of hurting people online without ever having to show their faces. Find the little X at the top of your webpage and click it PDQ!

## Close to home is where your heart is

I would also consider that the very closest people to us, our significant other, soulmate or best friend may be a valuable form of support. In theory, and depending on your relationship, there may be the one or two people in your life who won't let you down and can offer you a listening ear and a shoulder to cry on at times too.

You may even be surprised to learn that the people you are confiding in are suffering in similar ways and that is very helpful. You can share your experiences, even laugh at them, and feel extremely comfortable talking about them. This is awesome. But remember that no two lives are the same. Talk about what works for you both but *never* recommend anything. Part of the healing process is realising our power to make our own decisions – about healing, about life, *and* eventually about food. The only exception to this would be if you feel strongly that your friend is in danger.

Agree and set some ground rules in your conversations about your plans. Ask your friend or relative to do the same at the outset, so there is no hurt and no disappointment. Remember that help and support is a reciprocal thing. Whatever we give out we get back in equal measures or more.

*"Surround yourself with people who provide you with support and love and remember to give back as much as you can in return."*
*~ Karen Kain*

It is extremely important to remember that this programme has no destination. You will finish this book (I hope!), you may find you are at your target weight (if you still feel you need to visit the scales), have run your marathon or now fit into a dress three sizes smaller than you were when you began. These are all great achievements that deserve celebration. But the real goals are the ones that you dared to dream of with your vision board and there are, and will be, others. You really are limitless. Your weight loss and your fitness goals, as big as they may seem, are just the results that will happen when you find your happiness, confidence and faith, so that you can have whatever the heck you *really* want in this life! Having lifelong effective relationships with people you can trust and share the ups and downs with is a valuable part of realising your vision.

You will have many successes. But as life is a journey, so are your emotions. The way you react to these emotions may change, and you will be more in control of the emotions that don't serve you. The work in this book is a *lifetime* practice that will sustain you through even the most difficult of times and challenges. You will come to value your practice, your **health**, your **healing** and your **happiness** in that way. Food will not then be your 'go to' escape from the realities of life.

This is not an impersonal weight loss plan where one size fits all (excuse the pun!). It is a lifestyle and attitude shift that *you* are making just for *yourself*, according to *your* needs, to ensure you are healthy in mind and body, now, *and* for the rest of your life. So it's worth noting that, unlike a diet, you are likely to appreciate some authentic and individual help on this journey towards your vision, that goes beyond reaching your target weight, recovering from illness, no longer binge eating or even swimming the English Channel!

# Exercise

1. Who do you really trust in your life?

2. Are they close enough to be able to offer you support?

3. How do you think they will react when you explain what it is you are working through?

4. What professional support can you ask for and afford that you consider suitable?

5. Make a plan to contact these people specifically to discuss your plans and goals.

*"Negative emotions like loneliness, envy, and guilt have an important role to play in a happy life; they're big, flashing signs that something needs to change."*
*~ Gretchen Rubin*

## Chapter Seven

# Food Facts

*"It's bizarre that the produce manager is more important to my children's health than the paediatrician."*
~ Meryl Streep

## Knowledge for MAGIC!

This book is not a nutrition book. But if you are to **Know Yourself** and **Know Your Worth**, then it would make sense to check in with your knowledge of what food can do for you. This is all part of the **7 Spells of BodyMAGIC!** The **Idea** and **Intention** is for you to consider what food can do for your **health, healing** and **happiness**. This chapter is a little bit of **Focus** so that you can check and possibly deepen your **Understanding**. In turn this will give you **Confidence** about what you are eating and rekindle your **Enthusiasm** around food. Food should be enjoyed, not just by the tongue but by the whole digestive system, as it shares its nutrition with every cell in your body. When emotions have controlled our eating patterns, we haven't cared about what the effects of our eating have been, even if we have known what was good for us and what wasn't so good. But as that knowledge deepens, we can develop more compassion for each and every cell we have. The benefits to this are plenty – physical, mental/emotional *and* spiritual.

Trends in diet and food health generally have changed radically over the last few years. You can pick up a health and recipe book from the 1980s and will see very different takes on what is healthy and what is not. There are very good reasons for this – some of it I will explain in detail in *Chapter Twelve* - Fads and Fallacies.

## Health v Weight

The danger that we have nearly all fallen prey to has been keeping healthy eating and weight loss dieting separate. Keeping them separate means prioritising 'diet' foods over healthy foods. Not only has this shown very little long-term success, but it has also had the real potential of making us ill. The emotional overeater will go through very difficult phases of obsession with losing weight. And at times it will be at any cost, notably to health. When we look at what food decorates the shelves of our supermarkets, the millions of pounds fast-food giants are making every day, it is not difficult to realise that there is a huge proportion of so-called developed populations, at every size from skinny to obese, who are definitely *not* healthy. And what we determined as rare diseases 30 years ago are now commonplace and increasing rapidly – cancer, diabetes, Alzheimer's, heart disease and more.

It's just a matter of time.

## The Slimmer's Sacrifice

As well as the stress I endured from emotional overeating and years of being unhappy with myself, and *those* stressor effects on my health, I spent years eating rubbish food, full of unnatural ingredients, i.e. chemicals, that also added to the stress on my body and the effects on my health, especially my immune system. I remember never really knowing why, throughout winters, I would catch cold after cold, resulting in sinus infections, ear infections and coughs that would go on for weeks. And what did I do? Take painkillers, antibiotics, cough medicines, nasal sprays and throat lozenges, of course! A huge cocktail of even more chemicals that did nothing for my overall or long-term health. I feel quite sorry for my digestive system, and I am grateful it came through! Now is the time for me to reward it with real food choices and natural remedies wherever needed, that serve every aspect of myself, my growth, my life and my planet.

There is also the philosophy that having stuck rigidly to a dull and under-nourishing diet, and ended up feeling exactly the same – dull and under-nourished – that we are convinced that we therefore deserve a treat! Yes, that's right, more unwholesome chemical-laden stuff – cakes, cookies, bars and biscuits full of nothing that our bodies can use. Slimming clubs endorse this approach until we believe that losing weight is the key to health, and this is so not true! We are encouraged to 'fill up' on fizzy drinks containing proven harmful sweeteners. We are happy to eat and drink them because they fall within our allowance for the day. Although they have fewer calories, the truth is, it isn't *real* nutrition. Far from it. There is evidence to show that these everything-free drinks are increasing our appetite and food consumption (1).

*"Let Food be thy Medicine."*
*~ Hippocrates*


It is still commonplace for dieters to consume processed foods such as slimmers' microwave meals because they have the fat, carb and calorie values on them. Moving aside, without discussing the reported dangers of eating food cooked in a microwave, almost always the dieter is completely unaware of the additives, sugar and table salt that are added to make them flavourful and favourable over other foods. The perception is that they are healthy, quick and satisfying. Neither is the dieter aware that with just a little more time in the kitchen, she would most definitely be able to buy the raw ingredients and cook the same dish with much fewer calories and harmful ingredients and probably just as cheaply. I have experimented with these comparisons myself, many times.


**The Love of Food for the Love of God**

Recent years have seen me turn in a different direction. I have always known and loved basic nutrition as far back as senior school. It has fascinated me how every morsel of real food we eat has a purpose. At some point however, my misery from overeating overpowered my health's need for me to eat properly.

Now, I love to shop for food and to cook! It's a hobby of mine, and whilst I used to think that cooking was a hindrance to me as an overeater (and I guess it can be) I have found in recent years the opposite to be true. Not only does the food that I cook taste real, it *is* a real experience. Selecting, buying, peeling, chopping, mixing and cooking raw ingredients gives us a very valuable connection to our food. This, you will see, is extremely important. If we honour and respect our food, it will honour and respect us, pure and simple.

You may think that is a bit airy-fairy, and I don't blame you, but food does have power. The yogis call it life force (prana). It has the power to nourish you in ways even scientists are still discovering. It can stimulate or suppress your appetite, it can affect your mood, your sleep, your energy, your body and your weight *extremely* quickly. So you see why a connection with your food is an essential part of this book. It's time to make friends with our food again!

Our body may need to lose weight for health reasons, but if we don't feed it with the stuff it needs to be well, it will become ill anyway. We will have no energy, be forever fighting with our emotions because we are depressed, and find ourselves eating more bad stuff than ever. It's a cycle that has filled the coffers of the slimming industry's bank accounts for years, and it is time to step out of it and into *your* power and the power of your food!

## Are your servings serving you?

Your power here is some essential knowledge. This is a brief overview of the basics of nutrition. When people talk about a balanced diet, it means you need a balance of all of the following elements. This fact hasn't changed, but the recommended proportions of these elements in overall daily intake *have* changed over the decades of my life. I believe a basic knowledge is crucial to enhancing our health, as is understanding some of these changes. They are all based on scientific research, and some of them may surprise you. If you want to go deeper, I have listed some resources to further detailed information.

As you get to **Know Yourself** – your body and mind – and you truly believe that you **Know Your Worth**, eventually you will develop your intuition around food and you will know what is serving and not serving you.

## Protein Principles

Protein is needed for growth and repair. It is formed of a set of amino acids that are needed to fulfil the role of multiplication and regeneration of human cells. Twelve of these amino acids can be made by the body. The other nine are called *essential* amino acids, and they need to be obtained from food. When a protein contains all of the nine essential amino acids, it is considered a 'complete' protein.

Protein seems to have been *the* fashionable nutrient since the turn of this century. But actually we don't need as much as we have been led to believe. Eating too much protein is not thought to be harmful except that, as with overeating anything, there is a level beyond which we will gain weight. Recent scientific research shows that we need about 0.83 g per kg of body weight of protein, per day (2). Most of us can get at least that daily, just eating a reasonably healthy balanced diet.

Good protein sources have always been thought of as animal products (meat, fish, dairy and eggs) and certain plant sources (nuts, beans and lentils, seeds and quinoa) because they contain a good proportion of all of the essential amino acids. However, *all* plants have protein. Even fruits have some! When we consider how much protein we really need, as long as we eat a diet of fresh and whole foods, protein intake should not be a huge concern for most of us. We don't need expensive protein shakes and supplements. Real food has it all! Spend your hard-earned dollars on nuts and seeds for protein snacks, keep the rest of your diet fresh, wholesome and natural and you need not worry about your protein intake.

For example, here is a sample diet without meat, showing how easy it is to get the right amount:

If I weigh 60kg (132.2lbs), and I am in average health, I require 49.2g (1.74oz/0.2 (1/5th) cup) of protein per day. What does this look like? Well, if I ate:

1 cup of oats with 1 cup of soya milk for breakfast, I would get 13g of protein
1 cup of cooked lentils and 1 cup of brown rice for lunch, I would get 23g of protein
1 cup of broccoli, 5oz tofu and 1 cup of carrot, that's another 15g
This gives me a total of 51g, without other vegetables or fruits, sauces, dressings, snacks or drinks.

On the Vegetarian Resource Group's website, there are some protein amounts shown in various foods, and I have used these figures for illustration purposes. Most whole food contains protein and there are many healthy choices to be made. The point is, we don't need to 'count' our protein intake. Most experts now concur that eating a varied, whole food, natural diet will ensure we get more than enough for most needs, even with statistics giving a lot of room for variance.

At present, research shows that there is no difference in the needs of men and women unless women are pregnant or lactating (2).

**On Protein and Vegetarianism**

There are many reasons for considering vegetarianism for your body, your mind and your spirit, some of which are highlighted in *Chapter Nine* - Nature Calls. But this book is not about trying to convince you of the merits of a vegetarian diet. It is for you to have more knowledge about the food you eat, so that you can become more connected to it and nature in general, in the most positive ways possible. If knowledge is power, then understanding more about your food will give you your power to make informed choices at every supermarket, restaurant and every serving. If you are interested in the philosophy of vegetarianism, whether you plan to eat meat or not, there are some resources you can tap into at the back of this book.

*"Nothing will benefit human health and increase the chances for survival of life on Earth as much as the evolution to a vegetarian diet."*
*~ Albert Einstein*

When I was about thirteen, I decided that I no longer wanted to eat meat. This may have done me a favour when it came to eating family leftovers, as I didn't want to eat anything with any trace of meat on it! It was hard for my mum. In 1979, there weren't many vegetarians. My high protein food was really just eggs and cheese. And lots of it. Now we know that all food has protein and my mum need not have worried. I became vegetarian because I realised what I had taken for granted all my life – that animals were being killed so that I could eat them! My limited view of vegetarianism was that I had no right to eat an animal if I didn't have the guts to kill it myself. I would never have been able to do that. However, I didn't really have much of a grip on nutrition then.

This book is not about trying to change your beliefs about what is morally right to eat, it's about your emotions. So if you feel that any emotions are prevalent when you choose, buy, cook and eat meat, then perhaps you might consider a vegetarian diet for a while. It really can do you no harm and may help you to practice stepping out of your comfort zone and effecting change. I cover some aspects of meat eating in *Chapter Twelve* - Fads and Fallacies too. Whatever you feel is OK, if it's conducive to your physical and emotional health.

**Carbohydrates Credentials**

Carbohydrates are needed for energy. They produce four calories per gram. They are further divided into:

**Complex Carbohydrates** – mainly natural sources – whole grains (wheat, oats, rice, quinoa, buckwheat) and vegetables, but also include refined foods such as white flour. However, natural sources provide more nutrition and are more slowly absorbed, keeping you feeling fuller for longer.

**Simple Carbohydrates** – processed sugars, milk and fruits. They provide energy to the body very fast but will also spike your blood sugar much more quickly, putting more stress on your pancreas. Only a few years ago, some weight-loss programmes and health officials generally damned fat but said sugar was OK. Sadly, there are many casualties from this era with Type II diabetes, who never managed to lose weight long-term either.

Nowadays, it is carbohydrates generally that seem to be the enemy. Some nutritionists believe that if we eat less of them, we are sure to lose weight. There are references to research all over the internet that seem to support this. I'm a great fan of research, but I'm an even greater fan of reality, tradition and experience. For example, it is a fact that the yogis in the Himalayas eat primarily a simple and high carbohydrate diet of pulses, rice and chapatis, fruits and vegetables. I have adopted this diet when I have been there in the ashrams and restaurants of Rishikesh in India over several weeks at a time. I have *always* lost weight effortlessly and felt a real shift in my health and wellbeing. That may also be because of the yoga practices (including lots of breathing exercises), increased exercise (walking everywhere), the altitude, the lack of stress and the general increase in self-awareness around food. But it certainly is not a question of eating less. I have had a good appetite there and have nearly always had second, very generous, helpings!

The challenge is that science and research has to include measurable factors such as age, sex, demographic profile etc. However, a person's emotions are difficult to measure. We all have a unique emotional history. It is almost impossible to measure one's degree of grief, sadness, anger or worry and therefore its relationship to the levels of cravings for certain foods. I have spent a great deal of time delving into arguments for high and low carbohydrate diets. I believe that healthy carbohydrate choices for the emotional overeater depend on two things:

1.  What type of carbohydrates we eat
2.  Whether we are using them as a comforter

If we truly believe that emotions are the drivers behind our impulse to overeat, then certain types of carbohydrates will not help our recovery. This is undisputed. These choices are proven time and time again to cause health challenges, allergies and addictions. I have covered them all in *Chapter Eighteen - The Seven Seldom Sins*, but I will make no apologies for introducing some of them briefly to you now.

Drum roll…

**Sugar** - by far one of the most readily-available-to-all-ages drugs on the planet. We are literally 'spiked' with this drug every day in our food *and* in our drinks. Just read the labels on any pre-prepared food you buy, remembering that 4g of sugar is a whole teaspoon. It is shocking. And also very addictive. I have done my own experiments with sugar over the years. I only have to have a dessert after dinner on two consecutive evenings and the third night, if one isn't available, I crave it. This is even more noticeable with refined sugar, such as in puddings. I find fresh fruit does not give me the same challenges. I can take it or leave it. I am no scientist but I have also worked out that once a regular sugar habit is established, for me, it takes a detox or a total change of eating habits for a while to overcome it again. And it's really difficult!

**Wheat** - in everything. An allergen that after years of over-consumption by sensitive eaters can cause bowel irritation, diverticulitis, bloating, gas, etc. There is a strong link between the gut and the brain – that is why when under stress we get irregular bowel movements or even a slight reaction like butterflies in our stomach (3). So if we eat large amounts of irritants to the bowel, it makes sense that these can affect our nervous system and brain. High amounts of grains, particularly wheat, have been linked to ADD, ADHD, Alzheimer's and more.

**Gluten** - in fact a protein, but found mainly in wheat, barley and rye. Gives bread flour its pliability (think pizza kneading). Dr. Perlmutter, in his book, *Grain Brain*, believes that 30-40% of the population have some insensitivity to gluten. Long-term intolerance causes permanent damage to the small intestine, called Crohn's Disease.

**Yeast** - feeds bacteria called Candida, which can become out of proportion to other healthy bacteria in the gut, causing major health problems throughout the body.

None of these foods is dangerous in small quantities now and again. But because of their addictive qualities, they can really hinder your recovery. If nothing else, do your research! You will see that all of these are present in commercially-bought bread, for example. When you consider that a western diet usually includes toast for breakfast, sandwiches for lunch and often pizza, pastry or pasta (with garlic bread) for dinner, you may start to identify a potential problem.

There are so many alternatives to bread for a healthy carbohydrate. Yes, they are often more difficult to find. No, they are not traditional Western cooking. But this book is all about change and looking at eating in a different way. So if you have been stuck in your food choices for a while, consider some of these, if you don't eat them already:

Brown rice, quinoa, buckwheat, amaranth, millet - use in place of rice or for pizza bases etc.
Potatoes (leave out the chips/fries). Try new varieties.
Sweet Potatoes.
Other starchy root vegetables e.g. carrots, beetroot, turnips, swede, parsnip, celeriac, Jerusalem artichokes.
Squash and pumpkin.
Fresh Fruits - try some new ones for your sweet treats such as papaya, pineapple, mango, bananas, pomegranate, grapes. Although some are high in sugar, they will always be better than refined sugar.
Beans - mung, black-eyed, aduki, black, kidney, pinto, borlotti, etc.
Lentils - red, yellow mung dhal, green mung split, white urad dhal, green and brown lentils.

More on these later on and in Resources. I have listed a totally inspirational vegan athlete, Brendon Brazier. He has amazing recipes for smoothies, pancakes, pizzas and burgers, all vegan and based on high-density nutrition. There are many other recipe authors and I have named a few later. Recipes for all of these foods are plentiful online, often without having to buy a recipe book.

*"You can do a lot for your diet by eliminating foods that have mascots".*
*~ Ted Spiker*

## Fat Facts

Fat is for energy and for processing fat-soluble vitamins. It is a very concentrated form of energy food, producing nine calories per gram. All fats have had a bad press for many years. And if you have looked for diet foods at any time over the last 30 years, you will no doubt have gravitated to the low-fat alternatives, as I did. But this has been a huge disservice to a healthy diet. Once again, we find there is a difference between diet foods and healthy foods. Usually we see a slim body as a healthy body. But weight loss alone does not guarantee health.

## Saturated Fats and Heart Disease

It seems that the official nutritional guidance has taken an about-turn on the use of saturated fat in the diet. The American Journal of Clinical Nutrition reports that from studies of 347,747 participants there is no evidence to suggest a link between saturated fat and cardiovascular disease or stroke (4). For many years we have been told to cut down on animal fats, eggs and full-fat dairy products, nuts and saturated oils like coconut, that have been wrongly reported to increase cholesterol and cardiovascular problems.

Whilst we are on the subject of eggs, research now shows that the cholesterol in eggs is unlikely to be bad for the majority of us and that eggs have many more nutritional benefits to health that we should consider (5).

## A little on Cholesterol

Cholesterol is a type of fat that is found mainly in animals. Its vegetarian cousins are called phytosterols. It is thought that phytosterols can compete with cholesterol in your body. Cholesterol, like fat in general, has had a bad press, but in my view most of it is not justified. It's worth noting that it's the lipoproteins that vary in their effects, not the cholesterol itself. As cholesterol is a fat, and the body is mainly water, it uses the lipoproteins to transport the cholesterol around the body.

There are two *main* types of lipoproteins that do this transportation:

**LDL - low-density lipoprotein** - this is considered to be the bad guy. But it can be further divided into good, large LDL and not so good, small LDL. Without getting too deep into this (and I do not profess to be an expert), it is generally a good idea to avoid foods that can increase the bad guys. A reduction in carbohydrates, especially sugar, can help with this (5).

**HDL - high-density lipoprotein** - considered to be the good one. We want to increase this and can do so by including a bigger proportion of good fats in our diet (e.g. nuts, fish), increasing activity, reducing alcohol and giving up smoking. The resulting weight loss will also help. In line with the principles of this book, however, our focus on healthy food choices and lifestyle changes is far superior to simply aiming to lose weight.

## Omega options

The body can make most of the fatty acids it needs, but not all. The ones it can't make are called essential fatty acids (EFAs). It needs linoleic acid (LA), an omega-6 fatty acid, and alpha-linolenic acid (ALA), an omega-3 fatty acid from food sources. They are important for many functions of the whole body because they are involved in cell growth and repair.

- omega-3 - can be obtained from oily fish such as salmon, mackerel, herrings and sardines, but also from flax (linseed), hemp seeds and chia seeds.

- omega-6 - from vegetable oils including canola, safflower, corn, sunflower, and from nuts, eggs and meat.

There is a lot of discussion (some conflicting), suggesting that there may be a problem with the proportion of omega-6 to omega-3 that we take in. This is because omega-6 competes with omega-3. Studies highlight that the ratio has changed radically from around 1:1 in the diets of our ancestors to, in some studies, 25:1. Too much omega-6 in our diet has been linked to inflammatory health issues, diabetes and even behavioural problems (7). My understanding is that if we are going to focus on optimum health from fats in the right amounts, we need to focus on trying to maintain a balance of omega-3 and omega-6 sources. Perhaps vegetarians or those who dislike fish may like to consciously increase their intake of omega-3 from other sources.

**You are what you eat, right?**

Well no, not actually. I always believed that if I ate fat, I would be fat. This is not true! We need to eat the *right* fats for health. They are responsible for helping to build each of the 100 trillion or so cells in our bodies. If I had only known that my dry skin conditions, brittle nails and stiff joints might have been relieved to get more of a greasing than I would permit, I might not have suffered so in my 20s and 30s. And the notion that fat makes you fat probably comes from overeating fats, particularly the wrong ones.

New evidence suggests that certain good guys can actually help you to lose weight. Coconut oil, for instance, has been shown to have encouraging results on metabolism, because it contains MCTs – medium chain triglycerides. A survey of 40 women who were given two different oils showed that coconut oil reduced abdominal fat and, because of the presence of lauric acid, improved good cholesterol and reduced bad cholesterol. (8). I love coconuts! I have a selection from coconut oil, milk, desiccated, chips and coconut water most days. It is alkalising for the body, and it balances blood sugar and thyroid function. It is also anti-viral, anti-bacterial and anti-fungal. So it strengthens immunity and helps out with gut health. Although this book is not about losing weight directly, coconut could be a great ally in your quest for **health, healing** and **happiness**.

Then there are nuts. These plant foods are high in protein and good fats and reduce LDL cholesterol, excellent for the heart and arteries. Each variety has different qualities but most contain good sources of omega-3, fibre, vitamin E, antioxidants and l-arginine. They also play an extremely big part in my vegetarian diet as a protein.

*"The belly rules the mind."*
*~ Spanish Proverb*

**So is all fat good for health?**

Definitely not! There is a wealth of research that shows that certain fats are a hindrance to health:

☐ Trans fats are found naturally in some foods including meats, but the bad guys are in hydrogenated oils. These are implicated in heart disease, death from cardiovascular problems, inflammation and behaviour challenges (9).

☐ When vegetable oils are cooked at high temperatures, they oxidise, which changes their chemical make-up. By-products include cyclic aldehydes and acrylamide, known to have carcinogenic properties and implicated in prostate (10) and lung (11) cancer.

☐ All fats deliver a high amount of energy and some of them taste so good! It is very easy to eat too much fat. One can easily get carried away drizzling delicious oils over superfood salads. Two to three tablespoonfuls per day of 'good' oils or a small palmful of nuts is sufficient for most dietary needs. It really is a question of substituting fats that probably are not giving you the nutrition you could get from your fats. For example, if you use sunflower oil in your cooking, which is volatile at high temperatures, try swapping it for coconut oil which is not. Consider this – if your body is getting a high level of nutrients from the food you are eating per calorie, spoonful, plate, meal or whatever, without your having to measure it obsessively, then your body will be content. In receiving its needs, it will slowly stop craving sugary or starchy comfort foods to get a quick fix. You can do this with reasonable amounts of good fats. Fats keep you satiated for longer.

## Low-fat foods

Most reduced fat foods are processed, usually with the addition of chemicals to reconstruct them to a product that closely resembles what we have been accustomed to. They are packaged as the saviours of maintaining a lifestyle diet. Take butter for example. Several decades ago, butter was the only fat apart from maybe dripping (solid fat left at the bottom of a roasting pan that had been used to cook a piece of meat) that anyone would put on their bread. When fat became a bad word, food manufacturers brought out low-fat spreads and spray oils. The problem with some of these products is that they contain artificial trans-fatty acids. They go through a process called hydrogenation that gives them a longer shelf life. Someone once told me that they are one molecule away from plastic and that flies won't land on them. This is not true apparently, but they have been through a pretty awful process to get onto your toast, so that you can pretend that it's butter! It's not necessary. In Spain, they put extra-virgin olive oil on their bread. There are many healthy alternatives that don't cost the earth, but will support health in your body, in your mind and therefore in your emotions.

## Vitamins

There are thirteen essential vitamins, which all have a unique name but are more often given a letter to differentiate them – Vitamin A, B1, B2, B3, B5, B6, B7, B9, B12, C, D, E and K. Some are more commonly known by their name rather than their letter.

All have slightly different roles to play in the body, but generally they are responsible for the body's function and protection. Vitamins help with chemical reactions, make red blood cells, help the nervous system and provide antioxidants to help rid the body of toxins and waste products. They are necessary for the healthy development of cells and work in alliance with other nutrients such as proteins and fats to maintain health.

Deficiencies such as night blindness, scurvy and rickets were greatly reduced from the 1940's with more knowledge of nutrition and greater availability of produce across the globe, in every season. However, nutrition education has been lacking in much of the developed world, with many people turning to cheap, processed food. Reduced soil quality is also thought to play a part in the reducing levels of vitamins found in non-organic produce. Deficiencies are once again being reported and more are forecast in the future (12).

## Solubility

Vitamins are micronutrients, meaning that they are only needed in small amounts. Vitamins A, E and K are fat soluble, so they require some fat to help to transport their properties around the body. But because they are held in fatty tissue in the body, they can be toxic in excess. Other vitamins are water soluble. Whatever the body doesn't need, it will excrete on an ongoing basis. They are not stored in the body in the same way as fat soluble vitamins, so a daily intake is normally required to maintain optimum health. Furthermore, water soluble vitamins can be more volatile as their properties are lost through overcooking in water and steam (into the air).

I have listed a few resources in the back of this book for you to read further if you wish. A really good piece of advice I was offered was to eat 7-9 reasonable portions of a range of vegetables and fruit in different colours. I would add a caveat to say that I limit my fruit intake to a maximum of three pieces per day. Occasionally, the sugar in most fruit can reinstate my cravings, especially if I am busy or facing emotional challenges. Eggs, nuts, fish, meat (particularly liver) and dairy and fortified cereals (if you can find any without added sugar) are good sources of some of the essentials too. It boils down to eating a wholesome diet every day and avoiding processed, nutritionally-empty foods.


**Sun's Double D-light!**

1. Vitamin D can come from food but it can also come from sunshine. In the UK there is barely enough sunshine during the winter months, but Vitamin D can be stored for some time. It is essential for bone health when we are young and to maintain our frame as we mature. Vitamin D works with calcium to help maintain bone density.

Regardless of where we live, it has been suggested that because more children play indoors nowadays than ever before, and when they do go out they are covered in sun blocks and screens, that the beneficial effects of the sun are also being blocked. Doctors are seeing a resurrection of rickets, even in the south of England, where greater levels of sunshine are possible (13). It seems that in response to skin cancer scares, we have again gone over the top to turn away from nature. Whilst too much sun *might* be the cause of skin cancer, what about the effect of the sun's rays on the chemical compounds of sunscreens? Personally, I no longer plaster myself with chemical-laden sunscreens and baste for hours. I take 30-60 minutes depending on where I am, the time of day and year, sometimes with a little therapeutic and alkalising coconut oil, then I simply cover up and get in the shade with a book or go off and do something else. Dr. Joseph Mercola has written a very interesting book about these concepts and more (see Resources). He not only highlights, with evidence, that the potential risks of the sun have been blown out of proportion, but also discusses the ways that the sun can, as it always has, improve health and prevent degenerative disease, *including* cancer:


*"careful sunbathing has the potential to radically reduce many of the chronic degenerative diseases that rank among the greatest health problems faced by the modern man"*
*~ Dark Deception, Dr. Joseph Mercola*


Interestingly, fair-skinned people need less sun to fulfil the same requirements than darker skins do (14). At the time of writing there is an app I quite like called **dminder**, which helps ascertain whether you are getting enough sunshine (and particularly vitamin D) for your profile and location.

2. If you've ever been on a packaged sun and beach holiday, you will know that despite an increase of intake of alcohol, ice cream and other 'treats', coupled with less exercise and late nights (yes that used to be me!), you still come home feeling fabulous. There was a time, not so long ago, when this was the *only* holiday I would consider. That feeling of glowing health wasn't just the suntan I proudly paraded through the arrivals gate, wearing the last white clothes I had clean and saved so I could be the envy of all at the airport! Nor was it just being away from a stressful job, and a change being as good as a rest. The glow was more than that. It was serotonin and dopamine (happy hormones). These are mood enhancers gifted to us by the big light in the sky. When we feel the joy of the sun's rays, we are uplifted. The opposite of

this would be SAD (seasonal affective disorder), a depressive condition caused by inadequate natural light, usually over the winter months and in cooler climates.

In some mystical traditions, light is considered an element, and it's maybe one we have forgotten about as an essential element of our overall health. The sun has been honoured, worshipped and respected for all time. Many of us still do in our own way. Yet again our instincts have been disturbed by propaganda and inaccurate information. As emotionally sensitive people with greater intuition unfolding, we need to consider whether are getting our share of sunshine, both for our physical and our emotional health. We don't actually need that much sun. We just need to make the most of it when it shines at certain times of the year, by taking short periods in the sunshine without sunscreen.

The sun can be a great ally in your quest to overcoming emotional overeating.

*"Millions say the apple fell, but Newton was the one to ask why."*
*~ Bernard M. Baruch*

## Minerals

These are needed for regulation and maintenance of the body's tissues and organs and their functions. They are further subdivided into major minerals (macro-minerals) and trace minerals (micro-minerals) because of the amount that is needed. Both major and trace minerals are essential to health.

Major minerals include calcium, chloride, magnesium, phosphorus, potassium, sodium and sulphur.

Minor minerals include copper, chromium, fluoride, iodine, iron, manganese, selenium and zinc.

Minerals play a huge part in bone and tooth health, fluid balance and metabolism. They also rely on other nutrients for these functions, in the right quantities, to keep the body in balance (this balance is called homeostasis).

Here are some examples:

- Iron can be more readily used by the body when it is combined with vitamin C.
- Potassium works with sodium to help to regulate blood pressure.
- Vitamin D helps the body effectively absorb calcium.
- Vitamin B12, iron and B9 (better known as folic acid) work in synergy with each other.

Eating plenty of whole and natural foods including a variety of quality proteins (meat, fish, legumes), fresh vegetables and fruit, will ensure that enough minerals are consumed for maintaining health. If you are eating a varied wholesome diet, and unless you have a health condition, supplementation is not normally necessary.

# Fibre - Friend or Foe?

This is another controversial nutrient. It is thought to be needed for elimination and detoxification. Fibre is strictly a carbohydrate. We need enzymes to process all food. There are carbohydrates that we humans do not have the enzymes to digest. These foods are what we call fibre. We have been told for decades to supplement with dietary fibre to help prevent some cancers, improve our chances of, or help to manage diabetes, help us lose weight and much more. But a lot of evidence to back up these claims is sketchy.

There are two types:

Soluble - this fibre dissolves in water. This is thought to slow down the digestive process. For the slimmer, that should mean feeling fuller for longer. However, without any supporting evidence, I doubt this. Why would I want to slow down a natural process? In doing so my stomach expands as the fibre multiplies in my stomach, my stomach is stretched, and after a while my stomach becomes accustomed to needing more food, including fibre, to get the 'full' sensation.

Insoluble - this fibre does not dissolve. This type is considered to speed up the digestion. So it allegedly helps to flush us out quicker. Personally, I don't think that is a good idea either. If we eat wonderful healthful food and then try to speed up the laws of nature, we could be passing nutrients out before they have had a chance to assimilate. Over a couple of decades or so of low-fat eating, I have come to realise that high-fibre diets (those including bran and other grains that have a high roughage content) can cause a lot of bloating and pain. I believe that most of my constipation was actually due to inadequate fat consumption, resulting in a dry bowel, making insoluble fibre very difficult to pass through.

Doctors are now questioning whether fibre may actually favourably affect the risk of colon cancer as was first thought (15). Like many other carbohydrates, fibre is being demonised and maybe with good reason. I have included a YouTube link for you to listen to and you can make up your own mind.

This new take on fibre makes a lot of sense. For years, I would have bran on my food. I have even tried psyllium husks and other dietary laxatives in a desperate attempt to lose weight. All I got for those years (and for my money) was constipation, irritable bowel syndrome and abdominal pain. I will add that those conditions were also caused by external stress, but I feel it's pretty likely that internal stress from my desperate dieting days as a whole had quite a lot to do with it. It wasn't until I started including healthy fats in my diet and practised some cleansing techniques (physical and emotional) that my digestive channels started to flow so much more efficiently. Nowadays, I do not have an elimination problem and I do not supplement with dietary fibre. I really trust that all of the fibre I get from foods like seeds and their oils, some non-glutinous grains, lots of vegetables, fruit and other fats are all the digestive fibre I need. I'm not alone in this back-tracking. In one study in 2012, constipation was actually relieved by *reducing* intake of dietary fibre (16).

## Natural Antioxidants and Superfoods

The word 'superfood' was unheard of a couple of decades ago. There seems to be a new trending superfood every couple of months. They are worth a mention because some of them fit very well with my philosophy of eating natural, wholesome and traditionally healthy food. However, I'm not talking about the packets of powders making up a whole new health industry. Below is a list of my favourite natural superfoods – my N-eat Nineteen. I have not included any of these trending commercially-packaged superfoods in this list, not because they do not have a great many benefits, I know that some of them do. I haven't listed them because they are usually processed (e.g. to make them into a powder), often imported and heavily packaged (which is not necessarily in the best interests of the planet). They are usually expensive, and they are not always organic. There are usually cheaper, locally-sourced and less heavily-processed alternatives to get the same health benefits. Even cutting out some of these new and exotic superfoods, there are still so many I *could* include here. Feel free to post your questions to me about these and any others on social media if you like. The following is my shortlist, with just a little about why I eat them, based on what I know and how they make me feel. There are links in Resources if you would like to know a little more.

*The body becomes what the foods are, as the spirit becomes what the thoughts are.*
*~ Kemetic Saying*

## My N-eat Nineteen

1.  Awesome **Apple** - I always remember, growing up, the saying 'An apple a day keeps the doctor away' and there may be some truth in this. Apples contain antioxidants that are thought to help protect nerve cells and prevent lots of diseases. The natural, small amount of soluble fibre in apples helps to manage weight, blood sugar, blood pressure, bowel movements and immunity. What a great fruit – low in sugar, keeps well and is versatile. It is, however, the number one food that you should always try to buy and eat organic.

2.  Lovely **Lemon** - apart from water, lemon could be the best thing you can put into your body when you get up in the morning. Contrary to popular belief, lemons are actually alkalising to the human body, so great for cleansing away toxins and controlling inflammation. I have often heard that disease cannot exist in an alkaline body. Lemons are high in vitamin C and have anti-viral and anti-bacterial qualities, so are great for helping to fight off a cold and for strengthening immunity. Lemon can boost energy levels, therefore may be an excellent alternative to caffeine.

3.  B-line for **Berries** - I was once told that these were the most important fruits to eat to raise my vital force. I was in a pretty tough space at the time. I go to these for their phytochemicals that offer protection for my cells, reducing damage and inflammation. They slow down mental decline and other common aspects and challenges of the ageing process.

4.  Perfect **Papaya** - not only does this delicious fruit contain more levels of vitamin C than oranges, it is also high in vitamin A – great for immunity and helping the health of the skin and eyes. And it contains several B vitamins too. Papaya has an enzyme called papain which helps to digest proteins and can help with acidity-related digestive disorders. It contains potassium and calcium. And that's just the fruit! The seeds have anti-parasitic, anti-inflammatory properties. I have included a link to a delicious, tried and tested smoothie for parasites. You'll read more about parasites in *Chapter Twenty* - The Gremlins in your Gut.

5.  Cool **Coconut** - I have already covered many of the benefits of coconut oil in this chapter, including its use in my life as a 'sun oil'. Coconut comes in so many forms. You can drink the water, alkalising and cooling on a hot day. You can use the milk to add depth and texture to curries and desserts. I use the water and the milk in smoothies and ice cream. You can also get creamed coconut that melts into hearty soups and casseroles. I often add desiccated coconut to healthy desserts and smoothies. It is a great alternative to some dairy products.

6.  Gotta love **Greens** - kale, spinach, broccoli, lettuce, rocket, watercress and more – I just had to bundle some of these all together because there are so many! Most of them have very similar nutritional benefits. They are good for vitamins A, B, C, E and K, calcium, potassium, magnesium and iron. Did you know that they are a good source of protein too? Raw they are rich in chlorophyll, a great way of getting more oxygen into the blood. How about sprouting your own

seeds to get fresh, living greens? This can be done in a large pickle jar with water and light, even if you live in the city.

7. **Celery** Call - I chop this into smoothies, soups, salads and stews. I also fill sticks with goodies such as hummus and veggie pâté for a healthy, light snack. It is a great substitute for a salty flavour but it can actually lower blood pressure. It contains phytochemicals called phthalides, which relax artery walls thereby reducing blood pressure in the arteries. A polysaccharide in celery known as apiuman is thought to give celery its anti-inflammatory properties. Celery is another antioxidant-rich wonderful food, providing a great deal of insoluble fibre which is more gentle than its grainy relatives.

8. Poor **Potato**! - I feel sorry for it and the bad press it has had along with most other carbohydrates. However, I have started to see its popularity return. Being brought up in England with an Irish father on 'meat-and-two-veg', I do believe that I have potatoes in my blood! It's usually the way that they are cooked that destroys their reputation and their nutrition. When cooked in their skins, either boiled, smashed, baked or as a starchy natural thickener for soups and casseroles, they are high in vitamin B6 and vitamin C, potassium and manganese. In sweet potatoes, there is a greater presence of vitamin A, so another great antioxidant. They also have a high water content compared with other starchy carbohydrates so are easily digested. Where some starches bloat me, potatoes do not.

9. Brilliant **Buckwheat** - this is my favourite pseudo-grain. So-called because it's actually not a grain. I could have also included amaranth, millet, teff or sorghum here too but I don't really buy them as much. I love buckwheat because it's quite easy to get hold of, not expensive, so versatile and gluten-free. It can be boiled and used like rice, sprouted and used in salads or used to make 'crackers'. Buckwheat flour is a great alternative to wheat and I use it in bread making and in pancakes. It even comes in flakes for porridge and healthy cookies. Rutin, a flavonoid in buckwheat, helps circulation and magnesium helps to lower high blood pressure.

10. Quirky **Quinoa** - a protein wonder containing all nine of the essential amino acids. It comes from the Andean region of South America and seemed to be a staple when I visited Peru. Extremely tasty and very versatile indeed. I use it instead of rice. Cooked, I put it into soups, pancake mix and pizza bases. I have also enjoyed red quinoa, which has a nuttier taste. Quinoa also has a good level of fibre, iron, magnesium and manganese.

11. Luscious **Lentils** - I have already highlighted the flexibility of this amazing legume and included them in some of my favourite recipes in *Chapter Twenty-Five*. They are the most alkaline protein source. They are cheap, low in fat and sodium, high in folate, iron, manganese, magnesium and potassium. Lentils are easy to cook and to digest. Love lentils!

12. Sexy **Seeds** - I love sunflower (for vitamin E), pumpkin (for iron), hemp (for protein), sesame (for antioxidants) and linseed or flax (for omega-3). But all seeds have varying quantities of excellent nutrition. I grind them fresh for smoothies or sprinkle them whole on salads, use as a porridge topping and put them in my Swiss muesli too. I can also make crackers and pizza bases with them. Sometimes I just grab a handful when I want a snack.

13. Nice **Nuts** - full of good fats, nuts used to get a bad press. But we have to understand that we don't need much of this high-quality plant protein to benefit from it. I love almonds for their calcium and vitamin E, but also for their versatility – they can be whole, skinned, sliced or ground and great in either sweet or savoury dishes, everything from burgers to biscuits! It is easy to make a milk alternative with almonds. I also love walnuts – more folic acid and antioxidants than any other nut, they spookily resemble the human brain and are thought to improve memory due to their high omega-3 content.

14. Excellent **Eggs** - their nutritional content makes them one of the most nutrient-packed natural foods you can eat. Depending on size, they have 6-7g of protein from around 80 calories, vitamins, minerals and depending on what the chickens were fed, some omega-3 too. I am conscious about buying eggs from 'battery' farms where the chickens have a cruel and short existence. If I can buy free range and organic; I will buy them every time. But even then the males are usually killed at birth, as they are useless to the farmers. It seems the only ethical way, if there is one, is to buy eggs from hens rescued from factory farms (i.e. they were about to be slaughtered because either they weren't laying enough or the farmer gets rid of them rather than feeding them over the winter months). We have rescued them in the past. There are people who rescue hens and sell them on to willing adopters. Chickens are so much fun and to give them a free-range retirement in exchange for a few eggs is a great experience. But it is a well-debated topic among some vegetarians and vegans. We have to ask ourselves how we feel but not judge others for their views.

15. Clever **Cinnamon** - medicinal uses include fighting bacterial and fungal infections, HIV, diabetes and Alzheimer's, I love it with my porridge, pancakes and hot smoothies and in eastern-style soups and curries. It gives a sweet flavour without having to add sugar.

16. Go to **Garlic** - not only does garlic make casseroles, soups and sauces taste amazing, it has a history of uses for health. It is anti-fungal, anti-bacterial, lowers blood pressure and strengthens immunity, amongst many other proven benefits.

17. **Ginger** Greatness - now a part of my life, this amazing tuber gets me through the winter months in great health. Every night, we finely chop up about a square inch into a Thermos flask with boiling water and a squeeze of lemon. Then in the morning we have ginger and lemon tea! Warms the cockles (not scientifically proven!), great for sore throats, nasal congestion and all manner of digestive disorders from flatulence to nausea. Also known for its anti-inflammatory qualities.

18. Top **Turmeric** - whose active ingredient curcumin is a well-known anti-inflammatory and antioxidant remedy and is also used for a whole lot of digestive disorders. It gives food a deep yellow colour. Of course I use it in curries and dhal but also in some Mediterranean-type rice dishes instead of saffron.

19. Super **Seaweed** - I am lucky enough to be able to order seaweed through the post from pristine waters off the coast of Scotland. It not only enhances the flavour of savoury dishes with a unique taste called umami, it also has some unique health properties. High in protein and delivering vitamins and all manner of minerals, this is one of my favourite superfoods. Not all varieties have the same qualities, but most support the thyroid function, including metabolism and immunity. Seaweed is great for the skin, both eating it and bathing in it. Varieties like Kombu are helpful in preventing bloating and flatulence, when added to lentil and bean dishes.

## Water

Last but by no means least, water deserves a section all of its own. In Chapter Nine - *Nature Calls*, I shall be talking about the principles of drinking the most natural water possible. But here, let's just have a look at why you should drink lots of it.

Dehydration occurs when the amount of your intake is less than what you excrete through natural bodily fluids like urine, faeces, sweat, saliva, bleeding and breath. Humans are roughly 60% water, so when ignoring the natural thirst call, can easily become dehydrated, especially for example, in hot weather, whilst exercising or eating a lot of salt. Proper hydration is necessary to keep the blood thin, assimilate nutrients, pass through waste products, fuel muscles, beat fatigue and maintain immunity.

A little 'old wives' tale' I learned a few years ago was to take a gulp of water after sneezing to avoid colds and flu. I really have no idea whether I would have caught a cold after that first sneeze, whether this is mind over matter or there is any science behind it at all, but it has worked every time! I do believe that warm water first thing in the morning is a great treat for the digestive system (added lemon and ginger optional).

A recommended amount to drink every day is half your body weight in pounds, as fluid ounces. So if you are 150 pounds, you might like to ensure that you are drinking a minimum of 75 fluid ounces per day. A general rule of thumb is to drink a quarter of this when you wake/get up, a quarter before lunch, a quarter mid-afternoon and a quarter before dinner. Try to avoid more than a couple of fluid ounces within an hour after eating food. It is thought to dilute the digestive juices.

It is a shame that water seems to be relegated to a back seat when people talk about the benefits of good nutrition. It is absolutely essential to have an appropriate fluid intake to help your body process all of those nutrients effectively. It is also a shame that water sits in the shade of diet drinks when it comes to weight loss. Research proves that artificial sweeteners in such drinks may actually cause glucose intolerance (17), so there is an even better reason to hit the water bottle! If you are not used to drinking water throughout the day, it may take a little effort to construct new habits. Get yourself a reusable cup, PBA free, and take it with you wherever you go. It will pay dividends within a short period of time.

And mostly, it's free!


*"Take a course in good water and air; and in the eternal youth of Nature you may renew your own. Go quietly, alone; no harm will befall you".*
*~ John Muir*

# Chapter Eight
# YogaMAGIC!

*"You cannot do yoga. Yoga is your natural state. What you can do are yoga exercises, which may reveal to you where you are resisting your natural state."*
~ Sharon Gannon

In many ways I have been itching to write this chapter, but now that it's here, I really don't know where to start! There is so much that I can teach you about the amazing effect yoga has had on my own life and on the lives of millions of men and women throughout the world. I'm going to focus on how it has helped me to learn to love my body and to understand the power of the mind-body connection, then share what *you* can do immediately to tap into that power and manifest the MAGIC! you need for finding **health, healing** and **happiness**.

## History and Philosophy in Brief

Yoga originates in India. Historians believe that its practices go back over 5,000 years. The word 'yoga' comes from the Sanskrit word 'yug' meaning 'yoke' or 'union'. We have come to know yoga as a 60 or 90-minute class of holding beautiful shapes, given the names of animals and other things in nature. What many people don't realise is that **asana** (postures or poses), is just one part of a holistic practice. And it's a superb part to start with! This aspect of yoga has swept the western world with a wave of healing so big, it's palpable. I thought it was just me, but when I started to teach, I began to hear, understand and realise just how powerful an effect yoga has on so many people, in so many ways.

About 2,000 years ago, the Yoga Sutras were compiled, by Patanjali. They are 196 verses ('sutra' means 'thread') representing, very specifically, the science of yoga. Of course, at that time the yoga sutras would not have been written, but chanted and passed down between master and student. There are many translations. Two that I have studied are referred to in the back of this book in Resources. The key thing that you can observe from these pages, is that yoga has more to do with the mind than the body. The only time asana or any physical practice is mentioned in these texts is with the aim of preparing the body to sit comfortably in meditation! The word 'asana' means 'comfortable seat' and it is believed that our word for our butt - 'ass' or 'arse' (if you're British) comes from it!

*"Yoga is the practice of quieting the mind."*
~ Patanjali

Patanjali talks about yoga as a path to enlightenment, freedom or a super-conscious state. There are seven steps before this that are clearly outlined in the texts. They are not only about a personal and self-centred practice, but also about how we interact with those around us. Patanjali realised that *how* we interact with the world around us is a huge factor in how we feel in mind and body.

For basic information, I have listed them here. There is so much more written about the Eight Limbs of Yoga, including on my website, www.chinmayimagic.com, that you can look further into at some point if you wish.

1. Yamas (abstinence) - non-harming, non-lying, non-stealing, self-control, non-greed
2. Niyamas (observance) - purity, contentment, self-awareness, discipline, devotion
3. Asana (posture)
4. Pranayama (breath/energy control)
5. Pratyahara (sense withdrawal)
6. Dharana (concentration)
7. Dhyana (meditation)
8. Samadhi (contemplation, absorption or super-conscious state)

*(taken from The Yoga Sutras of Patanjali - Sri Swami Satchidananda)*

You may notice that the Yamas and Niyamas read a little bit like the Ten Commandments, and maybe somewhere, deep in history, religions have shared philosophies and information. If you delve into yoga philosophy or any religious scriptures, you may find many similarities. However, yoga is NOT a religion or even a set of rules that must be followed in order to live a fulfilling life. It is a science. Yoga is a precise and comprehensive programme of change to enhance happiness and peace for anyone who seeks it. It does not profess to be the only way either. The yoga sutras will not tell you that you are damned if you don't follow them. You will not be judged or criticised by anyone else – any teacher, or any authority or any god or Higher Power, if you are practising any aspect of yoga. If you find yourself judged or feeling inferior, you're probably in the wrong class! These are merely codes of conduct for a happier and more fulfilling life. And who doesn't want that?

*"Without proper breathing, the yoga postures are nothing more than calisthenics."*
*~ Rachel Schaeffer*

## What does modern yoga look like?

If you live in the 'West', you will find yoga is mostly a physical (called **asana**) class. I use the term 'West' lightly, as now many cultures in what is considered the 'East' are finding a new wave of yoga in their communities. This is called **Hatha Yoga**. It is the yoga for improving health in the body and mind. The word 'Hatha' is made up of two words, Ha (sun) and Tha (moon). In yoga philosophy these represent opposing energies. Therefore, the purpose of Hatha yoga is to balance body and mind. An effectively-balanced practice will include warming sequences (including spinal movements in all directions), standing, seated, downward and upward facing poses, balancing and twisting poses, various breathing techniques to suit aspects of the practice (called **Pranayama**), a relaxation (called **Savasana**) and maybe a meditation or focus for the class.

Local yoga groups usually meet weekly as a class, hopefully held by a suitably trained and/or qualified teacher. The teacher is there to guide you through a practice, to help you to understand the benefits of different parts of the practice, whether that practice includes poses, breathing, meditation and/or relaxation techniques. You will learn how to enter and exit the poses safely and about any cautions that might need to be observed. The teacher should be able to adjust and assist all students where appropriate, with permission, with care and with confidence. A qualified teacher will know enough anatomy and physiology to help you to heal many different health issues, and what the limitations of yoga are for those issues.

A class is usually 60 or 90 minutes and is done in bare feet, usually on a sticky mat. There are sometimes props available to help you to adjust more comfortably or even to go deeper into a pose. It is important to be there at the start of the class and stay until the end, because a carefully planned class will offer the balancing benefits as it progresses. You should refrain from eating anything within 90 minutes to two hours before the start time, as most of yoga works really deeply within the digestive system. Make sure you are comfortably hydrated before your class and have water ready for after the class. Yoga is extremely detoxifying. Water will help this process continue. So it makes sense to avoid as many toxins as you can, for as long as you can, either side of your practice.

A weekly class is wonderful. You will learn so much. You will see many more benefits much more quickly if your overall aim of going to a class is to learn a home practice. It doesn't need to be a long practice and you will probably feel a bit lost in the beginning. But once you know a couple of sequences e.g. sun breath or sun salutation, you soon get into a flow. One of the benefits of home practice is that you can just move your body as it needs it. You find that your body needs some poses more than others and that may change day to day. What is certain is that you will never regret doing your yoga practice! Just get into some comfortable clothes and stretch! The MAGIC! in your personal practice is that you are moving from within the needs of your body. This connection is one of the main ingredients of BodyMAGIC!

Keep going to class so that you can learn the structure of an effective practice and acquire new information. You may also find some great classes online. Check www.bodymagic.website and www.chinmayimagic.com for my teachings. Yoga is a huge world all of its own and there is so much you can try, learn and incorporate into your routine. Try out different teachers too! You will find huge differences in styles and may feel judgement creeping in. Embrace the differences between classes. You will always take something new from every practice.

*"Yoga doesn't take time, it gives time."*
*~ Ganga White*

## What style of yoga should I choose?

Hatha yoga is really an umbrella term. Under it there are so many styles, to suit all tastes. I shall not be critical or favour any style, as I realise that the needs of the student are so varied. I would say that if you are following the general guidelines and the path of this book, try to find a class that has a philosophical, spiritual and/or traditional element to it. The whole path to BodyMAGIC! is a holistic one. This means your class should have practices for body, mind *and* spirit. If you are going to a yoga class that is purely physical, you are missing out on the healing that comes from being able to relax and understand your mind. You may like the idea of having arms like Madonna, but the real reason you are there is much more important. It is to learn about your relationship with your body, your mind and your emotions, so that you can find real **health, healing** and **happiness**, particularly in your relationship with food.

Yoga should always be fun. Yes, really! I spent the first 10 years of my yoga practice thinking it would be rude to smile or play in a yoga class. Some classes I have been to are *very* serious and solemn, which is a shame. Do you know that when you smile or laugh, whether it is natural or forced, your brain hardly knows the difference? You will produce endorphins, serotonin and dopamine just the same. These ingredients will supercharge your positive emotions beyond your expectations, giving you the healing you need in your relationship with food. And this teaching to me, doesn't come from some new age, inner-city yoga brand. This 'happy yoga' philosophy comes from one of my own great teachers in the Himalayas of India!

*"Yoga is not about touching your toes, it is what you learn on the way down."*
*~ Jigar Gor*

# What will it do for me?

I already wrote about my story of finding yoga in *Chapter Five* - MeditationMAGIC!, but suffice to say, yoga is a part of me. When I get on to my mat, I'm entering a sacred space where something very special happens. And the time I'm practising is sacred too! It's like stopping the world from spinning, getting off and taking a huge breather, literally as well as metaphorically. The benefits of yoga are *real*. Not just in my experience. I know this from the incredible feedback I get as a teacher. I now have hundreds of unsolicited testimonials from my students telling me what it has done for their lives. Yoga *HEALS*!

Here's an overview of some of those benefits:

1. Improves sleep quality and quantity where needed

2. Balances, and where needed, calms the nervous system, helps with headaches, migraines and diseases of the nervous system

3. Detoxifies the body through moving lymph more efficiently and massaging the abdominal organs

4. Encourages deeper breathing, sending more oxygen to the cells, improving all the body's systems, increasing lung capacity, heart health and lung detoxification

5. Slows down the ageing process by improving regeneration of cells

6. Boosts immunity by maintaining the proper intake of nutrients into the body from food and getting proper rest

7. Reduces stress by teaching us how to relax. Most of us can sleep, but rarely do we truly relax

8. Yoga asana lengthens and stretches tight muscles, reducing tension on joints, thereby preventing injury. The extra range of movement afforded by asana allows joints to shift toxins and welcome fresh nutrients that keep them supple

9. It is thought by yoga experts that the health of the spine has a direct link with ageing. It is not difficult to see why. A full range of movement through asana not only improves posture on and off the mat, it prolongs the life of the discs, encouraging the movement of healthy spinal fluids

10. Helps to alkalise the body, reducing the risk of all illness, disease and emotional imbalance

11. Helps to balance all of the emotions and stop us overreacting to situations beyond our control. This enhances our relationships and makes for a more fulfilling life

12. Reduces cravings for food and drinks that do not serve us, and other substances that are harmful to our long-term health.

13. Overall improvements in health can reduce our dependency on all medications and therefore their potential side effects are eliminated

14. Increases our confidence, which helps us stick to our goals and enhances our personal power to show us that we *are* in control. Yoga strengthens our instincts

15. Increases focus and concentration. Yoga helps to de-clog the mind so that we are able to find more creative solutions to life's challenges

16. Helps to balance all hormones. This is great news for diabetics (helps lower blood sugar and regulates insulin), for those suffering with PMT/PMS, menopause or difficult periods, and for stress sufferers (reduces cortisol *and* need for excess food)

17. Can balance circulatory problems, reducing hypertension and increasing circulation to extremities, strengthening the heart and cleansing the blood

18. Depending on the practice, yoga can be very strengthening and weight-bearing, so particularly useful in the prevention of osteoporosis

> *"Yoga teaches us to cure what need not be endured and endure what cannot be cured."*
> *~ B.K.S. Iyengar*

There are many more benefits, in more detail, available all over the internet and in books, magazines and DVDs. If you need any more information to inspire you, go and read! If you are already convinced and you're ready to go, here are some ideas for a beginner's practice. I acknowledge now that yoga is extremely difficult to learn from a book. Go to my website (www.chinmayimagic.com) and learn some of the basics. It's obviously much easier to listen to someone's voice when you're in a balancing pose than to look down at any book! One way around this is to record yourself reading through these instructions on your mobile or another recording device, or have someone do it for you. Still not ideal, because until you know what you're doing, you may not allow appropriate pauses between instructions, but it's worth a try.

Whether this is your first experience of yoga or not, I want you to get the very best out of it.

So I have a special gift for you!

Place the link below in your browser and follow the link to download a video on these sequences for FREE!

www.vimeo.com/127093199

Enter the code - **BeginYogin**

Please feel free to post any feedback or questions you have. I will do my best to answer them.

Please read the **Notes on Practice** before you start.

# Notes on Practice

It makes sense that if you have, or have had, any illness or injury, you should consult your doctor before starting yoga or any exercise. Do not hesitate if you have a reason to believe that *any* exercise in this book is unsuitable for you. Most doctors will agree that yoga can help out with most conditions, but there are still exceptions.

There is no substitute for guidance from an experienced teacher, especially if you have an illness or injury. Even if you only go to a few classes when you have the time, you will have the benefit of adjustments and assistance where necessary and your body will remember them after a few practices. You will also get the 'feel' of yoga and be able to recreate that space in your home.

If you are pregnant, please do not start practising yoga for the first time without consulting your doctor and your yoga teacher. Some classes are gentle and may be OK. Hot yoga, power yoga and Ashtanga yoga are very likely to be too much, especially if you are a beginner. There are special considerations in yoga during pregnancy. Yoga is extremely beneficial in pregnancy, but it is a very different and specially-focused practice that deserves guidance from a trained teacher.

Whether you are a beginner to yoga or a well-practiced experienced devotee, you will benefit from this next short sequence. I suggest you start at the beginning and do as much as you have time for. If you are new to yoga, read and/or listen to the instructions carefully. Don't rush through them. Maybe start with Tadasana and add a new pose in each time you practice.

Try to make it every day in your sacred space. When you get the hang of it, maybe step outside. Make it part of your routine. You will need 10-15 minutes at the most. And you won't even need a mat for most of it, so there is little need for much preparation.

I make no apologies for repeating that the MAGIC! from yoga happens when we let go of the goal. This was the mistake I made in my understanding when I started. I was a gymnast as a child and I had seen pictures of yogis doing some of the amazing poses I used to do, easily, as a child. I wanted to do them again. And as I said before, I was very achievement-driven around the time I found yoga. Once I got the hang of the breathing and beginners' poses, I wanted more. I resented having to go back and start a beginners' level course with my first teacher. I didn't have much choice though, as she was the only one in town! But as soon as got into the course again, I realised that there was *always* something new and magical for me to learn, that would go much deeper than my backbends and headstands. It came from the new connection with and respect for my body. A new, caring, nurturing and joyful appreciation of my body and **health** that would facilitate more **healing** and **happiness** in my life. If things happen for a reason, then *that* was the purpose of yoga coming into my life – for me to find emotional freedom, relieve stress permanently by realising what was really important, and eventually to teach others how to do so.

> *"Yoga is a way to freedom. By its constant practice, we can free ourselves from fear, anguish and loneliness."*
> ~ Indra Devi

The sole purpose of this practice is to help you connect with your body's MAGIC! This subtle healing energy is not found in the ego and the need to do more, achieve more and be better. It is moving *through* that illusion, letting go and simply allowing your body to heal through the health benefits yoga brings. Even if you have done these poses thousands of times before, take time to really work the subtle movements and notice the benefits as you practice them. I have gone into plenty of detail to allow you to do this. Feel for the shifts and changes in your body, your mind and your emotions.

## Tips on Breathing in Yoga

1.  *Always breathe through your nose.* There are a few exceptions which are advanced specific breathing practices through the mouth, but certainly in yoga movement and holding of poses, always breathe through the nose.

2.  *Never hold your breath.* It can be a challenge as a beginner. We associate holding a pose with holding the breath. Not so. Again, there are some breathing exercises in yoga where the breath is intentionally held. But in asana, the breath is extremely important for moving and balancing energy.

3.  *Inhale up and open, exhale down and squeeze.* You may notice that when you breathe in, your ribcage lifts. The lungs act like airbags to help you to extend your body upwards and outwards. Your inhale is the most energetic and powerful part of your breath, so use it to help you work against gravity. When you exhale the ribs fall and your muscles naturally relax. This is where you surrender to gravity, in a controlled manner. It is also the breath used for squeezing, for example in a twist. When the lungs are emptying, more room becomes available to go deeper into the twist

## Simple Yet Profound Yoga Practices

### Palm Tree or Mountain Pose – Tadasana

To improve posture and balance; to encourage proper breathing and oxygen to the cells for the body's overall efficiency; to improve concentration, confidence and general outlook.
Improves circulation, revitalises the nervous system.

Most books will call this pose the Mountain Pose, but Tad actually means Palm Tree. However, the qualities of the mountain are relevant – *stillness* and *height*, as are the qualities of the palm tree, *grounded* *with strong roots and a need to* *extend* *up to the sky.* So use whatever visualisation you like right now to breathe into this wonderful pose.

Work from the roots up, i.e. start at your feet:

1.  Stand with your feet parallel, with about a foot between the very middle of your feet. Your second and third toes will be pointing forward. This may feel a little pigeon-toed at first, but the square shape you are making with your feet will help your balance, strengthen all the muscles, and work all the tendons and ligaments of your feet as they were meant to be.

2.  Spread your toes as if you are trying to take up as much room with your feet on the ground as you can.

3.  Soften your knees. There is difference between a locked and a bent knee. Yours should be somewhere in between. There is no tension in the knees in this position, but the muscles will still have to work to hold you up. You should feel the thigh muscles engage.

4. Move your awareness to your lower back. Move your tailbone down towards the floor, without moving your legs. It's a kind of tucking action, but visualise it moving downwards rather than underneath. This will cause your abdomen to move inwards. Encourage this by drawing your navel inwards towards your spine. Hold this position with your core gently, as you move on and up.

5. Be aware of the centre of your chest, your breastplate/bone or sternum. Inhale deeply and feel it lifting, opening your chest, at the same time keeping your shoulders back and down. Do not allow the back to arch. Instead, feel a lengthening upwards.

6. Have your chin parallel to the ground and feel the lengthening in your neck. Visualise that there is a rope attached to the top of your head and it is lifting you up through the centre of your body.

7. Let your arms hang loosely by your sides, relaxing your shoulders, arms and fingers. Direct all your energy with your breath. As you inhale, feel the lift up through the spine. As you exhale hold that lift but encourage the shoulders to relax. I like to visualise a water fountain. The force of energy comes up through the middle and it cascades down the sides. Or you can visualise the shape of the palm tree in a similar way.

8. Hold this position for 5-7 breaths, longer if you have time.

Notice how much taller you feel. You will feel lifted in body but also in spirit. You are allowing for breath to reach all areas of your lungs, increasing oxygen to every cell of your body, improving every aspect of your body's health. And notice how you feel. It is extremely difficult to feel low when you are holding this pose. Thinking about the most confident people you know – how do they carry themselves? Sad people usually shrink their bodies to match their mood. Confidence thrives in an open heart. Try this the next time you feel below par mentally and notice the MAGIC! It will soon become a habit, and with practice you will move though these eight steps in a few seconds.


## Sun Breath - (Half Sun Salutation) - Ardha Surya Namaskar

*"Sun salutations can energize and warm you, even on the darkest, coldest winter day."*
*~ Carol Krucoff*

This short sequence introduces long, slow and steady breathing to a yoga practice. This aspect is fundamental to yoga. Without proper breathing, a practice is just some light gymnastics. This sequence is a shortened, beginners-level or half version of the Sun Salutation. But it has most of the same incredible benefits. It wakes up the spine and balances ALL of the body's systems and functions. It warms the whole body, especially the spine and the muscles in the arms and legs. It is an excellent way to start the day, and even more powerful if you can be outside facing the East, at sunrise. You won't need your mat for this sequence and if it's cold you can still wear your coat and boots!

Start standing with the hands in prayer, with the thumbs on the heart centre and the elbows lifted.

1. Inhale - raise the arms out, back and up into a prayer pose above your head, lifting your chest.

2. Exhale - fold your body in half from the hips, coming forward with a flat back, softening your knees to take the weight of your upper body as it comes down onto your thighs. Let your hands come to your calves, your feet, or to the ground.

3. Inhale - lift your upper body up to a flat back position, looking forwards, smile :-)

4. Exhale - lower back down to position 2.

5. Inhale - lift the chin and chest, unfolding the body, softening the knees to take the weight out of the back, raising the arms out and up to a prayer pose above your head as in 1.

6. Exhale - bring the arms back into a prayer pose at the heart centre.

7. Repeat up to 7 times and notice the change in your energy!


## Standing Twisting Breath

This moving twist massages the spine, relieving stiffness in the whole body, whether from sleep or sitting for prolonged periods. It does this by recirculating spinal and joint fluids. It detoxifies the digestive organs, particularly the liver, stomach, bowel and kidneys by wringing and pumping them. This movement, combined with full and fairly fast breathing, stimulates the metabolism and elimination. It's a wake-up for the nervous system, helping with the flow of energy, signalling vitality all over the body.

1. Stand with your feet hip-width apart. Turn your toes out slightly. This is to reduce strain on the knees as you twist.

2. Inhale as you lift your arms and turn to the right. You are using your shoulders to turn; your arms and hands are relaxed and floppy.

3. Turn your head to find a point to stare at as you exhale. The exhale is slightly forced, as if you are pumping the air out. I liken it to a steam train leaving a station!

4. Inhale, repeating on the other side and continue.

5. If you do feel any pulling on your knee, lift the heel up from the ground as you twist. If you feel dizzy, keep looking at a point in front of you instead of behind. With practice the dizziness will lessen.

Start with seven repetitions on each side. You can build up to 54 or more.


## Standing Side Bending Breath

This pose is often called Tiryaka Tadasana, meaning Swaying Palm Tree. It stimulates elimination, massages digestive organs, particularly the bowel, liver, stomach and kidneys. Helps to re-energise and detox unwanted negative energy by balancing the adrenal glands, relieving tightness in the spine and shoulders. This strengthens the upper core and tones the waistline. It opens you up to new possibilities!

1. Stand in Tadasana pose

2. Inhale and raise your arms to a prayer pose above your head, lifting your ribs upwards

3. Exhale and lean to the right

4. Inhale back up

5. Exhale to the left

6. Inhale back up the centre

7. Repeat until you have done seven rounds, then exhale back into a prayer pose, with your thumbs at your heart centre. Close your eyes and take a deep, lingering breath through the nose.

In time you can build up to 50 repetitions or more.

Note: The most important aspect of this movement is to imagine that you are leaning between two pieces of glass. There is a tendency to lean forward and for the upper arm to fall over the face. In this way, you are using your back muscles rather than the obliques (side muscles). You can use a wall as a prop to do this pose, to check and guide you in the beginning.

*"God wisely designed the human body so that we can neither pat our own backs nor kick ourselves too easily."*
*~ Unknown*

## Chair Breathing

This will get your heart pumping! It will work the strongest and the longest muscles in your body. It will overhaul and improve your cardiovascular health, strengthen and tone your legs, your back/shoulders and your arms. If you breathe deeply in this exercise you will supercharge your fitness, your lungs' capacity and your immune system.

1. Stand in Tadasana, but take your feet two inches further apart. This is for balance. When you look down, try to see and feel that your ankles, knees and hips are stacked above each other. Keep those knees soft!

2. Inhale, raise your arms up to shoulder height, palms facing down.

3. Exhale with a little force, bend your knees and sink your buttocks back as if you were going to sit on a chair, pulling your hands into your armpits as fists.

4. Inhale and stand up again, taking the arms up to shoulder height again. Don't lock out your knees at the top. This keeps the thighs engaged.

5. Repeat seven times, or as many as you can comfortably. You can build up to 50 or more, or even more than a hundred with a regular practice!

6. To finish, fold forward and witness your breath coming back to normal. Move slightly to feel a stretch in your back and your hamstrings.

## Staff Pose - Dandasana

This is what many call a 'foundation pose' for seated poses. Many seated poses start in this pose. It is excellent for strengthening the thighs, the back muscles and especially the spine. It is fabulous for hamstring flexibility and core strength. It improves posture and encourages deep breathing.

1. Start seated on the floor, on flat comfortable ground. Use a yoga mat, towel or rug if you need it to be more comfortable.

2. Straighten your legs if possible. If this is not for you just yet, don't worry. You should not feel pain at any time. You can modify this pose easily by placing a pillow, a bolster, small rug or rolled up towel under your knees.

3. Ease the flesh of your buttocks aside. One of my teachers calls these your personal pillows! You should feel your sitting bones on the ground. Then place your hands lightly on the ground next to your buttocks.

4. Inhale deeply, flexing your feet and lengthening up through your spine. If this is uncomfortable, for support you can use a wall or even your sofa if you are practising in your living room. As you get stronger you will be able to move away from it.

5. As you exhale, aim to try and hold the height from your inhale.

Repeat for seven breaths and build up according to your practice and strength.
Some days your practice will be more challenging than others. The reason for this may be obvious to you. Be kind to yourself. This is no boot camp! Accept where you are today, back off from straining in any pose or sequence and just do what you can. Your body will love you for it!


**Bird Flying Pose**

This is a prone pose. That means you are facing downwards, lying on your tummy. This falls into the category of back bending, but it's gentle. You are lifting against the mighty force of gravity and this pose will do wonders for your core and all of the other muscles in the back of your body. I always include a little visualisation with this pose, because the first time I ever did it in this format, my teacher did the same. You never forget the fantastic feeling you get from the sweetness of a challenging pose. Like most poses in yoga, it also works on the digestive system, by massaging all of the major organs and detoxifying stomach, liver, kidneys and intestines. Backbends are anti-depressant. They open the heart and your willingness to bring joy into every cell of your being.

1. Lie on your belly, on a flat surface, and on a towel or mat if you have one. Bring your arms by your side, palms down, and rest your chin on the floor. There are three stages in this pose. Try the next stage after seven breaths. If it is too intense, go back to the previous stage or bring your chin back on the ground.

2. Throughout the practice, visualise yourself flying over your favourite place in the world. It could be your favourite beach, park, lake or some other site you have visited and been moved by. Somewhere you found peace, joy, healing or some other positive emotion that you have held the memory of. Observe those feelings again. Notice the colours, the sights, the smells, even tastes. Be aware of the time of day, the time of year and who and what is there. Take in the experience once again. Create your own blissful moment.

3. *Stage One* - Inhale and lift your chin and upper chest off the ground. To relax your neck, you can look down. Keep breathing deeply, which will be a challenge lying on your front. This also strengthens the lungs. Repeat up to seven times.

4. *Stage Two* - Inhale and lift your arms off the ground. Breathe here up to seven times at least before moving on to

5. *Stage Three* - lift your feet off the floor. You will be balancing on your abdominal muscles and the bottom of your ribcage. Continue breathing here as deeply as you can, without straining.

6. Whenever you feel that you have had enough or finished, exhale and slowly lower your body down to the ground.

7. Move straight into Child's Pose (see below) from here. Bring your hands under your shoulders, inhale and push yourself up and back, resting your buttocks on your heels. After Child's Pose you can repeat Bird Flying again if you wish.

*"Yoga takes what you have and moulds and sculpts it, which is a much more natural way to look and feel." ~ Adam Levine*

## Balasana – Child's Pose

Child's Pose is known as a restorative pose, as it relaxes your heart rate and breath. It also relaxes the senses. It is extremely grounding and centring.

1. From a prone position, inhale and push yourself up onto your knees and then back further. You are aiming your buttocks back onto your heels. If this is too much for your knees and/or your feet, either place a pillow between your buttocks and your lower legs or sit on your bottom and stretch your legs out in front of you. This is a counter pose for a backbend, so you want to be bending forward in your spine in the most comfortable and convenient way.

2. Either bring your hands back to your heels, resting the elbows on the floor, or stretch the arms out in front of you, using the stickiness of the floor or your mat to ease you back onto your heels a little further.

3. Breathing here will also be a challenge in the front of your lungs. Try to breathe into your *rear* lungs. We actually have more lung capacity at the back of our bodies and the same ability to expand the rear ribs. Breathing here gives you a wonderful abdominal massage and is a great stress buster, since we hold most of our stress in our digestive system.

4. Another variation is to open the knees and rest your upper body between them. Great if you are pregnant or have a bloated, uncomfortable abdomen.

5. Feel the stretch across your shoulders and the forward bending stretch in your spine.

6. You can stay here for as long as you have available, or hold for just a few breaths.

7. To exit, inhale and use your arms to help you to sit upright, exhale and relax.

## Savasana - Corpse Pose

This is the relaxation bit! I will be covering the benefits and the art of relaxation in a later chapter, but suffice to say that few of us really know how to relax. This pose helps us to focus completely on physical relaxation. It is not something you can read from a book whilst you are in Savasana, but you can use the recordings I offer, or record yourself and play it back. The purpose of Savasana is to relax, not to sleep.

But you can use this practice to go to sleep if falling asleep is an issue for you. Otherwise, use it as a relaxation.

1. Find a space where you will not be disturbed for about 15-20 minutes. You should be warm, free from draughts and insects and if possible in a dimly-lit place. Have blankets, pillows and lots of comfort. It's better to do Savasana on the floor, rather than your bed, so make sure you are going to be comfortable.

2. Lie on your back with your legs outstretched. Have your legs about 2.5 feet apart (the width of an average yoga mat) and let your feet flop outwards.

3. Take your arms a little distance from your sides, so that there is space in your armpits. Turn your palms upwards and let your fingers curl naturally.

4. Move your shoulders down towards your feet an inch or two to lengthen your neck. When you lie down, your shoulders instinctively raise to protect your head. Then tuck your chin into your neck a little to lengthen the back of the neck further.

5. Close your eyes softly. Let your eyes fall back into their sockets. Your eyelashes are just gently meeting and sealing out the light, but there is no tension.

6. Be aware of your forehead. Notice any frown or tension there. Allow that tension to move by giving yourself a soft smile.

7. Relax your cheeks and your nose.

8. Is your mouth relaxed? Your teeth can be apart and your lips gently touching. Relax your tongue behind your bottom teeth.

9. Now become aware of your abdomen and become aware of your breath. You are going to practice abdominal breathing. Your breath is going to move all the way down to your abdomen. Allow the belly to rise and expand with the inhale, and fall and contract with your exhale. If you are new to this, you can bring your hands onto your belly to help and guide you.

10. Try to keep your awareness on the rising and falling of your abdomen and your breathing. Continue this for as long as you have time. When your mind wanders, do not analyse or judge the distraction, just come back to your breath and the rise and fall of your belly.

11. When you are ready to come back, do so slowly. Keep your eyes closed. First, be conscious of where you are and your surroundings. Start to lengthen your breath. Wriggle your toes and fingers and turn your head slowly from side to side. Inhale and raise your arms over your head, stretching your heels away from you, or if you prefer, walk your knees up to your chest and give them a hug.

12. Still keeping your eyes closed, gently roll on to your right side, taking a few breaths here.

13. Then use your hands to help you come up to sitting. Still try to keep your eyes closed.

14. Rub your palms together to build some heat in them and then cover your eyes. When you feel ready, open your eyes, letting the light in through your fingers and slowly drag your hands away from your face, into a prayer pose.

15. Namaste!

*"I lie to myself every day when I tell myself, 'I can skip yoga'."*
*~ Melissa Fumero*

### Chapter Nine
# Nature Calls!

*"Natural abilities are like natural plants; they need pruning by study."*
~ Francis Bacon

## How to honour the hand that feeds us

This chapter is humungous! And so it should be. It applies to everyone who feels that there is something missing in their life, whether they overeat or not. For me, it has been what people call 'finding themselves'. It is reconnecting with what is real, traditional and natural, whether that is:

> the food we eat,
> the water we drink,
> the air we breathe,
> the exercise we perform,
> the sleep we have,
> the medicine we take,
> the healing we need,
> the cleaning we do,
> the beauty we seek

and eventually the work we do, where we live, the friends we choose, even how we bring up our children.

Mother Earth is far from just the planet we walk upon. Like all nurturing mothers, she uses the resources of the sun with its light and heat, with the seeds of the earth and the water from her clouds to provide our food and keep us warm. She grows trees to take away carbon dioxide so that we may breathe the oxygen we need. The forests are her lungs, the rivers are her arteries and the relentlessness of nature to provide for us is at her very heart. She gives us what we need until our bodies come to the end of their days, and then she takes us back to her bosom as dust.

Traditions all over the world have honoured her gifts as long as humans have existed. They clearly knew the importance of her workings to their lives. Of course, now we have advanced. We can build shelters to withstand all weathers, process and store food with ingredients to make it last years, push a button for heat, buy a ticket or a tank of fuel to go anywhere we please. The world has become smaller by convenience, but its natural magnificence has somehow been forgotten.

One thing that has facilitated all of this change is money. Instead of ethically gathering her resources and sharing them with the poor, the sick and the world, we want more and more. We will do anything to get the money to buy things, when all we really want is more joy. Nature holds this already and most of it is just outside our front door.

I'm not suggesting that you give up your job, your home and belongings, and go and pitch a tent in the wilderness. I'm asking you to explore some neat ways of connecting with Mother Earth and allowing her to help you to heal. It's what she has always been very good at since man evolved. Our bodies haven't changed that much at all in the last 500 years, but our lifestyle, values and consciousness have changed beyond recognition. Small adjustments to these will help us to realign with who we really are – millions of atoms of energy, hyper-sensitive beings, super-intelligent minds, spirit-connected souls who can achieve just about anything, including joy. I have come to realise that when I don't get what I desire, it's usually because it's not for my highest good and not in line with what is around me.

When you realise just how amazing you are and the capacity you have for change, overcoming overeating will have been merely a sign-post in your life, directing you back to what is real, traditional and natural. That kind of **health, healing** and **happiness** is what is meant for you. Always has been. Always will be.

## What does all this have to do with BodyMAGIC?

The biggest shift I have found is when I have turned to nature for help. To get up close to nature, as often as possible, is really like seeing your mum or someone else who has had a great positive influence on your life for advice, guidance and motivation. It can start as a simple awareness.

## Energy Levels and Connecting with Nature

One of the most important aspects of getting to know ourselves is the recognition of our energy levels day-to-day. Sometimes it's difficult to understand why one day we feel absolutely on top of the world, with stacks of energy, and other days we just want to hide under the duvet and not speak to anyone!

As we become more aware, we can often be more sensitive to the energies of others, to variations in the weather, the food we have eaten or the amount and quality of the sleep we have been getting, even the phases of the moon and the sun. Some days we can feel really positive, and those are great. The problem for the overeater is the days when we feel negative emotions. Sometimes it's just a little frustration at everyday challenges. Other days it can feel like the whole world is against us, and we just want to give up altogether on our good intentions.

The indigenous Andean people of Peru believe that there is no such thing as negative energy. It is heavy energy instead that the human body does not recognise. This makes a lot of sense. As I have said before, the kind of stressors we are having to face daily are new to human beings. We haven't evolved quickly enough to cope with them. The body cannot process and detox these energies either quickly or efficiently. So they hang around us and feel as if they are bringing us down. The Andean medicine men and women call this heavy energy Hucha. It belongs to Mother Earth, and to her it is like nectar. When we feel this energy in or around us, we can give it back to Mother Earth. She wants to take it from us, as any good mother would of course! And we can do this simply by reconnecting with nature itself.

The light energy that is meant to be ours is called Sami. Hucha and Sami do not just hang around in our physical body. We have an energy body also that the Andean people call the Poqpo. This is sometimes known as an aura in modern culture – the yogis call it the Pranamaya Kosha (one Kosha of five) and it is loosely known in Buddhism as Sambhogakaya – a subtler part of our being. There are many beliefs and systems of understanding that cultures share in common all around the world. They just use different names. The fascinating thing is that they have all existed for thousands of years in indigenous tribes and cultures, totally independently of one another. The ancient yogis, for example, had amazing powers of perception and knowledge. They were able to 'see' and understand things that modern science has only just begun to research and confirm. It seems all traditional cultures know about the energy body. What is important is to be aware of it and know how to work with it to keep it nurturing, energising and protecting you at all times.

# Exercise

**Sami Chakuay** - cleansing and balancing natural energies

This is a simple Andean shamanic practice that really helps to shift Hucha energy out of your body and into the Earth, replenishing your energy system with Sami or light energy. It takes three to five minutes. This short exercise really helps to clear Hucha in and around you that doesn't serve you, replacing it with Sami or light energy. This is your natural state of being. Record this so you can work comfortably through the stages.

1. Stand in bare feet or without shoes if possible. Close your eyes. If you are outside, all the better! Feel the ground beneath your feet as close as you can. Get a sense and strong awareness of your contact with the Earth's surface. Be aware of your physical body standing on the ground.

2. Next, get a sense of your energy body, your aura or your poqpo. Still keeping your eyes closed, raise your arms a little and gently push your palms away from you. Can you feel or sense a kind of boundary or different sensation in your hands? Sometimes this layer is close to your physical body, sometimes it expands quite a way from you.

3. Now lower your hands and keep a visualisation in your mind of your physical and energy bodies. Allow your arms to relax by your sides.

4. Become aware of your breath. As you breathe deeply, visualise Sami energy coming down through your crown **into** your physical form, working its way down, taking with it Hucha, heavy or negative energy that you no longer want. Visualise it moving through your head space, your neck and into your chest and shoulders. If you become aware of physical tension, visualise it being dissolved by the Sami (light) energy.

5. Allow it to penetrate your whole torso and down your arms into your fingers. Often I feel a pressure here in the tips of my fingers. You can touch your thighs and visualise it moving down into the Earth via your legs and feet. Keep the awareness of light moving slowly down into your abdomen and hips.

6. As the Hucha moves down, replaced by the Sami energy, visualise or feel it moving down your legs into your feet and pouring into the ground, and Mother Earth willingly taking it from you.

7. Next go back to the top of your head and visualise the Sami energy moving down from above and over the **outside** of your body, but within your poqpo. You are cleansing your auric field, your energy body. Take your time and work your way down, taking Hucha into the ground as before.

8. Then visualise the poqpo closing at the top and the Sami light coming down and cleansing the outside of your poqpo, taking Hucha into the ground.

9. Take a few minutes to finish the exercise, then gently open your eyes. Move slowly for a few minutes to come back to your day.

This wonderful cleansing practice is one of many ways of energy clearing. Use it when you feel you need to – when you feel negative about anything and you know you are suffering because of it. It's useful to do some kind of space-clearing daily.

**The Elements** - connecting with nature for healing

*"Everyone else on the planet, from the lowest amoebae to the great blue whale, expresses all their component elements in a perfect dance with the world around them. Only human beings have unfulfilled lives."*
*~ Nicholas Lore*

We only need to step outside and use our senses to connect with all of the elements that we also hold within. This is one very powerful way of connecting with nature. There are no rules, so you cannot do it wrong. Be guided by your intuition. Each of the elements has a healing quality to offer when we are feeling a little out of balance. This connection can take minutes, or could form part of a long healing walk. It could be a walk in a park, taking a seat in the garden or making a trip to the beach.

I show you here how I might connect with different elements and what purpose that connection might serve:

My **Earth** is my physical body - my skin and bones, my organs and all my tissues.
Connect with soil or sand underfoot, pick a stone and feel its density, hug a tree! (yes you can!)
Purpose - grounding for times of frustration, fear, worry, loss of material things.
Follow-up actions - eat foods from below the ground e.g. potatoes, carrots. Do some balancing yoga poses. Lie on the ground for a relaxation. Do some gardening.

My **Water** is my blood, lymph, saliva, waste fluids from earwax to urine.
Connect with the rain or snow, an ocean, river or lake, the clouds.
Purpose - cleansing for strong tearful emotions like sadness, grief, upset, hurt.
Follow-up actions - drink spring water to relieve imbalances, take a salt bath, swim in nature e.g., the sea or a lake (where it is safe to do so). Take a shower.

My **Fire** is my digestion, my temperature, my drive and enthusiasm, personal power.
Connect with the sun (even if it is hidden behind the clouds!) or a fire, even a candle flame.
Purpose - strengthening for lack of confidence or personal power, hopelessness, helplessness.
Follow-up actions - build a fire, take a sauna or visit hot springs, relax in the sun for twenty minutes.

My **Air** is my breath (external respiration), the effect of oxygen in my blood (internal respiration)
Connect with the wind, outdoor air.
Purpose - nurturing for times of loneliness, relationship problems, disappointment, shock, trauma.
Follow up actions - do some Yogic Breathing - see Resources, fly a kite, sail a boat, hang out the laundry on a windy day.

My **Space** is the spaces in my body, e.g. throat, ear canal, vagina, rectum, abdomen.
Connect with the sky.
Purpose - to open up communication channels, speak the truth, let go of the past, to detox.
Follow-up action - visit a large park or other open space. Climb a hill. Look up and see that the possibilities are limitless, gaze at the stars, gargle with salt water, perform Lion's Breath (see *Chapter Twenty-Four*).

This also relates to the Chakras that we will be discussing later. Now we will have a look at some of the different ways that we can connect with nature.

# The Element Song

*I thank you for your Earth and all its glory*
*For giving me my birth*
*To start life's story*
*I thank you for my friends, the rocks and trees and plants*
*I thank you for your Earth, I thank you for your Earth, I thank you for your Earth!*

*I thank you for your Water and all its glory*
*For rivers, lakes and seas*
*To quench life's story*
*I thank you for your grace, washing over me in peace*
*I thank you for your Water, I thank you for your Water, I thank you for your Water*

*I thank you for your Fire and all its glory*
*For shining on my world*
*To fuel life's story*
*I thank you for your power, your courage and your strength*
*I thank you for your Fire, I thank you for your Fire, I thank you for your Fire*

*I thank you for your Air and all its glory*
*For whispering the wind*
*To breathe life's story*
*I thank you for the breath, of love so pure inside my heart*
*I thank you for your Air, I thank you for your Air, I thank you for your Air*

*I thank you for your Space and all its glory*
*For filling it with love*
*To hold life's story*
*I thank for the gift, to know and live my highest good*
*I thank you for your Space, I thank you for the Space, I thank you for the Space*

*I thank you for your Light and all its glory*
*For shining inside me*
*To see life's story*
*I thank you for the truth, I witness within me*
*I thank you for your Light, I thank you for your Light, I thank you for your Light*

*I thank you for your Spirit and all its glory*
*For moving me to Bliss*
*To know life's story*
*I thank you that you're there, in all I see and feel*
*I thank you for your Spirit, I thank you for your Spirit, I thank you for your Spirit!*

*Chinmayi Dore*

# Natural Food, Natural Health

*"It's very dangerous to mix up the words natural and habitual."*
*~ Gandhi*

Before I go into details about natural food, I want to dispel a couple of myths with regard to overeating and the kind of food we eat. Ponder over these statements for a minute or two.

i. A little bit of what you fancy does *not* necessarily do you any good
ii. You *never* deserve the kind of treats to which you have become accustomed
iii. Just because you've always done it, doesn't mean you *always* have to do it *now*

I have written these in reply to the many times I have used these and other excuses to go ahead and overeat what I want. They speak of powerlessness over our food choices. Yet when we make them we feel powerful in ignoring our original 'good' intentions. The point isn't to tell you to never ever eat unhealthy food or drink again. The point is to be aware, informed and conscious when you do. We can only make changes when we really know what we are doing and why we are doing it. Emotionally this strengthens your **Focus** and **Understanding** of the foods you eat, so that you can move on to new **Confidence** and **Enthusiasm** for your health, which then gives you more **Discipline** and **Willpower** etc.

When you do allow yourself these other less nutritious foods, whatever they are, do so with awareness. It will slow you down, you'll probably eat less (you won't overeat), you'll enjoy it more (maybe in time you won't), and you won't feel guilty or a failure. This stops the cycle of feeling powerless over food. It's not the eating of junk that causes the pain, it's the guilt, despair and hopeless feelings that knock us down.

If we are going to get all natural with our food, we need to understand a little about the effect man has had on the environment. You see, Mother Earth has a huge, reliable ecosystem for us, making everything work as it should. It is the intervention of human greed that is changing this system. We are almost literally biting and gnawing at the hand that feeds us. And much of it is irreversible.

We have the capacity to feed the whole world easily, but there is too much money involved in the corporations who want us to have more than we need, of the types of foods that we *don't* need. Despite the incredible amount of research and the knowledge we have in books, magazines and social media, we still put profits before health.

*"When chemicals that are designed to kill are introduced into delicately balanced ecosystems, they can set damage in motion that reverberates through the food web for years.*
- *Honeybee populations are plummeting nationwide.*
- *Male frogs exposed to atrazine become females.*
- *Pesticides are implicated in dramatic bat die-offs.*

*Pesticides wreak havoc on the environment, threatening biodiversity and weakening the natural systems upon which human survival depends."*
*Source: Pesticide Action Network (North America)*
*(www.panna.org/issues/persistent-poisons/environmental-impacts)*

It is so easy to get upset, even angry about the state of the world's food supply. However, that would defeat your personal goals, of overcoming the emotions involved with overeating. I used to become so upset about the abuse of our Mother Earth, and I still campaign where I can. But now I try to maintain my own emotional health and just do what I can for my planet, my home, my own health and that of those I cook for. The best advice a friend gave me in my highly-strung, I-want-to-change-the-world-now days was to just lead by example.

*"Cultivate clarity, strength, vitality and power from natural, beautiful and organic living foods."*
~ Bryant McGill

## General Rules of thumb

*1.  Back to Basics*

If it hasn't had a life of its own, then it won't have any life force for you!
The yogis talk about the vital force that keeps us alive as **prana**. This prana fills every aspect of us. In the physical body, it travels through 72,000 energy channels called nadis. The prana that flows through these nadis determines everything about our health and wellbeing. One of the best ways we can ensure our vitality is by eating **basic** food. And I don't mean bread and wine! Natural food is food that has not been modified in any way. When you bring it into your kitchen, it looks the same as when it was harvested. I know how hard this is to do if you have a hectic life and work in urban areas. You cannot walk through many high streets and find basic or clean food. Some big cities offer healthy food, but at a huge cost. It is much better to make your own where you can.

*2.  Keep it Clean!*

Organic is nearly always best. The food will be certified and in its growth, it will have had no pesticides or other chemicals used. It should also mean that it hasn't been genetically modified. It is **natural**! This is a huge gift that you can give to yourself for your long-term spiritual health and your relationship with food. It is also probably the best thing you can do for your family's health and wellbeing. It was a huge shift for me. It's one of those things where you don't realise how big a difference it makes until you have done it and then you have to go back for a while. When I go long periods without organic food, maybe because I'm travelling, I really feel it in my body, and my immunity suffers. I am literally starving myself, not of calories, but of nutrients and life force. My body is having to work harder to clear out the chemicals before it can get to any of the nutrition from the food.

An analogy:
You want to make some tea. You go to the teapot to find it's still got yesterday's stale tea in it. You have to empty it and clean the teapot or the tea will not be fresh and hot. So making the tea has become a goal of two tasks! And if the boiling water loses heat while you are cleaning the teapot, it's going to be more difficult for it to brew thoroughly. It's the same with your body. When you eat synthetic food, with chemicals and non-natural additives, your body recognises them as toxins, so its job is to get rid of them first before it can get to its proper work and use what's left for your health. It puts extra work on your kidneys, liver and bowel.

When we eat organic, we are getting better quality nutrition that will improve and sustain your health (body and mind) for the rest of your natural life. This is natural preventative medicine!

Here are some more goodies:
- ☐ Organic food can be fresher, especially if you eat in line with the seasons
- ☐ It usually has a lower carbon footprint (many organic outlets don't use air transport), so you are strengthening your relationship with Mother Earth
- ☐ It generally tastes better and flavours are stronger, so you may need less to get the same taste

- You tend to get some rarer varieties of foods than in the supermarkets, who don't want to stock small supplies for short periods. I have tried Jerusalem Artichokes, Kohl Rabi, Tomatillos etc.
- Because of the superior quality of the food, you will want to eat less to be satisfied
- You generally know where it's come from and that it's grown in natural soil

Try local farmers' markets too. Most local farmers cannot afford the chemicals used by the big producers. But equally, they cannot afford to get organic certification. Ask where and how the food is grown. Be aware that some vendors on local markets are merely retailers for the big wholesale mass-produced growers that are probably not organic.

Some non-organic, fresh produce tends to have more chemicals used in its growth than others. Below is a very general list, and it will vary depending on where you live and the propensity for mass farming. So if organic isn't available to you for whatever reason, you can choose wisely for yourself in the meantime. I love these two great lists from the Environmental Working Group in the USA, showing clearly who the bad boys are for chemicals. The EWG reiterate on their website that "the health benefits of a diet rich in fruits and vegetables outweigh risks of pesticide exposure." However, it's good to know what to eat more of and most of when you can't find organic. I have a note of these in my purse for when I go food shopping.

| Dirty Dozen Plus | Clean Fifteen |
| --- | --- |
| Apples | Avocados |
| Strawberries | Sweetcorn |
| Grapes | Pineapples |
| Celery | Cabbage |
| Peaches | Sweet Peas - frozen |
| Spinach | Onions |
| Sweet Bell Pepper | Asparagus |
| Nectarines | Mangoes |
| Cucumbers | Kiwi |
| Cherry Tomatoes | Aubergine (Eggplant) |
| Sugar Snap peas | Grapefruit |
| Potatoes | Cantaloupe |
| Hot Peppers | Cauliflower |
| Kale/Collard Greens | Sweet Potatoes |
|  | Papaya |

*Source: Environmental Working Group*

*"We discover that concern for the happiness and well being of others, including animals, must be an essential part of our own quest for happiness and well being. The fork can be a powerful weapon of mass destruction or a tool to create peace on Earth."*
*~ Sharon Gannon*

Eating organic may be a huge step for some of us. Just eating more fruit and vegetables, organic or not, and other healthier foods, instead of processed foods or takeaways, would be a major change in the eating habits of most western cultures. It isn't that long ago that I made that change, little by little, and I'm still evolving. When I worked long hours in the office, I would find myself ordering food in or picking up quick pre-prepared food, several times a week. After a few months, I would start picking up bugs, colds and whatever was going around easily. I had no energy, carried extra weight, and suffered from bloating, constipation and cellulite.

Simply cooking your own food from scratch *can* make a real difference. It just needs a bit of planning. Some of the best investments I have made in my kitchen are a slow cooker (stock pot), a pressure cooker, a coffee grinder and a food processor/blender. In order to buy in what I need and use up what I already have, I spend about 30-45 minutes a week writing a food schedule. We don't always stick to it exactly, but we waste nothing in our household!


## But doesn't it cost a lot more to eat healthily?

On face value, organic food and healthy food generally is more expensive. But is it?

Is his article 'Health Costs: How the U.S. Compares with Other Countries' (http://www.pbs.org/newshour/rundown/health-costs-how-the-us-compares-with-other-countries/), Jason Kane highlights that in 2010, the US spent $8233 per person on health care. Is it therefore worthwhile establishing whether eating a more healthy diet might prevent the illnesses that these millions of dollars are needed to treat? What is the net cost of eating a balanced diet? Especially in countries where health costs are high, we find that healthy eating may produce a huge saving in the long-term likely health costs for us and our families. Add to that the other costs from ill-health – less mobility, shorter lifespan, time away from work, time in hospital and away from loved ones. Doesn't it make sense to spend a little more now to ensure a healthy, happy life, free from disease?

In another study, it was found that Americans at all income levels allocate too little of their food budgets towards healthy foods. It's around 6%, the lowest in the world. In 2012, Gallup revealed that the average American spends $151 per week on food – that's $7852 per year (1). Even without allowing for rising health costs, it's clear that the average American is spending $381 more on health costs than on food. With the dramatic increase in diabetes and other diet-related degenerative diseases, the journey away from nature is going further. In another study, it was found that just another $1.48 per day was all it would cost to eat healthful food. This translates to $550 higher annual food costs per person (2).

In the UK, most of the population relies on the National Health Service. It is a government-backed organisation. But its standards are nothing compared to private health care. As a UK citizen, even though the healthcare is 'free' (well, funded by taxes), I would still rather stay out of hospital, not have to take synthetic medicines and enjoy a vibrant, healthful, and hopefully long life! My experience of the British NHS has been that they are stretched well beyond their means.

The cost of organic food, including produce, is more of course, but it has taught me not to waste food. I order what I need and if my weekly delivery hasn't been used up by the fifth day, I'll use likely leftover produce to make some soup or something else and I'll freeze it.

Instead of spending money on health *insurance* – something that *might* happen – should we not spend it on something that *will* happen, i.e. assurance? Assurance that you will see and feel huge improvements in your health, not just freedom from illness and the war over your body weight. You will enjoy *life* more and have more energy for living in the most efficient body available to you.

Will that make you happy? I should think so!

# Exercise

## - Getting Closer to Nature

i.   What can you do to improve your connection with food, and therefore nature?

ii.   What can you change now to eat a little healthier? We can always do something.

iii.   Write a journal note of your first thoughts and plan to take a small step closer to nature

### *A Prayer to Mother Earth*

*Help us to give thanks for your bounty,*
*taking only what we need,*
*sharing that which we don't*
*and always in gratitude.*

*Help us to walk gracefully on your carpet,*
*honouring your gifts of all of the elements.*
*Help us to act honourably,*
*respecting all our relations*
*– fellow humans, animals, plants & rocks.*
*Help us to understand the cycles of life and death*
*in nature and all aspects of our lives.*
*Help us the see the magnificence and beauty of all that is,*
*as that which is also within ourselves.*

*~ Chinmayi Dore*

## 3.   The Meat Issue

Another big consideration is about eating meat and fish. As I have said before, this book is not about the ethics of vegetarianism. It's about the merits of natural food. There are many debates about whether eating meat is a natural habit. You must decide for yourself. What is *not* natural is the mass-produced, factory farming methods of bringing meat to our plate. Inform yourself please. Know where your meat comes from and how the animals have been treated. This is a major part of developing a positive relationship with the food you eat and with Mother Nature.

Dr. Peterson, in an interview with Project Camelot (YouTube) reveals that when a lion eats its prey, it will usually go for organs and other tissues before it eats muscle flesh. This is thought to be because muscle flesh is full of toxins from the stress hormones that flooded the muscles before the prey was killed. Muscle is the bit we eat first! That aside, if the meat is not organic, there is a good chance that you are ingesting antibiotics, steroids and other growth hormones with your meat.

In the 1950s, a hormone called DES was widely used to produce more meat from cattle at an earlier age. This was later withdrawn as it was found to cause cancer. (See Resources). Eating organic meat ensures that the meat is chemical-free and the grain fed to the animals is free of pesticides. To keep the animals free from antibiotics and hormones, they usually have to be kept in very small groups and need exercise to develop lean muscle for good meat production. So the animals usually have a far better life. Check with your organic butcher. They are usually very proud of their practices and happy to share them with you.

# Natural Water, Natural Hydration

*"By looking to the Source, to the Creator of nature, we can remember how to navigate life organically, with less struggle, and less suffering."*
~ Jeffrey R. Anderson

What do you know about the water you drink? It's extremely difficult to drink natural water in the developed world. It is essential, however, that you are hydrated. Often we can feel hungry when in fact we are just thirsty. There are many ways to drink water. I have given considerable thought to the merits and challenges of each. Here are the main sources of water:

**Tap water** - UK water suppliers profess to supply some of the best water in the world. And yet tap water has had a bad press over the last few decades. I can't help feeling that this has been fuelled by advertisements for bottled mineral water. It is true to say that most tap water has been recycled several times. While filtration systems are extremely effective, some chemicals such as hormones (e.g. those in the contraceptive pill) and antibiotics cannot be filtered. It is also true that the actual quantity of the chemicals that may be ingested from this water source is so very tiny that no-one is at risk. All up for debate I guess. In Lake Michigan in the USA, levels of the diabetes drug Metformin have been high enough to affect the hormone balance of fish, so we need to consider the bigger picture (3).

**Bottled water** - a safer option, especially when travelling in developing countries. The downside is the amount of plastic waste. You can select your accommodation taking into account whether a water filter is available. Then you can use a reusable bottle for your water. Never leave plastic bottles in your car or in the sun. Plastic chemicals can leak into the water. If your tap water is really not suitable for drinking and filtration is not an option, you could consider investing in a water cooler. The larger bottles in theory are less likely to leak chemicals from the plastic and they are a good reminder to drink more. When I worked in an office where we had these, I always drank more water during the day.

**Filtered water** - I use this all the time at home, even in Spain where the water is from a natural source, because our water has some limestone. The filter helps prolong the life of my kettle and I don't have a settling white film at the bottom of my glass! Filters will take out some of the chemicals from your tap water, such as chlorine, often making your water taste better, but not usually fluoride, unless you have a reverse osmosis filter fitted to your tap. Neither boiling water nor freezing it will remove fluoride.

I feel that when all is said and done, it is probably best to get the most natural that you can. Drink more of it, regardless of your chosen sources and if you can, try to 'connect' with its origin in some way – the rain, the rivers, the lakes, etc. Treat it with respect, whatever its source, and try to express gratitude for it in your own way. Be aware of how you might waste water, e.g. leaving the tap on while brushing your teeth.

Choose water as your first thirst quencher. Avoid fizzy drinks. Give them up! They are about as natural as acrylic fingernails! Only they do much more harm. If you are having lots of diet drinks, especially colas, you are ingesting aspartame and caffeine, which as Christine Northrup, one of my favourite health experts highlights, is a deadly combination. It destroys brain cells and can mimic the symptoms of multiple sclerosis and cause neurological problems. You may find that you have an addiction to these because they give you a lift. It's very possible to kick the addiction to fizzy drinks quickly, depending on how much and how often you drink them. Christine says that just three days of drinking lots of water will do it, to come off this addiction. It's really worth it, and you will feel awesome within a week.

# Natural Air, Natural Breath

*"Who will tell whether one happy moment of love or the joy of breathing or walking on a bright morning and smelling the fresh air, is not worth all the suffering and effort which life implies."*
~ Erich Fromm

I know in the past I have taken the air that I have been breathing for granted. It was not until I travelled to India and the Far East that I found out what real air pollution is. I consider myself so lucky to live in the mountains in Spain, for many reasons, but none of them comes close to the air quality here. We are at 3500ft. so it took a while to get used to it, but it is the definition of breathtaking. Like many other places, I'm sure, once you get out of the city or other industrial areas, you can literally breathe a sigh of relief for your lungs.

Please don't get me wrong here. Our lungs are magnificent things. Some people can smoke twenty cigarettes a day for their whole life, spend their working life in a coal mine or live in a smoggy city and never have so much as a cough. Our ability to get rid of the toxins we breathe is nothing short of incredible. The thing to remember always is that your healing will happen regardless of where you live, work or play. This is but a piece in the jigsaw of your health. What is important is to get outside as much as possible, especially on clear or windy days. This is working with the air element and is heartwarming stuff. It will help you with self-love, the energy needed for motivation, and will help you to be open to new possibilities in your journey through this book, and indeed your life.

Do you know that for most of your day, you breathe unconsciously and naturally into just the very top of your lungs? If you aren't particularly active, and you spend most of your day sitting, you are unlikely to get much action in the rest of your lungs. When we are stressed, whether we are just concentrating hard on something (that can be good stress), or whether we are really angry or upset, we are likely to be breathing in a very shallow manner. And you will not be aware of it. It is part of the automated nervous system that keeps going without any deliberate effort from your mind. When you are aware of your breath and you change the pattern and the length of each cycle, you are using a different part of your brain. So unless you increase your heart rate, say by exercising, you have to deliberately make an effort to lengthen your breath.

The benefits of deep breathing are huge! When we breathe fully, we take in more oxygen and we take it deeper into the far reaches of the lungs. These alveoli (little lung sacs) need a good deep breath now and again to remain clear and supple. Furthermore, in the lower part of the lungs we have more blood vessels, so our intake of oxygen and prana (life force) is increased even more. When we breathe more deeply, we are also massaging our abdominal organs, including the digestive and eliminative organs too. This massage will also help to balance the hormones of the reproductive system (and help you out with those monthly cravings), benefit the nervous system, relieving stress (when you are stressed you tend to breathe less and eat more) and help you to detox what your body doesn't need (reducing inflammation) and so much more. So take a deep breath, *often*.

There are so many breathing exercises, and almost all of them will encourage deeper breathing. The traditional yogis believe that everyone has the same number of breaths in their life. So if we can lengthen our breath we can lengthen our life!

The basic keys to efficient and healthful breathing are:

1) Try to always breathe through the nose. This warms and filters the air so makes it more usable by the body. The mouth is for eating and the nose is for breathing.
2) Breathe long and deep whenever you remember.
3) Never hold the breath unless it is part of a practice where you have the guidance of a qualified breath-work teacher.

Here is an exercise to encourage the healthy effects of proper breathing, to calm the mind and increase overall vitality. It is natural and simple. You could do it anywhere you want to connect with your body and recharge your energy levels. But in the beginning, take some time out to master it and feel it in your body.

You will also find some online (see Resources)

# Exercise

## Conscious Deep Breathing

Most of us naturally breathe about 15-20 times per minute. When we become aware of the breath, and with just a little practice, we can slow the breath right down. This reduces pulse rate and blood pressure. It calms the whole body and mind.

Try to reduce the number of breaths per minute slowly. You can reduce it to six per minute by working with 10 second breathing cycles. There is a natural pause at the end of each inhale and exhale. So your breathing at this pace might be something like this:

> Inhale for 3 seconds
> Hold in for 2 seconds
> Exhale for 3 seconds
> Hold out for 2 seconds = 10 seconds (6 breaths per minute)

There are a couple of metronome apps available for mobile devices that can help you keep pace. But for this one you just need a good old fashioned ticking clock! You may find this really easy or quite difficult, so adjust the pace according to your abilities and decrease your breaths slowly, increasing your practice time over several weeks.

Never ever strain. This will only work against you, putting unnecessary stress on your systems. The most important thing to remember is to relax. It should feel pretty darn good!

This exercise assumes that you are in good respiratory health. Please consult your doctor if you have any reason to believe that that *any* exercise in this book is unsuitable for you.

# Natural Exercise, Natural Fitness

*"If we could give every individual the right amount of nourishment and exercise, not too little, not too much, we would have found the safest way to health."*
*~ Hippocrates*

If you already have a fitness routine, consider how much of it you currently do outdoors. Could it be more? Do you really need to drive to the gym to run on a treadmill, when there's a beautiful park or walkway nearby? Get out and discover what nature is already there.

## Walking

It's easy to discount walking as an effective mode of exercise, especially as an overeater. We want to burn calories, break into a sweat and do the most we can in the least amount of time possible. But walking can offer all of this and so much more. You get to see places of nature that you miss when you're in a car. You get to notice the changing seasons and appreciate the cycles of nature in all its glory.

Use your senses when you are out. If you are with others, don't just natter the whole way round! Look around you, share your observations with your friends and also make your own private connection with the nature that warms your heart. I often like to take a camera out with me most times when I walk. It helps me to capture the moment and remember the MAGIC! from that walk throughout the whole day.

## Cycling

I remember that my bike was my lifeline as a child or a teenager. Before I learned to drive I would go everywhere on my bike. I rode to school, to friends' houses, to the shops, on errands and to the local pool for a swim every week. I never thought it an effort and I was fearless. Somewhere down the line. after driving for a few years, a whole load of new reasons NOT to cycle came about. For a start, my hairstyle would be ruined. I couldn't wear a short skirt. It was raining, cold, windy. No-one else rode a bike.

Then there was fear. Drivers didn't allow enough room. and I could get knocked off and killed. As an adult it seems so much cooler now to be riding a bike. However, it is still a pain in the bum sometimes. You can't wear full make up and high heels! You really do need a helmet and a secure lock to leave your bike anywhere. You might arrive somewhere a little sweaty if you have some tough hills to climb.

On the other hand, you are getting your heart pumping, you are breathing fresh air and there are paths and routes especially for bikes that take you off the busy roads and help you to get to know your area better. You can take it easy or you can push yourself a bit. The key is always to make it fun. You can cover a lot of miles in an hour, an afternoon or a day, so can get to see places that you would miss in the car and might never reach on foot. As for the weather, you can find waterproofs, mud guards, gloves and clothing especially for cycling without spending a fortune.

Even the bike itself doesn't have to cost a fortune. Second hand bikes are pretty cheap and plentiful. Also consider your huge saving on planetary resources. Check out organisations that provide excellent information – maps, routes and events to support and encourage you. Sustrans (sustainable transport) is one such organisation in the UK that has a map of all routes suitable for bikes, on or away from main roads. Give it a go and get pedalling!

## Other Outdoor Activities

There are literally hundreds of activities you can do outdoors. Here are some suggestions that are kind to the planet and that give you the opportunity of connecting with nature. Some of them are physically challenging, others not. Remember the goal is not weight loss, it's connection with nature, perhaps making changes to your exercise routine, and definitely having fun:

Archery, Wild Swimming, Abseiling, Rock Climbing, Gorge Walking, River Rafting, Dinghy Sailing, Windsurfing, Bird Watching, Nature Walks, Gardening, Zip Lining, Canoeing, Hiking, Potholing, Nature Photography, Tubing, Horse Riding, Skipping, Hula Hooping, Rowing, Snorkeling etc.

Not forgetting that there is a whole other list of competitive games and sports that are done outside, such as football, netball, tennis, beach volleyball etc. I have not included these as there is probably less of a connection with nature. Your awareness is largely on the game. Of course, these are an excellent way of getting out in the fresh air, so don't discount them if you are inclined.

If you are going to change your relationship with food and exercise and if you are going to connect with nature, it's probably going to involve a change of attitude towards life in general. Look towards trying something new. Make it a fun challenge. Involve a few friends or family if you can. If you've always wanted to do a parachute jump, then make it happen! Do it for yourself, or maybe do it for charity if you need another reason to stick with it.

## Exercising for weight loss

As a long-term emotional overeater, in response to you sharing your concerns over your weight, you have probably heard many people say "Just eat less and move more." It makes sense. If we eat a certain number of calories and we use up a few more than we eat, we lose weight, right? Well that has been a common understanding for decades. New research proves that there are many variables to this philosophy that make it a difficult one to rely on.

I had nine months of training for the Edinburgh Marathon in May 2014. In those months before the 'race' (with just the mileage I recorded with my running monitor), I ran 858 miles over 149 hours and allegedly burned 91851 calories! I was running four times a week, practising yoga nearly every day and eating very well. Around the fourth month, I started to lose some weight. This probably coincided with increased distances and times, but until I was running nearly twenty miles a week, I lost nothing. So you see, exercise helps you in many ways. It increases wellbeing, gets you some fresh air, improves circulation, digestion, nervous system (stress reduction), improves muscle tone and so much more. But you have to do an awful lot of it for a long time before you start losing weight. Even then, the appetite increases and you eat more (especially carbohydrates). I did lose about eight pounds before the marathon and I felt great. Looking back though, the great feeling was more to do with my wellbeing than my weight. I drank virtually no alcohol and loads of water, got proper sleep and looked after myself. I knew I had to be in the best possible condition if I was going to run 26 miles.

The whole purpose of the marathon was to push my limiting beliefs, expand my self-imposed boundaries. However, when I started losing weight and being able to eat exactly what I wanted, I was extra-charged and motivated. This was great because it got me through the second half of my training. The week after the marathon, it slowly dawned on me what my body had adapted to. It had taken four months before my excess weight started to come off, but only a few days before the weight started to go back on again. My lean legs and trim waist were covered with layers of new fat within weeks, even though I was still running 2-3 times a week. There are lots of reasons for this pattern, most of them beyond the scope of this book. But there are a few huge learnings I'd like to share with you:

1. You have to do a *lot* of exercise to burn more calories than you use and over a sustained period of time. There are other factors involved too such as:

- [ ] your weight at the time
- [ ] your movement for the rest of the time
- [ ] your lifestyle habits - smoking, medication, other drugs
- [ ] your hormones
- [ ] your stress levels
- [ ] your dieting history

2. As an emotional overeater you are also a habitual eater and probably have addictions too. So if you are training for an event or a big milestone, you may lose weight. After the event, during your recovery and reduced training routine, you will need to give up any addictions you have developed, such as sugar, and change the habits of what and how much you eat. This is extremely difficult for an overeater. I fell into the trap of relying on energy gels for my long runs. They really gave me a boost. But they also introduced refined sugar back into my diet in quantities not taken since I was a teenager. I started to crave sugar after every run. I remember going out to a restaurant once and really not wanting a starter or main course, just a dessert!

3. When you exercise to the point of stress, you release cortisol. This encourages your metabolic rate to fall and what little you do eat to be converted to fat around your torso. Long-distance running, pushing through pain, injury and a general unwillingness to be exercising *causes* stress. In a nutshell, unless you are enjoying yourself, you are not going to be losing weight, no matter what exercise you are doing or how many calories your phone app tells you that you have burned.

4. Your success with weight loss now is powerfully influenced by the dieting you have done in your life so far. This determines the strength of the **famine response**. If you have been a regular dieter and/or binge eater in the past, your body will have interpreted these patterns either as a feast or a famine. So when you decide to diet, your body thinks you are in a famine and will slow everything down and store fat as fuel. When you binge or overeat, your body thinks you are in a feast situation. Because of previous famine, your body again will store fat in case it needs it again for a future famine. I know – it's so unfair! I was heartbroken when I learned about this. And it was only recently. It brought back even more feelings of failure than I'd ever had before.

The same works with exercise. The more you do, the more your body will want you to eat to maintain its fuel stores. There will be a point when you will lose weight, but it is after a lot of regular exercise and unless that level is sustained, the weight will return.

In the frenzy and panic of weight gain, say after Christmas, it has become almost customary to join the gym. It's like we are punishing ourselves for overeating and we think that a few weeks on the treadmill will make all the difference. The only good thing it does do is to dedicate some time to ourselves. If you really and truthfully enjoy the gym, then there is a chance that you will find some benefits. But there is good reason why 67% of gym members don't use their membership (4). In my experience, most people see it as a chore. It's a novelty in the beginning and seems like a solution to the guilt of overeating and the laziness that tends to follow eating unhealthily, maybe for a couple of weeks over Christmas or a summer holiday, but for most it's short-lived.

# Natural Sleep, Natural Relaxation

*"And if tonight my soul may find her peace in sleep, and sink in good oblivion, and in the morning wake like a new-opened flower, then I have been dipped again in God, and new-created."*
~ DH Lawrence

We have all heard the term 'a change is as good as a rest'. And a change to anything is nearly always for the better. For some, a rest is going for a beer at the local bar, playing cards with friends, dancing the night away in a club, playing sport, visiting a museum or going to the cinema. This *feels* like a rest because it takes us out of our routine, away from the mundane and into a place of escape, where we can forget about our cares for a while. It's respite, and it *is* great to have that change of scenery and energy regularly in our lives. However, this is not the kind of rest that I'm talking about. Real rest and relaxation are things we seem to have forgotten about. Traditional and natural relaxation is a conscious practice to connect with the body and mind and encourage a letting go of tension in both. It's sadly missing for most of us.

Yet it is more important than ever before. The Mental Health Foundation report that 59% of British adults say their life is more stressful than it was five years ago. The main causes of stress in Britain are money and work. People are three times more likely to drink alcohol to help deal with stress than to visit their doctor (5). With stress-related illness at an all-time high, quality relaxation is one thing that can be extremely health-changing. The results are rejuvenation and revitalisation, giving us long-lasting health benefits to keep us feeling good inside. When we feel good inside, we want to put good stuff in. Our diet improves, our health improves. MAGIC!

We also tend to assume that relaxation is what we do when we go to bed. Again, I would say that sleep and relaxation are also radically different. Yes, you are resting your body and mind, but not consciously. It is in the conscious practice of relaxation that the MAGIC! can happen.

## Abdominal Breathing Exercise

This is a skill for better sleep, helping you to really relax, beating stress and increasing your awareness of your body and its connection with your mind. It is done in Savasana (covered in *Chapter Eight - YogaMAGIC!*). Once in Savasana, bring your hands on to your lower abdomen. Breathe deep, slow and silently, allowing your abdomen to rise with your inhale and fall with your exhale. Unlike normally breathing, you are not breathing into your chest.

I find it the most relaxing way to breathe and it makes sense why. When we breathe naturally and automatically, the body realises that it is running out of oxygen so it calls for you to inhale. Then when it is ready to get rid of carbon dioxide, it will trigger an exhale response. This is a tiny bit of stress response from within the body with each breath to transport the messages for you to breathe. When you take control of your breath in exercises like Abdominal Breathing, your nervous system gets a little break. In addition, breathing into the abdomen allows the oxygen to get to the bottom of the lungs where there is a higher concentration of blood vessels, making oxygen intake much easier for the body. Therefore, you are able to relax more deeply. Furthermore, you will feel more relaxed because of the internal massage you are giving yourself, without any effort from your hands! Try this for 10 minutes or more, any time you feel stressed or emotional, you are struggling to 'let go' of the day's challenges, and/or you are struggling to sleep. It's MAGIC!

## Sound Sleep

Sleep is very often disturbed by eating habits. If we don't get enough of it, we can feel lethargic and low in energy. The brain can then send signals to you for energy that you can often misinterpret as food calls! Evidence shows that lack of proper sleep is one of the key reasons for weight gain and obesity (6).

I believe that almost all of us need 7-9 hours per day of good quality sleep. It's the body's time not just for rest, but for regenerating cells. It's the chance you get for a new body every seven years! Most of that renewal takes place at night.

If you are having trouble sleeping, consider the following:

### Things to change

The two-hour rules:
- avoid eating within two hours of your planned bedtime
- for five days a week, rise and retire with the sun, or within two hours of it
- stay away from your laptop or mobile device within two hours of bed (blue light can be confused with daylight by your brain)
- cut out coffee, or at least try, for a month. Avoid any other caffeine two hours after lunch
- finish your main water intake two hours before your planned bedtime
- apart from relaxing yoga or stretching, avoid exercise within two hours of bedtime
- switch your phone off two hours before bedtime. The time before bed is for winding down

### Things to start

- put 3-4 drops of lavender on your pillow
- if your head is spinning with thoughts, try a few drops of Rescue Remedy by Bach
- if you are going through some difficult times, try chanting or simply listening to a slow mantra for ten minutes or more. There are loads on the internet, but one of my favourites is Om Nama Shivaya by the Singers of the Art of Living Foundation. It's releasing, soothing and calming
- seek guidance from books, or find professional help for trauma, bereavement or major life events - you deserve to be free
- sip a small cup of chamomile tea an hour before bed

# Natural Medicine, Natural Healing

*"Our primary health care should begin on the farm and in our hearts, not in some laboratory of the biotech and pharmaceutical companies."*
*~ Gary Hopkins*

When we have faith in nature to help us heal, it can give us a real sense of independence and power. Modern-day medicine has made some great advances in finding treatments, even cures, for some illnesses and we should always turn to it in emergencies or when we don't have a natural alternative. However, we have to remember that there are hundreds of diseases for which there is no cure. More often than not, doctors and hospitals have to resort to treating the symptoms, for example managing pain. Most drugs have a long list of possible side effects, some of which require another medication to relieve. It's not surprising, therefore, that from a USA study, 87% of 75 year-olds take prescription medicine and 72% take over-the-counter drugs. On average they take 4.2 different drugs by prescription and 2.5 over the counter (7).

But there are alternatives. Even in some developing countries, people live to over one hundred years without medication. They are active and healthy until the day they die. Deterioration and disease in the West seem to be a given, but it's not necessary at all. A greater connection with nature and a positive attitude to ageing can make the difference between a vital, happy and healthful old age and an immobile and sick one. Christine Northrup, a leading authority in the field of women's health and wellness, promotes the ageless mindset and says that when we get to 50, we have a choice – we can either get moving or get sick. It's about a balance between all of the facets of this chapter (food, water, exercise, medicine, sleep etc.) but it's also about staying young in the mind. This includes having a purpose, having fun, having social interactions and having peace of mind.

I shall focus on two alternatives to non-prescriptive, modern medicine and then highlight some complementary therapies. As you get to **Know Yourself** and **Know Your Worth**, you will notice and act sooner when you feel a little out of balance. All too often, we wait until we are almost incapacitated before we go to the doctor. Often, we can nip sickness in the bud if we treat it early and just check in with how we are living day-to-day. Food intake is obvious, but are you getting enough rest, drinking enough water, having enough fun, etc.? Make some changes early on and you might just avoid being out of action for a time. I do believe that if we don't listen to these signals, the body makes it almost impossible for us to carry on. We get ill, and we are forced to heal by resting. Far better to look to nature for help than the paracetamol or ibuprofen that mask symptoms that are really only the body's messengers to nudge you to rebalance your health and lifestyle habits.

## Food as Medicine

In *Chapter Seven* - Food Facts, I list some of my favourite foods, and not just for their flavours, their versatility and their nutritional content. Most of them also have a wealth of healing abilities. I shall give you some ideas now so you can think of the right food in times when you are a little off balance. Of course, if you are already taking medication you should always talk to your doctor if you intend to reduce your medicine and should never suddenly stop taking prescription medication. However, there are some wonderful stories around from people who have used food as medicine, and with care and collaboration with their doctors have not only managed to stop long-term medication but have improved their overall health beyond their dreams.

It goes without saying that it will never be enough simply to eat all of these foods on a regular basis. If you are eating food that is not serving, or even destroying your health and if you are living a lifestyle that does nothing to serve your vitality and quality of life, these foods will not stand a chance. Keep in mind that it is up to you to first start respecting your **health, healing** and **happiness**. When this powerful switch goes on, you will gradually change your lifestyle and your diet to fit these new values.

There is absolutely no need to draw a line under all of your eating and lifestyle habits and make changes suddenly. If you understand that your eating patterns are influenced by your habits and your emotions, then both will take time to adjust and replace. Forcing yourself into an instant change is being cruel to yourself and if you **Know Yourself** and **Know Your Worth**, then why would you want to do that?

What you can do now is to start adding some of these healing foods to your recipes and meals and maybe replacing a few of the ones that don't serve you, if and when you feel ready. Please remember that these are suggestions. They have worked for me many times, as they have for our ancestors and in some places in the world where they have no painkillers, antibiotics or other modern medicines. I realise that until recent years I have always run to the chemist with an ailment. But we are only just starting to realise the effects that taking some medicines such as analgesics and antibiotics can have in the long term. We don't need to discard them altogether, as they will always be welcome for serious illness.

There are links to further information in the Resources section. This list is really just the tip of the iceberg, designed to give you a flavour (excuse the pun!) of how food can heal.

*"Let food be thy medicine and medicine be thy food"*
*~ Hippocrates*

## Eight Greats
- a few medicinal foods for your natural medicine cabinet

| Food | Add to | Can Replace | Some Benefits |
|------|--------|-------------|---------------|
| Chia Seeds http://healthyeating.sfgate.com/top-10-health-benefits-chia-seeds-6962.html | baking, smoothies, pizza bases, burger mixes | Eggs - 1 tbsp with 3 tbsp of water soaked for 15 mins | Antioxidant - protect cells from free radicals - cancer and ageing, detox and reduce inflammation from food reactions/overeating |
| Cinnamon http://news.health.com/2014/11/21/health-benefits-of-cinnamon/ | breakfast dishes, soup, desserts, fruit recipes, hot drinks | sugar in sweet dishes | Candidiasis, diabetes, concentration issues, Parkinson's, heart issues |
| Clove http://naturalsociety.com/health-benefits-of-cloves-super-spice-healing/ | make tea, oils, curries, bean dishes, winter soups, ground in smoothies, fruit desserts | painkillers, chemical insect repellents, skin creams for acne and warts | Toothache, anti-viral, anti-bacterial, asthma, insect repellent, insomnia, acne, warts |
| Garlic http://authoritynutrition.com/11-proven-health-benefits-of-garlic/ | all savoury dishes - curries, stir fry, casseroles, soups etc. | sugar in savoury dishes, painkillers | Common cold, lowers blood pressure, reduces 'bad' cholesterol, detox heavy metals, fungal infections, headaches, dementia prevention |
| Ginger http://www.medicalnewstoday.com/articles/265990.php | hot water and brew to make tea with optional lemon | coffee/teas, throat sprays, painkillers and anti-inflammatory medication | Exercise-induced muscle pain, colon and ovarian cancer, hypertension, migraines, sore throat |
| Manuka Honey honeyhttp://www.theaustralian.com.au/news/honey-i-killed-the-superbug/story-e6frg6n6-1225737035676 | drizzle on fruit, pancakes, take off the spoon | sugar, care with quantities as will still increase blood sugar. Use for medicinal reasons early stages of infections | Antibiotic - use to ward off secondary infections when immunity is compromised, use directly on skin for healing, sore throats, chest infections, coughs, allergies |
| Pomegranate https://www.drfuhrman.com/library/article19.aspx | juice, smoothies, desserts, breakfast cereals, pancakes | dried sweetened fruit such as dried and sulphured cranberries, apricots, sultanas and raisins | Helps to reduce arterial plaque, lower blood pressure, increase bone density, reduce the risk of stroke |
| Papaya http://www.whfoods.com/genpage.php?tname=foodspice&dbid=47 | on its own, as a starter, smoothies, juices | sweeter more acidic tropical fruits such as pineapple, banana, mango | good for digestion, improves health of the digestive tract, treats parasites, anti-inflammatory, |

I realised in writing this that I haven't taken a painkiller, an antibiotic, an anti-inflammatory or used an antiseptic cream or an antihistamine for some time. Food can be preventative medicine as much as it is a treatment for sickness. As you get to know your dietary and medicinal needs better, you will find that the preventative stuff is just your normal diet and your health is maintained without much therapeutic intervention. You will probably still want to hang on to your home first aid kit as insurance, until your faith in nature strengthens. Ironically, my first aid box is actually an old biscuit tin that has started to rust around the edges. I should really check its contents!!

Please visit and Like our Facebook page - **Food Facts and Fallacies, Myths and Magic** where you will find regular posts of useful information about the magical properties of food.

## Healing Oils - Aromatherapy

I learned aromatherapy long before I learned the power in connecting with nature more deeply. I really only realised just how important this connection with nature was to my healing when I studied shamanism and shamanic healing methods. For many years, I underestimated the power of nature to heal. Now it gives me great joy to use these oils in so many aspects of my life. Essential oils used in aromatherapy are extremely potent.

In *Chapter Fifteen* - Traditional Medicine, I have given another small list of some oils that you can use to help with your recovery from emotional overeating. Here, I'd like to share some of the benefits of essential oils as a natural way to treat some common health issues for you and your family, as opposed to automatically reaching for over-the-counter remedies.

Here are just five that are widely available, which you will probably find a need for sooner or later.

**Please note:-**
- Refer to *Chapter Fifteen* for ways to use the oils
- Note that children under fifteen should use half the stated dose
- Never take oils internally without the guidance of a suitably qualified aromatherapist

*Tea-tree* is like first aid in a bottle. It's a very powerful oil, cheap, natural and easily available. You can put it directly on your skin. It's good for cuts and scrapes and even infestations. Tea tree is anti-bacterial, anti-fungal and anti-viral. Use it for warts, acne, ringworm, athlete's foot, head lice, dandruff and common colds.

*Lavender* is another first-aid oil. And it smells good too! Use it directly on skin for all burns. Mix with aloe vera for sunburn. Lavender is anti-viral and anti-bacterial. Use it for insomnia, relaxation, stress relief, eczema, psoriasis and headaches.

*Clary Sage* is an excellent oil for all manner of hormone imbalances – everything from libido to PMS, painful periods to menopausal symptoms. Have this in your cabinet when you feel out of sorts.

*Eucalyptus* is my choice for colds, coughs, congestion and even cold sores. Also good for aching joints, including arthritis and rheumatism. It's good for cellulite, insect bites and stings. Eucalyptus is also very helpful for fluid retention, cystitis and kidney problems.

*Peppermint* is the digestive oil. It helps by cooling the digestive fire that overworks in constipation, diarrhoea, flatulence, indigestion and nausea.

## Healing Traditions

My rule of thumb is this. If something is not from nature, but I still want to pursue it because it's good for me and it works in the long term, I will try and reach out to the most traditional (because I'm a slight purist) and convenient (because I only have so much time) way of doing things as possible. This might be yoga, meditation, massage, energy healing or herbal remedies.

Take yoga for example. There are many styles of yoga. The most recent styles are those that are usually more physical challenging. I believe that this is because most people see a yoga class as mainly an exercise routine where they wish to improve their physical health and/or their appearance. And there's nothing wrong with that. But it's not the traditional meaning of yoga. In more traditional styles, physical yoga is for looking after the body as a means to the purification and health of the mind. The yogis would cleanse the body through many yogic practices, asana (poses) being just one of them. They would do this as a means to preparing the body for meditation on the path to enlightenment. It's conceivable that in our need to improve the body for fitness or vanity reasons, we have missed the real point of yoga in its traditional form. That's totally fine if it's all that you want. I'm not trying to criticise any style of yoga here but to illustrate a point.

So you could go to a physically demanding yoga class, lose lots of weight and tone your thighs, and this would no doubt improve your confidence. But if you stopped going for any reason, you would get out of your routine, eat as much as before but not work out as much, probably put your weight back on again and your confidence would fall. Sound familiar? You would then look for a new way of getting those results and the cycle would continue. Why? It's not because you didn't try. You stuck with it, dedicating your time and money into getting results.

The problem is that you only ever got temporary relief from your real issues. These are the real reasons why you gained the weight in the first place. Your 450/hr calorie-burning yoga class may have felt like the answer, but you never connected with your body or your mind. You tried to take control of a situation and your body with all your good intentions by telling your body what you wanted, but you never listened to what it was telling you, and therefore you never found your way to the root cause.

Like a wound, it's not the Band Aid that stops the bleeding, it's the keratin in your blood that clots to stop the flow. The Band Aid just makes it look better for a while. If the wound doesn't stop bleeding, you can keep changing the Band Aid but sooner or later you are going to want it to stop. So you need to find out the reason why. Maybe your blood is too thin, maybe you are pulling the scab off every time you take off the dressing, or maybe you have an infection. Only when you know the cause of the problem can you find the solution. So the traditional path of yoga (to enlightenment) is arguably the more relevant path for the emotional overeater, because it goes within to find the solution. It helps you to **Know Yourself** and therefore **Know Your Worth**.

All too often we subscribe to new and trending solutions to our health and wellbeing that cost us dearly, in time, money and effort. Some of them are so far away from traditional methods of health and healing. This is often because these methods are not tried and tested over time and sadly, often because there's more money in a brand than in a tradition. We love to try new and exciting solutions. However, just like diets, some of them are crazes that show no real benefits over time.

# Natural Cleaning, Natural Waste

*"Our house is clean enough to be healthy, and dirty enough to be happy."*
*~ Unknown*

If we are going to have more faith in nature's gifts to feed us with life force, be it from food, air, water or medicine, we might also be aware of what we use in our environment, in particular how what we use can affect our natural balance. If we are inhaling fumes from harsh detergents and potentially absorbing traces of these through our skin, it's definitely worth looking at alternatives. If we believe that the rivers and streams are the arteries of Mother Earth, we also need to accept that we *do* depend on her for the life blood of every single being in existence. Then it would make sense to take some responsibility for what has the potential for pollution.

In Resources I have included a link to a very interesting article about the dangers of toxic chemicals in the home. There is so much information, research and testing going on. Please become informed.

The multiplied danger of these chemicals is their potential effect on children. It really isn't enough to lock these poisons away in a cupboard. Traces of them are left all over the house. The first time the bath is filled with water after chemical cleaning, the fumes rise into delicate little lungs. The younger the child, the more delicate their lungs, their liver and their skin are and the more time they spend on the floor and with stuff in their mouth. Add to that the fact that even experts don't know the real dangers of these products. They get away with it by putting a warning on the bottle, depending on parents to always be vigilant. Most parents know that these are dangerous to anyone but they know little about how mixing these products could be fatal. For example, mixing ammonia with chlorine can cause permanent lung damage. Individually the gases from these and other chemicals are damaging to the eyes, nose and throat. They may be very harmful to those more sensitive, such as those with asthma or other lung problems. Other chemicals or chemical combinations penetrate the skin and are known carcinogens. Why do we still buy and use them?

The great news is that alternatives are available. From dishwasher tablets to floor cleaner, laundry bleach to toilet cleaner. And they smell so good! OK, so they are a bit more expensive, but when you start to use them, you realise that you don't need as much of these products as you may have thought. And you can take comfort that you are not exposing yourself, your loved ones or your planet and its natural inhabitants to any unnecessary harm.

You can also make your own and use this stuff around the house to help you to clean. The main ingredients to natural household products are:

**lemon juice, vinegar, bicarbonate of soda and salt**

Again, I have included a link in Resources to just one website of many that itself has links to other surprising household cleaners. For example, you don't have to throw away all those unnatural foods from your larder, you can put them in your cleaning cupboard! Your leftover cola will clean and shine your toilet, your tomato ketchup will make your silver sparkle, and coffee grains take away strong smells. Freeze your white bread and defrost a little for dusting off your oil paintings and picking up tiny fragments of glass from joins in your floor tiles. I live in an area where the water is naturally high in lime. Every week, we put lemons in our kettle, boil the kettle before we go to bed, and voilà! The kettle is as good as new in the morning. No need for harsh expensive chemicals. Nature has everything you need. And Google will point you in the right direction!

Some essential oils that you can add that work extremely well include:

**tea tree, lavender, pine, lemon, eucalyptus, peppermint, grapefruit.**

Most of these are anti-fungal (good for mould and mildew), anti-bacterial, anti-viral (for hand washing, work surfaces, laundry) and therefore disinfectant (good for bathrooms and drains).

Combine these to make up some gorgeous products that you will be proud of. You can also buy eco-friendly base preparations, like liquid soap, that you can then use for washing dishes, showering, cleaning your floors and surfaces and even washing your hair. They are so gentle; your health will love them!

Many people I know who have made the switch, either to commercial eco-friendly products or using their own, have noticed a change in their health, either improvements to their skin, a reduction in headaches, even a greater willingness to clean! I think the TV and other advertising mediums have thrown us into sheer obsession about cleaning over recent years. I have found very little difference in the propensity for sickness from a household that cleans every day to one where there are several pets and cleaning is not a priority. I have also heard that many hospitals have stopped using bleach in their cleaning products because it's thought to kill a lot of the protective bacteria. These hospitals have seen a reduction in infections after a period of time.

I think a lot depends on what we are accustomed to. I have nearly always become sick when I have gone to India because I'm not used to the bacteria there. That's pretty extreme I know, but it shows how maybe we are losing our resistance by feeling that everything in our house needs to be sterilised. We simply do not need to use these harsh cleaners in our homes. They can do more harm than good and are really unnecessary. A high level of food and bathroom hygiene can be achieved with the assistance of natural products.

Also remember your garden. Weed killers are strong because they have to kill weeds, right? But they also kill insects and good bacteria in soil. They are proven to be harmful to all species, including pets and humans. And they can also seep into water supplies. Please be mindful. Use alternatives like vinegar, salt and boiling water or just pull them out of the ground regularly with your hands.

It's easy to feel that we alone can't save the planet from pollution, and that is true. But you can effect change in your home, share the joy (even pride) in your new choices and the reasons with your friends and relatives. You will change someone else's mind. No-one can do everything, but everyone can do something to change the future of the world we live in. Mother Earth's resources are limited. It's our children's children who may have to face a world without real nature. A friend of mine cleans houses for a living using only eco-friendly products. She has no problem finding new customers. Once people realise how harmful these chemicals can be to them and especially their children, they make the switch and never go back.

I have listed some resources in the back of the book where you can buy ready-made eco-friendly products and oils online. But there are many. Once you have the containers, you can also order bulk refills. Why not ask your friends to share and cut costs?

## Waste Not Want Not

I never understood this saying until recently. I thought it only really referred to eating and food, but I have discovered that not wasting anything develops a deep gratitude for everything we have, from clothes to furniture. Until a few years ago, I would always be happy to toss out old styles for new trends. It made me feel worthy, whole, even connected. But what was I connected to? Advertisements, materialism, my ego? Just a few years later, through what can only be described in one sentence as a deep realisation, I have come to appreciate everything I own and use it fully until the end of its useful life, and even then look to reuse its parts or recycle it in some way. It pains me to throw stuff away. At the end of the day, there is no 'away'. Mother Earth eventually takes it into her belly as landfill.

> *"Willful waste brings woeful want."*
> *~ Thomas Fuller*

And we hoard! Boy do we hoard! Most of us have so much more stuff than we need. We consider variety of choice to be a necessity, or we live in fear that we might need that something one day, so we'll hold on to it as clutter. This is a very interesting and emotive subject. The need to connect with nature as a path to overcoming emotional eating can be aided by disposing of our rubbish more consciously. Furthermore, I think there is a reason for decluttering as a way of letting go of the emotions, the traits and even the weight that no longer serves us. Detoxing your home, little by little, is a great way to help your healing. The freedom from severing long-standing attachments to your possessions is not unlike the freedom you seek from your overeating emotions. It's the same willingness to let go that's involved and it's the same knowledge that despite whatever has happened in your past, you'll really be OK. By letting go of stuff, whether physical or emotional, we create space for the new – whether that's new space in your cupboards for healthy foods, new space in your wardrobe for clothes that fit you properly, or new space in your life for new people and activities.

I try to do one of four things with stuff I really don't and probably won't need:
- sell it
- donate it to charity, to a friend or family
- recycle it myself or give it to the authorities to recycle
- reuse it - rather than buying a replacement, can it be used for some other purpose now?

There are also steps I try to take when I buy new stuff:
- can I buy it second hand, i.e. recycle it myself?
- can I adapt or reuse something I already have?
- can I buy a more natural or biodegradable alternative?

The only thing that I really struggle with these days is plastic bags. I try to reuse them when I go to the market and try not to get any new ones. This is really the only thing that goes in our general waste. Plastic bottles, glass, paper and metal are all recycled. Food waste goes on our compost heap. Because our cleaning products are eco-friendly, we pour our grey waste water on the plants too. There are lots more ideas on the internet for you to try and it really involves no additional time or effort.

The point could be to view your idea to declutter your home as a way to connect better with your planet rather than simply tossing your unwanted possessions in a landfill site. It does give you a bit of a warm feeling that you are doing your bit for Mother Earth! But most of all it can help you to be really mindful of what you buy. I understand better now the difference between wants and needs and it is certainly true that the less I waste, the less I want.

## Natural Beauty, Natural Skin

*"Beauty is only skin deep.*
*I think what's really important is finding a balance of mind, body and spirit."*
*~ Jennifer Lopez*

Call me 'ole suspicious' if you like, but the more I read and hear of the corporate illusion we have bought into, the more I wonder how long some industries can last before we all wake up and realise how harmful the stuff is that we cover our skin with. It would be a brave newspaper or fashion magazine that refused advertisement income from these unethical organisations.

How many more millions per year do we have to spend on beauty products, before we appreciate the real potential costs there are to our health of using these products?

How many more animals have to suffer the agonising pain we enforce upon them every time we buy a beauty product from a company who just won't bite the business bullet and stop their mindless and heartless cruelty?

How many more years will we continue to spend our hard-earned cash on perfume, without a care in the world about what is in the bottle, how it got there or what it can do to our skin?

In the USA in 1989, the National Institute of Occupational Safety and Health found that of around 3,000 or so ingredients used in the fragrance industry, 884 are known to be toxic. These are known to cause birth defects, cancer, neurological problems, allergic respiratory problems and eye irritations. They can also cause migraines, circulatory problems, concentration problems and fatigue. I wonder whether any of the many people I have known with chronic fatigue and serious debilitating headaches have ever considered this? The disaster here is that fragrance companies aren't required to list their ingredients because of trade secrecy laws (8), (9). To think that for years I spent a small fortune on buying these toxic cocktails for my friends and family. I feel totally misled. But I never thought to question their integrity. We are a world obsessed with brands and totally swept along by advertising.

It's crazy!

Of course, fragrances are not the only products we put on our skin in the hope that it will keep us younger and make us look and smell more beautiful. Every day, most of us cover our hair, our face, our body and our teeth with them. Do we even think about the substances to which we are exposing ourselves? If you knew the danger that the thousands of chemicals, most of them never tested on anyone, might have on your health, would you put yourself at risk? Make-up has also been found to have mercury compounds and lead among ingredients that are not declared on the packaging (10). Even when they are declared, they are often listed by their Latin names and we have no idea what these terms mean.

What to do? Well, I'm going to give you the opportunity to consider some alternatives of course! Fortunately, there are many, including some Resources in this book and on my website. I review certain products myself, so please keep your eyes on www.chinmayimagic.com and www.bodymagic.website and subscribe for updates and freebies. I know you will have learned a lot from this book, but my websites will have the most up-to-date information to support you on your journey. Even several of the resources I recommend as I write, whilst they have excellent information now, can often be a little behind as great new knowledge emerges.

## Wonderful Ways to Wash and Moisturise

The first thing to realise is that we do not have to wash our whole bodies thoroughly every single day. Unless we are really sweaty or working in 'dirty' environments, often a short wash will suffice. Many of the commercially-bought, synthetic shower gels and bath foams are degreasing, so they take a lot of the good oils off the skin. Sometimes a light body wash with traditional soap will ensure that these stay in situ. Even the 'nourishing' or 'hydrating' ones strip your natural moisturisers off first and leave a layer of chemicals on your skin, so that it feels soft, but actually it's just designed to coat your skin. You can buy organic base preparations in liquid soap form including shampoos, base creams and plain body lotions and conditioners, and to those you can add health-giving carrier oils and therapeutic essential oils, depending on your skin or hair type, your mood and your preference.

If you do not want to mix your own for any reason, there are lots of great options online. See Resources.

## Some ideas

Carrier oils will help the moisturising qualities of your washing liquids and body lotions. Always try to buy organic ones if you can. They are unlikely to have chemical preservatives in proportions that you might be sensitive to. Here are three of my favourites:

*Coconut oil* - good for normal to greasy skin. Is cooling and alkalising for skin in the sun and absorbs really well. Coconut oil is only liquid above 24C or 76F, but makes a great make-up remover without the risk of getting chemicals in the eyes. Solid, I use it as a lip balm for the same reason. Because of its anti-microbial qualities, it can be a useful, natural treatment for dry skin conditions such as eczema, psoriasis, even cracked heels. I have heard it's particularly effective when applied to affected areas after soaking them in warm water.

*Moroccan Argan Oil* - a thick oil, known for its deep moisturising and reputed anti-ageing qualities. As useful as any oil in your beauty cabinet, but it's not as greasy. It can be used on greasy skin conditions such as acne. It has also been a feature of hair products recently as it can help to condition hair and calm frizzy types. As with all oils, not much is needed for them to work their magic. Be aware of any argan oils that have been processed or have chemicals, including fragrances, added for use on hair.

*Almond Oil* – again, all of the aforementioned benefits. This oil is thicker and softer. It's my favourite for massage. It's also thought to clear up dandruff, slow down hair fall, clear scalp inflammation and help with splitting ends! Obviously not a choice for anyone with nut allergies.

Essential oils, as mentioned before, can be extremely therapeutic for the skin. Their molecular structure means that they are absorbed into the bloodstream and can help with just about any ailment known to man. You can use them to make your own personal fragrance too, with the addition of alcohol and water. Again, see Resources. Here are a few common ones that are great to add to base products:

*Peppermint* - tired feet, sunburn, broken capillaries
*Lavender* - sunburn, oily or dry skin, scars and stretch marks
*Geranium* - mature skin and dry skin conditions e.g. eczema
*Juniper* - cellulite and congested skin
*Clary Sage* - mature skin, hormone imbalances and inflammation
*Chamomile* - sensitive skins
*Tea tree* - acne, head lice, cold sores, mouth ulcers

If you decide to buy ready-made products, you can still look out for these ingredients if you have specific needs.

A good rule of thumb is not to expose essential oils to the sun's rays as they may cause a reaction. But coconut oil, whilst it doesn't have an SPF/sunscreen content, does not become toxic at high temperatures as other oils can do.

*"I love to think of nature as an unlimited broadcasting station, through which God speaks to us every hour, if we will only tune in."*
*~ George Washington Carver*

## Om Shanti Shanti Shanti

Oh great Universal Vibration!
Peace for ourselves,
peace for those around us
and peace everywhere
for everyone and everything!

## Chapter Ten

# Eating Habits and Addictions

*"You know you are addicted to a food if despite knowing it is bad for you and despite wanting to change, you still keep eating it. Addiction means that a craving has more control over your behavior than you do."*
*~ Kathy Freston*

Recognising our addictions is a fundamental part of the healing process in this book. All addictions are founded in emotions and/or the desire to escape from emotions. As they take a hold of our life, they sap our power and our **Intentions** for better health and happiness. They take us from a thriving life to a merely surviving existence. BodyMAGIC! is not just about getting through your challenges with food. It's about finding peace, joy, bliss and happiness, every day for the rest of your life. It's about realising that this life is a gift, a miracle that *will* be enjoyed rather than endured. Addictions have the capacity to wipe the MAGIC! out of your dreams, your hopes and all those around you whom you cherish.

## What is an addiction?

Many rehab websites, government departments, advice lines and charities refer to defining addiction as the four Cs. I have given examples of addictions around food to illustrate them:

**C - Loss of <u>Control</u> over eating -**
"I cannot just go into a store and buy one bar of chocolate, I have to buy three or four"
"I try to stay away from the kitchen in the evening, but I can't help myself. If I know there is cake in there, I won't stop until it's all gone"
"When I take one slice of my homemade bread, I swear I could eat the whole loaf within an hour"

**C - Continues to overeat despite harmful <u>Consequences</u> -**
"I will hate myself tomorrow but for today, I'm not going to worry about it"
"I know I'm overweight and this is putting added stress on my knee injuries. It's as if I'd rather eat than walk"
"I know that sugar/alcohol/bread/junk food/coffee may cause me psoriasis/eczema/bloating/IBS/candida/acidity/headache/diabetes but I still can't help myself"

**C - <u>Compulsive</u> eating**
"All I think about is food - what we are going to eat for the next seven days, what I'm going to eat next and what I've just eaten"
"When I'm invited to an event, my first thought is whether there is going to be food there"
"I treat food shopping as a serious chore. I don't want to forget anything. I usually end up with more than our family needs"

**C - <u>Craving</u>**
"I salivate over the thought of eating my favourite foods"
"A last-minute plan to go to my favourite restaurant sent me into an excited frenzy! It changed my mood dramatically"
"Once I get the idea of chocolate in my head, I can't let it go. It eats away at me until I eat it!"

*(Taken from a definition of addiction by Savage et al, 2003)*

*"From food addiction to food serenity - freedom tastes great!"*
*~ Vera Tarman*

You may recognise yourself making similar statements. Don't be surprised. I have said all the above myself in the past. Maybe not exactly word-for-word. Healing has a great way of helping you to forget some aspects of your pain. But I remember the feelings behind them well. I share these with you because they are typical of a food addict, and I know I have felt each and every one of them, many, many times.

On top of that, I had years of waking up every morning feeling really awful about myself. Hating myself for not sticking to my diet the previous day. Dreading some event that was looming, by which I planned to lose a stupid amount of weight in a silly amount of time, just to feel 'good' for a while. Those targets were, of course, unrealistic. I would have to go out and buy another dress, a size bigger. But it would feel like I was buying one ten sizes bigger. I felt so huge, bloated and ugly. Then a little spark of hope would come up. Maybe if I ate only salads today, or fruit, or cabbage soup, or if I drank lemon water, I could still do it. So I would start the day with my plan in mind. Then I would remember that I was meeting a friend for lunch. I would *plan* to have soup, but by the end of the meeting, I was convincing myself that a summer pudding would be fine, because it had so much fruit in it! Then I would arrive home, feeling sick to my stomach and my heart. I would give up altogether by drinking wine and eating far more than ever. And so the cycle would roll. I would gain weight because I was down, and I would be down because I gained weight. It's so sad, but that is the nature of an addiction. A downward spiral of self-hatred and failure. The only spark would be the next new diet pills that melt away fat, or a new way of eating that would guarantee that I can burn cellulite off the back of my thighs.

It seems so cruel to me now. These dieting companies are making millions out of our desperate misery. It's nothing short of mental abuse. It goes on because we all have been so desperate that, like any addict, we've wanted a quick fix. And the fix is not just the reduction on the scales but the feeling of having done it. We know that some diets can work in the short-to-medium term and we are convinced that we are going to be part of the tiny minority who can succeed, maybe even longer.

If this scenario rings bells for you, have another look at the four Cs. I realised that as well as being addicted to food, I was also addicted to dieting! My diet would give me some reassurance that I wasn't letting myself go. That at least I was doing something. But I now know I was doing absolutely nothing for my self-esteem, my mental or physical health, and certainly nothing for my relationships. The closest people to me had to listen to my constant moaning about myself. I don't think it set a brilliant example for my daughter. Luckily she sees and hears the changes now. I lost count of the engagements I cancelled because I got myself into such a state of panic and sadness that I just couldn't go. I often fell ill prior to these gatherings too. It seemed my immune system just couldn't take the strain anymore. And I'm not at all surprised!

**Frying Pan to the Fire**

There is another huge hurdle that can very often present itself when overcoming emotional overeating. It's likely to have come up when you have been *successful* in losing weight and even keeping it off. Emotional overeaters will often unknowingly replace overeating with another habit or addiction. Examples of alternatives include smoking, drinking alcohol, sugar/sweeteners, diet drinks, coffee, diet foods and drugs. It makes sense. If I force diets on myself, lose weight, but don't do any healing work on myself, the harmful emotions will still be there. I tell myself that I can't *eat* what I crave, so to escape the painful emotions, I'll find another comforter.

This has come up for me several times since my earliest memories of overeating and weight loss. When I look back at the times I've been successful in losing weight, I have often replaced healthy food with something that doesn't serve me. It might not always be another food either. That habit might be drinking wine, getting up late or spending hours on the internet.

I might be feeling new and positive emotions from losing weight and increasing body confidence, but these are short-lived, because I've developed another dependency that creates a new physical or emotional imbalance. It's like robbing Peter to pay Paul. This inevitably results in returning to former eating habits. The unconscious mind (instinct) and the subconscious mind (behavioural patterns) tell my body to get back to what it knows as fast as possible.

So the process goes something like this:

1) Unresolved emotions become unmanageable
2) Overeating and/or food addictions suppress emotions and soothe temporarily
3) Weight gain takes place to support the stress and famine responses
4) Dieting seems the only answer to fix the physical problem, but challenges the emotions further
5) Enter new emotional support/dependency that alleviates difficult emotions
6) Weight loss gives emotions a positive boost, things seem to be going well
7) New dependency increases, disrupting life and eventually emotions
8) Overeating returns to soothe emotions
9) New dependency still remains
10) Emotions are still unresolved and become more unmanageable

So what's the answer? It goes back to the keys once again.

If I **Know Myself** and **Know My Worth**, I will recognise my behaviours sooner and will react in a way that nurtures my **health**, facilitates **healing** that will lead to real **happiness**, without further struggles. That nurturing way for me has been my daily practice, especially meditation, but actually all of the practices and learnings of this book. If I miss my practice, after a while those unmanageable emotions will return and it will often feel like I am in a worse place than before I started.

The *only* way to overcome overeating is to work on the emotions. Then the addiction can be overcome too. The **7 Spells of BodyMAGIC!** will give you the knowledge and skill to prepare you for all the challenges you face in working towards your vision, by strengthening your **Discipline** and **Willpower**. They are all linked by your practice. Without practice, this book is just a collection of facts. Habits and addictions are practices themselves, so they can only be adjusted by other practices.

*In theory there is no difference between theory and practice. In practice there is.*
*~ Yogi Berra*

## Other Addictions

Look within yourself and see if there are any other habits or addictions lurking. Consider anything that keeps you from your daily practice, from healthy behaviours, from your self-care and your commitment to the **7 Spells of BodyMAGIC!**

If you are aware of any addictions, I beg you to find extra help as soon as you have finished reading this paragraph. Sometimes definitions like the Four Cs can help us to realise that there are other addictions going on that we have not have realised or resolved. There is no time like the present to take action. I'm neither endorsing nor discrediting any organisation, for I have little expertise in the area of addictions, other than food and cigarettes (see below). But get in touch with any of them *today*. Have the courage to let go of your ego and surrender yourself to the experts. You will never regret it. If one method, organisation or professional doesn't suit you, find another. But just do it!

## My Smoking Story

Here's one of my earliest examples of replacing overeating with an addiction.

From my mid-teens I was a cigarette smoker. I remember the time, in my mid-twenties, that I realised I was hooked. As cool as I had thought it was to smoke in my teens, it was just as cool to give up in my twenties. But I tried, time after time, and just couldn't stop. It was so hard. Then in my thirties, I realised that if I didn't give up soon, I was going to make myself very ill in old age. My grandfather smoked from the age of twelve and he suffered badly at the end of his life from emphysema and COPD. I was terrified. I tried everything from hypnotism to tablets. But nothing helped me. Why? Because I wasn't using my power to access my unconscious mind. This is where the real addictions reside, and the only place from which they can be removed. There were two parts to my cigarette smoking – one was **habit** and the other was **addiction**. I managed to break the habit (in several places) by stopping smoking in my car when I got a new one and stopping in my home when we moved. Then I got a job visiting customers in their offices and hated smelling of smoke, so I stopped there too. The habits were easy to change little by little. But the addiction didn't move away quite so consciously. It just happened, as my body realised that smoking cigarettes was unnatural and was destroying my health and vitality. So it was an unconscious shift into a new and more nurturing way of life. It has been the same process for most of the foods that, in reality, do not serve me.

> *"Not feeling is no replacement for reality. Your problems today are still your problems tomorrow"*
> ~ Larry Michael Dredla

## Addiction to Food

Most of us would never think of any individual food, or even food as a whole, as an addiction. Some people may argue and say that they are addicted to chocolate, ice cream or other single foods, but they are more likely to be addicted to sugar than to just one sugary product. Sometimes it comes down to being more of a habit than an addiction. It's a point that I have studied many times in different ways and with different clients. Habits usually relate to circumstances.

When I worked in a busy city, every Friday I would treat my team to a breakfast baguette. It was my thank you for their hard work throughout the week. I would be super-excited about having one myself on a Friday too, salivating thinking about it on my way to work. It became a habit. But when I left that job, I didn't even think about finding a new supplier for my weekly Friday treat. Habits with food and drink are very common and they become a habit simply by association.

Take alcohol for example. It's a western custom to drink champagne to celebrate, to have wine with a meal and liqueurs after, to find punch bowls or pitchers at parties and to have mulled wine at Christmas. But we don't do those things every day. They are association habits. If we did drink all of those every day, without the association, we might well be on our way to a serious alcohol addiction. And there would likely be some emotion present that we cannot deal with.

> *"Whether you sniff it smoke it eat it or shove it up your ass, the result is the same: addiction."*
> ~ *William S. Burroughs*

Medical News Today highlights the difference between a habit and an addiction:

- ☐ with an addiction there is a physical or psychological element, where there is no control
- ☐ with a habit one can stop easily and successfully when they want to (1). Using these parameters, overeating is definitely an addiction, as there is physical feeling of lack in the body that is brought about by psychological conditioning. So we can change our habits by fasting, supplementing meals and going on diets. But for the overeater, it is the addiction that needs healing, or the weight eventually goes back on again. All too often, we then put on even *more* weight than we had to lose in the first place. Why? One reason is that we have new emotions to deal with, such as feeling a failure, sadness, guilt, worry, self-loathing, hopelessness and helplessness. Where do we go with these feelings? To food.

I remember when I was about sixteen and I went to visit a hypnotherapist to help me to lose weight (alarmingly without any necessity for parental consent). I went on the recommendation of a friend who had gone to him to help her to give up smoking. For her, the treatment was very successful. Not so for me. For me, it was nothing more than relaxation. The hypnotherapist said that it was far more difficult to hypnotise for weight loss, because eating is a *natural* thing the body has to do, whereas smoking obviously isn't. It made sense at the time. Funny how he said that after he took my money!

However, my experience, knowledge and healing have helped me to realise that *overeating* is definitely *not* natural. It's quite separate from eating for nourishment. The vital difference is whether it's necessary for health or not. When we are hungry, we eat to satiate a physical need. When we overeat, we eat to satiate an emotional need. I make no apologies for stating the obvious, because it's *that* subtle difference that actually gives us **hope**.

We will always need to eat, and that driving force needs to remain intact for our health. We know how important it is to eat a healthy balanced diet for sustained energy and vitality and to prevent illness. Unless we live in any kind of real poverty, we have been brought up and accustomed to the habit of eating at certain times of the day, usually certain foods. These are good habits and they shouldn't be played around with too much, simply because it is not the habits that are the problem, it's the emotional overeating addiction. This is why diets, fasting and pills don't work as a way of losing weight. When we swap meals for chemicals, supplements, shakes or other commercial diet foods, we are trying to change a habit (as well as disconnecting from nature). But it's not the habit that needs changing, it's the addiction.

## Hope for the Overeater

If we can understand our emotions, where they come from and whether they are relevant, appropriate and necessary, in those moments before we overeat, they lose their power. And we gain back the power we need to heal our relationship with food. You will find no emotional healing power in any slimming pill or diet products that I have ever seen, tried or heard of.

You may ask why some people succeed in losing weight with these kinds of products and are even keeping it off? It could be that in getting to their goal weight, maybe getting fitter and staying fit, getting a new job or partner through increased confidence, they have (inadvertently maybe) worked on their emotions. But it's usually more luck than judgement. I would be very interested to see any life-long results without constant effort. Unhealed emotions will always reveal themselves again in some way. whether it's through an addiction, an illness or in a relationship.

Never forget that all of these fat-busting pills, supplements, appetite suppressants and other gimmicks are part of a multi-million dollar industry. Most of them don't hang around too long because they *don't* work in the long term. I tried my share of them over the years, probably spending more money on them than real food at times. I really don't think they are good for our health either. Despite getting these things through testing and regulations, I have concerns about their long-term effects, and especially when combined with other medications, supplements and food and drink. No laboratory can cover all of that. Stick to the solutions *nature* offers. You will have more money in your pocket and you will be following a system of healing that has been tried and tested and been around forever.

> *"We love our habits more than our income, often more than our life."*
> *~ Bertrand Russell*

# Exercise 2

**Eating Habits**

Have a little fun with this self-analysis exercise of your eating habits:

1.  How many meals do you feel you want to/need to eat per day?

2.  Do you feel you need a snack at some point during the day? What is it normally and when?

3.  What food(s) do you feel sustain you most at:

    i.    Breakfast
    ii.   Lunch
    iii.  Dinner
    iv.   As a snack?

4. If you don't have time to cook, where do you usually go for food?

5. How much water do you drink per day? When in the day do you tend to drink the most water?

6. How much tea/coffee/other drinks do you have?

7. Where do you usually have your meals?

8. Who do you eat with?

9. Do you have a favourite:

    i.    seat at the table?
    ii.   plate, cup or glass?
    iii.  brand of some foods?
    iv.   store where you like to shop?
    v.    place you like to go to for food treats?

10. What quirky eating habits do you have? e.g. the way you organise your food on your plate etc.?

11. Do you do other things while you are eating?

Decide which of these, if any, you might change if you feel that it will improve your health and your relationship with the food you eat. They may be quick wins for you. Some habits are very easy to change and the new, novelty factor to your routine is why so many diets seem to be successful in the beginning. They can give you a jump start. But remember that these are eating **habits**. They can be changed, but they are not the total solution to long-term weight loss or overeating.

If changing them wouldn't really improve your health, might they change your emotions? For example, if one of your habits is to have a green smoothie every morning, but you had to miss it, how would you feel? You are having to break a habit for one day or maybe more, but would you be terribly fraught? I'm not suggesting that you give up anything that is truly good for you. But look at those habits that have maybe got you stuck in a rut and any that bring up some emotion inside you. Be curious. There is no right or wrong way here. Take some time to contemplate your habits before you move on with this book.

*"Our daily decisions and habits have a huge impact upon
both our levels of happiness and success."*
~ *Shawn Achor*

Let's look at this a little deeper now. I shall share part of my eating history with you to illustrate what it took me years to realise – the difference between habits and addictions.

Until recently, there were very few times when I had finished my meal and not wanted to carry on eating. This is a habit, a pattern based on my eating ways of the past. Even as a child, I would never have been satisfied with just the meal on my plate. I would wait for my very skinny sister, who was extremely picky and ate her food like a bird, to finish her meal and I would say "Do you want that?", "Can I have it?" My dad used to call me the 'dustbin'. Not helpful in retrospect, but that's what I was labelled and what I believed. I was encouraged to finish my plate because of the 'starving children in Africa'. Perhaps that also encouraged me to finish everyone else's plate too! This was a habit I was taught, and it developed from a young age. I do not blame my parents at all. They probably wanted me to be nourished by the food they had lovingly prepared, not waste it and then come back an hour later saying I was hungry, asking for sweets.

I also know that for most of my childhood, especially after my brother was born, I felt I had to fight for my parents' attention. So perhaps on some level I thought I would win their approval if nobody's dinner went in the bin, when there are 'starving children in Africa'. It became a way to gain approval. I was feeling rejected by my parents and having to share their attention with my siblings, when previously I had been an only child. The key thing we realise here is that as children, we are all profoundly sensitive. A parent can make a fleeting comment to twins and it can affect them both totally differently throughout their whole lives.

Until I started work on those emotions (the need for approval, viewing eating everything as an achievement, guilt, etc.), this compulsion to clear the plates was an addiction. Now, through the practices which I'm sharing with you in this book, which are for life-lasting healing, I no longer feel the need for constant approval, I no longer need to achieve anything to feel loved, and I *know* that overeating the food left on my plate will certainly not help children starving in Africa! The emotions behind wanting to carry on eating have now been resolved. I am not compelled to overeat by the emotions. Occasionally I still want to carry on eating despite being full and satisfied. But this is a mere pattern from the past and is extremely easy to recognise and manage. I have more power in those and other situations, because I have worked through my emotions. The desire usually doesn't extend beyond one or two more bites.

Obviously these are not the only emotions involved in overeating, but they were biggies for me and changed my patterns of eating forever. Some changes were profound and sudden, others subtle and slowly unfolding. The really good news is that we don't have to deal with every single emotion that has caused us to overeat. We just need to make a start on one or two. By working on our emotions, we set up new patterns that serve and support our resolve for wellbeing, instead of sabotaging it. The comfort we seek from food comes from the new care we are offering ourselves by doing our practices. This accelerates the healing of all the emotions we have struggled with.

*"I believe that parents need to make nutrition education a priority in their home. It's crucial for good health and longevity to instill in your children, sound eating habits from an early age."*
*~ Cat Cora*

# Exercise 3

## Reasons for Overeating

What do you feel are your reasons for overeating?

What are the emotions behind them?

I have laid out some typical examples here for you to tick or cross through. There are hundreds of reasons why people overeat, but there are some common ones, simply because we live in similar cultures. You may not agree with some of the emotions behind your overeating habits, and that's OK. Use it to contemplate *your* situation. Then close your eyes and really feel that emotion if you can, in the context of the reason why you overeat. See if you can find a similar habit, routine or event in your past that might connect with your different emotions.

Take some time with **Focus** on this exercise. Allow it to stimulate some **Self-Knowledge**. In your progress through the **7 Spells of BodyMAGIC!** it will pay you dividends on your journey.
Please be sure that you have completed this exercise thoroughly before you move on. Make further notes on any 'A-ha!' moments you have, here and separately if necessary.

| Why do you emotionally overeat? | The Possible Emotion | Where does it come from? |
|---|---|---|
| I want to give up at that point | Hopelessness | |
| I deserve it | Lack of self-worth | |
| One time won't do me any harm | Denial | |
| I hate waste | Guilt | |
| I don't want to miss out | Insecurity | |
| I need comfort food | Lack of love | |
| She went to so much trouble | Approval (give and receive) | |
| The dessert looks so good | Fear of scarcity | |
| I ate too quickly | Fear of hunger | |
| I needed energy | Tiredness | |
| It helps me to forget | Grief | |
| I was bored | Sadness | |
| Sometimes I don't even think! | Anger | |
| In case I don't get time later | Worry of scarcity | |
| It's too expensive to leave | Need to justify oneself | |
| It was too good to miss | Fear of scarcity | |
| | | |
| | | |
| | | |
| | | |

## Sugar Addiction

There are genuinely addictive foods. This chapter would not be complete without another mention of one of the most highly addictive yet legal substances known to man. This substance is killing more people than anything else. The fact is that if we eat a diet with a high volume of simple carbohydrates, including ice cream, pastries, jams and jellies, cakes, pancakes, puddings, biscuits, sweetened cereals, candy, sweets and chocolate with high fructose corn syrup, maple syrup, treacle, caramel and custard and all those other chemically-coloured sauces, we are going to find it very difficult to give these things up, no matter what our circumstances or emotions. And it's not just in our food. We may have sugar in every hot drink. Sugar is in colas, sodas, lemonade and other fizzy drinks. Even fruit juices are often laced with added sugar.

Anyone who says sugar is not an addictive substance wants to see young children compete for sweets. They are obsessed! But we don't see them falling over each other for bananas or honey. Yet they can walk into a store and buy this drug at any age. Diabetes is the single biggest and still fastest-growing disease in the world. Even in developing countries, people are turning to sugar for cheap food, with disastrous consequences for health, and with no healthcare to either educate *or* help them.

If there were only one food I could mention that is extremely likely get in the way of your **health, healing** and **happiness**, it is sugar. There are many ways to overcome a sugar addiction, and many alternatives. But please don't even consider artificial sweeteners. They are highly toxic. And they have even been proven to stimulate appetite! In a study that was published in a journal called Appetite, rats gained more weight when they were fed artificial sweeteners than those fed with sugar over a 12-week period. (2).

This is just for starters. Other difficult ones to kick are coffee, alcohol and dairy. They are addictive, and in large quantities and with regular sustained intake, they will hinder your progress. They are so important that I have dedicated a whole chapter to them. But most importantly, I want to share some real solutions for kicking these in the butt, replacing them with much healthier and non-addictive alternatives. You will feel much more empowered if you can conquer these seven things.

Importantly, if in reading this chapter, you realise that you do have other addictions not really covered here, can I please recommend that you seek professional help? This journey will be fueled by letting go of all of the patterns that no longer serve you. But the help and care you need to move on from them is most likely to be beyond the parameters of this text.

Love yourself enough to recognise what is holding you back and to take action, without wasting any more of your precious time.

*"The only proper way to eliminate bad habits is to replace them with good ones."*
~ Jerome Hines

## Chapter Eleven

# Intuitive Eating and Mindful Munching

*"Be a lamp to yourself. Be your own confidence.*
*Hold on to the truth within yourself as to the only truth."*
*~ Buddha*

## Lifelong Healing

As emotional overeaters, we have the potential to develop so much positive intuition around food. Being emotional means that we have the capacity to be more sensitive to our feelings and therefore to what is nourishing or not. However, for whatever reason, somewhere on our weight loss journey we lost the power of our intuition. We surrendered to a set of rules. We trusted these rules to guide us to weight loss. They were meant to help us, but in reality, they didn't. The emotions became our downfall rather than our asset.

The **Idea** has now changed. It changed for you when you started reading this book. The **Intention** here is to just stop and listen. The **Focus** is on healing your relationship with your body, your mind and your food. You are not going to force yourself out in the cold rain for a run when every cell of your being is screaming "NO!" I don't want to!" You don't have to sit with a packet of rice cakes at the end of your day when you are hungry and you have no 'allowance' left. You will come to **Understand** what your body needs and what it doesn't.

We are going to rekindle and redevelop our innate instincts – the individual and unique processes by which we are all able to balance **health, healing** and **happiness**. These are the natural attitudes, beliefs and relationships to food that we have somehow allowed to be manipulated over the last few generations. It's time to get back to what we already know.

In this re-acquaintance you will find new **Confidence** around food and **Enthusiasm** for the freedom this brings. Here's how to get started:

## Awareness of the Diet Trap

1.  Be aware of thoughts about needing to watch your weight, eating less of certain foods or all food. Be aware of analysing what you ate yesterday and thoughts of making amends today or in the near future. Be aware of thoughts of having to take exercise to burn off something you ate. Allow your body to adjust itself. Trust that you have your own internal mechanism for balancing your body's health and its weight. Your emotional intervention in this process is more likely to disrupt its natural ability, both now and in the future.

## Understanding your Appetite

2. Why are you hungry? Is it because you haven't eaten for a while? Or maybe because you didn't eat very much at your last meal? If you are hungry and it's been more than three hours since your last proper meal, honour your body's request for fuel. Never ignore your hunger, try to suppress it, or ever try to fool it by giving it food that has no calorie or nutritional value. It's like giving a baby water instead of milk. Try not to go without food for more than five waking hours, or miss breakfast.

*"The best way to predict the future is to invent it."*
*~ Alan Kay*

## Friendship with Food

3. Make friends with the food you eat. When you choose, buy, prepare, cook and serve food, honour it as one of the most important things that you do for your health, because it is! Be curious as to how that food got to your plate. Care about how it was cared for. Invest your time, effort and money in food that comes from conscious sources that support your planet, your home. The energy used in harvesting the food is the energy you will be eating! If you like, bless and 'heal' the food with gratitude as you bring it into your home. Find a deep, positive connection with your food.

## Respect for Cravings

4. Honour your cravings. Apart from the addictive substances found in some processed foods, your body is very likely needing something your conscious mind doesn't know about yet. Something for your health. If there is anything unusual going on with your cravings, why might that be? Consider a change in the weather, your immune system, the moon cycle, unusual stressors, even the food you ate earlier. Is it natural, e.g. wanting warm carbohydrates on a cold day, or unnatural, e.g. craving sugar or coffee to cure a hangover? If you are regularly craving sugar, alcohol, coffee, junk/fast food, and not getting them affects your moods and clouds your thinking, they could be addictions. Work through them slowly and with gentle self-care. Get help if necessary or find healthier alternatives until the cravings come less frequently. Respect yourself enough to feed your body the best you can, most of the time.

## Peace in the Present

5. Ask yourself whether you have truly ever been starving, and getting food was really difficult. And take account of times when you have been really hungry because you have been starving yourself. Forgive yourself for the times when you have denied your body's signals and replace any guilt with gratitude for the food you have easy access to now and in the future. People are truly starving in this world, not because of a scarcity but because of inequality and poverty. There are many positive ways to help those who are unintentionally deprived of food in the world. But nobody will be saved because you didn't finish everything on your plate at your favourite restaurant.

## Knowledge of Hunger

6.  Are you aware of the difference between being peckish, hungry and ravenous? What is your body really saying? Are you tempted to indulge out of habit, emotion or stress? Or do you just want to enjoy a muffin and coffee with your friends now and again or fish and chips because you're at the seaside for the day? Is that OK? Don't deny yourself what you enjoy or the events involving food that you want to remember in life. Is your body going to really enjoy this food? Is it what your body needs to feel satisfied right now? Are you going to feel like you are missing out if you abstain from something you actually really enjoy eating once in a while? There will be more on this in *Chapter Twenty-One - Going Hungry*.

## Learning to Leave

7.  How much of what's on your plate do you think your body needs to satiate your present hunger? Even if you are really hungry when you sit down to eat, take your time to eat mindfully. Notice how much food you really need to satiate your hunger. Don't worry about when you will eat again and if you might get hungry. Don't refill your plate at the buffet table, just in case you might need something later. There is no need to store food. We live in a society where there is more than enough to go round. Have healthy, non-addictive snacks or even leftovers in your refrigerator, nuts, seeds or fruit in your car and a healthy snack in your bag if you want to.

## Nature's Way

8.  In this age of fast communication, we're constantly being bamboozled with new ideas and trends for everything. This includes ways to lose weight, ways to get fit, get healthy, get sleep, get love, get happy, get rich, etc. The problem is that we are letting go of our inbuilt ability to find these things ourselves. We have come to believe that the more we pay for something, the better or more effective it is likely to be. You have a huge muscle in your toolbox called intuition that will be slowly waking up with the practices in this book. In the meantime, if your intuition doesn't seem to have the answer and before you go and pay someone else to tell you what *they* think is the answer, look for the answer in nature. Our body's cell memory is familiar with working with and in nature, eating naturally, breathing naturally, sleeping naturally, healing naturally, communicating naturally and even being entertained naturally. It will welcome the familiarity of these traditional practices that may have lain dormant in your cells for too long. And your body will respond accordingly, with bliss and health.

## Emotional Healing

9.  We have not evolved to deal with emotions like the ones we face in the 21st century. Almost all illness, disease, even injury can be attributed to stress. Stress from life's events, from the environment, from our lifestyle, it all adds up. Top it off with an eating disorder that is directly attached to the emotions, where in its extremes we starve or binge, and we are asking a heck of a deal from our bodies. If we want to be happier, we need to focus on our health. If we want to have good **health** we need to focus on our **happiness**. That is done through **healing**. The three are beautifully interconnected and yet inseparable. Hence they form the principles of this book.

Eating itself is a **practice** in BodyMAGIC! You can't take your yoga mat, your meditation stool, or even this book out to dinner with you, but you can take your practice. And it is just that, a practice. What you believe to be perfect now is going to change. You will come to realise that you have always been perfect. Your body and mind have the capacity to quickly bring you back into perfect balance every time something knocks you down. It's a miracle! This time, you are working with it, not swimming against the tide. Your practice will reveal to you the perfection that you have always held, in body mind and spirit. And you won't need it confirmed by the scales.

There is no question that when we eat emotionally we are barely aware of how much, what and how fast we are eating. After years of overeating in this way, these habits spill over into normal mealtimes. If we are going to increase our **Discipline** and **Willpower** over food, we need to find **Commitment** to a practice of mindful eating at each mealtime. This heightened awareness, whether we are peckish at the buffet table or ravenous in a restaurant, will give us all the discipline we need. And if it doesn't kick in quickly enough sometimes, we will at least know why. Remember it is a practice. It takes 21 days to create a habit out of a practice. But there will still be times when, with the best intentions in the world, we decide to indulge, maybe without thinking. We will be totally fine about it because we trust that the body, because it is a perfect miracle, will bring us back into balance. It will do this for us because we are focusing on health.
So here's to the practice!

*"Do what you can, with what you have, where you are."*
*~ Theodore Roosevelt*

# Exercise

## How to Munch Mindfully

### 1. *Prepare to impress*
Prepare your food as if you are preparing it to impress someone. Take time, take care and take pride in your task of bringing nourishment to yourself and your family. It's such an amazing thing to do for everyone when you think about it!

### 2. *Use your senses*
In preparing the food, use sight, sound, scent, taste and feeling. Be present throughout the process. Share these observations with those who are preparing the food with you. Be aware of negative energies in conversations in the kitchen. Keep awareness with the food. This will make the experience of peeling and chopping vegetables like nothing you've ever done before!

### 3. *Sit in super surroundings*
Sit down to eat, if possible at a table. This does not include your car. Make the table colourful and bright, almost like an altar to your food. If you cannot eat at a table, use a tray or a special chair. If you are on the run, find a table to sit at to eat. Or stop the car and eat. Never eat while you are driving. Not only is it dangerous, but it's impossible to eat mindfully. Change family habits slowly and get the family to see the benefits of this, as a social occasion.

### 4. *Dodge Distractions*
Remove distractions to mindful eating. Turn off the TV, radio or loud music. Leave mobile phones on silent and not on the table. If anyone rings, don't answer it, don't even look! Don't read the newspaper at breakfast, check your email or update Facebook while you are eating. Give your food the respect that you expect from your food. It may take others in your household a while to change, if ever. Work on *your* patterns first and see what happens.

### 5. *Grace for Gratitude*
Consider saying a prayer or 'grace' before you start eating, or using a mantra or a chant. It may not be easy to introduce this into the family home, but you can do this silently and without anyone noticing if you want to. I have a few suggestions in Resources, but write your own if you want to. Focus on gratitude.

### 6. *Shut up and Chew!*
Try not to talk when you are chewing. When you do this, you hurry it down and don't chew it properly. Finish your mouthful slowly, put your fork down and then speak. There's really nothing worse than having to rush down something delicious to answer a question. Chew your food until it is totally mashed, like baby food. Not only are you releasing powerful enzymes to help with digestion, you are slowing your eating down so your brain will get the fullness signal much more quickly and you will have eaten less. Chew your smoothies too. Yes really! Get those enzymes flowing by moving your mouth a little before you swallow each mouthful.

### 7. *Wait a while for the wash-down*
Avoid washing your food down with a big drink. It dilutes the enzymes that your digestive system has naturally produced. Sip only a little if you need to. Warm water is ideal. Drink a glass of water 10-15

minutes before you start eating and wait for 45 minutes at least before you have another big drink. You will feel fuller for longer as your stomach and intestines have more work to do.

## 8. *Take a break and contemplate*
When eating, try having a little break when you start to feel satiated. Wait 3-5 minutes if you can, when you have eaten half to two-thirds of your meal. Have one more mouthful if you like when you feel satiated, then push your plate away. Stop if you feel full, no matter how much is on your plate. Those extra mouthfuls may be delicious, but in your heart you know that they can turn a pleasant eating experience into an uncomfortable and regrettable one.

## 9. *Love your leftovers*
You can do something with the food you have left. You can freeze it, put it in the refrigerator for a couple of days as a healthy snack, make it into something else, give it to the dog, cat or fish (if appropriate), put it on your compost heap or bury it in the garden. You have no need to ever throw food away! And if there's one thing I've learned about buying organic and whole food, it's that in the end, it didn't cost me a whole lot more than the usual supermarkets, because now I appreciate it much more, use only what I need and waste virtually nothing.

You will no doubt find some of these stages more difficult than others. Take your time. Find the quick wins and integrate them first. Then gradually, when those become a habit, work on the rest. See them as an experiment rather than a rule or even a chore. They may be a huge change for you, so be patient with yourself.

Make it fun. If it's fun, you will smile, and that **happiness** will help your **healing** and your **health.**

*"Feelings are much like waves - we can't stop them from coming*
*but we can choose which one to surf."*
*~ Jonatan Mårtensson*

## Chapter Twelve
# Fads and Fallacies ~ Myths and Truths

*"Happiness cannot be traveled to, owned, earned, worn or consumed. Happiness is the spiritual experience of living every minute with love, grace, and gratitude"*
*~ Denis Waitley*

I have tried a lot of diets. I have been to hell and back and at the end of my tether with nearly all of them. That cycle of dieting has gone around more times than I care to remember. It starts with a good intention, almost excitement and hope that this one is the one that's going to change my life. The genuine commitment and motivation in those first few days or weeks is beyond what I can ordinarily muster. Then comes the realisation that it's really hard to do, that life's goodies get in the way and I may not be able to stick with it after all. I'm hungry, I'm not enjoying the food that I'm eating and I'm miserable. When I can take the struggle no longer, I let it all go. All my enthusiasm and commitment seem futile. All that time, money and effort wasted. The ensuing disappointment, even despair, is a dark and depressing hole. All I have left is a feeling of total loss of any self – self-esteem, self-worth, self-love. And then the questioning starts? Why can't I do it? Why am I so weak? Why can't I just eat normally? I'd try again the next day, week or even pick it up again months later, but the cycle was the same.

It is not my intention to encourage you to abandon diets that *are* working or you feel *have* worked for you. But if the diet, eating plan or supplement you tried had really and truly worked for you, you wouldn't be here. Something is missing. This book will help you to find it.

You have come so far with this book already and in the spirit of 'knowledge equals power', I would like to give you a little diet industry overview. This is a brief, general look at just a few of the diet types that have been around us for the last 30 years, although forms and variations of them have been documented for a hundred years or more. My comments and opinions are based on *my* experience. This chapter is not just for you to know more about diets throughout recent history. I'm sure you have heard about, if not tried, some or most of them in your eternal quest to lose weight and/or overcome emotional overeating. I want to show you how and why *my* experience of what works sometimes and what doesn't work (short-, medium- and long-term), has influenced the message I have for you in this book.

**Calorie Counting Diets or units, points etc.**

People have been counting calories for weight loss since the 1920s. But there are other 'counting' diets. These are diets whereby the *quantity* of food is monitored and an allowance is given, usually per day. In more recent years these diets have evolved whereby some foods are often allowed in unlimited quantities and do not need to be counted. Usually there is no food that is forbidden. All foods have calories, but some of these diets use other units of measurement and some foods need not be counted.

These diets appeal because in theory we can have anything we like as long as we count it. The challenges with these diets are with the whole preoccupation around food. For example, at special social occasions, especially where alcohol is involved, if I am having to count everything, then weighing scales and measures are needed. Not normal handbag accessories! This kind of diet can create an obsession, as it did for me. The whole long-term aim of losing weight is to keep it off. But this involves a change of thinking and lifestyle, and help with the underlying reason for overeating, prior to the diet. Most of these plans do not allow for the bigger picture. This obsession with points/calories/units or whatever and the number that is showing on the scales keeps us away from what's really going on. The diets often don't encourage us to eat things like healthy fats that are necessary for long-term health in mind *and* body.

More often than not, weight returns when we come off the diet.

My experience of a counting diet was with Weight Watchers. I was with them for over 10 years. I lost 19 pounds in the first 10 months, but when I came off the diet, gradually the pounds came back on. As I gained weight, my relationship with food became very tough indeed. I went back to Weight Watchers several times, but I just couldn't find the appeal any more. I became disillusioned at the paradox of a half-hearted approach to health and the weekly sale of cakes, sweets and chocolate bars that had no contribution to make to my health. It was all about points, not what those points consisted of. They appeal to the masses, across a massive demographic, and sadly in doing so, they haven't taken enough brave steps to encourage people to eat more healthily. The perception is that healthy foods cost more money and aren't always readily available. Weight Watchers want to make it as easy as possible for as many people as possible. There is an education gap here, because people need to learn about the long-term costs of ill health from a cheap diet, such as medical costs, having to take the medicines, time off work, inability to live a full and vibrant life, having to rely on relatives and friends in old age and losing independence.

At one of my last meetings, I asked why there was no points listing for seeds in the booklet. The meeting leader didn't know, but she suspected that they were excluded because they are high in fat. I continued to receive text messages from my meeting leader after I stopped going to meetings. One day she sent a reminder to her list to ask everyone to buy or bake a Weight Watchers cake and bring it to the next meeting in aid of their chosen charity – Diabetes UK! It was the final straw. This was a national Bake Off. It did nothing to raise awareness about health, only to totally contradict it!

**Low-fat Diets**

It wasn't so long ago that we were told to cut out fat. The supermarkets were and still are full of low-fat foods. Even butter substitutes were low-fat! It was an easy win for food manufacturers. The saying 'you are what you eat' made a lot of sense to us. If we ate fat, we would be fat! But we could eat all the sugar, simple carbohydrates and starch we wanted to. I still have a book of a diet plan with a cake recipe containing a small amount of flour, an egg, a shed load of dried fruit and three cups of white sugar! I don't know how many times I made that for a treat! And I know a few people who battled with low-fat diets 15-20 years ago and who are diabetic now. Diabetes is life-changing and can be life-threatening. Some of us didn't realise we were adding another addiction – sugar – to the food addiction we already had.

It is now widely recognised that there are certain fats that are full of very important nutrition. We were probably denying our bodies with this one. I did for many years. I love avocados, nuts and seeds but I wouldn't touch them while on this kind of diet. I remember using a processed, refined oil in the form of a spray for frying and I also remember having at least one of those sugar-laden or sweetener-packed low-fat yogurts a day. I had to restrict eggs too, and I shudder at the thought of all of the egg yolks I threw away because they had fat in them. Saturated was a swear word.

I don't remember any long-term weight loss from these years. But I do remember that during this time I was in a difficult marriage with a man who had his own addiction. The diet may have given me hope that I could look and feel a better person, but my emotions were what really needed the healing.

*"They hype up the urge for gratification by providing an unattainable goal and inevitably provoke a vicious cycle of self-loathing, constipation and bad breath. But still we buy into them, all it requires is a spankingly good line in self-delusion."*
*~ Louise Foxcroft, Calories and Corsets*

## Low-carb Diets

These are not a new phenomenon. Dr. Atkins wrote about his personal success with a high protein, low carbohydrate diet at the end of the 1960s. His first book was published in1972. The low-carb diets have bubbled under for decades, but with Atkins' New Diet Revolution, released in 2000, a whole new generation sampled the low-carb methods. This also brought attention to the Paleo Diet – a theory about the diet of humans during a period in history that ended 10,000 years ago, where dairy is not allowed, and nor are grains or legumes, coffee or alcohol. Many of its driving factors are disputed. The diet mainly consists of meat, fish and seafood, and non-starchy fruit and vegetables. The Stone Age Diet was published in 1975 by Walter Voegtlin, with similar beliefs. The Dukan Diet follows principles in the same vein again, but is also low-fat. The struggle with these diets is that the body craves carbohydrates, for whatever reason, making these difficult to stick to.

All of these have worked well for some people. Especially for meat eaters. Not eating carbohydrates has never been easier, especially in North America. There is as much evidence to say that these diets are good for health as evidence that they are bad. It depends what aspect of health we are discussing. For example, saturated (fat) was a devil's word for many years. Now we are learning that not all saturated fat is bad. Avocados and coconut oil, for example, are extremely good for our health, with many benefits.

I have read reports that low-carb diets help with a reduction in cardiovascular conditions, but an increase in osteoporosis has also been reported. There is conflicting research everywhere. I personally found all of these diets extremely difficult. I did lose a bit of weight in the beginning, but eventually the pull back to carbohydrates was so strong, I would binge or overeat. It was as if my body was trying to play catch-up. Not a great situation for an emotionally-driven eater.

In my quest to become more connected with my food and nature in general, my personal preference for the last decade or so has been to cut down on animal foods rather than increasing them as a calorie replacement for carbohydrates. I haven't eaten meat since I was thirteen years old, so on a low-carb plan I found myself eating lots more eggs, dairy and fish. However, that didn't sit well with my consciousness either. I found I was having more pre-menstrual symptoms, heavier periods and bloating. My intuition told me that it was dairy. I usually find that people say random things out of the blue, but at the right times. I found I was reading more and more about potential problems with dairy products at that time. Then, for the first time, a famous nutritionist highlighted that we are the only species who purposefully drink the breast milk of another.

I also have values and concerns around the environmental issues associated with eating so much animal protein. If we appreciate a connection with all things, then at some point we will consider that the health of our planet has a direct or indirect connection with our own health. Here is revealed a different aspect of our healing. If food is our medicine and we rely on Mother Nature for its continuation in its purest and most nutritious form, we have to educate ourselves as to how best that can happen in the future. Kathy Freston, best-selling author and veganist, writes, "the meat industry contributes to land degradation, climate change, air pollution, water shortage and pollution, and loss of biodiversity." (1)

Awareness is everything. Make informed choices. This will accelerate your healing path to greater health in body and mind.


## Supplementation Diets

There have been many wonder pills, creams and potions over the years that promise to help you shift fat, lose weight, reduce cellulite like magic, and also promise you that you can have a body like a catwalk model. There are synthesised exotic herbs, spices and plant extracts from all over the world that have somehow managed to get through legislation and out onto the shelves of drug stores and health shops.

They promise an answer to all of your prayers. But they come at a price, both a hefty financial one and in terms of possible risks to health. Here's one example.

Orlistat came out as a fat-burning pill called Alli a few years ago. It blocks up to 25% of fat eaten from being digested and can save 100-200 calories. Obviously manufacturers claim great successes, but they can have a very embarrassing effect on bowel movements, often being out of control if the dieter eats too much fat while taking the pills. Loren Wissner Greene of New York University School of Medicine says this may interfere with vitamin absorption as a certain amount of fat is needed in the diet for vitamins such as A and D to be absorbed by the body (2). Not surprisingly, all of them require you to adjust your eating habits and incorporate exercise. Of course, if we eat healthily and exercise more, we will probably lose weight anyway, without the fear of pooping our pants!

Another way of supplementing is having a shake instead of a meal. The Slim Fast Diet is one example that has been around much longer than I care to remember. It came to my attention when I was working in an office full of women during the late 1980s. It was expensive to me then. But I would try anything. I would have two shakes replacing two meals and a calorie-counted meal in the evening. Looking back, I don't really see the point of it. The shake itself was unhealthy and unsatisfying and what I would now call 'wasted' calories. It had a long list of additives, flavourings and synthetic vitamins. It was punishment for my body and especially for my mind. I wanted and craved food! I must have lasted less than a week. There was nothing satisfying in drinking a powdery drink. It gave me a bloated stomach and terrible flatulence! And I wasn't the only one in the office who readily admitted this! Maybe, if I had stuck with it, I might have lost some weight. But I do remember calling it a day and going out for a curry with wine at the end of that week. Why I put myself through this misery is a mystery. Perhaps it's like trying a new fashionable clothing item, like huge stiletto heels. I know I can't walk in them and they feel ridiculously uncomfortable, but I wear them anyway because I want to be 'in touch' with the latest trends.


## Research


Most of the research on the success of diets is the same. There is no evidence to support that diets are successful at sustaining weight loss or preventing heart disease, diabetes or other obesity-related illness. Dr. Mark Eisenberg, Professor of Medicine at Jewish General Hospital/McGill University in Canada, who conducted clinical trials on four popular diets in November 2014 said,

*"Despite their popularity and important contributions to the multi-million dollar weight loss industry, we still do not know if these diets are effective to help people lose weight and decrease their risk factors for heart disease."*

The diets trialled were Weight Watchers, the South Beach Diet (a phased, low-carb diet), Zone (30:40 ration of protein to carbohydrates) and Atkins. Weight loss can be achieved, and statistics show an average weight loss for up to the first year. But this is definitely not as much as you were probably led to believe or hoped for when you started the diet. In nearly all cases, some or all of the weight is regained within the second year. He goes on to say,

*"A broader lifestyle intervention, which also involves doctors and other health professionals, may be more effective. This also tells doctors that popular diets on their own may not be the solution to help their patients lose weight."* (3).


When you first heard that diets don't work, you probably had a moment of defending your position. I remember when I first heard this statement, I was totally blown away. I didn't know whether to laugh or cry. I felt a huge wave of defence coming out of my mouth. "How can that be when Weight Watchers have been running for nearly half a century?" and "Yes they do! I lost fifteen pounds and kept it off for six months." We all know someone who has lost lots of weight, even kept it off for a long period. There will always be exceptions to everything in life. For example, it is much easier for a woman to lose her temporary baby weight than to lose the same amount of weight that she's been carrying around since puberty. Her eating habits only changed for the time she was pregnant (probably influenced by her hormones) and the body will remember those previous habits more easily.

It's long-term weight loss that makes a diet truly successful. Unfortunately, this long-term analysis is hard to find on *any* weight loss organisation's website.

I would also suggest that if organisations *were* very successful in helping most of their subscribers to lose weight, they wouldn't have these customers for long, and therefore wouldn't have the success that they have as a *business*. Weight Watchers are listed on the stock market, so one could argue that their success depends on people *failing* to lose weight!

Sadly, when we regain those hard-earned pounds, most diet organisations would have us believe that *we* are the failure, that we had the tools and we just couldn't make it. That it's up to us to find the discipline. But that is nearly always *not* the case. An addiction is an emotional dependency and it takes much more than willpower to overcome one.


## The Famine Response


In 2012-14, there are still over 804 million people in the world who do not have enough food to eat – about 13.5% of populations in developing countries (4). Although enough food is produced to feed the world one and a half times over, there are many people all over the world who are starving, even in some of our own communities. The reasons are inequality and poverty, rather than scarcity of food (5).

On the flip side, for the first time in our evolutionary history, most of us are lucky to have a year-round abundance of food. But it was not always like this. If we take a look at the survival of animals, we can see how they adapt to seasons of scarcity by overeating and/or storing food. We did the same. It was the basis for our continuation as a race.

The brain itself has an inbuilt mechanism for making sure that we don't starve. It doesn't know that we have supermarkets we can go to when we run out of food. Our human genetics haven't quite evolved to complement the availability of food we enjoy. When you are hungry, the brain will send overwhelming signals through your chemistry to get you to eat. Think for a moment. You know that feeling when you are really hungry and after waiting for a while, you finally get the opportunity to eat?

You've finished your meal in a flash
You realise that you hardly tasted it
You wish you had more
And sometimes you get more. Much more. More than you need.

Then you realise that you were out of control. And you were. The unconscious mind runs many times faster than the conscious mind. It is your safety mechanism, your protection and your instincts working to get you out of all kinds of danger, including famine, and as quickly as possible.

The body doesn't like to feel hunger. This is another reason why diets fail. When we go on a restrictive diet, the metabolism slows down by up to 40%, transit of food slows down in the digestive tract to take out more nutrition from the food, and instead of providing us with energy, the calories are stored as fat (6).

*"What you resist not only persists, but will grow in size."*
*~ Carl Jung*

And the more we diet, the worse it gets. So the more times our brain is aware of a lack of food, the more it will want you to overeat when food is available. It's trying to protect you from starvation, and you are trying to take control of a 200,000-year-old instinct designed to look after you. That instinct is the reason you and your fellow human beings are still here! You don't understand it, so you start to see it as your weakness. You punish yourself further by trying diets, plans and programmes whose advertising and shiny offers all seem to offer the solution. But as the hungry periods increase, the instinct just gets stronger and the binges more frequent. So consider now how that might affect your emotions. No wonder we struggle and we feel out of control!

If the famine response is called upon regularly in a diet situation or if real long-term starvation is experienced, its power is strengthened and increased. Worse still, it is passed on to future generations with some of the same strength.

During the winter of 1945, Hitler cut off food supplies to Holland and many thousands of people starved. Because of the famine response and a process called epigenetics, the children of then pregnant mothers went on to become obese, by having an increased appetite and ability to store energy as fat. During Mao's Great Leap Forward in China, many starved. Epigenetic modification is thought to explain why the children of that generation are now obese in middle-age (6).

So it could be that our misunderstandings about dieting are making natural weight management more difficult for our children and grandchildren. Are we sending signals to our children, born or unborn, that this world holds the risk of famine? We have another reason to back off diets *now*. This is a force we cannot and should not reckon with.

What is the answer? Well fortunately there is more than one. All of the practices of this book have been included because they work with kindness on the unconscious mind. They have helped my brain to relax about the possibilities of me starving myself or making myself go hungry again. Some of them will work better for you than others because we have all had different journeys. Try them all, please. All of them are methods of self-care rather than self-harm. When we turn kindness on ourselves, all of our stress responses relax, including the famine response.

## The Novelty Factor

This book is about emotional eating, and this chapter specifically is about why diets cannot work. However, even emotional eaters will claim lots of success. The emotional eater wants to believe that it can work for them and will often stick to a diet for long periods of time. Those emotions will even work in her favour in the beginning, giving her all the rock-solid intention and enthusiasm she needs to succeed.

This is the novelty factor.

Eventually she will come off the diet and put some, if not all, or even more, of the weight back on. She will consider the diet was a success because she had originally lost weight. However, in reality, it would only have been a success if she had kept it off. She will view the weight gain as her problem, her failing, not any shortcoming of the diet, plan or programme. She goes back on the diet because she believes it had worked before and it can work again. But this time, she struggles. Why? Because the diet isn't a novelty anymore. It's tinged with failure in her unconscious mind. Her body and mind instinctively know that it didn't work and don't want to play that game again!

## The Latest Offerings

You receive an email or see a catchy advert on a website, and you are curious. From that moment you are mesmerised. Sometimes you even know in your heart that it's just another fad, but a little part of you wants to know more. They claim to be different this time. They seem to get you to a place of such misery, telling you about all the diets that failed YOU. It goes something like this...

"It's not your fault, the other diets were no good. But this one is! Here's the science behind this one. Look at all these endorsements by film stars! See all these before-and-after weight loss photographs! This incredible testimonial page! You too can have this! And if you sign up today you will get this extra bonus!"

Remember, diets don't work, *none* of them, in the long term. Your issue is your emotions, and depending on your dieting history, your body's famine response. They are the driving force behind every morsel you put in your mouth that you don't need to satiate your hunger, or to keep you healthy. A pill might suppress your physical urges for a while but it's not working with your emotional profile. Only you (or a trained professional who has all your details and history) can do that. So as soon as you stop taking the pill, the problem comes back out to bite you again. Often then it's morphed into something much more. Remember the keys to emotional freedom:

**Know Yourself**. You *do* have the power to do this work for yourself. You have everything you need. You can move from a place of trying to control your eating addiction to more intuitive and mindful eating by understanding the patterns of your body and mind.

**Know Your Worth.** Keep coming back to this book and your practices. Be patient, and find your personal power to keep going. It's your time for you to celebrate life-long **health**, **healing** and **happiness!**

Smile and feel that **Knowing** deep inside of you.

Watch this enlightening summary, a TED talk by Sandra Aamodt of some of the principles outlined in this chapter. Note the results overall of incorporating healthy habits into the lives of all people, whetheroverweight or obese. Either key in this url or search for her name on You Tube and the title of the video:

Why Dieting Doesn't Work
https://www.youtube.com/watch?v=jn0Ygp7pMbA

## My Time for Change

There are one or two of these diets that I persevered with over the years and went back to many times because, in theory, they seemed good for me, they suited my lifestyle and they seemed to offer genuine support. But sadly none of them lasted for me as an emotional overeater. It was only when I realised that my troubles with food actually had a name and my feelings were a key component of my overeating that I knew that no diet would ever help me permanently.

*"If you keep on doing what you've always done, you'll keep on getting what you've always got."*
*~ Unknown*

I just reached a point in my life where I wanted to get to the heart of the problem. I'd had enough of it. I was sick to my bloated stomach, my fat butt and my thick thighs of it all! Sometimes you have to hit rock bottom before you can stop falling. And boy how I'd fallen! I'd fallen into the trap of nearly every diet opportunity that had come my way for over 30 years. That's like a life's term imprisonment! Well, a long time to be stuck in a trap anyway! The only thing that hadn't fallen was my weight overall. That was all I wanted. It was to have thighs like Jane Fonda, a waistline like Rosemary Conley and a bottom like all those partygoers on Miami Beach. It was all that mattered. I would have done anything. And once or twice I had it. But like everything superficial, I desperately hung on to it, going into emergency action mode whenever I put on a pound. That kind of fear is not living. And the belief that being thinner would make me happy is just so wrong.

When my mum passed away, my priorities changed and my emotions were redirected to grief. In those dark nights of the soul (there were many), I realised that huge change was not just what I wanted, but that it was critical to my health and maybe my life. The bottom I hit was what some call a nervous breakdown. I had to pull over on the motorway one time because I thought I was going to have a heart attack. I suffered with strong panic attacks, palpitations or dizziness every day for months. I spent days in bed, hardly able to move. I had a broken body, with aches and pains, no energy, found myself shaking and had a whole load of digestive issues, from heartburn to IBS. I wasn't doing well at all. I had no purpose and no motivation to find one. Much less did I care.

It wasn't a sudden turn for the better, it was a subtle change. I started realising that when I practised yoga and meditation, I would feel better. It was the incentive to keep going back week after week. Even after the most stressful days, I would walk out from my evening class feeling joy and bliss. I was able to rationalise issues much more easily. The more often I practised, the better I felt. The analogy I still use is that my practice is like a washing line. Every practice is a prop. The longer I go between practices, the lower I hang and therefore feel. But a practice lifts my energy right back up again. Little by little, I began to open the doors to a whole world that I'd ignored for most of my life. It was a world of real **health**, **healing** and **happiness**.

## The world of pure energy and bliss

In the metaphysical world some call it consciousness, universe, source, higher self, higher intelligence, prana, chi, ki. In the spiritual world some people call it Higher Power, God, Allah, Jehovah, Rama, Krishna and many others. They are all words. The Peruvian shamen call it 'that which is known by a thousand names, and that which is the unnameable one." It is the universal life force that links us all. This force is unconditionally loving, supporting, accepting and giving. And we have it within us, every one of us, in every cell, all of the time, without cost or sacrifice. It is our essence, our true nature. All we have to do is be willing to go within and see it.

I had turned my back on religion and dogma many years before, so the idea of godliness freaked me out! I could feel my defences going up at the very mention of the word God. If I had read this book ten years ago, I know that I might have thought it was really 'out there.' But here I am writing one! *Now* I understand. God is not a person who sits on a cloud with a white beard, judging and punishing me. The *energy* behind every religion is God, or one of the other names. I had rejected God (or at least its human interpretation in religion) and therefore its energy, for so long. Yet it was the very force that has always supported me, past, present and future, regardless of whether I go to church on Sundays or pray for forgiveness for all my sins. *Now* I get it. It's the meaning that's important, in fact it is **vital** to my healing. My learning about universal energy is much more scientific than religious this time around.

*The essence of religion: Fear God and obey God.*
*The quintessence of spirituality: Love God and become another God."*
*~ Sri Chinmoy*

One of the greatest influences I have had in my spiritual life has been through my Catholic upbringing. It gave me many gifts, especially as a child – learning the difference between right and wrong, an understanding of devotion, surrender and faith, a respect for a Higher Power than myself, the value of honesty, the necessity for communities as a human race. Religion has so much to offer but many, including myself, have become disillusioned with the abuse of the control and power that religious leaders have had. If you are able to see and feel beyond this, then your faith will continue to be a valuable support to you, as you work through this book. If you can't, like me, then you always have your spirituality. In spirituality, you make your own rules and this gives you the power to evolve in your own way.

Through yoga, meditation and all of the other practices in this book that really *do* work, this is what happened for me:

- ☐ my health in mind and body improved
- ☐ I allowed deep emotional healing to take place and I found real happiness in my life
- ☐ my relationships shifted and they became more open and meaningful
- ☐ I was able to see my life and soul's purpose much more clearly
- ☐ I let go of so much fear attached to my future, based on my past
- ☐ a huge depression lifted and I became so happy, even joyful, most of the time
- ☐ I had more energy and zest for life

If you were offered a commercial diet, plan or method that could offer *all* of that, would you take it? Of course you would! If on top of that, and because of all of that, you found yourself at your natural weight, without counting a single calorie, unit or point, what would you say? I hope you would say

"YES PLEASE!!"

Because that's exactly what happened to me -

**My weight stabilised!**

This is how and why I lost the weight so effortlessly. For the first time in my life that I could remember:

- ☐ I found I was happy to leave food I didn't want
- ☐ I found that I wasn't thinking about food *all* or even *most* of the time
- ☐ I found that I didn't salivate at the thought of chocolate, cakes or even ice cream! (a big one for me)
- ☐ I was able to go for meals and not eat to bursting, and without guilt
- ☐ I was able to watch someone eat a dessert without wanting to try it, because I'd already had enough

- ☐ I was able to make a loaf of healthy bread and only have one or two slices of it
- ☐ I was eating more slowly, tasting more and not wishing I could eat it all over again
- ☐ I was frowning less and smiling more
- ☐ I was struggling less and thriving more
- ☐ I was sad less and happy more
- ☐ I wasn't craving simple carbs like sugar when I had low days
- ☐ I had a stock of healthy snacks in the house, most of which I made myself
- ☐ I could make a shopping list, look at recipes, plan meals without having to eat afterwards
- ☐ I knew exactly what to eat for health if I wasn't at home
- ☐ I looked forward to spending time with my friends more than I did the food I was going to eat

And I didn't panic if I was hungry

But most importantly…..

**I understood my emotions, why I had them and how to heal, nurture and care for myself**
*and*
**I realised my worth and my importance in the world**

And what's even better, I had a message of MAGIC! and the confidence to share it with the world!

I want that message to have real meaning, structure and guidance. I want it to be honest, open and clear for you to see. There are no gimmicks, no hidden extras, there is no catch. I found the truth about my pain around overeating and I found my healing solutions. It took me over 30 years to find it, to know enough about it and to have confidence to share it. With your work on the practices in this book, you need waste no more of your time, effort or money.

Here it is in a nutshell:

## The 10 Principal Understandings of BodyMAGIC!

*Health*
*Healing*
*Happiness*

1. Improved **Health**, an integrated practice of **Healing** and finding **Happiness** facilitate life-long freedom from emotional overeating.

2. Improved Health is achieved by reconnecting with Mother Nature through the elements of Earth, Water, Fire, Air, Space. This connection is through eating, drinking, moving, breathing, sleeping and other day-to-day practices in a NATURAL way.

3. Practices of traditional Healing offer holistic solutions to the challenges of emotional overeating.

4. Real Happiness is the true meaning of life and can only be found within oneself.

5. Diets, including chemical appetite suppressants, meal replacement plans, fasting, nutritional adjustment methods are not effective in the long-term to treat emotional overeating.

6. Exercise is an important part of the principles of Health, Healing and Happiness, not a direct method of losing weight.

7. Most emotional overeaters have a food addiction, a diet addiction or an addiction to one food, or a combination of these that usually results in sub-optimal mental and/or physical health.

8. The basis of addiction is emotional. Therefore, the most important work for this programme is that which focuses on healing the emotions of past trauma, being aware of harmful emotions in current day challenges and having tools to manage negative emotions for the future.

9. There are food and drink types that can hinder or help progress, based on current medical research. Therefore, it is necessary to make informed choices about food and drink that is bought, caught, harvested, prepared and eaten. Eliminating or including a food may contribute to health, healing and happiness but it does not guarantee weight loss.

10. The basic Keys to Emotional Freedom are to **Know Myself** and **Know My Worth**.

*"You have been criticising yourself for years, and it hasn't worked.*
*Try approving of yourself and see what happens."*
*~ Louise L. Hay*

# Exercise

## Affirming Energy

1. Read through the following statements, written in the present tense (because that's where they are!). I have also taken out any negative words. Read through them slowly, with real certainty and faith in your voice. This is one of the techniques of the Law of Attraction.

2. At the end of each line, and however you choose, visualise or imagine the energy from each of those statements permeating your energy body and into your physical body. Imagine that you had written them yourself. Pause and witness the shift in your energy, how you feel. Use your creative mind. Perhaps you see this energy as light, magical twinkles, medicine or fairy dust. Whatever you like, there is no wrong way to do this:

   a) My health in mind and body has improved, I practice
   b) I give permission for deep emotional healing to take place, I allow
   c) I find real, true happiness within my life, I rejoice
   d) My relationships are open and meaningful, I trust
   e) I see my life and soul's purpose clearly, I know
   f) I let go of fear and there's nothing but love, I release
   g) I am so positive about my future, I see
   h) I have limitless energy and zest for life, I feel

3. We'll be covering affirmations again in *Chapter Nineteen* - See it! Say it! Give it! Get it!, dedicated to their life-changing MAGIC! In the meantime, choose one of these and write it on a sticky note. Place it on your bathroom or bedroom mirror and every time you look into it, say those words, but more importantly absorb them into your body. Change it after a while if you like. Or place another somewhere else.

## Chapter Thirteen

# Stress and the Mind

*"A feeling is no longer the same when it comes the second time. It dies through the awareness of its return. We become tired and weary of our feelings when they come too often and last too long."*
~ Pascal Mercier

## Recognising Stress

For the recovering emotional eater, awareness of stress is an incredibly important aspect of the journey. Stress is so common that it is often incorporated into life as a norm and nothing unusual. But prolonged stress *isn't* normal for the human body, the mind or the spirit.

Some people seem to manage stress quite well. For example, in an office full of people with the same tasks, it is likely that everyone will react to stress in a slightly different way. Some will internalise their stress, pretending it's not affecting them and, for their own reasons, not want to let anyone know that they are suffering. Some even seem to be able to let it go quickly. Others will externalise their stress in some way. Everyone has a different way of feeling and dealing with it.

As an emotional eater, your way has been through food and maybe other habits or addictions too. This is a form of escaping from what you can't control and possibly don't want to face. It's been *your* way of dealing with *your* stress. You are here with this book because it's time to find some answers to the mystery and meaning of your life without hurting yourself any further. Stress has been a major factor in your emotional eating. As the pure and perfect being that you entered this world as, you have a chance to reclaim that purity. You have the right to access change and the birthright to a blissful life, but ultimately of course, it is up to you (with a little help and support along the way!) to resolve your stress.

☐ This is *your* journey, and recognising your stressors and subsequent reactions is probably one of the most important aspects of **Knowing Yourself**.
☐ A regular practice helps you to understand yourself better, clears away the veil of doubt and delay in order that you can make the necessary changes to your life, so that you are living life at its very best. That is the essence of **Knowing Your Worth**.

## Types and Causes

Some stress is **acute** – a sudden impact factor that the body responds to. This would be the typical fight, flight or freeze response. We have carried this reaction with us for all of our existence. We would have needed it to run away from animals who saw us as dinner and to run after animals to get our own. The effects on the body are the same as any stress – they are sudden and can be quite severe – but they can fade as quickly as they came. For example, exam stress, having to make an impromptu speech, a dental appointment, a car accident. The body reacts by triggering the sympathetic nervous system, but when the stressor has gone, it kicks in the parasympathetic nervous system to bring it all back to normal again.

Other stress is **chronic** – this is a relatively new phenomenon to the human race. It is the stress we feel when we are in an unfulfilling job, a challenging relationship, a demanding routine, when we have no time to relax, there seems to be no fun in life. We find ourselves complaining more, have little to say that is positive, struggle to laugh or smile and generally feel sadness, worry, grief, fear or anger most of the time. It is usually the result of a life change event that evolves into long-term stress. It is gradual and possibly less severe at its peak, but it lingers and has the potential to do more damage. Recent studies for this kind of stress have cited chronic stress as the most common cause of absence from employment today (1).

## What Happens When You Stress

The natural reactions of stress in the body are the same whether it's acute stress or chronic. This is the work of the sympathetic nervous system:

1. increased heart rate
2. breath rate increases
3. immune system shuts down
4. perspiration and heating in the body
5. reproductive function stops or is reduced
6. higher blood pressure as blood vessels constrict
7. muscles tighten, noticeably in the thighs and core
8. the digestive system stops and bowels are often evacuated
9. the liver produces more glucose for increased energy release
10. brain signals stress hormone release from the adrenal glands - adrenaline, cortisol

But over an extended period, as with perpetual, unresolved chronic stress, these initial, sudden and short-term responses become more extended and therefore it's more difficult to adjust back to normal. The resulting effect is an imbalance, dis-ease or illness. It's then quite easy to see what an extended time in a state of fight, flight or freeze may have on our health.

Compare this list with the one above to see the possible results of long-term stress:

1. heart disease, heart palpitations, irregular heart rate, heart attack
2. panic attacks, asthma
3. increased occurrence of colds, flu and infections, eczema, psoriasis and other skin reactions, hair loss
4. dehydration, reduction in uptake of nutrients, kidney and bladder problems
5. reduction in libido, erectile dysfunction, fertility problems
6. arteriosclerosis, risk of stroke, blood clots
7. neuro-muscular disorders - MS, muscular dystrophy, headaches, neuralgia, migraines, back pain, cramps
8. indigestion, diabetes and associated problems, food intolerances, IBS, diverticulitis, ulcers
9. cravings, addictions, need for energy rush
10. obesity, eating disorders including binge eating and emotional overeating

When the body is in a stressful place, it becomes acidic. Think of acid reflux, stomach ulcers, mouth ulcers and indigestion. We can take medication for this obviously, but that is not advisable in the long run. An alkaline diet can play a major part in healing the body during stressful times. But even then, if food is eaten while stressed or eaten too quickly without proper mastication, it cannot be digested properly and will only exacerbate digestive problems, including acidity.

So what is the solution? You can try to establish the root cause, possibly where this reaction has come from in your life, acknowledge and accept it, then work with the emotions in the present and try to establish new patterns of reaction. When we effect this kind of change, the body can do what it needs for you in perfect harmony with every aspect of your life.

## Causes of Stress

**Work stress**
unemployment, work pressure, not enough work, bullying, interviews, redundancy, retirement

**Financial**
lack of income, spending addictions, economic influences, losing money, divorce

**Family**
bereavement, wedding, relationship breakup, family behaviour, new baby, adoption, illness

**Education**
exams, study schedule, learning difficulties, bullying, personality clashes

**Time**
clock-watching, distraction, delay, perfectionistic/black & white/all-or-nothing tendencies, boredom

**Physical**
overtraining, overworking, competitiveness, drugs, alcohol, overeating, lack of sleep or self-care, accident, injury, illness

**Mental/emotional**
anger, jealousy, worry, fear, sadness, grief, panic, shame, sorrow, disgust, hate, hurt, greed

**Spiritual**
lack of self-worth, self-esteem, confidence, purpose, connection, drive or enthusiasm


These lists are general of course. And there will be a great deal of overlap between them. Many of the physical, mental and spiritual causes are also symptoms of another cause. How you work through the stressors you recognise will largely depend on your beliefs, values and what other stressors are present in your life. Some people manage and work through stress very well, one stress factor at a time, others try to ignore it, accepting it as normal life, then find it compacts and builds up until something has to give. What gives is usually health!


*"Many of us feel stress and get overwhelmed not because we're taking on too much, but because we're taking on too little of what really strengthens us."*
*~ Marcus Buckingham*


## Stress and Eating

I used to wonder why people said that they couldn't eat when they were stressed when it was all I ever wanted to do! When we are stressed about something, the brain sets off the fight or flight response by producing adrenaline. As well as other responses in the body, it shuts down the digestive system so that it can prepare the body to run. This can mean elimination too. It is where the term 'shitting oneself' (pardon the expression) is derived from. In total fear, this might be the body's way of getting rid of unnecessary weight to enable it to run faster and away from danger. This was a necessary reaction to the stress of our ancestors. It's sudden, it's quick and then it's over.

This is *acute* stress.

However, if the stress continues, the opposite is more often true. In all stressful times, the body also produces cortisol, which is an appetite stimulant. And it's self-perpetuating. The stress causes weight gain and weight gain causes stress. Remember that the body wants to remain balanced (homeostasis) at all times. If the stress is on-going, the body will make provision to protect itself from the possibilities of harm. It does this by asking you to eat more fat and more carbohydrates (which it can turn into fat). So that it can protect your major organs from danger, it will be deposited around your middle. Sounds so unfair doesn't it? This is a downward spiral because as the weight increases, so usually does the stress. Therefore, people who say they can't eat when they are stressed are probably suffering from acute stress. Most overeaters are suffering with chronic stress. For me, because of my crazy lifestyle and pre-existing challenges with eating, I already had a base-line chronic stress level, which would encourage me to eat more than I needed to satisfy normal hunger.

One of the reasons you are stressed is because you cannot see a solution to your problems or see a way of avoiding them, so you will turn to the stuff that helps you to forget, like comfort and convenience foods, sugar in its many guises, alcohol, even drugs. Long-term stress is usually involved in addictions. Again, the exercises and practices in this book will help you to find the solutions you seek to heal and move on with **Confidence** and **Enthusiasm**.

## Back to the Old Ways?

There is recent research to suggest that the negative effects of stress can be overcome if we change the way we look at stress as a whole. Experiments show that when we can see the benefits of stress, our health is no longer affected. This is interesting, because it is only in recent years that it seems stress has impacted our health so much. Is this because we are more aware of the dangers of long-term stress on our health? Or because we worry more about stress and our health, which in turn exacerbates it? It appears that stress is more of a threat to our health now than ever. But is it? For example, how stressful was it for our grandparents and their grandparents who lived through the effects of war? Did it affect their long-term health? Was it related to their eventual cause of death?

The new research shows that we are only at risk if we believe that stress is bad for us (2). In other words, if we believe that the physical reactions we have to stress, such as those listed above are there to help us, that they will only be temporary, and that there will be no need to panic or worry, our overall health will be maintained despite how much stress we face. This is yet another reason why it is so important to connect our body, mind and spirit – to **Know Yourself**. We have a super-caring intelligence, a deep intuition within us that has somehow been overruled by the media, modern medicine and many beliefs that are based on fear and worry.

## Mind over Matters

We have covered a lot in this book about the body's natural ways of looking after us. On the physical and scientific side, we know that the brain has great power in organising chemical messengers (hormones) to adjust the body's workings, so that we can operate as efficiently and healthfully as possible in all manner of circumstances. When people say "it's all in your head", they are right. For everything starts with the brain. It's like your central processing unit. But it is better than that. It has the capacity to work through all sorts of challenges, from broken limbs to decades of self-abuse, including eating the wrong foods, smoking, drinking and drugs. We truly are marvellous, highly intelligent beings.

If we apply that same capacity for change to our mind and spirit, we need never worry about the future of our health and wellbeing. Our potential is virtually limitless. I'm not talking about winning races in sport, building a multi-million dollar business or taking a holiday in the Caribbean, although that is possible of course. I'm talking about your personal growth, change and transformation. The internal shift. A huge opportunity presents itself, every day, for finding peace in your body, mind and your soul. A belief in this possibility is all you really need. That comes with your practice.

*"We are what we think. All that we are arises with our thoughts. With our thoughts we make the world."*
*~ Buddha*

In ancient philosophy, some of which I have studied, the mind really has three facets:

## 1. The Conscious Mind

This is the mind that you are always aware of. You may forget things of course. But the conscious mind is the one you rely on most of the time. It has your best interests at heart. It is the one you use to think about your goals, your plans, your actions and your desired results. It the mind you have used to set intentions with the workings of this book. It is a solution finder. It takes in information and turns it into possible actions. It serves you well as an emotional overeater. It's going to get you to where you want to be. It is going to help you to bring some of the theory of this book and put it into real-life practice. It is where the first four of the **7 Spells of BodyMAGIC!** are working:

1. **Idea** which becomes an **Intention** leads to
2. **Focus** which becomes **Understanding** leads to
3. **Confidence** which becomes **Enthusiasm** leads to
4. **Determination** which becomes **Commitment**

## 2. The Unconscious Mind

This is your instinctive mind. It knows how to keep you safe. When there is a car coming at you at 50mph, it is the unconscious mind which gets you out of the way. It is hugely powerful. It is where all of your reactions come from, including your emotions. Some of these reactions you were born with – the ones that save your life. Others are taught to you by the people who have been around you during your life and the experiences you have had. Whilst most of these reactions are useful and necessary, some of them are not serving you as an emotional overeater. The challenge is that, most of the time, you are not aware of them.

The other challenge is that the unconscious mind works many thousands times faster than the conscious mind. It must do this to keep us out of danger. It is full of your instincts. When that car is coming at you, it doesn't think "well if I go that way, I'm going to get wet in that puddle, but if I go back, I may not have time to turn around and therefore I'll trip over, hmmm what should I do? Maybe I should ask that man over there to save me?" No, of course not! You don't know how you get out of the way, you just do it. It's fast, it's simple and it's very powerful indeed. But it doesn't always know what's best for you because it's not conscious. It's your programming. It's like a wellbeing app that has had some peculiar updates over the years! When you set off to a restaurant with good intentions and come away having eaten totally differently and wondering "Why did I do that?" it was your *unconscious* mind that reacted.

When someone tells you that "if you carry on losing weight like this, you are going to fade away" and that drives you to the bakery to over-indulge in what you like until you are almost sick, the unconscious mind has taken over the conscious mind. At this level, you believe that you can eat and overeat as much as you wish because someone has told you that don't need to lose weight. Your unconscious mind actually thinks that if you don't, you will fade away! It's an irrational reaction. It may seem like you are out of your mind and you are (well the conscious mind is anyway!). In an ideal world you might have taken on board the compliment and then made your own conscious mind up. But before you could even think about it, you had reacted. It was like you had permission to indulge in your addiction, but really it was just your deep-rooted unconscious beliefs about survival coming out to 'help' you. Therefore, it is necessary to work with the unconscious mind to work the other three spells.

5. **Discipline** which becomes **Willpower** leads to
6. **Self-Knowledge** which becomes **Patience** leads to
7. **Tenacity** which becomes **Success** leads to

This is where the MAGIC! starts to happen. When you are able to catch your reactions to the things people say and do, however normal those words are in conversation, you are paving the way to real healing. Your body will love you for it but first your unconscious mind needs to be shown the way and reassured that you are taking care of yourself.

As an overeater who says she has no discipline, this is one of the most challenging parts of this process. But it is totally doable. The practice of Anapanasati meditation is one of the most effective ways of accessing the unconscious mind. However, all of the practices of this book will help.

*"When I look back on all these worries I remember the story of the old man who said on his death bed that he had had a lot of trouble in his life, most of which never happened."*
~ Winston Churchill

## 3. The Subconscious Mind

This is your routines and habits arena. If you have always gone to a restaurant at a certain time each week, sat in a certain chair being served by a certain waiter and had triple chocolate sundae with cream and marshmallows, it's what your subconscious mind has come to expect. So when you go in one week and they have no ice cream, how do you feel? Rationally and consciously, it shouldn't matter. But part of you, out of seemingly nowhere, isn't happy. With practice we can laugh at this. It's just an attachment to a habit and can be changed.

We are *creatures* of habit. We love continuity. It gives us comfort and makes us feel safe. As a yoga teacher I used to see the face of a student who arrived late for class and couldn't put her mat in her usual place. Of course, consciously these things don't matter. But the unconscious mind's reaction can be so strong. It can often give us a knee-jerk reaction that we later regret. But it can be trained and it can work more in favour of our **health, healing** and **happiness**. The secret is to **Know Yourself** – your habits, your routines and your attachments – and make changes *slowly*. Have some fun with these patterns and never force anything.

Recognise that some of your patterns are healthy and support your healing. Certainly the sooner your practice becomes a habitual pattern, the better! Even in the early days of your practice, you will start to see things more clearly, you will understand yourself and your worth much more, you will feel the benefits of the healing you are doing and realise that your level of happiness is going up. At this point it is quite likely that your subconscious or unconscious mind will step in again. You may get a sense of achievement, destination and that you've 'made it'. Most of us have been brought up to believe that there has to be a finishing post. Sometimes a few things can happen within the trifecta of your mind:

- The *subconscious mind* wants you to go back to what it has known for the majority of your life. It has been trained, through your experience, that you go on diets and programmes but eventually you go back to the 'way things were'. So it may trigger thoughts of giving up and going back

- The *unconscious mind* just wants to keep things safe and normal. So it may bring on thoughts of discomfort (feeling outside the comfort zone). Sometimes it may recognise change, however positive, as a threat. It likes the status quo because it has the attitude of 'better the devil you know'. It can often see change as risky business.

- This work is an amazing journey that runs alongside the journey of your life. For life-long emotional healing we need to remain conscious. The practices within this book, particularly Anapanasati meditation will help to grow your conscious mind. You will recognise these kinds of reactions and that will give you all the **Discipline, Willpower, Self-knowledge, Patience, Tenacity** and **Success** you so readily deserve. It may be hard work at times, depending on your age, your life story and your history of disordered eating and dieting. But it does get easier and the more you come to **Know Your Worth**, the more this practice becomes as necessary a part of life as eating itself.

For me, these practices are fuel for my conscious mind. I have come to think of my practice as food for my soul.

"*When my mind gets out of my way, I believe that anything is possible.*"
~ Chinmayi Dore

# Exercises

1. What have been the effects of stress on your physical health?

2. What have been the effects of stress on your mental health?

3. How do you think chronic stress affects/has affected your eating habits?

4. Do you crave certain foods or anything else only when you are stressed?

5. What are your reactions or patterns when you are stressed? e.g. When I get stressed, without thinking, I nearly always…

6. Taking into account all stress, what are the top 10 stressors in your life now?

7. Who do you find yourself blaming for your stress?

8. What acute stress have you had in your life that may have a bearing on your reactions now?

9. How might you be able to think differently about each of your top 10 stressors?

10. If you didn't feel tied to the situations that are stressful e.g. your job, your relationships etc., what would you do?

11. When you feel stressed, where do you feel it in your body? What is your body trying to communicate with you? Is it trying to help you?

12. List 5-10 people who you can talk to about the stress in your life. How might you spend some time with one of these people per week over the next few months?

13. Of your top 10 stressors, what is totally out of your control? You have no influence over these.

14. Have a little ceremony for the people who have hurt you. This is a way of cutting emotional ties, sending forgiveness and love because that's what you want and need in return. It is extremely powerful. I have done this while in the bath! Light a candle for the person you wish to release. Write their name on a small piece of paper. Set fire to the paper and repeat these words (by Doreen Virtue) as many times as you need to, until you feel that the hurt has gone:-

'(name),
I forgive you,
I release you.
I hold no forgiveness back.
I am free, you are free.
I'm sending you all my love'
~ Doreen Virtue

**Chapter Fourteen**

# A Review - Time for Reflection

*"He who would learn to fly one day must first learn to walk and run and climb and dance; one cannot fly into flying.*
*~ Nietzsche*

I love reviews!

They prove to me what I can do and inspire me to go onwards.

As well as my journal pages, I actually keep a little diary that has my intentions broken down into smaller plans and tasks. I don't just use it to remind me of what I need to do, like going to the dentist and what I'd like to accomplish; it serves as a simple reminder of what I've *managed* to do. And they are often not the same thing. Life throws the unexpected at us and sometimes, frankly, it's silly to decline! All too often, we can ask "where has the day gone?" or "I had so much to do today" and feel dejected. But for me, when I consider what I *have* actually managed to get done, and everything unexpected that has happened, I feel so much better.

What I try not to do is give myself a hard time if I don't achieve my plans. I call them intentions rather than goals because I feel it gives me more power. If I don't get them done, then there's always another time. I also believe in fate. I've missed planes, trains and even boats to go to important occasions, because something else cropped up. I've never lost any friends over it and with hindsight, I've usually been able to see why. This is an important aspect of this review. If you need to go back and work with some of the chapters again, do so. There's no time limit with this book. Obviously the sooner you integrate some of the practices of this book, the sooner you can advance on your healing journey. But everyone is different.

However, it is only practice that will make a difference to your BodyMAGIC! For that you need time.

For many of us, time is a more valuable commodity than money. My experience of the two is that it's hard to achieve a balance. When we get more of one, the other seems to diminish. I admire people who can find a happy medium between them. My very nature is to get distracted when I have the time to do so and I can very easily sit and spend hours daydreaming or surfing the net. For some people their free time is television. A big part of knowing ourselves and our worth is how we spend our time and money. Life has so many riches and a little investment in the direction of something for your personal growth and healing is never wasted. I quit TV some years ago. I still watch movies, but only if I think they are going make me feel good. I rarely watch the news or read newspapers, not because I want to hide away from the world in my ivory tower, but because of the drama around its content. It doesn't serve me or my emotions. It causes me stress, grief, anger, sadness and worry. Even the commercials! It seems good news doesn't sell newspapers or products or get high TV ratings. We have become obsessed with drama. If it disturbs *your* peace, then you have to manage that in some way that serves you.

Anyone on this path will tell you of a book or books that made a difference to their life. But they won't have just read them once and BOOM! they are a different person. If you could see their copy of the book, it's probably got scribbles in the margin, sticky notes in it and is what Amazon would call "Used - Poor!" Make *this* book your own. Don't give it away. It is a gift to yourself. An opportunity for the ownership of lasting change. It's a workbook and it's your guide. You can keep coming back to it over and over again. We rarely remember what we have read until we have fully worked on its messages.

Since my first life-changing book, I have invested several thousand pounds and months of time in courses, retreats, training programmes, workshops and classes. This takes no account of the books, papers, articles and blogs I have read around my healing and development. This book is like a specially-chosen selection of my learnings that will help you to heal emotional overeating.

You don't have to spend too much more money or time on such things, unless you want to and you have the resources. What you do have to do is the exercises and the daily practices, the best that you can. That is the priority. It is so easy and quite typical (because I have done it myself) to read a book, feel that the book has helped you and then move on to another. But this is not a novel with a dramatic ending. This is setting the stage for the rest of your beautiful, happy and healthy life.

You've spent your money. It is *time* that is needed with this book. And if you prioritise, you will find it. You cannot invest money in your happiness anyway, but you can invest your time in the healing that will give you the happiness that you desire. And I make no apologies for the amount of time I have invested in emphasising that practice is what makes things shift. I don't want you to tell people you have read this book. I want you to tell them you are living BodyMAGIC! Well, that is maybe a bit corny! But the difference is the difference it's going to make to your life.

Grab yourself some tea and five minutes to hop back over to the Contents Section at the beginning of this book to see, at a glance, what we have covered so far. Make some notes here, in your Journal and/or Gratitude Diary of what you observe.

*"One of the most dangerous forms of human error is forgetting what one is trying to achieve."*
*~ Paul Nitze*

*And to sum it all up:*

# The Keys to Freedom

Know Yourself &
Know Your Worth

# The 7 Spells of BodyMAGIC!

1. **Idea** which becomes an **Intention** leads to
2. **Focus** which becomes **Understanding** leads to
3. **Confidence** which becomes **Enthusiasm** leads to
4. **Determination** which becomes **Commitment** leads to
5. **Discipline** which becomes **Willpower** leads to
6. **Self-Knowledge** which becomes **Patience** leads to
7. **Tenacity** which becomes **Success** leads to

Lasting, lifelong **health, healing** and **happiness!**

# The 10 Principal Understandings of BodyMAGIC!

*Health*
*Healing*
*Happiness*

1. Improved Health, an integrated practice of Healing and finding Happiness facilitate life-long freedom from emotional overeating
2. Improved Health is achieved by reconnecting with Mother Nature through the elements of Earth, Water, Fire, Air, Space. This connection is through eating, drinking, moving, breathing, sleeping and other day-to-day practices in a NATURAL way.
3. Practices of Traditional Healing offer holistic solutions to the challenges of emotional overeating
4. Real Happiness is the true meaning of life and can only be found within oneself
5. Diets, including chemical appetite suppressants, meal replacement plans, fasting, nutritional adjustment methods are not effective in the long term for emotional overeating
6. Exercise is an important part of the principles of Health, Healing and Happiness, not a direct method of losing weight
7. Most emotional overeaters have a food addiction, a diet addiction or an addiction to one food, or a combination of these, that usually results in sub-optimal mental and/or physical health
8. The basis of addiction is emotional. Therefore, the most important work for this programme is that which focuses on healing the emotions of past trauma, being aware of harmful emotions in current day challenges and having tools to manage negative emotions for the future
9. There are food and drink types that can hinder or help progress, based on current medical research. Therefore, it is necessary to make informed choices about food and drink that is bought, caught, harvested, prepared or eaten. Eliminating or including a food may contribute to health, healing and happiness, but it does not guarantee weight loss
10. The basic Keys to Emotional Freedom are to **Know Myself** and **Know My Worth**

# Exercises

Having read the first thirteen chapters of this book, completed the exercises and integrated the practices into your daily life as much as you have been able, it's time to officially acknowledge some progress! The following are reflections, contemplations and practical exercises to bring together what you have covered in the book so far. This is a really important chapter. Even if you are beside yourself with excitement at what the rest of the book will reveal, please take your time with this bit. It may take you several hours, days, even weeks to work through this chapter, and that is great. This is an important milestone in this book because:

It is an important phase of **Knowing Yourself**
It plants positive experiences in your unconscious mind that will work your **Discipline** muscles, strengthening your **Willpower**
- Reviewing your progress increases your **Self-Knowledge**, giving you **Patience** with this process
Your proven success and **Knowing your Worth** will lead to **Tenacity** and life-long **Success**
and you will be super-excited (I hope!) to move on to the next phase of this healing journey.


## 1. Emotion Evaluation

Your emotions are evolving, transforming and developing as part of your healing.
This is a repeated exercise from *Chapter One* so you can see some progress.
Don't peek back at *Chapter One* until you have completed the exercise again!

| 1 = no importance |
| 10 = extremely important |

How much importance, on a scale of 1-10, do you put on:

| | | rating (1-10) | | | order of importance |
|---|---|---|---|---|---|
| a) | your weight | | | 1) | |
| b) | your clothing size | | now list them in | 2) | |
| c) | your diet | | order of importance | 3) | |
| d) | your exercise | | here > > > > > > > | 4) | |
| e) | your sleep | | 1) = most important | 5) | |
| f) | your health | | | 6) | |
| g) | your healing | | 8) = least important | 7) | |
| h) | your happiness | | | 8) | |

Compare the results with your answers in *Chapter One*. Note here any changes in your priorities and observe the reasons for these changes.

## 2. Emotion Elevator

Go back to your table in *Chapter One*. Take a little time to review each of the emotions. Do you still agree with where you wrote the date when you first did the exercise? Write a new date in a different place if appropriate. Note the progress you have made with any of your emotions.
Note the positives on your progress here.

## 3. Emotional Self-Imagery

a) Write down five words that describe how or what you *want* people to feel when they look you in your eyes and face.

b) Take a photograph of your face with your mobile device or digital camera. Do not pose for the camera! Upload the photo on to your computer, or better still print off the picture.

c) Write down five words that describe what you can see in your eyes and face from your photograph when you look at it.

How do the two answers compare? What can you identify that is still evolving and growing?
Note here or journal your reflections.

## 4. The 7 Spells of BodyMAGIC!

Using your journal to jog your memory if necessary, and referring to the **7 Spells**, have a think about some of your journeys through these spells. Then answer the following questions:

a) How strong is your **Intention** now for this book?

b) Is there anything that you need to **Understand** better to continue on with this book?

c) How **Enthusiastic** do you feel about the benefits of BodyMAGIC!?

d) How **Committed** are you to continuing with the practices and the rest of this book?

e) How powerful do you feel when your **Discipline** is challenged?

Make a note of difficulties you have encountered with **Discipline** and what you have learned about overcoming them.

f) How **Patient** do you feel with yourself that your healing is coming?

g) What **Success** have you already had with overcoming emotional overeating? This doesn't have to include weight loss.

## 5. Vision Visuals

Have you been having a good stare at your vision board? If it needs to be moved, then do so. You want to be looking at it daily or more often.

Take one aspect of it now. One of your visions. When you close your eyes, you are going to visualise that it has already manifested. Make this into a huge daydream. You can lie down to do this if you like and/or do this exercise every night before you go to sleep. Set the scene, the time of year, the surroundings, the people, all of the senses. Then make it happen in your daydream. As it happens, notice how you feel. All of the emotions and the most prominent one. When you really feel it, reach out your hand and grab it as if it were gold and gently bring it into your heart. Take several deep breaths and feel that emotion drenching every cell of your body. When you are done, gently open your eyes and smile. Journal about your experience.

Repeat this regularly to step into your visions.

## 6. Journal Review

Spend some time looking through your journal. Notice your difficult moments and days. How do you feel about them now? Are they getting fewer? Notice any difference on the days when you journal and the days when you don't. Write about the missed days now if you like in the blank pages.

## 7. Meditation

a)  Review the meditations in *Chapter Five*. Write a few notes about your progress.

b)  Have you tried both practices? Which one are you finding the most challenging?

c)  Maybe you are finding it difficult to find the time for meditation. Considering that meditation is the most important practice in this book, what changes to your routine can you make to ensure that this takes priority?

Some people prefer to meditate with others. Perhaps you can find a meditation group close to you to help and encourage you to meditate more frequently.

d)  Take a few moments throughout the day to just stop and breathe. Just bring your awareness to your breath at the tip of your nose for 1-5 counts. If you have ever heard the term 'stop the world, I want to get off!', then this is your chance! It literally gives you a break from any stress. Try it also when you are tempted to overeat. Put a tiny sticker on your phone or mouse to remind you to breathe deeply more often.

One of the Swamis I studied with used to say that we are lucky in our offices as we have little caves we can go to for a quick meditation. We were all puzzled until we realised he meant the toilet cubicles! Well I guess they are usually fairly clean, very private and extremely convenient!

## 8. Support

Are you getting the level of support you need?

Consider joining the BodyMAGIC! Facebook Page. Look out for forums and community pages that support healing from emotional overeating. There's loads of free stuff on the internet to keep you motivated. Refer to the Resources in this book. Or go to YouTube and have a lucky dip! Make it fun, but if it doesn't sit well with you, don't do it. Sometimes they are not all motivating or even informative but they can clarify what you don't want. Be an eternal optimist! Try to surround yourself with positive people who are willing to listen to your **Enthusiasm** and **Commitment** to the work in this book. They don't have to get involved, but maybe a few words of encouragement are all that you need. Don't hesitate to ask those close to you for what you need. We thrive on good support, so seek it out wherever and whenever you can.

*"Success is a journey, not a destination."*
*~ Ben Sweetland*

## 9. Food Facts

Are you eating a balanced diet most of the time which supports your health, healing and happiness?

Remember this is not about eating more carbs, less protein or any of the other rules of diets. You are learning intuitive eating and mindful munching. And although you don't have to suffer with cardboard crackers and low-fat cheese anymore, your body still needs nutrients. Are you eating 5-7 portions of vegetables in various colours and 1-2 portions of fruit per day? This will strengthen your immune system, clear your skin and make your eyes sparkle. It will also fill you up and help your digestion. Have a salad and/or smoothie every day if you can. If it's too cold, have soups and/or casseroles. And if you find things moving a bit faster than normal I can tell you that emptying your bowels 2-3 times a day is not unusual, it's healthy. It keeps your gut clear and your whole body detoxed, and ensures your energy levels are high.

## 10. Yoga

Do you have a regular practice now? Or have you preferred to attend a class? It doesn't have to be a major deal. A few of the practices in this book will do. Just start.

If you have started, how do you feel afterwards? Visit the BodyMAGIC! website to look for videos you can download for free and others you can purchase if you want to go deeper. YouTube has hundreds for you to choose from.

If you're still not convinced, ask someone who goes to yoga regularly or read some reviews. Find yourself some proof that it works!

For getting so far with this book, and to encourage you to continue, I have a little surprise for you! I have a free beginners' class for you to practice at home. So find an hour, somewhere warm, where you won't be disturbed, put on something stretchy and enjoy!

Put this URL into your browser to access the class:

www.vimeo.com/127386844

Key in your password **BeginYogin2** and enjoy!

Leave a review please. It really encourages others!

## 11. Nature

Of all of the ways of connecting with nature I have suggested, which have you found the easiest to integrate into your life? Are you feeling a little more connected with nature now?

1.  Are you able to step **outside** at least once a day and see something of nature?

2.  What changes have you made to the **food** that you buy and eat away from home? Make a note of these. Even one small jump towards more natural eating will help. Tell others what you are doing too. It's surprising how one change to your habits can trigger a small revolution within your work and social groups. Granted, family can take a little longer, but be creative with your adjustments and make it fun. Don't be disheartened if they are rejected at first. This is your book, remember! You will be

taking a small step towards a big change that is positive healing for yourself, your family *and* Mother Earth. And you will be strengthening your connection with her further.

3. How is the **water** flowing? Remembering to drink plenty of water is one of the most challenging habits to get into. What can you do to help you remember to drink water? Can you have a jug or bottle on your desk, a glass next to the sink, an alarm on your phone? Whatever works is good for you.

4. Are you able to practice deep **breathing** during the day? Like drinking water, it's difficult to remember. But there must be hundreds of times when you can do this. Whether it's while on the bus, driving your car, making your dinner, taking a shower, even just before you go to sleep. List all the times today when you might remember to do this. Or set an hourly beep on your mobile device and take at least one deep breath when you hear it. No-one need ever know! With practice, deep breathing will become second nature.

5. Are you able to **exercise** in nature? If the weekdays tick by and you never seem to get out (especially in winter), make a date with yourself, your partner, your friends or your family to get out *this* weekend, come rain or shine. If you have been struggling to exercise at all, just a 15-20 minute walk three times a week will make *all* the difference. Cycle, walk, run or even swim! Nature is nature, so wrap up when it's too cold, waterproof when it's wet, and cover up when it's too hot. You don't need to go far to appreciate beauty, even when it's throwing it down!

6. With all of this practice, are you getting enough **rest**? How is your **sleep**? You need a quantity *and* quality of sleep. There is no doubt that exercise, meditation and yoga really help with both. When sleep evades you, get up and try an extra meditation. You don't need to go far. Sit on the floor using your bed as a prop and do Anapanasati. You can easily crawl back in when the Zs start to flow again! And don't forget that **relaxation** is also important. Abdominal breathing can be done almost anywhere once you have mastered it. It calms and soothes everything.

7. Have you had an opportunity to consider natural **healing** alternatives to medication? It's important to consult your doctor if you are considering stopping any medication. But if you have a headache or a sore throat, a cut or a graze, think about nature's offerings before you run to the medicine cabinet. You will have heaps more on this in the following chapters.

8. Are you **cleaning** up your cleaning act? Have you used up all those harsh bleaches, chemicals and detergents? There's no need to throw them away. Switching to eco products is a quick win. They are available in most good supermarkets. Yes, they are more expensive. But they work well, they last for ages and they smell fabulous. You are doing your health and your family a great service by switching. And Mother Nature will love you. What's the recycling like where you are? Are you composting? Make this a bit of fun in your home if you can.

9. And last but by no means least, your personal pampering! Have you found any alternative **beauty** products and cosmetics? There are some wonderful lotions and potions around. Skip to Resources if you want a lead. If money is tight, how about asking for these for birthdays or Christmas presents?

## 12. Addictions

Having read more than half of this book, do you understand the nature of an addiction? Are you able to realise any that you have yourself?

And are you able to separate out your habits? These are things you can change if you feel that they would help you on your journey.

Do you feel that there is any area other than overeating that maybe needs your attention and that might be holding you back? Consider coffee, sugar, cigarettes, drugs (prescribed or recreational), relationships, sex. Check these against the four Cs.

Please check out appropriate Resources in this book for information and links, and take action to help you move further along your path without delay. You deserve freedom from all addictions.

Remember - this is your time.


## 13. Fads and Fallacies

In this chapter, we reviewed some of the various types of diets and we talked about how easy it is to believe the promises offered by the diet industry. If you ever feel like going back to a diet plan or programme, that's quite common. Please do your research. Look at the statistics. Understand how the famine response might mean that you are destined to fail. Don't punish yourself – you deserve peace.

Go onto the **BodyMAGIC!** website and get some help and inspiration. Try out a new healthy recipe, exercise or spiritual practice. There are lots of ideas.

If you haven't already, print off **The 10 Principal Understandings of BodyMAGIC!**

Read and contemplate them when you feel low or short on energy, over a hot cup of tea. Have a warm bath, with oils and salts. Massage your skin with healthy soothing oils. Honour the vessel that is your body with warm, nourishing and wholesome, satisfying food. Repeat a mantra that says how special you are over and over until you truly believe it. Listen to some uplifting music that makes your heart sing along too.

How are your affirmations going? Have you got one on your bathroom mirror right now? Apparently it takes 30 days for something to shift in your consciousness. Do it as an experiment! Do it now! If you haven't got 10 seconds every time you brush your teeth to affirm your worth, then you need to ask yourself why!

You are now going to take this one stage further. Here are the affirmations again:

| Statement | Score |
|---|---|
| a)  My health has improved; I practice | - |
| b)  Deep emotional healing is taking place; I allow | - |
| c)  I find real true happiness within my life; I rejoice - | |
| d)  My relationships are open and meaningful; I trust | - |
| e)  I see my life and soul's purpose clearly; I know | - |
| f)  I let go of fear. There's only love; I release | - |
| g)  I am so positive about my future; I see | - |
| h)  I have limitless energy and zest for life; I feel | - |

a)  write a number score 1-5 for how much you believe that what you are saying is true. For example, if it is difficult for you to say the words at all, score a 1. If you can easily say them into a mirror with conviction, looking straight into your own eyes easily, score a 5. Be honest. You may already be way off the starting blocks if you are already doing a lot of affirmations. But *if* there's more benefit to be had, let's get it!

b) write out all of the affirmations onto sticky notes as many times as you want.
c) put them in your diary, the pages of books you are reading, on your phone, on your desk, on your dashboard, in your pockets, on the refrigerator, in your purse, your underwear drawer, your wardrobe, everywhere!
d) for the next 30 days, whenever you see a note, read it, out loud if you can. Into a mirror if you can. Say it with passion and put some of your great power behind it.
e) after 30 days, go back to your scores and reassess your progress. Make a diary note to do this.
f) if you feel you can go further with this for longer, write them out again on different coloured sticky notes, replacing the previous month's with the new ones (the brain gets bored after a while and doesn't see them).
g) repeat the exercise for another 30 days.

This doesn't have to be a chore – make it fun, laugh at yourself. Get all of your inhibitions out so that these statements can replace them with pure personal power. The mind works better when you are having fun.

This really works!

## 14. Intuitive Eating and Mindful Munching

Here is a summary of the components of Intuitive Eating. This is really an overview of your relationship with food. It will serve you well to remember the message behind each of the components. Use this to check in with your memory now and again or let it pop up on your calendar every week or so:-

a) awareness of the diet trap
b) understanding your appetite
c) friendship with food
d) respect for cravings
e) peace in the present
f) knowledge of hunger
g) learning to leave
h) nature's way
i) emotional eating

And so to Mindful Munching! You should have had a few meals since you read this chapter so take a while to reflect on your practice, at the table or elsewhere. Here's a summary that you can copy or print out from the BodyMAGIC! website. When I eat alone, I often turn it into a ritual. I have my mindful munching notes with me and I practice each one as diligently and as slowly as I can.
It feels so awesome and liberating to do this!

1. Prepare your food to **impress**
2. Use your **senses** in preparing the food
3. **Sit** down to eat always, if possible at a table
4. Remove visual and loud **distractions** to mindful eating
5. Consider saying a prayer, a mantra or a chant of **gratitude** before you start eating
6. Avoid talk when you are chewing and **chew** it to mush!
7. Don't wash your food down with your **drink**
8. When eating, try having a little break when you start to feel **satiated**. Have one more mouthful if you like when you feel satiated, then push your plate away. Stop if you feel full, no matter how much is on your plate.
9. Do something with the food you have **left over**, aside from eating it!

Refer back to *Chapter Eleven*, to revisit more information and tips on practising these at the table. Remember a change in habits takes 21-30 days and is more effective when you change one thing at a time. If it takes a year or more to integrate these practices into your life, so be it. It's still a turnaround from emotional eating and is on the path to happiness.

## 15. The Mind and Stress

As this was the most recent chapter before this review, we shall leave out any further exercises.

This book is about the emotions related to destructive patterns and issues around food – overeating, food addictions, other addictions, body image, bingeing or dieting. Of course, your physical body will be under chronic stress with any of those. But they all mess with your head and can make the rest of your life unbearable too.

Please be extremely mindful of *any* stressors you have in your life that affect your eating habits and any food addictions. It may be that your only major stress is your relationship with food. In some ways that will make it easier for you. But if there is anything else major going on and the practices in this book are not helping, get professional advice or extra support somewhere.

If nothing else, please try to find time for yourself. If you don't like what is happening in your life, you can change the way you look at it, or you can change that aspect of your life. Only you will know what and when is appropriate. But you must give yourself time to reflect on it.

Time to contemplate your life.

Your success with this book depends on consistent, healthy habits and conscious commitment to the practices of the **7 Spells of BodyMAGIC!** In the end the biggest stressors will disappear because the overriding cause of your stress is your emotions. When the emotions are balanced, you will be able to make better decisions about your life. Even effect radical change.

Your future is now!


*"The greatest discovery is that a human being can alter his life by altering his attitudes of mind."*
*~ William James*

## Chapter Fifteen
# Traditional Medicine

*The body is a miracle waiting to happen,*
*if only we optimize its ability to do what it's made to do naturally."*
*~ Lissa Rankin*

What is traditional medicine? As modern medicine has developed over the last fifty years, you may not know much about ancient health care practices. Guardians of traditional medicine will call modern-day health care allopathic or contemporary medicine. When we are ill, we go to the doctor. He is our medicine man, she is our nurse and they are our healers. If, however, you have spent any time with holistic, alternative or complementary therapists, you may have realised a subtle yet radical difference in nature between the aims of a healer and a modern doctor. Generally, a healer's overall aim is to establish and find the deeper *cause* of illness when presented with a set of symptoms. A doctor's goal is generally to treat symptoms – with modern, laboratory-tested, synthetic medicine or with a referral for physical surgery. Doctors are usually the first port of call when we are sick, yet most of them have only 5-10 minutes to question a patient and establish a treatment plan. It's hardly enough time to establish emotional and stress factors connected with an illness.

Of course, there are many exceptions in both channels. Many doctors now acknowledge the merits of mind-body medicine. They frequently refer patients to complementary therapists to support recovery where needed. Holistic therapists too, having undergone some meaningful training and certifications, should always try to complement the medical profession's advice and know of contraindications to their therapies. They will also offer relief from symptoms.

There are hundreds of therapies not included here. Some of them are covered briefly in other chapters of this book. There are many variations on just about all of them, including those that link two or more traditional therapies together into a new one. Most of them are ancient in origin. Sizeable books have been written on any one of these therapies. This chapter is to give you an overview of just some that have helped me enormously on my journey to overcoming emotional eating and some that I have experience of, or training in, as a therapist. I have given some specifics where appropriate. The reason for putting these in this book is to encourage you to invest in yourself. And they don't all involve a pot of money. Simply getting an old bowl, filling it with warm water and adding some therapeutic oils to soak and massage your feet in can make you feel like a million dollars!

I consider myself lucky to live in the UK where we don't have to pay for health care. The only thing we do have to pay for is prescriptions. However, I cannot remember the last time I had to buy antibiotics or any other prescriptions, cold and flu remedies, painkillers, anti-inflammatory drugs or anything else. Most of these drugs are solutions to symptoms, not causes. It is only by improving the situation, lifestyle or environment that caused the dis-ease in the first place, that we can be sure of improved long-term health and vitality. The medicine will only make us feel better, but it's not healing the real problem. Drug companies are making millions from our symptoms, but most modern chronic diseases are on the increase. Very little accurate information is given on how we can prevent these diseases, especially in low income families. Sadly, charities too are driven and backed by drug companies who are more interested in finding a cure that finding out the cause.

I enjoy perfect vibrant health nearly all of the time. If my health or happiness is ever sub-par, I *always* know why and what my triggers have been and I can usually nip sickness in the bud before it takes a hold. I have so many natural medicines in my 'cabinet', from herbs to crystals, healing foods to special breathing techniques and yoga poses to specific meditations. A book of mine would not be complete if I did not share some of this wisdom with you! It's a part of my jigsaw in overcoming emotional eating.

How nice would it be to be able to spend money on a one-hour massage treatment rather than a 10-minute doctor's appointment or expensive medications! It's hard to do this when we are ill and I'm not suggesting you give up any treatment or medicines you have been prescribed. But please look after your wellness. These therapies are preventative medicine! They can also assist the body and mind in healing itself. The following offer you real assistance in your healing and recovery from overeating because they are holistic. They work on the *whole* mind, body and spirit system, bringing balance to the health of all of you.

## Relaxation mode

One of the most important benefits of all of these as a treatment is that, for the duration of your appointment, you are in relaxation mode. Remember this is a lost art for most of us. These treatments give you permission to just let go. And you start to remember how to relax elsewhere, when you have other opportunities to do so.

They are relaxation MAGIC! They let go of the stress response in your body and mind and replace it with pure healing. Science is now confirming what traditional medicine has always known. When you invest time, money and/or effort in yourself and allow others to help you, your recovery accelerates. With all of the therapies here for you to investigate further, I have listed some Resources at the end of this book.

## Yoga Therapy

This is prescriptive yoga. The therapist will offer specific yogic practices for your health and wellness needs. A class will help you enormously, but a one-to-one yoga therapy session will give you what you need *particularly*. This will speed up your healing as you will need only practice what you need to assist you in your recovery, or to enhance your health. The therapy will usually include individual diet, lifestyle, breathing and meditation techniques specific to your needs, as well as a physical asana practice. This is not the same as a one-to-one yoga class.

One of the most relaxing practices in yoga is Yoga Nidra. Nidra means sleep, but it is not to help you to necessarily go to sleep, although it may assist you to do so if you struggle in this respect. It is total body and mind relaxation. It takes your brain activity into what is known as the theta state (1).

I have another special gift for you!

Because the world needs to relax more and because of the proven scientific benefits of Yoga Nidra, I have recorded a 40-minute session for you to practice at home. Although there are quite a few books on Yoga Nidra, it can be quite difficult to find Yoga Nidra classes. So this will give you the chance to try it for yourself. Remember yoga is a science and this is your experiment in relaxation, just for you. Yoga Nidra has been scientifically proven to enhance many aspects of your health.

Enter  https://soundcloud.com/chinmayi-2/yoga-nidra/s-YI3xO

Or  https://goo.gl/c6cRBo

No password is required. Be curious, but let go and enjoy!

# Aromatherapy

Essential oils are extracted from plants and trees and are mixed with carrier oils or water, depending on their administration. They are extremely potent and should never be taken internally, without the advice of a highly-trained and experienced aromatherapist. Usually they are either massaged into the skin, where their small molecular structure allows absorption into the body's tissues, or inhaled through the nose with steam using a diffuser or a bowl of very hot water. A bath with oils would deliver the benefits into the body in both ways. Having an aromatherapy treatment usually involves massage, but not always.

There are ways you can incorporate oils at home that can really support you on your journey with this book. Try to get organic oils if you can. You may find it easier to buy some of them online where you will read about which ones are likely to help you the most, checking contraindications. Beyond that, trust your instincts as to which will benefit you. Although it's not possible to try when buying online, in my experience if you like the scent of an oil, it tends to work better. It's that sense-connection thing again! So try and sample some in a specialist store if you can. There are also many different varieties of the same oil. For example, I have found that many people don't like the scent of lavender. But there are several varieties from many different countries around the world. As an oil, lavender has great value to health and healing, so it's worth finding the one you like most.

I have chosen some common oils specifically for the emotions and stress-related symptoms. But there are lots of alternatives that have the same benefits. If you want to delve deeper into the awesome power of this connection with plant medicine, there is stacks of information on the internet. However, books are usually better-researched and written by qualified professionals.


## Easy uses

Add a total of 8 drops of one of, or a combination of oils to a bath
Add 1 drop to 1ml of a cold-pressed carrier oil such as melted coconut, almond, grapeseed or apricot kernel for massage
Add 2-4 drops in a large bowl of water for bathing feet or hands, or in a small bowl to inhale steam
Add 2-6 drops to a small amount of water in an oil burner or diffuser

- Lavender - for insomnia, relaxation, depression, acute stress, anxiety
- Peppermint - for indigestion, bad breath, flatulence, tiredness, headaches
- Chamomile - helps withdrawal from tranquillisers, nervous tension, depression
- Geranium - helps with menopausal symptoms, diabetes, relaxation, good for grief
- Rosemary - good for migraines and headaches, fatigue, diabetes, physical and mental stimulation
- Basil - an uplifting oil, great for digestive complaints including constipation, flatulence and cramps

For digestive issues, massage the blended oil slowly in a clockwise direction around the navel over the whole abdomen.

*"You're only here for a short visit. Don't hurry, don't worry.*
*And be sure to smell the flowers along the way."*
*~ Walter Hagen*

## Crystal/Chakra Therapy

Like all of these therapies, there are reams I could tell you about the wonders of crystals. They have been used in ancient healing techniques for thousands of years. All crystals help you balance the emotions. If you are a beginner to crystals, I'm going to suggest that you get a set of seven chakra stones. Each of the stones I have chosen is particularly useful for matters around overeating, but together they are also a balancing therapy for the chakras. This will serve you as a brilliant little crystal first aid kit or starter kit, if crystals are something you would like to go deeper with. All of these crystals, when used for healing, want to be near to your body. This can be in your pocket, even your purse. Some can be taped onto your skin. For this reason, tumbled stones work well as they are smooth and you will forget they are there.

Crystals are like batteries. They need to have clean connections and need recharging before and after use. You can cleanse them in many ways:

- washing in natural water (the rain, a well, stream, river, lake, sea, mineral water or water infused with sea salt)
- passing quickly through a candle flame
- smudging with sage or incense.
- using sound like tingsha bells or a tuning fork

The crystals can be recharged by putting out in the sun, under a full moon, or when there is a comet shower. A good way to celebrate the full moon is to put your crystals out for a few days in all weathers. Note, however, that some stones (not these listed here) should not be put into water as they can dissolve. Dark stones can fade in full sunlight if left out too long. I also bury my stones in the ground after use, sometimes for a day or two to clear the hucha (heavy or negative energy) after working with them and I have found this works well for any stones used on an altar or in healing, but particularly some of the darker stones and for crystal quartz.

Quartz crystals and also Carnelian will charge the other crystals when stored with them.

| Chakra | Colour | Stone | Healing - Physical | Healing - Emotional |
|---|---|---|---|---|
| **1st - root** | Black/ Brown/Red | Tiger's Eye | digestive disorders especially those of elimination - intestines, bowel, cystitis | overcoming addictions, balancing metabolism, aids depression and increases willpower |
| **2nd - sacral** | Orange | Carnelian | stomach, upper and lower intestines and gall bladder, liver and kidneys, healing candidiasis, menstrual problems, strengthens immunity | aids depression, despair, exhaustion and lethargy, balancing with forgiveness, releasing tension and increasing personal power |
| **3rd - naval/ solar plexus** | Yellow | Citrine | constipation, liver and stomach problems related to acidity, diabetes, hormone imbalances incl. menopause, menstrual cramps | reducing anger, frustration, self-doubt, replacing them with clarity, self-confidence and optimism |
| **4th - heart** | Green/Pink | Rose Quartz | migraine, clearing toxins and sluggishness in the body's systems, for sexual health, fertility and childbirth, good for cardiovascular and respiratory problems | cleansing, heals trauma including PTSD and abuse, guilt, enhances self-esteem, love, acceptance and trust in oneself and in others, good to assist in finding natural weight |
| **5th - throat** | Pale/ turquoise blue | Blue Apatite | chronic fatigue, metabolic syndrome, thyroid imbalances, tonsillitis, glandular problems, immunity, allergies | enhanced creativity and imagination, appreciation of abundance; creative solutions, enhanced communication, deeper understanding, concentration |
| **6th - 3rd eye** | Indigo | Lapis Lazuli | concentration/memory, eye/sight, ear/hearing problems, mental illness, diseases of the brain, seizures, strokes or tumours, headaches and migraines, withdrawal from addictions | balances obsession, disappointment, confusion, over-indulgences and feeling hopeless with deep knowing, clarity, objectivity |
| **7th - crown** | Purple | Amethyst | all round healer - relaxes symptoms of stress, nervous system including insomnia, headaches and migraines, clears negative energies, helps withdrawal from addictions by reducing stress | connects with your divinity, helps you to experience inner peace and equanimity, great for helping with meditation, releases all emotional traits that do not serve your higher purpose |

I have suggested some common crystals here that are not expensive. Sometimes you can be drawn to some crystals more than others. This is because you and they have vibrations that either resonate, repel or something in-between, maybe even just at that moment. I have included the colour here so if another leaps out at you for that chakra, you can be flexible with how you feel.

If you are not drawn to work with a particular crystal, you can take a 'lucky dip'. Sit with each of the crystals in turn and meditate to connect with it. For throat and heart crystals you can buy an inexpensive silver wire cage so you can keep the crystal with you all day. You can also put them in your underwear (i.e. close to your skin), your pockets or purse and under your pillow. You can even tape them to your skin for on-the-spot healing. In relaxation, you can place them adjacent to the chakras and allow them to balance while you simply let go.

## Massage

There are many different forms of massage, both traditional and modern. Massage is present in most cultures throughout the world and it's not difficult to see why it may help with overcoming emotional eating. It is balancing for all of the body's systems – digestive, cardiovascular, respiratory, nervous, reproductive etc. It replaces the stress response, whether acute or chronic, with the relaxation response. All of this rebalancing will calm and release harmful emotions, reduce cravings, increase self-esteem and strengthen immunity and resolve.

I have learned many techniques as a practitioner. And I have received many different types of massage in my travels around some of the planet. Some have been extremely gentle and with some I have felt like I've been through a mangle afterwards. For some I've been fully clothed, others naked as a jaybird! Some have been pretty scary, even excruciatingly painful. Others, I've wondered whether anything actually happened!

As a therapist, most of my clients have received massage treatments because of an injury, muscle tension or maybe back problems. Most of them come with the belief that the firmer the massage the better the results. This may be true for long-standing tightness in the shoulders or for deep tissue massage of the thigh muscles due to over-working them. But even those results would take more than a couple of treatments to really see a marked difference.

However, to have a firm, hard, stimulating massage for stress is a bit like adding fuel on to a burning fire. Stress is one of the most common triggers for overeating, so you really need to take every opportunity you can to relax. And relaxation is not easy. Maybe the first time you go for a massage, you are a little tense. But once you make a connection with the therapist and you know what it's like, you can relax a lot more. The misconception is that massage is a waste of time unless you need something fixing, even stress. But the fact is that a massage helps you to relax and prepares you for life's challenging times. There are so many benefits, physically and mentally, but they all bring the body back into balance, and that's important on your journey of a healthy, healing and happy life. That hour a week or fortnight, alongside your other practices, could make or break any of your **7 Spells of BodyMAGIC!** but especially your **Patience** and therefore your **Success**, when life throws you challenges. What's more important is to remember that you deserve it! If you feel money is an issue, learn a simple routine with a partner or friend and have a weekly exchange. Visit massage schools and get treatments from students at a reduced cost.

Here's the 'rub' down on just some of the many massage therapies you can have. All of them are worthy of individual discussion and are complete treatments in their own right, but you may find you get a combination of these:

*Swedish* - gentle and relaxing using base oils or cream.

*Aromatherapy* - gentle and relaxing incorporating essential oils to help you with physical problems and emotional imbalances.

*Hot Stone* - can be deeper and firm, uses the heat within stones to massage and relax muscles more. A therapist can also use cold stones to encourage circulation or to reduce inflammation. I have also had a similar variation of this with Bamboo Massage. With either it is necessary to ask for the massage to be light if possible.

*Lymphatic Drainage* - usually a very gentle massage to drain toxins in the lymphatic system. A useful treatment to aid detoxification.

*Reflexology* - a massage of the hands or feet. Points and areas on the hands and feet relate to different body parts and organs. Very relaxing and therapeutic for many injuries, illnesses and emotions.

*Indian Head* - usually starts with the back and shoulders working up to the head and face. Can be quite vigorous, but is extremely balancing for stress, the hormones and circulation. Oil can be used on the head but is usually optional and the treatment is done seated, fully clothed.

*Thai Massage* - is done using a combination of pressing palms, thumb presses and manipulation. It can be quite gentle or quite vigorous. It is often called Thai Yoga because of its similarity to some of the yoga poses. But all physical movement is passive. You remain fully clothed and the treatment is done on a mat on the floor.

## Kinesiology

I have found this a very useful treatment to have when trying to work out food intolerances. As you get to **Know Yourself** and what your body needs, by the practice of intuitive eating and mindful munching, you may find that you do have intolerances to certain foods. Sometimes, finding out what they are can be like finding your way through a huge maze. This treatment uses muscle testing to establish allergens and whether certain foods are raising your vital force, maintaining it or lowering it. Other ways to establish allergies and intolerances are invasive, expensive or inconclusive. For me it proves that your body knows what you need. With practice you will tune into its messages too. It has been spot on for me and my clients.

## Reiki

Increasing in popularity over the last decade, Reiki is a universal energy healing where it is sent to physical ailments or emotional imbalances via the hands of the therapist. It is simple and very effective. A therapist will often be able to 'read' the body and help you to understand what your body is trying to tell you. Reiki heals by bringing energy back into balance. The therapist has had training and an attunement to the Reiki vibration, so that he/she can pass it on to you for your highest good and wherever the healing is needed.

*"Those who can't remember the past are condemned to repeat it."*
*~ George Santayana*

## Shamanic Healing

Your willingness to try any of the following treatments will really depend on your belief system. They are neither a religious nor a new age concept. They have been passed down from ancient cultures over millennia. Evidence of shamanic healing has been discovered in the Czech Republic, and estimated to have been from 60,000 years ago. Most of these practices and treatments in their various forms were practised in different cultures throughout history, all over the world and before international communication, as we know it, existed. The rituals and healing methods were very similar between nations, although they would have had no way of sharing their philosophies. That allows me to feel that these practices are intuitive. Part of a shaman's role within a community would be like a local doctor's is today, to serve and heal people. The major difference is that a shaman's job is to find and eradicate the underlying energetic cause. The 'patient' may not be aware of this in their conscious mind. And it is often not necessary to know the cause consciously. But by removing the energy associated with the illness or pain, the person's own natural energy comes back into balance and health is regained.

This healing can be done in any time from about twenty minutes to two hours, depending on the work. Most are done face-to-face, but often some can be done remotely. The following is to give you a brief introduction to the potential of these treatments. They are extremely powerful and profound ceremonies that are done within a sacred space. It is absolutely essential that, if you are interested in any of them, you seek out a properly-qualified and suitably-experienced shamanic practitioner, whom you feel a connection with.

I have included some Resources at the end of this book if you would like to know more.


## Hands On Healing

This is healing with the power of intention. Ultimately the universal consciousness wants us to rebalance everything and everyone. The healer is merely a conduit. With the healer's intention to give healing and the subject's intention to receive it, the energy for it can flow.

If anyone ever needs any proof of this, in 1939 Semyon Davidovitch Kirlian discovered a special kind of photography that shows the life force around plants and human beings. Here, one can see an aura of light in and around both parties during a healing. And we can also see the light flowing into the subject from the healer. In removing the corner of a leaf, the aura around the original leaf shape remained. This is thought to be why amputees still feel that their limbs are present. All up for scepticism from critics of course, as with anything like this. You have to feel this energy for yourself (as in the Sami Chakuay exercise in *Chapter Nine* - Nature Calls).


## Soul Retrieval

During trauma in someone's life, sometimes a part of the soul can leave. We often see this in abuse. The person can seem to be left numb, empty and soulless, as if something is missing. Often, when the trauma happened at an early age, the person forgets what happened and doesn't know why their life seems incomplete or they are unable to move on. I believe this can sometimes be the cause of long-term depression. There are two methods of retrieving the soul part that went missing, which I have practised with clients. Both of them involve a journey to the spirit, using a rattle or drum. A journey is like a visualisation that takes you into a very deep state of consciousness.


## Past Life Therapy

Sometimes it seems that no matter how hard we try, we seem to be destined to do or not do something. It could be a past life lesson that wasn't learned that can be cleared once we know what it is. It helps our understanding to be able to heal the past life lesson so that we can learn it back in that past life and be free of it, to grow and live fully in this one. For example, in the case of an overeater, it might be that the person was starving in a past life. The therapy goes back to the past life and heals it, so that this life can be free of the fear of hunger.

*Entity Removal*

This is a very powerful treatment where energies that don't belong to us have somehow attached themselves. Often seen in users of alcohol, drugs and other toxins, the entity looks for a way into their energy field, when the recipient is vulnerable. It is believed by many healers that an entity may be the cause of some mental illness such as schizophrenia. The shaman will be able to feel and see the entity and will empower helpers to be able to feel it also. Using a special crystal, the entity is removed. It is a very powerful ceremony usually involving a fire.

*Ancestral Healing*

The shamans believe that ancestral traits go back and last for seven generations. We know that some family values, beliefs and ways are not always in the best interest of our health and happiness in this generation. This is another powerful journey to spirit to find these traits that are not serving us and heal them so they are removed from this life. It is usually done in two sessions, one for the mother's ancestry and one for the father's. It is powerful healing for our future generations too.

*Illumination Process*

This is a different approach to healing, by moving out the energy with which the problem exists. It is often not necessary to know why we experience strong emotions or feel stuck. Using one of the elements such as fire or water, a special breathing technique is used to move the energy out. It can be a very emotional experience and an amazing release. The void left by the energy is replaced by light, hence the term illumination.

The next two chapters focus on Emotional Freedom Technique and The Enneagram. I have given credit to these with their own chapters because aside from assisting your healing and increasing your level of self-care, they can be particularly beneficial for overcoming emotional eating. They differ from the therapies above in that once you understand their concepts and know how to work with them, you can practice them without a therapist because there is so much knowledge available for you.

*"Courage doesn't happen when you have all the answers.*
*It happens when you are ready to face the questions you have been avoiding your whole life."*
*~ Shannon L. Alder*

## Chapter Sixteen

# Emotional Freedom Technique (EFT)

*"Clouds open up into rain, You too should release your pain."*
*~ Terri Guillemets*

## Why I resisted EFT

There was a long period in my seeking of spirituality where I had the opportunity to learn more about EFT. I resisted because I think of myself as a traditionalist. I don't knock many modern interpretations of healing at all. But my philosophy has always been that if I want to get to who I really am, why I'm here and how I can find inner peace, then I need to find out what is the most natural way to get there. My view is that if a healing method has been tried and tested throughout many hundreds or even thousands of years, then it *must* work. And if it has been passed down from the ancients who, let's face it, probably had a greater connection with nature than we do as a civilisation today, then all the better. That philosophy has determined the essence of this book. However, when I finally did get round to finding out more about EFT, I learned that although EFT is a relatively new concept, it does have traditional roots.

You may be wondering why I have included EFT with a chapter all of its own. I came to EFT only when I realised that my insurmountable problems with food were solely and totally down to my emotions. The phrase and concept of emotional overeating came to me quite late on in my journey. I had read and almost literally digested(!) hundreds of diet solutions by the time I realised that what, and *how* I ate had very little to do with my weight. I remember reading a description of emotional overeating in the resources section of a nutrition book somewhere. Words cannot describe the sense of relief I felt. How could I have missed something so obvious? Even then I thought,

"OK! So I now know that I'm overeating because of my emotions, but I really can't do anything about it. I still have to go to work, feed my daughter and pay the bills. It's normal to be stressed and emotional, right? Isn't that just life?"

Although I had what some would call a high-powered job, a lovely home and even a *powerful* car. I was *powerless* over food. I was *powerless* over my emotions. I understood very little about true happiness back then. Happiness was a promotion at work, a day at the races, a holiday in Mexico or maybe getting a manicure. Looking back now, this proves so well to me how we can change our life, by simply opening ourselves up to new possibilities. It took me a long time. I have listened, learned and practised the teachings of many inspiring people, who talk about how changing your mindset can change your life. It's just a concept until it really happens to you. But happen it can. It happens gradually over time. So if you feel like some or even all of these concepts are way beyond you while reading this book, it's normal and it's a process. Please don't give up!

If you are travelling somewhere, it's easy to want to get there as soon as possible. So you may fly rather than driving or taking the train. It might be that you have to be somewhere quickly and that is fine. What you miss is a million views of nature, chance meetings with different people and experiencing different places with their own stories. It's hard to take photographs from the porthole of an aeroplane! But imagine the memories you can create and the gifts of beauty you can receive when you take your time.

In most of the diets you have tried, you have been set a goal weight, a goal dress size or the goal of a pair of jeans to get into. There is nothing wrong with goals, but when we make them, we have to take account of the challenges we are going to face, especially with addiction. If you are going on a diet to lose weight, but like me you have an addiction to dieting, then wanting to be a size 0 by your summer holiday is in no way nurturing for your soul. You are feeding your addiction, not choosing health. It is destined to end in more sadness, self-deprecation and disconnection from who you truly are. It's totally missing the point. There is no destination with BodyMAGIC! Its philosophy, practice and benefits are a life-long journey of **health, healing** and **happiness**. So take small steps on the journey and enjoy every day. It is no longer a task or a harsh punishment for giving in to food. You can find BodyMAGIC! in every step on that journey, in every moment. And anyway, the journey is nearly always much more fun than the destination!

The saddest thing about my life so far, when I look back, isn't giving up my fancy house or car, or giving up my job. It's not even losing my grandparents or my own mother to cancer. If it were, then I could have written a book about how, emotionally, I got back on my feet after these huge losses. On close reflection, the *real* sadness I have about my life so far and the thing I ask my mind and body forgiveness for, is all of the *real* living that I put on hold 'until I lost weight.' I was constantly fooling myself that a weight goal would make me happy. Make me a success. Make me loved. That's what we all want at the end of the day. An emotional eater wants praise for managing to lose weight, no matter what the journey was like getting there. I remember only too well the fear of meeting up with a long-lost friend, knowing that I was heavier than I was the last time we met. That I could maybe stall her and get some weight off first, so that she wouldn't judge me. Or the opposite might be true. When I had lost weight, I would hope and pray that she would notice my weight loss and compliment me on my success. It's so sad that I judged myself and others by our ability to stay slim. Even sadder that I punished myself so harshly when I didn't live up to my unrealistic expectations. Forgiving myself for ignoring real living in pursuit of weight loss has been a major and ongoing facet to my recovery.

In dieting, I was starving myself, not just of calories and healthy nutrients, but of the essence of life itself. The amount of happiness I blocked because I hated my thighs, my bloated stomach, my hips and my eating habits! The health that I blocked because I ate rubbish, processed food simply because it was calorie-counted! I refused to have any fats in my diet. And I would turn down a salad at the end of an overeating day because I thought, "It really isn't worth it now."

It's a crying shame!

*"Before you can live, a part of you has to die. You have to let go of what could have been, how you should have acted and what you wish you would have said differently. You have to accept that you can't change the past experiences, opinions of others at that moment in time or outcomes from their choices or yours. When you finally recognize that truth, then you will understand the true meaning of forgiveness of yourself and others. From this point you will finally be free."*
*~ Shannon L. Alder*

EFT has helped me to recognise many of my behaviours and most of the strongest influences in my life. It has given me the power to take the sting (emotion) out of all of my regrets and my issues with myself and others. I have gained an insight into what is really going on and how to let it go, once and for all. EFT is a gift of new life. Be open to receiving it now, as a very useful and convenient tool in your practice.

Although it is a modern concept (it has been around since the 1980s), it is rooted in the traditions of acupressure and talking therapies. Remember from *Chapter Six - Support or Solitude?* our ancestors had the benefit of a strong support network. EFT allows you to do this for yourself. It's like a combination of psychology and Traditional Chinese Medicine. EFT is often called **tapping** because that's exactly what you do with your fingers. In a certain order, you tap on certain energy points on the face and chest as if you were giving yourself an acupuncture treatment, but without the needles. It's far more convenient and carries no risk.

It's quick and is so easy to learn! It's free and it's available to anyone who wants it. You can go on courses to learn it, but to be honest, there is so much information about how it works and how it has helped so many people on the internet, you can learn it right now, in your own home, office or in nature. I did a 2-day practitioner course in the beginning and I shifted so much in that weekend, I hardly believed it myself. I have gone on to practice, study and learn from Dawson Church, Gary Craig and Nick Ortner. They have all inspired me. But it is Nick's sister Jessica Ortner who has tapped (no pun intended!) into the absolute value of EFT for women who battle with emotions and food. Her book *The Tapping Solution for Weight Loss and Body Confidence* has really nailed down how tapping can access emotional eating. She rightly says that weight loss was really a side effect of loving herself more and feeling more powerful and beautiful in her body through practising EFT.

As women, we have come to believe that power over food means being able to say no (willpower). But if that power is forced, then it's not really power at all. It's nothing but extremely hard work that just raises our stress levels further. When we are stressed, unhelpful emotions take us back to food. So all the time we were asserting our *lack* of power. EFT helps us to clear the emotions, so we can stand back into our power, release the stress and focus on health. The byproducts are everything we need to be naturally healthy and happy. The healing will be a reduction in illness, better sleep and weight loss, loving ourselves, mind, body and spirit, every step of the way.

It is MAGIC!

## Some Benefits of Tapping for Health

*Emotional* - It cleanses the body of negative emotions, i.e. the ones that don't serve you, such as fear, worry, anger etc. Instead of trying to avoid talking about them, suppressing them or just talking about their positive opposites, we go right *through* them. We can let them all out, every single last bit of the raw material that we feel! What a release!

*Physical* - It balances the chemical effects of stress and pain (1). EFT reduces cortisol. When you are stressed, your body's metabolism shuts down, so anything you do eat is stored as fat. EFT reduces these effects substantially.

*Acceleration* - EFT seems to support and amplify the benefits of other practices to address stress, such as meditation and yoga (2).

*Fertility* - stress can cause a reduction in libido, an imbalance in the sex hormones and subsequently sexual performance. The impact of EFT on stress will increase the chances of conception and reduce the chances of miscarriage.

*Sleep* - Cortisol can have a major part in keeping you up at night. Lower it with tapping and you may see a marked improvement in your shut-eye time. When you sleep well, you feel great, resulting in a more positive outlook, fewer negative emotions and unhelpful reactions, especially overeating.

*"It's all a matter of paying attention, being awake in the present moment, and not expecting a huge payoff. The magic in this world seems to work in whispers and small kindnesses."*
*~ Charles de Lint*

# How to Tap!

1.First of all, decide which of your emotions or feelings you want to work on. Consider all of them. Here's a prompt that might help you to identify, as close as possible, how you feel. But you may feel something different. Do your best to name it.

| | | | |
|---|---|---|---|
| Angry | Irritable | Regretful | Ignored |
| Depressed | Moody | Ashamed | Tired |
| Anxious | Panicky | Shy | Beaten |
| Frustrated | Sad | Worried | Overwhelmed |
| Hysterical | Stressed | Bitter | Stressed |
| Desperate | Low | Hopeless | Incapable |
| Insecure | Claustrophobic | Helpless | Unworthy |
| Lonely | Fearful | Lost | Heavy |
| Negative | Guilty | Scattered | Depleted |
| Restless | Punished | Old | Resentful |
| Shocked | Indecisive | Sick | Lazy |
| Exhausted | Jealous | Forgotten | Embarrassed |
| Grieving | Disappointed | Unloved | Neglected |
| Impatient | Forgetful | Insignificant | Hurt |

Choose one. And then think about the situation that is causing this feeling – the event, person and/or reason why *you* feel like this. If you don't know, that doesn't matter. It may be that you do not recognise exactly which emotion(s) you need to work on, but you may be able to see what the challenge is in that moment.

For example,
- ☐ "I'm really full and I still want to eat the rest of this big meal."
- ☐ "I'm taking a spoon of ice cream every time I go in the kitchen."

2. Go right into that feeling just for a moment and give it a rating between 1 and 10 (1 is hardly anything, 10 is extremely severe). This is called an SUD, which stands for Subjective Units of Distress.

3. Make a set-up statement. It goes something like this:

"Even though I _____ because of (optional), I deeply and completely accept myself."

Repeat this aloud **three times**, while tapping on the karate chop point. Use the tops of your middle three fingers. These are the ends of energy lines too.

Here are some more examples related to eating:

- ☐ "Even though I feel the need to overeat at the moment, I deeply and completely accept myself"
- ☐ "Even though I want to eat more, because it's so tasty, I deeply and completely love myself"
- ☐ "Even though my heart is longing for that X, I love and respect myself totally"
- ☐ "Even though I feel I might lose control, I totally respect and accept myself now"

Change the words to suit how you feel. You could write down a few examples of your own, if you like, to help you get used to this.

4. Then you are going to move through a sequence of tapping points. In my experience with the different teachers I have worked with, there are two starting points. Neither of them is wrong. I'm going to start with the crown, so that the sequence begins at the highest point and finishes at the lowest. It may be easier for you to learn the points this way. Whilst you are tapping, you are going to talk about how you feel. The points are as follows:-

## EFT Points Map

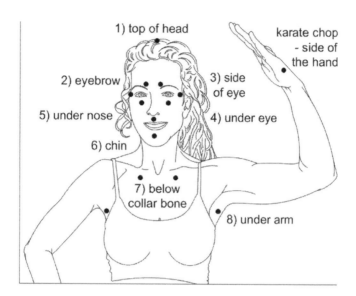

I call this the ranting phase! Get it out! You will tap whilst you speak of your emotions. To give you some ideas, you can say things like:

"Why did she do that? Say that?"
"It hurts my heart, my head, my family"
"I'm sick of this mess, cycle"
"I want to run away, hide, eat"
"I'm tired of trying, dieting, fighting"
"I hate myself, my body, my life"
"I'll never be any good, slim, happy"
"I'll always be fat, obese, dieting"
"Why does life have to be like this?"
"When is it ever going to stop? Get better?"
"I've really had enough of this/dieting"
"It's always been the same"

So you will tap for just a few seconds on each point. It's about 2-3 taps per second.

Giving you these examples makes me smile at the paradox of EFT. In most healing techniques, we are encouraged to be positive and affirm the most positive outcomes and speak with the best emotions that we would like to manifest. But in EFT we really get the chance to express ourselves and the truth about how we feel now. Sometimes with clients I can 'see' those burning emotions actually queueing up to finally get the hell out of their mouth and their life, once and for all. It is very powerful indeed.

Now is *your* time for this work.


5. If after one round or maybe two you feel a slight shift, stop. Take a deep breath and reassess your emotion level with an SUD. If it hasn't dropped down below 4 or if you feel there is more to get out, then do it again. There is no need to do another set-up statement. Just tap again through all of the points stating how you feel. If you can't think of anything to say, then repeat, repeat, repeat.

Keep saying what it is that you feel. Notice the changes. It might go something like this. Notice the shift in this example. It is important to get the worst 'stuff' out before you can feel the shift.


- □ "I want a pudding"
- □ "I could murder another glass of champagne"
- □ "Another spoonful won't hurt"
- □ "I've been good all week; I deserve it"
- □ "I'm trying to indulge my feelings"
- □ "What's really going on is......"
- □ "I can see why I feel like this"
- □ "The emotions behind this need to eat are...."
- □ "I'll probably regret it"
- □ "I am actually ok"
- □ "I'll feel better for not eating it"
- □ "I know that I'm overeating because......"
- □ "I feel helpless"
- □ "The real problem here is...."
- □ "What I really need to do is....."
- □ "I really need to talk to"
- □ "I'm so proud of myself and my growing willpower"
- □ "My practice is paying off"
- □ "I have control over my health"
- □ "I am no longer tempted"
- □ "I can try just a spoonful if I still want to"
- □ "My healing is so important to me"
- □ "I feel in control of my body and its health"


Keep tapping until there is nothing more to rant about it. Then check in again with a score. Once you are at 1 or 2, you are done.


**Getting to the Real Reason**


It may be that while you are tapping on one thing, which you thought was the most important thing to deal with, you discover that there is something bigger and more important underneath. You can stop, go back and do another set-up statement, repeat it three times and tap on all of the points in sequence once or twice until you clear this too. This is very common and is one of the benefits of the technique. It goes in, digs deep and finds out what really needs to be worked on.

*"If you don't deal with your demons, they will deal with you, and it's gonna hurt."*
*~ Nikki Sixx*

Be brave, face your fears around the emotions of your past and you will move forward with new hope and love for yourself beyond your dreams. I have some shamanic wisdom to share with you.

## Free Learning Resource

If you want to see a brief overview of the incredible results of EFT which can be found in every aspect of health, check out this seven-minute video on YouTube :
**EFT (Tapping) Intro by Gary Craig, EFT Founder.**

Also look for a demonstration to help to get you started. One I recommend is again on YouTube and is well worth 9 minutes of your time to get a great idea of the practice:
**The EFT Basic Recipe by Founder Gary Craig**

There are many other videos on You Tube specific issues that EFT has been proven to be very effective. Have a route around and you will be encouraged to give it a try. You will note some slight variations in practice with the EFT points and order. This is not important as the results are as effective.

It costs nothing to learn and practice EFT but it will enhance your self-worth by millions!

## Wise Words

Apologies for the language, but there is really no other way of putting this. A few years ago, at a shamanic retreat I attended in the UK, a Native American Indian said something to us all about fear in healing. He said that most of us have shit that needs working through, but we avoid it because it stinks really bad. And no-one wants to walk through shit, even if it's our own! However, the truth is that the shit is not the huge deal that we think it is. It's just a thin layer of ourselves that we believe is huge because of the emotions attached to it. On the other side of that stinky veil is paradise. We are so close to it all of the time. But the emotions fool us into thinking otherwise. When we face it, work with and through it, we realise that it was pretty easy really and future healing becomes not only possible but absolutely inevitable. What a revelation!

EFT is like that for me. It gives me the opportunity to work through what I consider are huge issues, when really, it's just my unconscious mind trying to protect me by getting me to suppress my emotions, as it perceives them as harmful. This can go on for years. This programming means that we avoid our personal and spiritual growth because we fear that the stress will be too much. This shaman made a further point to us about avoidance. He said that if we don't work through these problems, either as they happen or when we realise the effect they are having on our happiness, they travel all the way around the Earth and hit us again. Only the next time they hit harder. EFT is a great way to heal a lot of stuff in a very short time, with minimum effort or pain. Healing doesn't have to be hard work. But you have to have an **Idea** and **Intention** for the healing to begin with.

## Integrating EFT

This may seem like a long process but it can be done in just a couple of minutes. I have tried to give you as many examples as I can. But after a couple of times you will know what to do by heart. The thing most people forget is to give the emotion an SUD. This helps you to realise the effectiveness of the practice and the amount of transformation that can take place in such a short time. It is MAGIC!

There are a couple of ways of getting more EFT in your life.

1. **Purposefully** - spend a few moments before or after your affirmation in the mirror, morning or night, working on some emotion that you feel ready to identify and move through.

2. **Incidentally** - when a strong emotion comes up, whether it is driving you to eat or not, stop what you are doing, get yourself some privacy and move through the process.

I have included a brief summary of EFT in *Chapter 24* - Emergency MAGIC! as it is perfect to use in 'emergency' situations, i.e. those where your **Discipline** is exercised. It is a useful tool in your 'first aid' kit and with practice, can give you the willpower you need without effort.


*Joy and woe are woven fine,*
*A clothing for the soul divine.*
*Under every grief and pine*
*Runs a joy with silken twine.*
*~ William Blake (1757-1827), "Auguries of Innocence"*

## Chapter Seventeen

# The Enneagram

*"Courage doesn't happen when you have all the answers. It happens when you are ready to face the questions you have been avoiding your whole life."*
~ Shannon L. Alder

## Introduction

If one of the keys to overcoming overeating is **Knowing Yourself**, then the Enneagram is an extremely useful tool to developing **Self-knowledge**. For me personally, it was one of those light bulb or 'A-ha!' moments that really helped me to identify my *helpful* characteristics that I could develop more, and the *less helpful* traits that needed a little work. Acting on both ends of the spectrum and everything in between, working through the **7 Spells of BodyMAGIC!** will also reveal to you, unquestionably, **Knowing Your Worth**.

The Enneagram is an angular symbol within a circle. Where the points terminate at the edge of the circle, a number is given. Each point has a number, clockwise between 1 and 9, representing the nine different personality types.

The Enneagram started to become popular from the 1970s, and its popularity has spread, probably with the development of communication, the internet and the amount of business modelling that has evolved out of this kind of work. However, its philosophy is thought to have developed out of the Pythagorean era. What matters is its ability to help you see the intricate detail of yourself and yet your biggest and brightest self also.

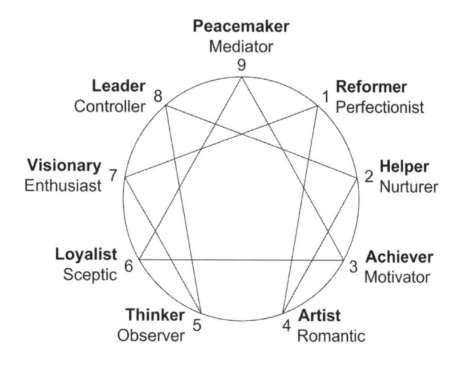

# My Enneagram Experience

I stumbled upon the Enneagram, some would say, by accident. Now I realise that it came into my life just at the right time (by MAGIC!). I was at an Emotional Freedom Technique weekend retreat in a beautiful area of Scotland, learning and sharing EFT techniques, when the facilitators introduced the Enneagram to the group. I was moved to tears, as were most of the others in the group during that weekend. We know that we are a body, a mind and a soul. When we are born, they all work in perfect harmony. As we grow up and learn how to communicate with others, it is our personality or ego that then separates body, mind and soul and causes suffering. The *reactions* to these divisions and therefore, *conflicts* between the body, mind and soul, are our emotions. This was a huge revelation for me as it was for everyone which sent me on a new, broader journey of understanding and healing.

The Enneagram will give you a new insight. It's that recognition of yourself, your challenges and your qualities, that will really help you on your journey to BodyMAGIC! If knowledge is power, then the Enneagram will supercharge your healing in overcoming emotional eating.

# Basic Observations of the Nine Enneagram Types

## Type 1 - The Perfectionist

These types will set high standards in everything they do, and expect others to do the same. They do not suffer fools gladly and have a tendency towards anger and resentment when things are not done their way. They have trouble accepting situations and people as they are. In extremes, perfectionists can become critical of others and themselves hypocritical as they struggle to perform and live by their own ideals. However, their intentions are for integrity and doing things in a just and proper way. They want to be seen as hard-working and committed to what they feel is right.

## Type 2 - The Giver

Givers go out of their way to help others, often to their own detriment. They want to feel loved and appreciated and when imbalanced can be quite manipulative. Then their love becomes conditional. They hurt when people don't show them the love that they feel they give to others and this can manifest in resentment and bitterness. Givers have trouble looking after their own needs, looking to others to define their worth. They believe that love has to be earned. They want to be known as helpful and kind.

## Type 3 - The Achiever

Image is everything with these guys. They usually dress to impress and put a brave face on all of their internal challenges. They set clear and tough goals and always seek recognition and reward. Threes will do whatever it takes to get the status they desire, often appearing harsh, unfeeling and even deceitful. On the flip side, they can offer a great deal of hope and inspiration to others. They are busy people and get things done. They hate to fail at anything and easily dismiss their shortcomings. They want to be known as successful and affluent.

## Type 4 - The Individualist

Fours are self-aware, analytical and sensitive. They usually tend to be quite shy and often like to retreat into the background when in groups. They can be demanding emotionally and obsessive. They are great at self-knowledge and when they are ready will find creative solutions to finding spiritual and emotional growth. Events are often epic dramas. They can overlook the simple pleasures and routine joys in life. They want to be known as individual and unique.

## Type 5 - The Observer

These are the information gatherers. They like to research, and believe wholeheartedly that knowledge is power. However, they make a lot of assumptions and can often fantasise. Out of balance, they seem to be detached, aloof and a loner. They can withhold their gifts and hold back from sharing what they know. In balance, they are innovative and wise with great ideas and constructive problem solving. They want to be considered competent and well-informed.

## Type 6 - The Guardian

Sixes generally err on the side of caution and try to forecast trouble before it happens. They tend to be pessimistic, although they would see it as realistic. Their main focus is safety and security, but they will often have moments of breaking all the rules. They can be defiant with authority. They tend to be skeptical of change and new relationships but once they trust someone or a process, they are helpful and faithful. They like to be known as loyal and reliable

## Type 7 - The Enthusiast

These types are playful, fun and cheerful. They love to take new ideas and plan every detail. They know how to make things happen, but they get bored easily and have trouble finishing tasks. This can lead to a lack of discipline and focus. They love to be around people and discuss new ideas and plans and are optimistic They have a tendency to avoid pain. To avoid this they will often over-indulge in pleasures to escape the uncomfortable. They want to be known as fun and a nice person to be around.

## Type 8 - The Leader

Eights are articulate and confident people. Their strength of will pushes them to do whatever is necessary to get what they desire. They are more than willing to challenge injustice and people who procrastinate. They can however be defensive, confrontational and overpowering, although they believe that they are trying to help and encourage. Their fear is being vulnerable, as they hate not being in control. Eights hate asking for help. They want to be known as strong and powerful.

## Type 9 - The Mediator

These types will do whatever they can to keep the peace. They hate confrontation and will resist discussing problems that are uncomfortable. People-pleasers, they will often give in to the demands of others, ignoring their own views and preferences. They hate taking sides and prefer to sit on the fence. If they feel cheated they will often withdraw rather than defend themselves. Difficult situations can make them anxious. But they are positive people with a bright outlook and great sense of humour. They want everyone to think that they are OK.


Not only has it strengthened my EFT practice by knowing myself better, it has absolutely rocket-fuelled my power to recognise the emotions that had, for most of my life, driven me to the overeating picnic site. This subtle piece of knowledge has catapulted my personal, spiritual and emotional growth into overdrive.

Don't get me wrong, I'm no expert. I've taken on this knowledge fairly recently compared with the other practices given in this book. I've read a lot (please see below and the Resources Section), but initially embraced the teachings quite light-heartedly. In the beginning, I thought of the Enneagram as just a bit of fun, rather like reading my horoscopes in the newspaper. Very quickly, I realised that it is far more accurate than anything I have ever studied. What's more, it doesn't just tell you what you are like *most* of the time, but what your other influences can be *some* of the time. It allows perfectly for the variations that life brings and the strongest influences around you. Even better than that, you can find heaps of developmental coaching available to help you to unfold the mystery of yourself and blossom into each beautiful aspect of your potential being.

## Delving into Discovery

One of the most comprehensive books I have read on this work is *The Wisdom of the Enneagram* by Don Riso and Russ Hudson. They also have a great website – www.enneagraminstitute.com where you can take a full and comprehensive test to discover your personality type. For me, it was fairly obvious from their Quick Test. Read through the paragraphs, choosing one from GROUP I and one from GROUP II that most accurately describe your personality. The weightings may give you a more accurate result, but for me it was fairly obvious without them. If you find that this test is inconclusive, please take one of their more in-depth tests. The first thing is to discover what type you are.

## Incorporating the Enneagram into your Practices

Once you know what type you are, what can you do about it? Of all the methods in this book (and I urge you to try all of the practices at some point), there will be one or two that you find easy to practice and one or two that you just can't get to grips with. This is likely to be reflected in your Enneagram type. It might be that one of the methods is actually bringing up unhelpful emotions, for example. The Enneagram will show you why that might be. There might be a practice that you find very easy, but is really not helping you much with overcoming overeating. Perhaps it's not giving you the change that you need to shift your paradigm, because it's something you have done a lot of already. You will learn why some things work and some things don't from the Enneagram type you are, and your biggest influences.

I love the Personal Growth part of the Enneagram Institute's website. If you sign up for their mailings, they will also send you a 'Thought for the Day', giving you just one aspect of yourself to be aware of over the course of each day. And it's free! It could be something you write in your diary or on a sticky note on your computer, to encourage you to reflect frequently during your day. For me it's just a little reminder of my challenges and how I can work with them.

This work, for me, has become a bit of a hobby. I take its philosophy seriously, but it gives me a chance to laugh at myself too. That's an important part of **health, healing** and of course **happiness!**

The Enneagram helps me and my tendencies, but it also helps my relationships. I recognise the types in many of my friends and family and it allows me to develop a great deal of understanding, empathy and learning in my interactions with them. There are other great resources for this listed at the end of this book, within which the relationships between types are discussed.

On the Enneagram Institute's website, they show a very useful table of the types and their usual eating disorders and addictions (1).

# Exercise

1. If you have been able to wait until the end of this chapter without doing the test, then now is the time to discover your type. Go to the Enneagram Institute website or any other resource and take a test. If the results are inconclusive, there are more in-depth tests available, some for a small fee.

2. Write down (below) some of the key words from the descriptions above (The Nine Personality Types of the Enneagram) that describe your **challenges** and are possibly affecting your relationship with food. Next to these words, write an emotionally-driven **action** that could heal these traits.

3. Then write some **affirmations** based around the opposites of your most challenging traits, using the Emotional Action words you have selected.

| Challenges | Emotional Action | Affirmations |
|---|---|---|
|  |  |  |
|  |  |  |
|  |  |  |
|  |  |  |

For example:

**Type 1 The Reformer** - the words *might* be

| Challenges | Emotional Action | Affirmations |
|---|---|---|
| Impatience | Compassion | I allow things and people to take the time they need. I understand that my idea of perfection is different from others. Where I am today is also perfect. I'm grateful for the opportunities I've had for my personal development. I am doing the best I can. I understand that I am human and I make mistakes, as do others. Life has many colours besides black and white. This gives life its beauty! |
| Perfectionist | Acceptance |  |
| Self-critical | Gratitude |  |
| Resentment | Forgiveness |  |

4. Incorporate one or two or more of these affirmations into your daily affirmation practice for 21-28 days.

5. Journal about your findings about your Enneagram Type and your affirmations. Notice the change over your affirmation period.

## Chapter Eighteen
# The Seven Seldom Sins

*One man's pleasure is another man's poison*
*~ Lucretius*

From the words and meanings in this book so far, we already understand that being told to eat *this* food and not *that* food is what we have come to know as a **diet**, and they don't work, right? So you may be wondering why, on this beautiful Earth, I am asking you *not* to eat seven *things*! Notice, if you will, that I'm not calling them foods. Most of them are sometimes called 'non-foods'. They do more harm than good in the majority of people and they have all gone through some pretty radical processes to end up either on your plate or in your cup.

Granted, some of us can smoke, drink alcohol, eat a sugar-loaded diet *and* live a stressful life until we are in our 90s, but these are exceptions. The truth is that although we are living longer (because of advances in medicine and knowledge of very basic nutrition), an increasing majority of us are spending old age in ill-health. The way the next generation is eating, they are unlikely to live as long as we will. In the USA, there has been a massive increase in health insurance costs. Claims are becoming more prevalent for lifestyle-related diseases such as diabetes. Alzheimer's and dementia are also on the increase and research is demonstrating that the western diet of processed and refined grains probably has an impact (1).

This has been a very interesting chapter to write. In my research and my experience, there are many differing views on eating 'policies'. Even some vegans who eat the same foods argue about their reasons for doing so. It is such *personal* thing. And as overeaters with emotions, arguing our beliefs about food can add even more fire into an already volatile environment.

Then there's all the conflicting research about the foods I have listed here. Each one is strongly debated. You only have to read a blog on something about healthy food and there are conflicting comments underneath. It seems that a piece of research on one food can be completely and understandably revoked in favour of other research. It's a minefield.

Rats are often used in research and experimentation with diets, certain foods, even exercise. In another journal however, the use of rats can be totally refuted because of the very differences between our growth and development and a rat's. So in that case some, like me, would call this a waste of suffering. I totally disagree with the abuse of any animals for *any* reason. However, if the results are there, then it is my view that those animals should not have been abused in vain. The campaigning for this practice to stop is for another time and place. In writing this book, I have an opportunity to share some of the results of their sacrifice.

The words in the last paragraph may stir some reaction in you and that is totally fine. We are all allowed our point of view. It is in the acceptance of others' views that we find peace and freedom from emotional reactions, such as overeating. If you are to evolve as a person in a positive way that nurtures your body and mind's health, then you have to practice acceptance. There is so much suffering in the world and we can only do so much in this short lifetime to effect change. If we are to love, respect, serve and change the world (including for rats), we need first to love, respect, serve and change ourselves. A life of emotional overeating shows not only a great imbalance in those traits, but also that we need to learn more about ourselves, our values and therefore our worth.

## Know Yourself and
## Know Your Worth

As we become more connected to nature and develop our consciousness, we don't have to read journals and bibles to know what is helping or hindering our progress. Even in my strict Catholic upbringing, I was taught that I have a conscience – the power to know what is right and what is wrong. That was in regard to **doings** - our deeds and our words. But we are more than doers. We are human **beings**. In our being, as we become more in tune with ourselves and our place in the world, we are able to make wise and profound decisions about what serves us *and* our world and what doesn't.

I am sharing my thoughts with you as they have formed *their* part in *my* journey. It is my view of the world. It may not suit your morals, beliefs or understanding of what is right or wrong in your world. I accept that totally. And you do not have to change anything until you are ready and if you feel it is right for you. All I ask is for you to consider the information you have access to now and make changes if you feel it is necessary.

*"Magic is a matter of focusing the disciplined will. But sometimes the will must be abandoned. The secret lies in knowing when to exercise control, and when to let go."*
*~ Marion Zimmer Bradley*

## Personal Power

As we have discussed already, in working through the **7 Spells of BodyMAGIC!** the biggest challenge with any **Intention** is the **Discipline** stage. By working with our practices regularly, we are flexing and strengthening our **Discipline** muscles, which ultimately give us the **Willpower**. In that moment of choice, not only are we able to catch and intercept those addictive tendencies and habits of our past, we are able to consider how we will feel afterwards.

Once you decide that you are not going to beat yourself up the next day and week, then commit to that, relax and just enjoy it! You will also realise you've found some BodyMAGIC! when you can foresee any guilt following an indulgence and you can happily refuse, abstain and move on.

That's what I call personal power!

You may have more than those here, or you may think some of these are fine. Try to let go of any attachment to these concepts. If you are not sure whether you have any attachment or not, try going without them for a week. Notice your cravings. Is this habit or is it an addiction? If you are unsure, check in with the four Cs in *Chapter Ten* - Habits and Addictions. Give yourself permission to work through these if they are troublesome. Go inside and find out for yourself whether these things are working with or against your **health, healing** and **happiness**.

## Never Say Never!

You may be thinking, 'Here we go again, more restrictions. Is this not a diet?' And you might be right. If you live on these foods, I won't lie, this is going to take a bit of time and effort on your part. I have called then seldom sins because that is what you are aiming for. Some of these, you may in fact be happy to see the back of. Coffee has been a quick win for me. I realise that I only want it because I don't want to be the odd one out. Now that doesn't bother me. I don't consider myself odd but rather unique, so drinking coffee doesn't matter. It's incredible how you can reverse a trend too. People are always interested to know why I don't drink coffee and what I love instead. Often they follow, especially when they know the facts.

Whatever you set as your parameters, aim to stay within them 90% of the time. The 10% allowance is there for you to enjoy without remorse and won't be enough for you to sink back into any old non-serving ways.

I'm no angel. There are certain times when I allow myself one or two of these. As the years go by, I *naturally* seem to want all of them less and less. There are rare occasions when I do and I find that as long as I don't repeat them day after day, my health and healing are unaffected. The reason for this, I believe, is that I have become so detoxed and my systems are working so efficiently now that I'm able to work anything like these things out of my body very quickly, without too much damage and with minimum effort. Paradoxically, when I do have them, sometimes I get a small reaction. I'm likely to feel some hangover, such as a little puffiness, lethargy, bloating, indigestion, mucus or headache. Nothing serious – just a little reminder from my body that it's happier without them. I always enjoy them without guilt and shame, and without any possibility of regret. My peace with myself remains intact.

Other sins are seldom indulgences and some still present a challenge. I no longer berate myself when my best intentions deteriorate. It's all a fantastic journey. My **Self-Knowledge** is to see how far I've come and congratulate myself. The *only* way forward now is improved health. This gives me **Patience** and **Tenacity**; however small those steps are towards my **Success**.

I have listed just seven 'sins' that will quite possibly hinder your progress with BodyMAGIC! But of course there may be more or less for you. You may find you have to do some personal searching within yourself. If nothing else, in the spirit of a changing relationship with food, your habits and lifestyle, try some of the alternative suggestions I offer. You may be pleasantly surprised!

*"Habits are safer than rules; you don't have to watch them. And you don't have to keep them either. They keep you."*
*~ Frank Crane*


## Seven Sins (because none of us are perfect!)


### 1. Coffee

I recently spent a month in the USA with friends and family, and I'm afraid it is my observation that in all the world that I have seen, coffee is one of most defended legal addictions I have ever known. And I'm not surprised. Corporate coffee shops and francises sure know how to load in the caffeine! They are changing the expectation of the masses to wanting long, strong coffees with sugar and milk. It's a total health nightmare. And it's the same in cities all over the world. When I worked in a big city, people would bring a huge coffee to work with them and claim that they wouldn't be able to function without it. It's not until you take a huge step back that you realise just how addictive it is. It's an expensive addiction too. Just two large ones cost more money than smoking ten cigarettes a day!

While I was in the States, I had a few cups in gorgeous coffee shops. These places are no different from bars serving alcohol, or parlours serving ice cream. I'm no scientist, but I did a little research of my own. After just one cup I felt jittery, awkward, even paranoid. My pee smelled (yes, I know, disgusting!) and I felt poisoned. This was strong stuff! I repeated this over the next couple of days, having on average two cups of organic, fair-traded coffee a day for three days, with no change to my diet. I felt very strange. My thighs felt sore to touch. Was this the cause of my cellulite? Far from coffee being diuretic, I actually felt inflamed and bloated. By the third day I had an upset stomach and the symptoms of IBS, which I hadn't had for a decade or more.

This stuff is toxic. It's a drug. Just because it's legal doesn't make it healthy. I'm very dubious about any of the research to the contrary. I do believe that in a few years, coffee will be as socially and healthfully unacceptable as sugar is becoming today. And most of my coffee-drinking friends don't take sugar, so the caffeine *is* the addiction. If you drink it regularly, try coming off it. You are likely to have withdrawal symptoms. Most people have headaches for days or weeks. If that's not an addiction, then I don't know what is.

Coffee is a dried and roasted product, some would argue processed food, that sends the adrenals into overdrive. That cannot be good for anyone, especially in light of the increasing levels of diabetes in the world. If you drink more than three cups of strong coffee a day, I suggest that you cut down first. Have two per day for one week and one per day for the following week. If this is merely a habit for you, you may be able to quit a lot sooner.

For some it is the ritual of it all - meeting a friend mid-morning, a business meeting in a hotel foyer or a nice way to round off a dinner. Try tea instead. There are lots to choose from and black tea has a little caffeine, so may help you to come off coffee more easily. Once you are detoxed from caffeine, you will feel better. If you are at home when you drink it, you may be wondering what to do with that very expensive piece of furniture called a coffee machine. How about these for some alternatives?

*Yerba Mate* - a tea from Argentina. Has huge benefits to health as it is high in antioxidants and can give the same 'awake' feeling as coffee, without the crash. When sweetened with a little natural green stevia power, I find the taste quite palatable. Use it like ground coffee or tea leaves. But don't go mad with it as it can keep you awake if you drink it later in your day.

*Dandelion Coffee* - one of my personal favourites. The root of the dandelion is slow roasted until it is brown. It can be put into the coffee machine as you would do with whole coffee beans, or you can grind it up with a coffee grinder and make it in a cafetière. It is particularly nice with coconut milk and a tiny bit of stevia if extra sweetness is needed.

*Green Tea* - these days the supermarket shelves are full of green teas and their blends with other teas. There is loads of choice. I have enjoyed a few of them. Some I don't like too much. I think the secret with these, if you are using a tea bag, is to take it out within about seven minutes. After this they can be really bitter. Again, stevia to the rescue if they need some healthy sweetening. I really enjoy green tea with grapefruit and green tea with goji berries. The fruit seems to balance the bitterness of the tea well.

*Black Tea* - this is still a great tradition in the UK. We'll forget that within that tradition, it's usually served with white bread sandwiches and cakes or scones with jam and clotted cream! If coffee wasn't so convenient on the streets of the UK and we weren't so addicted to the large amounts of caffeine we get from even a medium cappuccino, I believe that many local independent cafes and tea shops would not have gone out of business. I have seen many local businesses struggling to compete with the corporate coffee shops on the high street. It's such a shame, because the money from all those expensive coffees doesn't go into the local area. We can often forget how important it is to buy local.

Tea is a great alternative to have when you are meeting up with friends. Most places offer herbal alternatives if you are going cold turkey. You can often get a pot to share with friends and I think it makes a really nice way to socialise. If you like a milky drink, try a Chai Latte, a decaffeinated black tea, Earl Grey, Darjeeling, Honeybush or Rooibos. They are all good with or without milk or milk alternatives.

*"The easier it is to do, the harder it is to change."*
*~ Eng's Principle*

## 2. Processed food including unhealthful fats

Elsewhere in this book I have discussed the balance of time and money. It seems that when we have an abundance of one we lose some of the other. I have been on both ends of the see-saw and I have to say that for me, having less money and more time is far preferable. In an ideal world, we will all be time-efficient in making more than enough income to sustain a fulfilling and healthy life. For many that seems like a dream. However, when we put **health**, **healing** and **happiness** first, then time has to be the most important aspect. No matter what you are earning, even if it's only temporary, when earning it affects your health and wellbeing then either you can't enjoy your income or you are striving for the next 'thing' that never gives you the **happiness** you expect it to. Overcoming overeating becomes almost impossible, because you relinquish the opportunity to **Know Yourself**. Furthermore, **Knowing Your Worth** becomes a judgement only of what you deserve financially, not your level of **health** and **happiness**. Unless you are already really wealthy and have a cook, time constraints mean that often you 'make do' with fast food that is rarely healthy and involves the minimum of planning and effort. We can often convince ourselves that we deserve such a treat, in effect that we would rather drive to a restaurant or collect a takeaway or purchase a microwave or oven-ready meal, than stir-fry a few tasty vegetables with herbs and spices and boil some brown rice. And don't forget the stress factor will increase adrenaline and cravings so our **Willpower** will be stretched to the max. Often we are too tired to give a damn about what we eat. We just want to eat. But you can STOP! - step back and have a think about alternatives. I've become very good at this now, and it doesn't take much practice.

Here's why it's important:

I.   Most fast food contains flavour enhancers. This can be anything from table salt (with its own additives), refined sugar (that's what you are really craving, although you probably don't realise it) and stuff like Monosodium Glutamate (MSG). A few years ago, I thought it would be a good idea to go to a Thai restaurant for my husband's birthday, but we were very ill the next day – stomach upset and abdominal pain, dizziness and brain fog. We both had different dishes. So I called the restaurant and every other Thai restaurant in my home town and they all admitted (without reluctance) to using MSG in their food. We had just returned from Thailand after a five-week trip and had no problem. This stuff is toxic! It's a known carcinogen and can mess with your hormones, your brain and your heart. Dr. Frank Lipman, founder of the Eleven Eleven Wellness Centre in New York, says that the only way to ensure that you don't eat MSG is to cook for yourself (2).

II.  Very little of what you buy is actually food. Even putting aside the long-term costs to your health, these businesses make hefty profits from rubbish. The reason why they are so cheap is simply because of the quality of the food. Most of it is non-food or mass-produced in appalling conditions. More and more we are discovering that ingredients are far from what they claim to be. Even blueberries (ordinarily the healthiest part of a muffin or breakfast cereal) are being faked (3). If you truly knew what went into your fast food treat you not only would avoid them yourself, you'd be telling your friends!

III. Little of what you get, even in restaurants, is fresh. Many eatery pubs in the UK seem the perfect solution for families. They have children's portions, unlimited fizzy drinks and play areas. My daughter has worked in several of these places and most of the food has been prepared in a factory, delivered frozen and then microwaved by the staff. The sprig of parsley and salad garnish might make you think it has been freshly prepared. The truth is that there is only a small margin to be made from fresh local food, so to get customers in the door, they have to cut corners. I'm sure that there are some great independent pubs and restaurants around where the food is freshly cooked but you usually have to pay a lot more for them.  Which leads me to…

IV.  The cost is so much higher! When you look at the cost of your weekly food shopping, you get really good value from doing it yourself. When you add up the cost of the ingredients without buying soft drinks, snacks, biscuits, cakes and sweets, you realise that it is so worth it. The shocking fact is that I spend the same amount of money on food as I did twenty years ago. Yes! Really! Why? Because I very rarely buy any of the items listed below. Next to each of them I have given one alternative option, but there are many. The important thing to consider is the amazing amount of nutrition I get from the replacements. Furthermore, we always have an abundance of produce all week. Often I'm making stir-fries, salads, soups and smoothies to use up what's left before market day.

V.  Quite often when we make an impromptu decision to eat out or get a takeaway, we end up wasting food in the refrigerator that was planned for cooking. We are then disconnecting from our food, rejecting food that is good for us and throwing away our great **Intentions** for health. And while we think that we don't have enough time, we are getting in our car, driving to the supermarket or restaurant, queueing for goods or a table and afterwards, driving home again. Usually we could've prepared and enjoyed the most nutritious and delicious meal in the comfort of our own home and washed the dishes in that time!

VI.  You will find that many processed foods are cooked with trans or hydrogenated fats. As with many other additives, they are toxic. As I have discussed before, they were introduced to offer a low-fat alternative to butter but they are really not good for you. Be aware of cooking with most vegetable oils also. They become rancid (and toxic) at high temperatures. The best one is coconut oil which of course gives you loads of other health benefits, already covered in this book. It is unlikely that they will have been used in takeaways or restaurants because of cost.

# Sexy Substitutes

| | |
|---|---|
| pasta sauces | fresh tomatoes, olive oil and herbs |
| pasta | rice, buckwheat, quinoa |
| bread | homemade soda bread (usually non-wheat) |
| cakes | fruit, rice cakes, nut butters |
| biscuits/crackers | make your own e.g. buckwheat bakes |
| crisps | occasionally fresh popcorn |
| fries | potato/sweet potato wedges - own spices |
| Chinese dishes | own stir-fry |
| Indian dishes | homemade curries, dhals and rice dishes |
| pizza | own, using seed and nut flours |
| supermarket vegetables and fruit | farmers' market (local) or organic box (demand) |
| soft drinks, colas and fruit juices | fresh fruit, smoothies, water filter! |
| tinned and packet soups | make own using seasonal vegetables and herbs |
| butter, margarine | avocado, extra virgin olive oil, coconut oil |
| dips, spreads and pates | home-made using legumes, lemon, herbs and spices |
| burgers, sausages | vegetarian alternatives using nuts, seeds, good fats |

*"Don't let your sins turn into bad habits"*
*~ Saint Teresa of Avila*

## 3. Alcohol

Unless you have been living in a cave, you are probably well aware of the dangers of addiction to alcohol. I grew up in a country where drinking, even binge drinking is still fairly acceptable. In the USA on the other hand, I found it pretty socially unacceptable. I'm not sure that either philosophy works in the aim of cutting down alcoholism. I do believe that people drink excessively to escape from the stuff in life that hurts them, or from some lack of fulfilment. Beyond a healthy average daily intake, it is certainly an addiction. Anyone who has a family member or friend with a drink problem knows how difficult it is. It wrecks lives, and the sad thing is that it is legal. If you suspect that you might have an addiction to alcohol, then *please* get help. Until you do, you are unlikely to be able to find much of a solution in this book with your overeating. Alcohol encourages overeating, period, and it is a depressive so it will do little to help your challenged emotions.

However, if you drink regularly and you think that you have developed habits around alcohol, you may be able to work them out with some gradual substitutions. The thing to remember, whether you are an alcoholic or binge drinker or someone that likes a bottle of wine to chill out on a Friday night after work, is that you are only ever in control of your first drink. Whatever your values, permissions or ideals are around the amount of alcohol or food you plan to consume, they have the capacity to fly right out of the window after your first glass.

Energetically, alcohol lowers your vibration. This makes sense, as everything about alcohol involves going down. As a depressant, the force of excessive drinking comes from the lower chakras. It reduces consciousness in mind, body and soul. It cannot help you in pursuit of BodyMAGIC! A 'night off' this awesome path can set you back a lot further than you think. If you drink excessively tonight, what do you think you are going to want to eat tomorrow? It's unlikely to be anything healthy, that's for sure. It weakens your good intentions in your relationship with food.

If you find it hard to say no, ask yourself:

☐ What is it that I fear if I don't drink?
☐ What might I lose if I don't join in?
☐ What are my priorities in my life right now?
☐ What sacrifices am I prepared to make to succeed?
☐ Do I really believe I can succeed?

So what can you do instead?

Well, you can avoid bars like the plague and miss out on nights with your friends. You could volunteer yourself as the designated driver, so that you can't drink (this is a very insightful and sometimes a very funny practice indeed!). Or maybe you can find other things to do on a Saturday night besides drinking alcohol. You can try drinking tonic only, with lemon and ice, and no-one need know that you have left out the gin. You can do the same if you are a vodka, rum or other spirit drinker. There are alcohol-free beers now in most bars. Don't be tempted to go for diet sodas. They have been proven to increase appetite and are really bad for you (see below). Try a soda water or sparkling water with a generous squeeze of lime and ice. This is my favourite. Not trying to substitute alcohol works well for me and this drink is really refreshing!

Make any big changes slowly. If you find yourself giving in to temptation in the early days, don't be hard on yourself. Sometimes we have to fall a couple of times before we work out how to stay on the blessed wagon!


## 4. Sugar, Artificial Sweeteners and Soda

You will have already read about the addictive qualities of sugar in *Chapter Seven* - Food Facts. As I was growing up, the only danger of eating sugar I feared was the effect on my teeth. Sweets were everywhere! They were treats for being a good girl and we all loved them. We didn't care that they were full of additives and gelatine. *Nobody* cared! I would buy a bag of treats for a penny each at the local shop and they would be gone by the time I got home. Thankfully, slowly, the public are really starting to understand the dangers of sugar to health. This problem has been creeping up on us for the last 70 years or more, since the industrial revolution when we needed cheap energy foods to fuel manual labour. Only now, a much smaller proportion of us are doing manual work and instead of reducing sugar and other cheap carbohydrates, we have increased them. Massively.

Every time we eat sugar, the amount of glucose rises in the blood. To balance this, the pancreas releases insulin. What most people don't realise is that insulin is a stress response that tells your body to store fat. Insulin rushes to the rescue and then when it's done, sugar levels often fall below normal and so we crave sugar again. This is the reason why sugar is considered so highly addictive.

Sugar comes in many natural forms. Simple sugars include fruit, raw honey and milk. Other simple sugars are processed, such as white sugar and high-fructose corn syrup. Nearly all processed sugary foods contain more sugar than the body needs, especially in such concentrated form. Therefore, they have an extremely high impact on blood glucose very quickly, causing it to 'spike', and yet they have little or no useful nutritional value, whereas fruit, milk, potatoes and natural grains have nutrients that are great for health and healing. Sugar is also converted from starch. Natural starches include carrots, potatoes, swede, turnip, peas, rice, wheat and oats.

*"Roland could not understand why anyone would want cocaine or any other illegal drug for that matter, in a world where such a powerful one as sugar was so plentiful and cheap.*
*~ Stephen King, The Drawing of the Three*

It's important to note that if we are not already diabetic or allergic to some foods, it's perfectly OK to eat all manner of fruit, vegetables and carbohydrates in proportions needed for a healthy life, as long as we avoid the processed stuff. The abundance of sugars in processed food and drinks is responsible for the health problems. The body has worked very hard over the last few decades to keep up with our sugar intake, but for an increasing number of people it has worn itself out.

Diabetes is the single most prevalent disease in the world, and it's on the increase in almost every country. In 2000, there were 171 million people in the world reported to have diabetes. Estimates for 2030 are 366 million, based on present increases (4). This is not limited to the developed world. South East Asia is expected to show the greatest increase (155%) and Europe the smallest increase (44%). But even the smallest increase is staggering when you consider how much it costs in healthcare to manage.

In the USA, diabetes.org have reported that medical expenditure for people with diabetes is 2.3 times higher than for those without diabetes. The primary driver of increased costs is the increasing prevalence of diabetes in the US population. Recent estimates project that as many as one in three American adults will have diabetes in 2050 (5).

There are many alternatives to sugar that you can try, but please avoid sweeteners like the plague. Ingredients like aspartame cause a whole lot of havoc in your cells and mess with your metabolism (6). It is really counter-productive to any weight-loss attempts. They are just a mixture of non-natural chemicals. Agave nectar or agave syrup is a classic, once seemingly great alternative to sugar, but it seems that is far from healthy (7).

Honey is often branded a health product, but quality can vary. Cheap jars at the supermarket can often be a blend of really cheaply produced honey from anywhere in the world. Manuka honey has medicinal properties and I use it as such, rather than as a sweetener. It varies in quality but offers anti-bacterial properties and is anti-inflammatory, so good on the skin as well as down the hatch! Wonderful too, if you can get local honey, but all honey will spike your blood sugar and maintain your sugar cravings.

We are gifted with a wonderful natural sweetener in the form of stevia. It's a plant that grows in South America and is up to 150 times sweeter than sugar. The Japanese started cultivating it in the 1970s when we discovered that saccharin may cause cancer. Stevia was withheld from Europe until 2011. Interestingly, when it became available by law, the sugar companies had already made a weakened, white crystallised version in the form of Truvia. However, there is very little in common between the two. People buy Truvia or other brands claiming to be derivatives of stevia, thinking it's a healthy alternative to sugar, but this is really not the case (8). Stevia is a green powder. Just a tiny pinch will sweeten porridge, desserts and ice cream. It is thought to be helpful for candida, but check any added ingredients. For example, some brands contain inulin which feeds candida. In its most natural form it has some nutritional benefits, but the minute amounts used really don't mean much. However, it is one of the most healthy and natural alternatives to sugar on our planet today.

## 5. Factory Farming

I know, I know. We have already covered this in the Food Facts chapter, and I've told you that I'm not going to tell you that to lose weight or be healthy you need to eat a vegetarian diet. This book is not about weight loss; it's about overcoming emotional overeating. I'm not even going to say that you have to cut out meat. But what I will ask you to do, again, is consider the meat that you are eating. If you feel that meat should be a part of your diet, find out where it has come from. If we are to connect with the very nature that supports us, then having a good idea about how the food gets to your plate is extremely important.

I will share with you my experience, and you can take from it what you like.

I became a vegetarian when I was thirteen years old. After learning about cattle farming at school, I had a moment of realisation that an animal had to die to get onto my plate. Sounds pretty simple. I didn't stop eating meat straight away, but I started to have real nightmares about having to kill animals. In the end, the reason why I stopped eating meat is because I thought "well, if I can't or wouldn't kill it myself, I shouldn't eat it". I decided that I would probably kill a fish for my supper and therefore became a 'pescatarian'. This made life a bit easier for my mother, who really didn't know what to cook for me. I ate a lot of omelettes and cauliflower cheese in those early days!

Decades later, I decided to train for a marathon. I actually trained for almost nine months. As I said in *Chapter Nine* - Nature Calls, please don't even be tempted to train for a marathon to lose weight. But there came a point in my programme where I was craving meat. Looking back, maybe it was vitamin B12 that I was lacking, but I never thought about that back then. Every time I thought about meat, I would salivate. Normally, if I ever really thought deeply about meat I would feel sick. This was *very* strange!

### Knowledge is Power

I took it upon myself to investigate the availability of meat from sources where the animals were looked after, allowed to roam in pasture and were as humanely slaughtered as possible. I question whether any slaughter is humane most of the time. This was new for me. The company where I used to buy my organic veg and fruit box had put up a couple of lovely videos showing the animals skipping out into pasture in the spring. I contacted them because I wanted to know more about their slaughter. They very quickly responded, sending me a plain PDF document, an internal policy and procedure document that laid out the whole procedure for the treatment of their cows, pigs, sheep, chickens, and pigs. I was impressed at their openness and thought that if there was trust needed then this was a reliable source.

I didn't go on to eat meat again, although I resumed eating fish for a while. These days, I still run and love outdoor fitness, but the craving for meat came and went. About that time, I stumbled upon two extremely helpful authors – vegans and professional sports people – Brendon Brazier and Matt Frazier. And there are many others. They proved to me that we don't need as much protein as we think, even if we are fitness fanatics. It's a myth, and one that supports a huge industry of supplements, shakes and huge steaks! It's not necessary to eat meat to be healthy, to build muscle *or* to lose weight.

The other big fact that you need to understand as you connect more deeply with Mother Earth, and in your request that she support you with your **health, healing** and **happiness**, is what you give back in return. Agriculture is responsible for 66% of the UK's nitrous oxide emissions and 46% of UK methane emissions (9). There have already been numerous disasters from waste spillages in major concentrated farming operations (10). The world's cattle alone consume a quantity of food equal to the caloric needs of 8.7 billion people. That's more than the entire human population on Earth. In the USA, 87% of agricultural land is used for rearing animals, in pretty poor conditions. Also there, more than 260 million acres of forest land has been cleared to support a meat-eating population. Allegedly, each vegetarian saves an acre of forest every year! (11).

*"The second half of a man's life is made up of nothing
but the habits he has acquired during the first half."*
*~ Feodor Dostoevski*

## 6. Dairy

There have been many U-turns on the benefits or the bad aspects of eating and drinking dairy products. Many vegetarians include dairy in their diet (lacto-vegetarians). Most of the traditional yogis in India take milk products. Ghee, which is clarified butter, is honoured, and cows are worshipped as sacred beings in the Hindu faith. When I stayed at my teacher's ashram in the Himalayas, there was one cow kept behind the ashram. She was looked after well. The milk was either given to us at breakfast or made into plain lassi (a yogurt drink high in probiotics).

Unfortunately, this is a long way away from the milk we buy in supermarkets in the developed world. Consider further the treatment of the animals during their short life as a producer of breast milk. These cows don't just produce milk once a machine is attached to their udders, they have to give birth first. Their calf is taken away very soon after it is born. In mass-produced milk production, cows are often chained at their legs and cannot move within the confines of their concrete-carpeted cubicle. This is all stress that is passed into the milk that you pour on to your cornflakes. I'm not a troublesome, hooligan animal rights protester, and my campaigning history has so far been limited to the posts I have shared on Facebook and other social media.

Even if you don't really want to know about the treatment of animals that provide you with dairy products, maybe you could open your mind to the possibilities of the energy that you are consuming. It is well documented that the stress of a mother is passed through her breast milk to her baby. Her baby actually takes on the stress of the mother. Compare the stress of humans with the stress and suffering of cows in large-scale milk production and you are ingesting a huge dose of suffering yourself, unknowingly.

And if you still think that's a little far-fetched, let's look at the chemistry. Consider the hormones that cows need to continually produce this milk and the antibiotics needed to keep them from disease, being in such proximity to each other without any fresh air, and you yourself are taking in a considerable amount of drugs over your lifetime.

Cancer in reproductive organs is on the increase. In every single country in Europe, of all new cases of cancer, breast cancer is the highest of all in women. In Europe as a whole and in many individual countries, prostate cancer is the highest for men (12). Dr. Jane Plant, author of *Beat Cancer* speaks of her own journey with cancer and is convinced of the connection between hormone-related cancer cell reproduction and growth and hormone factors in milk products (13). She survived six diagnoses of cancer over 27 years before she discovered the connection. Her journey continues, but she knows that her findings will help many people. Breast cancer in China is extremely rare, where dairy products are rarely eaten or part of a balanced diet. Is this a coincidence? You will have to decide. As you connect more with nature, you will use your intuition and you will know. Inform yourself from unbiased sources. Then trust your intuition, for it will serve you well. Instead of looking for a cure for cancer (more drugs) we should be looking at the research to confirm possible causes. Unfortunately, this costs money, which is usually funded by drug companies. They are hardly going to fund research into causes of cancer when there is nothing in it for them. If a cure is found, pharmaceuticals will have to take a massive hit on their bottom line. Read Chris's story for more inspiration here (14).

## 7. Grains and Gluten

As a vegetarian, the reduction in certain grains, even carbohydrates in general, has been a challenging one. For several years now, low-carb, high-protein eating has dominated the diet world. From Atkins to Paleo, there are thousands of books around reducing carbohydrates to extremely low levels. I have tried low-carb eating several times, but have really struggled. I don't why. It's not the sugar. I rarely eat desserts, sweets, cake, biscuits or sugary snacks. They just don't appeal to me anymore. I have overcome my sugar addiction after several relapses, just by only eating natural food and making my own ice cream. I no longer have cravings. I enjoy a few squares of good quality dark chocolate now and again, but that's about it. I have found a compromise that has been working really well for some time.

I have found some alternatives to glutinous grains that give me the same satisfied feeling as a piece of crusty bread would have done, but at a fraction of the glycemic load. There are many of these so-called pseudo-grains.

Here are the ones I use 2-3 times per week and how:

- Amaranth - can be popped and used in crackers, cooked and mixed with nutritional yeast to make a vegan 'cheesy' topping for casseroles and moussaka-type dishes
- Quinoa - complete protein and can be used in pancake mixes instead of flour or as a base for salads
- Buckwheat - flour can be used to make gluten-free bread and pancakes, flakes for porridge and whole it's a substitute for rice or pasta
- Millet -same as buckwheat, has a more chewy texture
- Rice - wild rice is good

All of the above can be sprouted and used in salads, smoothies, pizza bases or burgers,

Why is this so important? Well, with extensive research, we have developed a deep understanding of the causes of diabetes. OK, if we didn't eat refined sugar and ate fruit instead, we probably wouldn't have a diabetes problem, but the fact is that a large proportion of us are hooked on sugar and getting off it is difficult, especially for the emotional overeater. In times of stress, we don't go for a banana or a bunch of grapes. If we crave sugar, we go for the hard stuff! Even if you don't turn to sugar when you emotionally overeat, it will be some other carbohydrate. Maybe it's a takeaway, bread, fries, crisps or savoury snacks. Carbohydrates are comforters, period. The trouble is that they all spike blood sugar, especially if we are eating them when we are stressed and we want more after, even the next day. Carbohydrates, at least most of them, have the capacity to take you away from your good intentions and create an unhelpful habit very quickly.

The other major consideration is brain health. In his compelling book, *Grain Brain* (1), Dr. David Perlmutter highlights the direct, long-term and irreversible effect of grains, sugar and gluten on brain health. He maintains, with supporting evidence, that diseases like Alzheimer's are not in our genes but can be prevented with a more ancestral and natural diet. Diabetes and Alzheimer's are tied together. If you are diabetic, you are twice as likely to suffer from Alzheimer's. Dementia too is linked to diabetes. As Dr. Perlmutter points out, it's not just growing old that we need to consider. ADHD in kids, depression, chronic headaches and migraine, epilepsy and even Tourette's can be linked to years of grain overload.

Wheat and gluten are particular allergens. The wheat our ancestors ate is very different from the varieties that we buy today. And we eat tons more than they ever did. Our bodies, however, have not evolved to eat them as fast. They irritate the bowel and cause digestive disorders, which produces more stress and guess what? Weight gain! Gluten, a protein, causes damage to the intestine wall. In extreme cases this is known as Crohn's disease, an irreversible condition where a sufferer gets very sick if eating anything with gluten.

In this time of change for you, try out some new alternatives. You don't have to go all out straight away. But if you have any neurological condition, you may like to investigate further, and I have listed some resources for you to do so. The recipes in this book give totally gluten-free recipes or options. I allow a little gluten in my diet because I do not have celiac disease and I find if I eat these foods occasionally in small quantities, I'm OK.

*"We are punished by our sins, not for them"*
*~ Elbert Hubbard*

### Chapter Nineteen
# See it! Say it! Give it! Get it!

*"You are the most lucky person in the world, only if you BELIEVE so."*
*~ Nitesh Aggarwaal*

We spent a lot of time in the EFT chapter talking through all the stuff that we don't like, don't want and don't have. And that should feel good. This stuff needs to get out! What it makes room for is everything that we dream about, everything we want for our **health,** our **healing** and our **happiness**. We can do this in so many ways. I'm going to share with you what has worked for me and what hasn't and why.

First of all, we need to find out what it is that we want. We need to have a clear **Idea** of what we want for our **health, healing** and **happiness**. We are planting seeds in our consciousness to allow for opportunities to come to us, which will allow us to get there. And it isn't just about dreaming and affirming what it is we want. It's about removing the blocks we have that stop the dreams from coming. This work is called The Law of Attraction. If you have ever seen the film The Secret, this explains fully how and why this law works. We are going to be using affirmations to help us to attract what we want, as we work through this book.

**Health** and **Happiness** are states of being that we aspire to. The purpose of this exercise is to get you to dream the best that you can for yourself. **Healing** is something that is done by you and for you. It is something you have to allow and work on through yourself. Take time to contemplate the answers to these questions and write down answers as fully as you can.

Use a separate sheet of paper to give you room to expand if you prefer, or write this in your journal or workbook.

## Defining Health Healing and Happiness

## Health

1. What is your definition of health?

2. What does it look like to others when you are in good health?

3. What does it feel like to you?

4. How does good health affect your working life?

5. How does good health affect your family life?

6. How does it affect your social life?

7. What might be the benefits of your being/staying in **ill**-health?

You may find the last question a bit weird. It's very common for us to block a positive change in our health because, on a subconscious level, we feel that it will change us, our relationships or perhaps we won't get as much attention and help. This can be a short-term thing where we string out an illness to get the help from others, or a long-term issue, for example where we have a habitual routine with a loved one and we fear that a change in health or lifestyle might alter that relationship.

I have known a woman who happily admits that she does not want to have an operation that might help her to walk again as she feels that it would change her relationship with her super-caring husband. Maybe they both feel that he might be redundant too. I'm sure that you know of people who stay in abusive relationships because it's what they know and they have repeated this pattern over and over again. They cannot imagine what it's like to *not* be a victim. Perhaps they have followed in the footsteps of parents. But whatever the influences, on some level they feel change is more of a challenge than staying where they are, despite how bad it is.

Some of my friends have had unresolved issues for years and years and even when they have the opportunity to move these out of their life, they back away. It seems part of who they are. It's sad, especially when it's someone you know and love. However, if any of this strikes a chord with you, please consider a new, brighter and healthier path. As I said before, the healing path is never as tough as we think. Make a firm decision to get help. We live in an age and a society where we have professionals who specialise in just about every trauma life can throw at you. And you are unlikely to be alone. It seems that in recent generations, like my parents, grandparents and probably a few generations before them, we have been taught to put up and shut up. But remember that the traditional way of dealing with our terrors in the *distant* past would have been to share them, and we would have had support. Even now, cultures and families vary so much.

Go back and answer question seven further if you need to before moving on.

*"No one can make you feel inferior without your consent."*
~ Eleanor Roosevelt

Some people I know have blocked out years of abuse because they say that it was so long ago, and to bring it out now would be too painful. "It's not worth it." But there comes a point where if you keep banging your head against the door of the joy and authenticity of life and you cannot get in, you have to break down the door! Because the party doesn't last forever, and this life is about learning, leaving the worst and living your best.

This is essential for the emotional overeater. We don't come into this world with emotional baggage, we pick it up along the way. Your true nature is one of peace, integrity and love for yourself and others. It will always be there waiting for you to come back to, but sometimes you have to free yourself from the stuff that serves you only as a life lesson. And you have to believe that anything is possible!

## Healing

1. What do you need to heal physically (in your body)? Give a rating of each aspect, 1-10 depending on its severity

2. What do you most need to heal emotionally/mentally? Use the Emotion Elevator in *Chapter One* to help you. Give a rating of each aspect, 1-10 depending on its severity now

3. What do you need to heal spiritually? Give a rating of each aspect, 1-10 depending on its severity

4. What *events* from your past bring emotional challenges? E.g. guilt, regret, fear, sadness, grief, shame etc. (this may be a similar answer to 2, but expand if you can).

5. Observe any underlying commonalities between your physical, emotional and spiritual healing

6. How can you start to heal one or two of these aspects and when? Consider the techniques outlined in this book (see below) and how you can incorporate them into a regular practice

7. How will you know that you are making progress?

**A summary of some of the proven healing techniques in this book:**

| | |
|---|---|
| Yoga | Emotion Elevator |
| Meditation | Journaling |
| Affirmations | Support Circles |
| Emotional Freedom Technique | Candida Detox - later in the book |
| The Enneagram | Rituals - later in the book |
| Natural Food | Professional Help (addictions, trauma) |
| Natural Exercise | Chakra Healing with Crystals |
| Natural Air | First Aid |
| Natural Water | Mindful Munching |
| Breathing Techniques | Intuitive Eating |
| 7 Spells of BodyMAGIC! | The exercises of this book |

*"What we must decide is how we are valuable rather than how valuable we are."*
*~ Edgar Z. Friedenberg*

## Happiness

1. What is your meaning of happiness? Write it out in a couple of sentences.

2. If the answer to 1. is a description of the happiest you can imagine, then that is 10. Where are you right now?

3. When was your lowest level of happiness - the event, year etc.?

4. What level of happiness do you think could be possible for you in this lifetime? Be more ambitious than you were in 1. Dream away!

5. Looking at *your* meaning of happiness, what do you need to change your mind about? What deep-rooted beliefs can you identify about happiness that need to be kicked out?

6.  What seven reasons can you think of to be happy right at this moment?

7.  How does this make you feel?

Draw a little picture of your happy scene. Include what you believe will make you happy.

*"I don't believe in pessimism. If something doesn't come up the way you want, forge ahead. If you think it's going to rain, it will."*
*~ Clint Eastwood*

# Be careful what you wish for!

By now you should have a good idea about what you would like to attract into your life to help you on this path to a healthful, healed and happy relationship with food. It's likely to highlight exactly the reasons for the emotions that lead to the overeating most of the time. It's one thing knowing, but it's the change in mindset that will make the most welcome difference. They say be careful what you wish for. You need to be very clear about your motives with affirmations. Is it for your highest good? Might it hurt someone if you get what you want? For example, I might affirm that I receive abundance, money, a nice house and a beautiful car, but

1. Is it what I really want? and if yes

2. Is it what I need? and if still yes

3. Can I truly believe that I deserve it?

Unless the answer is yes to all three of these questions, then it may not be for my highest good. For example, I may dream of a retreat centre in Hawaii. But maybe that desire is based on someone else's dream, maybe I don't really need a retreat to share my work. Maybe underneath the dream I don't feel like I deserve such a thing. So therefore, I could be blocking it energetically from ever getting to me anyway. Perhaps I feel that everyone who has a retreat in Hawaii is better than me, more powerful, more enlightened, more qualified. I could even be blocking it by thinking that anyone with the money to buy a property in Hawaii cannot be a good, kind or giving person. All rubbish of course. But could this be a value from my past? I know that I block wealth myself. Having had wealth and the power money gives, I feel that is part of my past, and to have it again would mean that I would be the same as I was then. This is obviously not the case. It's a belief that is firmly lodged in my unconscious mind. I'm not aware of it most of the time. But when I meditate, practice EFT, affirmations and other practices in this book, I realise that it is just conditioning. The really good news is that it can be shifted. It really is all in the mind, and in most cases like these, it needs to come out!

# Exercise

## How to Affirm to Attract

*"Dare to dream! If you did not have the capability to make your wildest wishes come true, your mind would not have the capacity to conjure such ideas in the first place. There is no limitation on what you can potentially achieve, except for the limitation you choose to impose on your own imagination. What you believe to be possible will always come to pass - to the extent that you deem it possible. It really is as simple as that."*
*~ Anthon St. Maarten*

Once you have established your position around **health, healing** and **happiness**, you then need to transform them into dreams. You will make them into bold affirmations, as if they were already yours. You can do this for each of the 21 questions above. Be creative but be clear. And write them out by hand in your journal. This is not a test, and there is no wrong way to do it. So just do it!

For example, for happiness, you might say:

1. I live my vision and true meaning of happiness which is…….
2. I'm achieving the highest level of happiness possible in my life
3. I'm healing myself from the past so that my true, well-deserved happiness can shine through
4. I know that my happiness is limitless and I can have it in every moment for the rest of my life
5. I let go of my beliefs about happiness and there are no blocks to my happiness
6. My instant seven reasons to be happy right now are: my daughter getting an interview tomorrow for the job of her dreams, my new book, an excellent night's sleep last night, watching the winter sunrise in a beautiful clear sky this morning, my warm woolly sweater, my lovely next door neighbour, our visit to a cultural city tomorrow to celebrate our wedding anniversary
7. I feel so grateful for these things and everything else I could list and everything yet to come. I am lucky and I know it in the core of my being. I deserve to feel this blessed.

Note: with healing from the past, there is no need to go into the detail. Keep the statements positive and in the present tense. Affirm how and why you are working on them and the benefits this work will bring.

Do this for all of the questions in **health, healing** and **happiness**. You may decide to change them around a bit and make sure they are affirming your highest good. When you are happy with them, write them out in the front or the back of your journal or somewhere you can access them easily.

Well done! You now have an affirmation practice.

You can do this for other aspects of your life, whether it is your job, your family, your romantic life or anything! Start with these statements, repeating them daily for 21 days. Choose a time when you are unlikely to be disturbed. Look into a mirror and gaze into your own eyes as you state them with conviction and the power they deserve. If you want to, after 21 days, feel free to change them, develop them or add to them. You might like to add some of the other affirmations in this book, if you feel they are appropriate. Be realistic with your time. It is better to affirm one thing every day rather than nothing because you have become overwhelmed. The least you deserve is 21 days of speaking your dreams and it will prove to you that this works. You have nothing to lose!

*"Most folks are about as happy as they make up their minds to be."*
*~ Abe Lincoln*

## Blocking

Blocking is something we do that means no matter how many times we affirm something we have a little bug in our hardware that needs fixing before the new programme can run smoothly. That bug is an outmoded belief. This belief might be inherited from our parents or guardians, but it is most likely now totally irrelevant in our lives. Sometimes it can take great courage to let it go.

I wanted to be a dancer when I was a child, but my parents insisted that I work hard at school and get a 'proper' job first. I had a terrible time in my first art class in high school where a teacher sneered at my efforts and have had a fear of a blank piece of art paper ever since.
I don't know how many times my parents told me that money was the root of all evil, and yet I was told that I should get the biggest house I could afford and pay as much as I could into a pension for my old age! I found out the hard way that nothing is certain or secure in life. I invested heavily in shares when I worked in a bank. I even saved to buy them at a discounted rate. The share prices crashed and they ended up worth a small fraction of what they had been worth at their peak. It hurt so much at the time. I felt bitter, angry and terrified that this could happen to me. This obsession with a nest egg stops us from living a varied, fulfilling and interesting life. The so-called security that my parents endorsed ended up being the kind of security that locks you up in a place of fear of the future and totally dependent on institutions outside your influence for that future.

Our attitude to change is one of the most common blocks we have to a more healthy life. It's essential to the process to make sure we really feel that, in every cell of our body, we deserve it. The changes in this book may be huge for you. The practices I suggest may mean that people are going to judge, criticise or question you. Watch out for people telling you that you are fine as you are, that you don't need to do this; that it's a waste of money or it won't work. Often, these people are jealous of your resolve and sometimes they feel that you are going to change so much that their relationship with you will be different. These comments are sometimes no less powerful as an affirmation than if you had made them yourself. Gently tell the person that their comments are not helpful and that you are really counting on them for encouragement and support.

## You Gotta Give To Get

As well as visualising our perfect life of **health, healing** and **happiness**, we also need to make sure that the channels for receiving these gifts are open. From my experience and the experience of others I have known, treated or taught, you have to give to get. By giving, without fear and reservation, you open a huge doorway that will also allow you to receive. All too often, we feel we can't give because we don't have enough to share. Even if we don't have money to give, we can give other stuff. Here are some suggestions:

- our clothes that we haven't worn for six months, to charity
- excess bedding, towels and toiletries we have more than enough of, to a homeless shelter
- over-cooking meals mean you could make up a portion for a neighbour
- a recipe to a friend
- a book we have read and liked, magazines we have read, to friends

- inviting a friend round for lunch or tea
- some of our time volunteering with a worthy cause
- using our skills to raise money
- displaced furniture, old TVs, stereos, radio, kitchen equipment, sell as a bargain or give away to someone who may need it
- unwanted gifts, give them to an elderly neighbour or relative

This is an extremely valuable exercise in letting go, not just of 'things' but of holding on to stuff out of fear of lack. This is one of the reasons why we overeat. It is an inbuilt reserve instinct inherited from hundreds of years ago to save us from starvation. It is buried deep within our unconscious mind. But it can be altered. We can let the unconscious know that we are going to be OK, but working in the opposite direction. Here are some ways that have worked for me:

- stop eating when you are full and store the leftovers in the fridge or freezer or give them to your pets (if appropriate) or back to the ground

- do not stock up on 'luxury' foods including meats, cakes, sweets

- do not stock up on any other food unless you live way out in the sticks and are very likely to get stuck in the winter without supplies and even then, make it *reasonable*. You don't need a cupboard full of out-of-date food. This should be eaten and a small supply of in-date food kept over the winter months. Anything more is either a hangover from your grandparents' wartime pantry philosophy or a deep-rooted fear you have of running out of food

- eat foods that are in season. Not only is this more natural, they are cheaper and probably haven't been transported half way around the world. Usually the farmer gets a pittance for these long-distance foods, so that the price you pay can be competitive. So this is giving back to your planet and is healthier for you too!

- cook less than you think you will need. Take note of how much of the ingredients you actually need to feed yourself and/or your family. As an overeater, we tend to cook more, eat seconds and then just finish off what's left because we might as well. By eating less, you are taking less. Less demand means less overproduction, waste and hunger for those who need it

- never overeat out of guilt or loyalty to the person cooking it, as a reaction to peer pressure or because there are other people who could have eaten it. You over-filling yourself at *any* meal does not save the life of anyone who is starving

I know in many countries it is illegal to give money to the poor. It makes my heart sink. We can destroy whole communities in favour of claiming natural resources and leave them with nothing but pollution. We want to drill the Arctic to ensure that we can still drive cars on petrol for another few decades, and now we can't give a man on the street a bit of money. It reeks of greed and we play into it every time. If you can and you feel inclined, maybe you can give them a blanket or hot soup or some clean water or a warm jacket you were going to throw out anyway?

> *"People want to know how much you care before they care how much you know."*
> ~ James F. Hind

*Most* of us can do more to share the many gifts we have, whether time, money, food, clothes, voice, energy, even a smile. Holding the door open for an elderly person and waiting patiently with a smile can change that person's day into something magical. For some, to receive this aspect of kindness is to receive hope again in the human race.

As we let go of the fear of lack, through sharing, we realise how little we need, compared with what we want. I went through a phase of actually making such thriftiness a bit of an obsession. It's amazing to discover how little we need to be comfortable and healthy. Most of our overspending, like our emotional eating, is borne out of fear. I'm not saying that provision for what *might* happen is not important. For example, it is prudent (and sometimes the law) in some societies to have car, house and contents insurance. But it isn't always necessary to have a pair of jeans in seven different colours or styles! When I stopped watching so many TV commercials, reading newspapers and trashy magazines, I started to realise just how hypnotised I had become. I would find myself saying "I've just got to have it!" We really do believe that life will be unbearable if we don't have the latest, the best or the all-new brand of some material item. Sadly, we often pass this philosophy and fear to our children. Sooner or later we have to realise that it is plain and simple greed. It's hurting someone, somewhere. It's just cause and effect.

And it spills over onto our plate. We want to eat whatever we like, no matter what the season, how far it has travelled, how much nutrition has been lost and in most cases, what the farmer who grew it got from your money. We demand to have whatever we like, whenever we like and in unlimited supplies. Supermarkets undercut each other to compete for our business, but the discount is often deducted from the farmer, who often works his land for little or nothing. Food is no longer a blessing and gift from Mother Earth. It is a commodity. And so much of it is wasted. It's hard for us to connect with food in this way. Be mindful of your food supply, trying to take no more than you need, and you will help to heal your relationship with food.

It's time for healthy change.

*Mother Earth,*
*help us to share your gifts,*
*taking only what we need and*
*always giving thanks for your bounty*
*~ Chinmayi Dore*

## Chapter Twenty

# The Gremlins in your Gut

*"I've learned that for many people, change is uncomfortable. Maybe they want to go through it, and they can see the benefit of it, but at a gut level, change is uncomfortable"*
~ Mitchell Baker

## Gut Instincts

I would like to congratulate you on reaching *Chapter Twenty*. I remember how I felt the first time I ever ran twenty miles; it was a milestone indeed! If you have been formulating a daily practice into your life and trying out some of the other practices in this book, you are well on your way now to life-long **health healing** and **happiness**. However, I want to discuss with you one of the huge blocks I have had to achieving health. This has affected my ability to lose weight over the years when I have been dieting, but it is more than that. The gut, or the bowel, is known as the second brain. If we have a lot going on in our head, i.e. stress, there is a pretty good chance that there's going to be a lot going on in our gut too.

There are two conditions that are really good to know about when it comes to overcoming emotional eating, following this book and its practices. You can be eating a healthy diet, exercising in nature, meditating daily and attending regular yoga classes and still wonder why it is that you feel foggy and have a lack of energy or enthusiasm. This can be so demoralising. Because of the link between our emotions and our gut, as an emotional eater you quite possibly have too many of these visitors in your gut:

1.  candidiasis/candida overgrowth
2.  parasites

They have both been a pain in the bum (literally!) to me, over my adult life and a huge hindrance to my health. Both conditions exist in everyone and are managed well by the functions of the digestive system and hormones. An overgrowth or too much of either of them can exist in someone for years, the symptoms just becoming part of that person's life as the candida and the parasites become long-term inhabitants of the body. The conditions are perfect for them. So they aren't going anywhere unless you evict them off your property!

Taking it one stage further, if you accept that generally, your health suffers at the same time that your emotions are out of balance, then you may be able to accept that there is a link between your ability to let go of your old eating habits, your addictions, even your excess body fat and hanging on to unwelcome bacteria and parasites. I have been around in cycles many times to come to really believe this. I'm hopefully going to save you lots of time and energy by not just dealing with them physically, but finding the energetic reason that they are there and letting that go too. We will address the physical aspect of these first.

## Diagnosis

There are not many accurate ways of establishing whether you have candida overgrowth or the pesky parasites. Most physical tests available are inaccurate. This is probably because we all have some candida and parasites; the question is whether they are a troublesome factor in your health right now. I first established that I had candidiasis when I went to see my healer, who used kinesiology to determine whether I was allergic to some foods. Now I am able to confirm it myself with a similar method, and also by dowsing using a crystal pendulum. But I just know, because the collective symptoms are so familiar to me. However, through the physical methods outlined here and some spiritual healing practices, candida and parasites are rare problems for me now. I do a cleanse for these when returning from travelling and at the change of the seasons. Of course, it's much easier to prevent than cure. This kind of detox gives me renewed energy, so why not!

# More About Both

1. **Candida Albicans overgrowth (Candidiasis)** and its noticeable effects is one of the most prevalent yet undiagnosed conditions of the time. It is thought that 75% of women will suffer symptoms of Candidiasis at least once in their lives. However, most research has been inconclusive. This is because most of the symptoms are treated as stand-alone conditions rather than as the symptoms of candida overgrowth. Symptoms can occur all over the body, especially in the reproductive, digestive and eliminatory systems. Here are a few:

   ☐ Brain fog, poor memory, inability to concentrate
   ☐ Thrush - vaginal or in the mouth
   ☐ Poor circulation, especially hands and feet
   ☐ Reduced libido
   ☐ A general feeling of heaviness, inflammation and/or weight gain
   ☐ Inability to lose weight
   ☐ Bloating and flatulence
   ☐ Cravings for sweet foods or foods containing yeast
   ☐ Breathlessness, easily out of breath with small amount of exercise, asthma
   ☐ Nasal secretion, congestion, sinusitis
   ☐ Vaginal discharge/thrush
   ☐ Abdominal pain, discomfort in bowels movements
   ☐ Irritable Bowel Syndrome, inconsistent bowel movements
   ☐ Lethargy, dizziness, headaches
   ☐ Tiredness, insomnia
   ☐ Acid reflux, heartburn
   ☐ Allergies and intolerances
   ☐ Frequent and/or lingering ear, nose and throat infections
   ☐ Muscle and joint pain or problems
   ☐ Yellow feet, toenails with disrupted growth

Candida Albicans is a naturally-occurring part of your gut flora. Most of the time, for most of us, it remains in balance and helps the digestion of our food. It exists in two forms – as a yeast or as a fungus. In the situation of overgrowth, the candida cells become a fungus and grow spores called hyphae that can lodge themselves in your gut wall. Candida gives off many toxins. Some, like ammonia, are poisonous to the body and once they enter into the bloodstream, many other more symptoms can prevail.

This list shows how so much long-term illness, discomfort or sub-optimal health may be attributed to Candidiasis. Dr. Mercola says in his special report (1), that if you are eating right and exercising and still not losing weight, it may be due to candida overgrowth, even if you have none of the other symptoms. Add to this other contributory factors such as:

- ☐ A high sugar diet including fruit, fizzy drinks
- ☐ A diet that is mainly non-organic
- ☐ Oral contraceptive or coil
- ☐ Antibiotics over the last 2-3 years

and you may be wise to check it out.

What makes candida overgrow? You may wonder why it seems like quite a new concept. There are many reasons for such a recent and high prevalence of candidiasis. One of them is sugar. Yes, that addictive drug that we seem to have taken for granted is finally taking its hold. If diabetes is not a problem for you, then candidiasis could well be if you eat a lot of sugar. If you have ever made bread, notice what happens when you add just warm water to yeast (candida yeast needs to be at body temperature to grow). You can see it grow slowly before your eyes. But add a teaspoon of sugar to another mix and you will have a good idea how hard the body has to work to find its balance again when you eat sugar. As I have said before, the body is a miracle, organic form with a very scientific piece of instinctive programming to help it recover as quickly as possible from things it can't use (like producing insulin for sugar). But it can only do so much. Candidiasis is one of the subtle slowly-evolving conditions in the gut where the body has been unable to recover from a consistent, long-term ingestion of foods that push the boundaries.

Another problem for Candidiasis is prescription drugs, including antibiotics. The unfortunate thing about antibiotics is that it kills off the good gut flora, the healthy stuff. If you have an infection in your finger, the antibiotics have got to go through your gut flora before they can get to your finger. These good bacteria are necessary for your immunity. So if our immunity is already weak and we drop a load of antibiotics in our gut, we are possibly going to feel 'ill' for quite a lot longer. It is one reason why I think that, in my teens and twenties, I had flu several times a season with sinus infections following course after course of antibiotics. It was a downward spiral, brought on by an already weakened immune system. I had no immunity to fight anything. I would be totally paranoid about working alongside someone with a cold, because invariably they only had to cough out loud and I would end up being off work for two weeks or more. Immunity-depleted individuals such as those receiving chemotherapy are also found to have a greater incidence of candidiasis.

We don't just take antibiotics when we are ill either. We drink them in our water supply. Traces of antibiotics, oral contraceptives, painkillers, anti-inflammatories, even cocaine have been found in water supplies in the UK. Most research shows that they are not in levels high enough to have any effect on our health. However, it could add up with everything else we ingest or are exposed to without knowing (2). Personally I also think it is shocking to think that most of us don't know what's in our water supply when we are encouraged to drink so much of it!

Then there is the issue of antibiotics not working anymore. They are an everyday part of factory farming now. Around 50% of all antibiotics produced go to cattle. Due to the crowded conditions of our cattle, disease can be rife. With the pressure to produce meat fast and in large quantities in a relatively small space, farmers administer antibiotics as a matter of course. It's not the risk of eating meat with antibiotics in them that poses a problem but the potential to eat bugs in the meat that are resistant to antibiotics. There are times when we need to have antibiotics. Ultimately they can save our life. More and more articles in newspapers and health magazines are stories about people who just cannot cure an infection because they are not responding to antibiotic medicine. The simple truth is that the more antibiotics we take, the more resistance to them we develop. If you do have to take antibiotics, always check with your doctor that they are absolutely necessary. If possible, take some strong *probiotics* before you start your course and a couple of hours after each dose.

I have had challenges with candidiasis for many years. It comes and it goes, but very rarely these days. I would forget about it, overdo the sweet stuff or some other trigger and then it would come back. I have learned how to master it quickly and without too much fuss. But the real mastery has come now that I am aware of my eating patterns and take heed before it gets out of hand again.

> *"Happiness for me is largely a matter of digestion."*
> ~ Lin Yutang

2. **Parasites**, often commonly called 'worms', are also very common. The first time I was aware of this problem was on returning from my first trip to India, but I now know that it is also extremely common in the developed world. Most of us have parasites, but we have become so accustomed to them and we don't have any noticeable symptoms or we attribute symptoms to stand-alone illness or to some other cause. Some can be pretty nasty nonetheless:

   ☐ Sleeping problems, fatigue, low energy
   ☐ Bloating, flatulence, indigestion, irritable bowel syndrome
   ☐ Food intolerances, allergies to food or chemicals
   ☐ Itching around the anus, genitals or feet
   ☐ Unusual weight loss or gain, loss of appetite or insatiable appetite
   ☐ Long-term cough, wheezing, breathlessness
   ☐ Depression, anxiety, low self-esteem
   ☐ Anaemia (lack of iron) or other nutrient-deficient illness
   ☐ Skin conditions - psoriasis, eczema, sores, rosacea
   ☐ Body aches and pains in muscles and/or joints

You will see that there is a huge overlap of symptoms between candidiasis and parasites. They often go hand-in-hand. When a parasite is scavenging your gut lining for its survival, the candida can replace some of the good flora. Both can get into your bloodstream, causing havoc in most of your body. Both cause nutritional imbalances, either because they are sapping the nutrients they need to survive (parasites) or lining the wall of your gut, preventing efficient nutrition absorption (candida). If you have been experiencing many or most of these symptoms in the last few months, you may have one or both of them. Yet, at least in my experience, your doctor is unlikely to recognise candidiasis in your gut as a root cause *or* test you for a parasite.

Parasites can come in all shapes and sizes. Some can barely be seen to the naked eye; others are several feet long. It is believed that those suffering with cancer and other chronic disease are likely to have parasites. They rob us of our nutrition and hinder our health. They also hinder our recovery from emotional overeating. These little guys need feeding and they will take all of the good nutrition we are feeding as well as the bad. So they will get in the way of our progress to **health, healing** and **happiness**.

As an emotional eater, this adds another growth area to our relationship with food and our body. Noticing the effects of candidiasis and/or parasites early and taking action accordingly is extremely difficult.

# Exercise

1. Take a thorough test or questionnaire to establish whether you are likely to have candidiasis. There is one online you can use in Resources, and there are many others on the internet.

2. If it is likely that candida may be causing health problems for you, in spite of eating healthily and exercising, please refer to other resources given in this book. Read further afield and consider the anti-candida diet for a couple of months, with supplementation and recommended herbs. Visit www.bodymagic.website for some solutions I recommend, as I have tried and tested them myself.

> *"Stomach: A slave that must accept everything that is given to it,*
> *but which avenges wrongs as slyly as does the slave."*
> *~ Emile Souvester*

## Recommended Treatments

I have offered some natural solutions to ease the burden at the end of the book. If you are unsure about whether you have any gremlins in your gut, these treatments are good for enhancing health anyway. When all is said and done, the treatments I have used have been a very useful detox, aside from candida or parasite treatment. All of them have great benefits for your **health and healing**, so can do you no harm.

These are just a couple of treatments that I have practised myself many times or have treated or supervised in others doing the same. Most you can read about and work through at home. Only Shankhaprakshalana should be done under supervision.

Please contact me for details via www.bodymagic.website.

## Going Deeper

Treatments for candidiasis and parasites will help with the physical symptoms, and you will feel better. However, there is no quick fix. The first time I self-administered an anti-candida diet and supplementation protocol, it took three to four months of careful monitoring and a great deal of commitment. But it was worth it!

It's a great opportunity to get to know yourself and your insides. On a physical level, your digestive health is one of the most important facets of your recovery. As I recovered from candidiasis, I was acutely aware of the cravings bought on by the 'die-off' syndrome, a phase where, as the candida fungus dies, it releases toxins that can make symptoms worse for a while. I now know that this can be managed easily. Tackling these cravings gave me a unique chance to really let go of my impulses and put my health first. It bought up a lot of emotions, almost like a grieving. I called on some of the other practices in this book, such as Emotional Freedom Technique (EFT) and affirmations to help to recognise where these emotions came from and heal them, permanently.

It wasn't easy, but it worked!

As an emotional overeater, this can be a useful addition to the practice of letting go of anything that no longer serves our **health, healing** or **happiness**.

# Exercise

## Letting go

1. Think of some of the most hard-hitting disappointments in your life. Times when you felt 'gutted', powerless and that a situation was out of your control. Two or three will do for now.

2. Pick one. Usually the first one to come up will be the one you still have strong attachments to. Close your eyes and ask yourself why it affected you so intensely. Who was involved? How did they make you feel? Why were you so upset? Take your time. Close your eyes and really go into that experience. Write down your thoughts here.

3. How intense is this feeling on a scale of 1-10? Make a note here.

4. Where can you feel this on or in your body right now? Does it have a form, colour or texture? Can you feel a lump in your throat for example? How big is it? Write it here. Just a couple of words will do.

5. Now begin to breathe as if you are blowing out candles on a huge birthday cake. Take several breaths as you imagine breathing out the feeling, whatever form it has. Breathe until you are tired, then check in with the score 1-10.

6. Repeat this until you feel that you have released it. This may take 3-5 rounds. Be patient, but be determined to let whatever it is finally go. Sometimes you can feel a little dizzy or tingly, so ease off if you need to.

7. Finally, when it has cleared, take several deep breaths through the nose with your eyes closed. Imagine that you are breathing in white light. Let it fill the void left by the space this issue occupied. When you feel calm and brighter, open your eyes and smile.

8. Work through other difficult memories this way when they come up and whenever you feel inclined. Be gentle but be brave in letting them go.

*"My soul is dark with stormy riot, Directly traceable to diet."*
*~ Samuel Hoffenstein*

## Chapter Twenty-One
# Going Hungry

*"The belly is an ungrateful wretch, it never remembers past favors, it always wants more tomorrow."*
*~ Aleksandr Solzhenitsyn*

## Fear of Hunger of the Overeater

At some point in **Knowing Yourself** you will realise that most overeating is borne out of a fear of being hungry. We know that our hunger is normally temporary. It is the unconscious mind reacting to hundreds of years of instinct. This connection can be broken so that we don't react to our feelings. In our panic we may have found ourselves diving into the nearest burger and fries takeaway because we have no idea where we can get anything better and, at that moment, much less do we care. We *can* care and we *can* stick to what our conscious mind knows is best for us. It's OK to be hungry for a while. We really *won't* starve. It is a good exercise to recognise our fear of hunger, experience and degree of hunger and ultimately put our hunger into perspective.

## Hungry, Starving or Peckish?

Let me share what I would call a magical experience with you. I once pulled over at a motorway service station to get fuel; something I rarely do because it's usually much more expensive on the motorway. I got out of my nice warm car to fill up with fuel and I felt an icy wind piercing through my body. I instantly thought about food. Specifically, *hot* food. Then I realised that I was probably not going to find anything wholesome in the kiosk. I was thinking that the only hot food, if there was any, was likely to be a sausage roll, a pasty or a bacon roll. Not mouth-watering for a veggie! But the food seed was already planted. I'd decided that I needed food and that was it. I was hungry all of a sudden. If I'd had a choice, it would have been vegetable soup. As a vegetarian I was probably going to have to settle for a cheese sandwich. I had to eat *something*. While I was holding the nozzle and filling up the tank, I looked over and saw three vertical flags, blowing in the icy wind. It's from those flags that I got my magic. One of them said 'Peckish?' Another said 'Hungry?' and the third one said 'Starving?' In that moment several powerful learnings came to me. These flags were there to encourage you to go in and buy their carbohydrate-laden, hunger-ridding, processed food. And they were covering all the options! Whether you were starving, hungry or even peckish, it was something that stopping here would solve. As if being hungry was an illness that needed treating and they had just the medicine! I remember this experience so vividly because I took a photograph of those blessed flags, not because they were aesthetically pleasing but because they allowed me to remember what I learned. I also realised just how little we know about *real* hunger. Assuming that the majority of people on that motorway have a car or are a part of a family or friendship with someone who has a car, they are unlikely to know what real hunger is. It blew my mind. Not because I have ever felt real hunger either, but because I realised how easily we can be convinced that we are feeling it.

*"Feel what it's like to truly starve,*
*and I guarantee that you'll forever think twice before wasting food."*
*~ Criss Jami, Killosophy*

# The Hunger Scale

This may not be the first time you have heard of the hunger scale. I know there are a few around and they are a great idea. If we are to practice Intuitive Eating and Mindful Munching, we need to have a good idea of what it feels like at different levels of hunger. Personally I have looked at several of such scales and found most of them to be too complex.

### NOT HUNGRY  >  VERY HUNGRY

More often than not, I go from 'not hungry' to 'very hungry', quicker than I can say "I need to eat." The amount of power behind that need is palpable. And it is that very power that I have tried to harness and use to train my unconscious mind. Remember, this part of your mind wants you to eat, only because it fears that you will starve if you don't. It works many thousand times faster than your conscious mind, which wants you to be sensible and healthy and knows what you *really* need. Your unconscious mind doesn't know that you have a cupboard full of healthful ingredients at home, just 20 minutes away and that you can have a good plateful of nutritious and satisfying food on your table within the hour.

That is, unless you tell it!

There are several ways to do this. I'll start with the easiest and work up to mastery. And you will vary between kindergarten and mastery more often than you might think! But it will become easier with time.

- ☐ Have a piece of fruit in your car and one at your workplace, save it until you crave something sweet or eat it when everyone else is eating cream cakes for someone's birthday. If you still want the cream cake fifteen minutes after the piece of fruit, then eat the cake too. Don't punish yourself, whether you eat the cake or not. Eat it if your body still wants it. Always have fruit around, especially if you are trying to come off sugar. It's nature's methadone!

- ☐ Think about what you have planned to eat and when. Will eating anything substantial now mean that you won't want your planned meal? Is that OK? So many times in my life, I would get hungry, overeat on rubbish food and miss the great stuff I'd planned. At my worst times, this would go on for days and the food would perish in my refrigerator. I know I'm not alone. Remember you have a relationship with food. In the end I felt like I was betraying my health partner. It was only my change in perspective that changed this habit. Having a healthy snack in moments of hunger, without the need to feel full, is a good practice.

- ☐ Make sure that in your waking hours, you don't ever go more than five to six hours without a meal or four to five hours without a snack. I'm not a great snacker myself, but if I get really involved with my work, or I'm busy doing something I love and don't want to stop to get a meal, I'll have a snack after four hours. It's just a little reassurance to my body that there is no shortage of food and that more is coming. More often than not, it stops me from getting hungry. When I'm hungry, I'm distracted and then I lose my flow.

☐ Ask yourself some 'W' questions:

a) why am I hungry?
b) what can I eat that will suffice now?
c) will I really keel over if I don't eat in the next hour?
d) when is my next planned meal or snack?
e) which mind is overpowering me: my *subconscious* (habitual patterns), *unconscious* (fear of starvation) or do I have a *conscious* and sensible reason for wanting/needing to eat soon?
f) who is trying to wreck my plans for health and wellness? Is it part of my old self or is someone not supporting me?

You do have to be kind to yourself and go with the flow. If you missed lunch because a meeting went on too long and you have another one in an hour, then it's simply unfair to tell your body that it can wait until after the second meeting, just because you know you're not going to starve. Your brain needs energy and nutrients so that you can think clearly and articulate yourself appropriately in the said meeting, but also to think rationally about food!

You may want to go to the gym later in the day. Don't be cruel. Give yourself some proper nourishment. If you don't, there's a pretty good chance your workout will be half-hearted or worse, forced, and that you'll overeat when you finally get home to your kitchen.

You may have a cold coming on or your period may be due, so you are maybe craving something that you normally don't eat. This is where we teach the mind to know what is real and what is not. This is where we get to really connect with our body and mind. Honour the cycles of your body and the variations in your hormones and health.


## Hungry or Angry?


This really expands on the *Why are you hungry?* question that you might ask yourself when you have the undeniable urge to eat.

It has to be an introspective process. For many years I'd ask my husband to intervene and 'help me' with my overeating. He would dutifully ask me why I wanted a third plateful of food. I would always have a great answer to justify my overeating. I would still overeat, probably regrettably, occasionally blame him, and feel as if I had fallen backwards in my progress. The sad fact is that it is *me* who overeats, *me* who makes the decisions and *me* who can step in before my intentions fall by the wayside. It *can* be done and it is the magic of the **7 Spells** that will get us there. As living, breathing and yes, normal human beings, it is unreasonable jump from an **Intention** to be healthy one day, to cast-iron **Willpower** the next. We have to wave the wand of BodyMAGIC! every day and in every interaction we have with food. Like any other relationship, it takes work and regular practice. Sometimes it can seem hard, but the good news is, it's not hard all of the time and *with* time it gets easier. Eventually we do it automatically and that's the MAGIC!

*"Hunger of choice is a painful luxury; hunger of necessity is terrifying torture."*
*~ Mike Mullin, Ashfall*

# Exercise

**Fantasy Feelings**

In **Knowing Yourself** you will come to easily identify the emotions that are propelling you towards overeating. In that lightning moment of wanting to overeat, with practice you will be able to intercept the unconscious cravings with the conscious caring **Discipline** you have developed for yourself.

1. Some people say that there is always a positive in a negative. Think of the last time you felt one of the emotions on the elevator table below. You may need to refer to your journal. Have a think about how you might have 'changed your mind' to consider that situation with the opposite emotion. Can you find any growth, learning or advantage in that situation that might take you across to its polar opposite?

### Emotion Elevator

| Unhelpful | Helpful |
|-----------|---------|
| Anger | Gratitude |
| Cruelty | Compassion |
| Disgust | Admiration |
| Familiarity | Surprise |
| Fear | Hope |
| Greed | Generosity |
| Hate | Love |
| Hurt | Relief |
| Loss | Gain |
| Panic | Knowing |
| Shame | Pride |
| Sorrow | Joy |
| Other | Other |
| Other | Other |

2. The next time you feel an overwhelming emotion, one that has you thinking about eating, drinking or using another method of escape, instead of turning those emotions on yourself by knocking yourself further, be your own guide. Find the underlying emotion(s) from the Emotion Elevator and try to imagine its opposite as an outcome. This will involve a lot of creativity and even fantasy. Hence I'm calling these Fantasy Feelings. The **Idea** is that with a little bit of effort, you will move away from the emotions that are

causing you harm, as well as the overwhelming desire to overeat. Your **Intention** here is to practice it when it arises.

Here's a fictitious but not untypical example of my former challenges with emotional overeating:

**What Happened**
- You didn't get to go to the theatre because your partner had to work late

**Overeating Result**
- You went to the shops, bought a huge pizza and a bottle of wine

**Your thoughts might be**
- Why should I go without? Why can't something go to plan for a change? Oh well, I'm still going to have a good night. I don't see why I should suffer. I'll go on my own. I don't need him! After all it was my night off too.

**The Emotions**
- Anger, Hurt

**The Opposites**
- Gratitude, Relief

**Fantasy Feelings**
- *Gratitude* - I'm grateful that he is such a committed person to everything. I'm grateful that it means we can go away for Christmas because of this extra work/contract/deadline. We can go to the theatre another time. I'm grateful that he doesn't mind me going on my own. He will be grateful that I didn't get mad or overeat. I don't really want him to feel guilty.

- *Relief* - I'm relieved that he didn't rush home and risk an accident to get here on time. I would hate to add to the pressure that he is obviously under at the moment. I want him to be relieved that I didn't get mad and that we can still enjoy the rest of our evening when he gets home. I'm relieved that I didn't follow my normal patterns and overeat or drink a lot of alcohol.

Whilst this is just an example and the transition is from one extreme to another, it is given to illustrate the absolute power in shifting the emotions. It literally will change your body chemistry by reducing stress – cortisol and adrenaline – and change your relationship with food and, one would hope, with your significant other! It is both powerful and empowering. It comes from a place of unconditional love and respect for yourself and others, and your powerful **Intention** for your **health, healing** and **happiness**. What a win that is!


## Water and Hunger

There is loads of stuff written in diet plans about drinking water as a way of fooling the stomach that you are full. I have to say that whenever I drink water on an empty stomach I feel even more hungry! I know that is not the case for some. Learn to trust your body's signals. Sometimes they will be a little confused. But if you are drinking a regular amount of water, you will know the difference. We have already discussed the importance of drinking water in *Chapter Nine* - Nature Calls. The most important thing to remember is not to play games with your body by drinking water to suppress your hunger. With the practices in this book, you are improving the relationship you have with your health and body. If the body tells you it's hungry at 3pm and you haven't eaten since breakfast, don't expect it to respond well to a pint of water. Water is for proper hydration, not a meal replacement drink.

# The Famine Response

You may remember the famine response we have inherited as a reaction from our ancestors. It wants us to overeat at times, because it feels that we need to stock up and if we don't, we might starve. Unfortunately, as I have said before, these instincts have not evolved as quickly as our diets and food supplies have, which is one of the ways we are driven to overeat.

The perfect illustration of this is when we go on fasting diets or cut out food groups for periods of time. You may be aware that the one of the reasons for the immediate success of these crash diets is that we lose weight from the muscles and we lose water, not fat. However, the reason why these diets are so ineffective in the long run is that when we cut out food, the body thinks that we are actually not able to get hold of it. This again is the famine response, which is a stress response. So this is what happens:

- anything we eat is stored as fat to protect the vital organs, around the middle
- the metabolism slows down even more to reduce the number of calories burned for energy

Years of being told to fool my appetite by shoving celery and carrot sticks down my throat when I haven't eaten all day has backfired. We are creating an unnatural response to a natural request. We can't replace balanced meals with low-calorie snacks. All that happens is that the metabolism slows down and we increase fat.

By eating more intuitively and mindfully we offer food to our body with grace and respect. This is the relaxation response. In that place, the body is able to let go of its protective layers and the metabolism is in balance.

> *"I saw few die of hunger; of eating, a hundred thousand."*
> ~ *Benjamin Franklin*

## Chapter Twenty-Two

# Ritual for the Soul

*"When you do things from your soul you feel a river moving in you, a joy. When action comes from another section, the feeling disappears."*
*~ Rumi*

## Ritual Revival

Long before religions tried their best to take over the world and our medicine women were burned at the stake, we were steeped in ritual. What religious leaders branded barbaric and uncivilised was a deep connection with nature, with consciousness and therefore with spirit. Naturally we are creatures of ritual and habit. We were an innately tribal race and were able to see the power of a group as being much more valuable than the sum of its members. These were days of humility, respect and honour. And connection with Mother Earth was paramount, not just for nourishment, but for survival.

The shamans were the medicine men and women of the tribes, like the family doctor is today. They had a deep connection with nature. They were able to forecast the weather, the location of food and the best place to build homes. They supported the natural environment and it supported them. Sounds ideal, doesn't it? They celebrated the passages of life with rites and rituals. The various stages of manhood and womanhood have been honoured in traditions all over the world since time immemorial. But many of these traditions were wiped out by religions and the need for man to control. For example, the seven stages of life have been replaced with the seven sacraments that no longer honour or celebrate the stages of the human body. Essentially, as in my experience growing up in a Catholic community, the main difference is that we were given a set of rules and told that we should fear and worship God as a separate entity.

In shamanic traditions, however, there are no rules, ceremony is done according to tradition, where there is nothing to fear, only love. They teach that God (or spirit) is within everyone and is reflected back to us. That therefore we should worship ourselves, those around us and all of nature. That every rock, tree, plant and animal is a relation. We are all connected by sacred divine energy.

As the decades have passed since these times, in most of our world connection with nature has been massively reduced, even lost. Is it any wonder, therefore, that we have some of the issues we face with food, addiction and emotions? Few of us have the support of a family, let alone a tribe. And we have become so disconnected from the elements of nature. We don't know where our food or water comes from, where our waste goes to, how and where our clothes are made, the cost to our planet of the fuel we use and the things we buy, or the abuse of our brothers and sisters around the globe. Some of us don't even know when one of our own family is in trouble.

This way of life can leave us detached, unfulfilled and extremely unhappy. It doesn't seem to matter whether we have money, have children or take luxury holidays, we still feel empty. Our instincts have not evolved at the same rate as our lifestyles. So we are left wanting. We just don't know what it is that we want.

Some people fill this void with a religious practice, and I totally respect that. A religious practice is a spiritual practice and it will give you what you need, if you are committed to it and you feel freedom, peace and support from it. If you do, then you hold something rare and beautiful that not many have. If you have no religious leanings but you feel that there is something missing, energetically or spiritually in your life, I have some suggestions for you. Again, these are based on my own journey from the church to atheism and back to my own faith. This is a belief system whereby you are able to make your own commitments and set your own guidelines.

This is done with a ritual. It should feel comfortable to you after a few times of practising, although in the beginning it may feel a little strange. You will be getting in touch with your spiritual side, love and compassion for yourself and others. That in itself is a challenge for most people. Depending on your upbringing, the concept of spending time on yourself may have been seen as selfish. And maybe you already do feel that way. Perhaps your rituals for working on yourself are treating yourself such as going for a manicure every week. And that's great. You are showing your body some love and attention and this should continue. This ritual is to nourish your soul. The truth is that without this practice, we can only give so much to the people around us before we find ourselves feeling empty. Here are some examples of rituals you can use for your whole being.

*Healthy Body Rituals*
- taking a slow bath, massage, pedicure, haircut, healthy eating, a daily smoothie, yoga, walking, other exercise that is fun, gardening, relaxation

*Healthy Mind Rituals*
- meditations, affirmations, EFT, Enneagram, chanting and mantras, music, reading, art, writing

*Healthy Soul Rituals*
- gratitude, prayer, devotion, love, compassion, joy, bliss

*"Those who danced were thought to be quite insane by those who could not hear the music."*
*~ Angela Monet*

You will notice that the rituals of soul are more states of being than actions. They are emotions! The soul cannot physically do anything. It just is! This chapter is about finding the rituals that will feed your soul. You don't have to go out and buy a feathered headdress and build a ceremonial fire in your back garden! You don't have to go to an ashram in India to find your spiritual path. This is the magical thing about your soul. All of the answers are right there inside you. They are in every conversation you have today, everything you read and everything that happens in your life, minute by minute. When you are open to the possibilities of spirit, then you also open up a channel for receiving so much support and help from it, from within yourself. There will be times when it will be so easy to forget the presence of spirit, but it is always there. The purpose of the ritual is to remind you regularly of this.

I'm not saying that you can do it all on your own easily, but you can have your own ritual easily. Reach out to like-minded people. Join groups, either in your local community or even online. There is no shortage of people just like you, seeking greater and more soulful fulfilment in life. There may be some big differences between your rituals and beliefs and theirs. That is part of the magic of life. Acceptance helps you to let go of non-serving aspects of your ego that have only brought man misery throughout history. You will find freedom away from the desire to change, control and persuade others, replaced by compassion for them on their own individual, unique journey. When I have been on retreats and workshops I have witnessed many different ways of practising the same ritual. I always try to be curious, without criticism, for then I get the most out of the practice.

The key things to remember about all rituals:

1. There is no right or wrong way, just your way, for your highest good
2. Energy follows thought. It is always your intention that matters, not what you do or don't do
3. Do them out of love for yourself and that is what you will get more of in return

# Exercise

## 1. How to Build an Altar

An altar is one way of doing some devotional practice. It can be surrendering or sacrificing something, physical or otherwise. It is like a focal point and an energy centre or vortex for your spiritual practice.

An altar is an altering thing (excuse the pun!). It can be changed depending on the season, the phases of the sun and moon, your mood or your needs. It is one easy and creative way of connecting with nature and celebrating the cycles of life. Even when there's six feet of snow outside or a heatwave going on, you can connect with nature through your altar. I'm going to share my ideas with you and you might copy them. You may also have some great ideas of your own. This is right brain stuff, so let your creativity flow when it wants to.

1.  Find a room or space within a room that can be used for your practice. Find a little table that is designated just as your altar. If you don't have one, you can maybe pick up something old from a charity or second-hand shop. I prefer something quite low so that when I sit on the floor, it is approximately at my eye or chest level.

2.  Set up the altar somewhere where it won't be disturbed by kids, cats or passers-by. Find a small cloth or scarf or mat to place on the altar. Grab a compass and find out which way is South on your altar. Maybe it's a corner or maybe a side. It doesn't matter.

3.  You can now work with the directions. I'm using the Andean tradition for the elements and directions. The elements for the Native American and other traditions are slightly different and that's totally fine too. There are no rules!:

| Direction | Element | Animal Totem | Qualities |
|-----------|---------|--------------|-----------|
| South | Earth | Serpent | grounding, shedding of the past, walking gracefully with strength |
| West | Water | Jaguar | clearing, protection, facing fear, integrity, cycles of life and death |
| North | Air | Hummingbird | wisdom, life purpose, oneness, ancestral and celestial teachings |
| East | Fire | Condor | higher perspective, ambitions, insight |

For each direction, you can place a small object that signifies the element, the animal totem or the qualities of that direction. Here are some suggestions:-

In the **South**, for the earth element, you could place a rock that holds some meaning for you, a crystal, a piece of ancient wood or a small plant or flower, a picture of a serpent or a small toy snake.

In the **West**, maybe a shell or some water taken from a holy well or sacred site for the water element, something to signify death, not necessarily of another person but something in your life you want to release.

In the **North**, you could place a feather or some incense for the air element or a little figurine or picture of a hummingbird. You could put an angel or a picture of your guru, grandmother or some other teacher, living, human or not.

In the **East**, how about a candle flame for the fire element, a picture or symbol of the sun, or a condor?

And finally, in the **centre**, I symbolise the space (ether) element, without which none of the other elements could exist. I use items that hold the potential for sound through music or voice. So perhaps a prayer, a mantra or the words of a song that I'm drawn to at that time. I also place my little rattle in the centre too. The indigenous people dance to music and song, rattle or whistle to call in the spirits before their ceremonies. The yogis too will chant an invocation to a deity such as Ganesha, the elephant God who helps us to overcome obstacles. Maybe you have a guru, deity, archetype or teacher who you can include in this space at the centre in some way. Your intention is that their energy fills your space with light. Or maybe you have been drawn to a symbol, such as a cross, star or pyramid. Follow your creative intuition.

It may take time to gather the items for your altar. Let things come into your life when they are needed. You will be surprised how things seem to appear in your life when you want them to!

So, what do you do with your altar once you have one started? Well, if I have space in front of it, I will do my yoga practice there. I will light a candle, do some cleansing (see smudging below), some yoga stretches, including sun salutations, and then meditate there. It is a way of connecting my physical and mental facets with the spiritual. I will sit here to contemplate when I have difficulties in my life, for example when I am worried about something or upset. Sometimes I will write here and ask spirit to guide me. It is very personal and with practice it becomes very natural.

> "*We are not physical beings having a spiritual experience;*
> *we are spiritual beings having a physical experience.*"
>
> ~ *Pierre Teilhard de Chardin*

## 2. Smudging

This is a way of cleansing with the air element.
Many different herbs or combinations of herbs can be used. The most common is Californian White Sage because it burns well and smells gorgeous. But you could also use incense.

You need a heatproof container to burn the sage and collect the ash and to avoid burning anything else. A clam shell is a useful container. It has little holes along the bottom edge that help to keep it burning. A feather can be used too, to direct the smoke in the direction of your intent. You can do it yourself, or ask someone else to help you.

Try to direct the smoke all over yourself, under your feet, your armpits and behind you too. Here is an old smudging prayer that works like magic in my life. Try it and see!

Its author is unknown but it is likely to be Native American in origin:

# Smudging Prayer

May your hands be cleansed,
that they create beautiful things.
May your feet be cleansed,
that they may take you to where you most need to be.
May your heart be cleansed,
that you may hear its messages clearly.
May your throat be cleansed,
that you might speak rightly when words are needed.
May your eyes be cleansed,
that you might see the signs and wonders of the world.
May you and your space be cleansed
by the smoke of these fragrant plants.
And may that same smoke carry all of our prayers,
spiralling to the heavens.

## 3. Gratitude for an Attitude

*"When I admire the wonders of a sunset or the beauty of the moon,
my soul expands in the worship of the creator."*
*~ Mahatma Gandhi*

We have already covered this **Idea** in *Chapter Two* - Journaling for Joy, but it is a ritual worth exploring further as to why gratitude is so magical.

My ritual of making a few notes at the end of each day in a Gratitude Journal gets me to think of reasons to be thankful. Even on the toughest days, we can be grateful for something. The secret is to have a little book or diary next to your bed and write one, two or at most three sentences about the great stuff that happened in your day. If you forget, it will be easy to catch up the next day. Interesting though, that if you go beyond a few days, you will tend to forget the small stuff. And it's the small stuff that makes the difference, the things that when you read back have a huge impact on your life.

Just recently I bought a five-year diary that only has a few lines for each day. It is perfect and it will be so good to look back over a few years and read how my attitude and growth have evolved. It takes minutes to do and really turns you into more of an optimist than you ever thought were possible! This is really important for your progress in overcoming overeating. We can so easily flip between positive and negative thought. The ritual of documenting the good stuff in your life helps you to switch a lot quicker when you have life's challenges come along. It is these that, if left unnoticed, can send you straight over to the refrigerator!

Gratitude works on your unconscious mind. The negative thought that comes up, that ordinarily we know we don't want, comes from the unconscious part of the mind. If we can turn a really tough and stressful situation into at least one positive thought, the unconscious mind is tamed and your chances of overeating are greatly reduced. It's not that you should shut off grief, sadness, anger or pain. Get them out! But before you go to bed at night, write down a couple of good things. Even if it seems really ridiculous, do it anyway. Your unconscious mind won't realise how unrealistic or silly it might be. But you are investing in the knock-on effects that previous and current stress has had on your health.

Other ways to find an attitude of gratitude:
- say a prayer before eating
- say thank you when things go right
- say thank you when you learn something from the things that go wrong
- do a 'deed a day' with food, cash, time, energy, prayer, information to someone, without expectation of a repayment
- say thank you to a picture of a teacher, sending them love. They need it too!
- give away clothes that no longer fit and you haven't worn for six months
- thank those who give you their time or energy

and place your hand on your heart when you feel gratitude.

It's an amazing feeling!

When we are suffering from loss, any loss, whether it's the death of a loved one or the loss of a job, it is very difficult to find anything positive to say. And you have the right to honour the pain and grief that you are feeling. It's natural and a necessary part of healing. But that is the conscious part of your mind. To limit the long-term effects of this or any other trauma in the future, do yourself a powerful favour. Accept any offers of help, seek counselling or take time out for other healing where appropriate. Writing may be the last thing you want to do in those times, but it really can help.

These are just three simple practices you can do and work with every day that will nourish your soul. There are many others. For some of you this may be easy or you may already be doing similar rituals already. If you have limited time however, these are perfect to begin your personal practice in the morning and to finish your day off on a positive note.

*"Let my soul smile through my heart and my heart smile through my eyes,*
*that I may scatter rich smiles in sad hearts."*
*~ Paramahansa Yogananda*

## Chapter Twenty-Three
# Energy and the Chakras

*That's the thing about magic; you've got to know it's still here,*
*all around us, or it just stays invisible for you."*
*~ Charles de Lint*


## Energy in Essence

Einstein established a very important fact that really helps us to understand energy within ourselves and the energy around us. He proved that everything we see is just that, energy. Just particles of atoms moving around each other in various densities. The more solid an item looks to us, the more dense those particles are. So if all matter is energy, then there is a connection between those energies. Some shamanic traditions have believed this forever. That everything has an energy or spirit. Furthermore, that this spirit connects us all.

We also know that transference of energy is possible. It's so easy to pick up others' energies, helpful or not. We know what it's like to walk into a room and be totally charged by an atmosphere. We know what it's like to be moved by someone's presence, even before they open their mouth. We can walk into an empty house and either feel welcome or not. As human beings we are hugely affected by energies all around us.

In *The Hidden Messages in Water* by Masaru Emoto (see Resources), we find that sound and even thought can change the structure of ice formed in water. We can play light music at the same time as freezing water and beautiful crystals are made. Or we can play heavy non-melodic music and have ice formed into shards. It's really fascinating. And if we are approximately 60% water then we can start to understand how stress suffered from our environment might affect our health.

This is the same energy that exists within each of the trillions of cells in our human physical body. In science we call this ATP (adenosine triphosphate). Yogis recognise this as prana, and further East it is known as ki or chi. It is the vital force, and we need a minimum to keep us alive. The principle of increasing vital force is to improve **health, healing** and **happiness**. This energy is taken in through the food we eat, but also from the air we breathe. This, sadly, is often forgotten. When we feel low on energy we go straight to food for supplies of vital force, but the breath has it too. We might change what we eat and drink and how much and in what proportions. Or we might take supplements or medicines. This is our basic human instinct, our reptilian brain. It works from our Root chakra, the very first chakra, from where we are born. As we expand our consciousness, we perceive, realise and understand more. We have a greater insight into our body and mind's possibilities. We can improve our energy through the breath. By working with the breath to improve our health, we are expanding the sphere of influence on our health.

The energy that we have moves through channels. In the yoga system these are called nadis. In Traditional Chinese Medicine, they are called meridians. There are three main channels shown in the diagram below – the Ida, the Pingala and the Shushumna nadis. I want to discuss these because they are keys to finding balance in life and helping us along our path to greater **Self-Knowledge** and **Tenacity**. With the breath, the Ida and Pingala nadis help opposing energies to flow. You will see how different the qualities are from the illustration. Both qualities are needed for balance. You will see how the channels leave the Third Eye chakra and weave and cross each other all the way down to the Root. It is these opposing channels meeting that causes a swirling centre and creates the chakras. Chakra means wheel. These swirling energy centres within and even just outside our physical body 'organise' different elements and forces. They spin like centres of light. This network of nadis and chakras make up the energy body that we have already referred to previously in *Chapter Nine* - Nature Calls.

> *"Let's not forget that the little emotions are the great captains of our lives*
> *and we obey them without realizing it."*
> *~ Vincent Van Gogh*

As a newbie to this path, on first hearing about the chakras I was cynical to say the least. But as I started to understand more, I realised that I have known about them all along, though not on an intellectual level. For example, your throat chakra is the chakra for communication and purification. When you struggle to listen or make yourself heard or when you hold back emotion, you will often feel a lump in your throat or a need to cough. It's like your energy body naturally wants you to speak out, cry or make another sound that reflects how you truly feel (even though you stop yourself for whatever reason). The throat is also usually where we feel a common cold coming on. As the purification chakra, the throat is usually the first line of defence for your immunity.

Nowadays, I find it all fascinating. It's a great insight into all aspects of ourselves from an energetic perspective and provides another method of healing to add to our bag. Remembering that energy follows thought, we are able to send healing energy to ourselves, specifically to the chakra that is out of balance, or all of them if desired. This is a whistle-stop tour of seven of the chakras. There are thought to be 22 chakras in and around the body, but these are the main ones and the ones that, for me, are easy to sense and work with.

# Map of the Chakras and Nadis

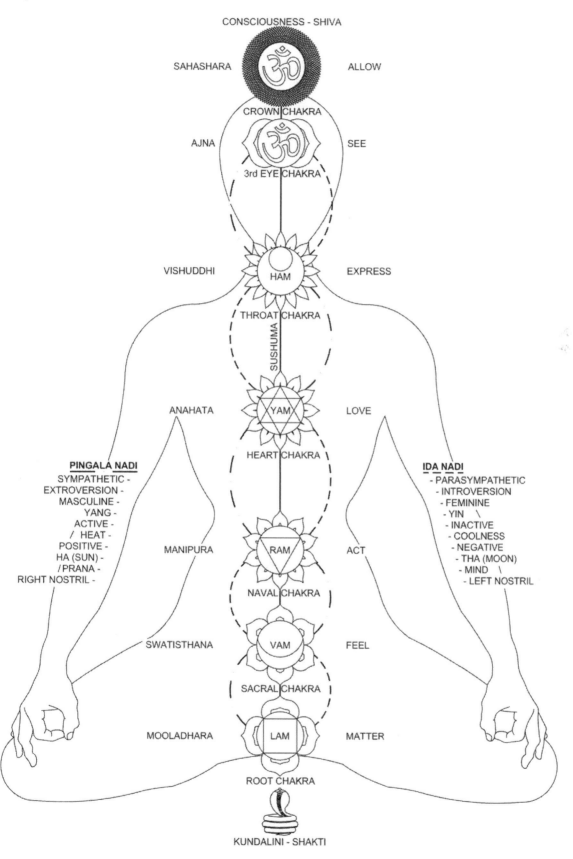

CONSCIOUSNESS - SHIVA

SAHASHARA          ALLOW

CROWN CHAKRA

AJNA          SEE

3rd EYE CHAKRA

VISHUDDHI          EXPRESS

HAM

THROAT CHAKRA

SUSHUMA

ANAHATA          LOVE

YAM

HEART CHAKRA

**PINGALA NADI**
SYMPATHETIC -
EXTROVERSION -
MASCULINE -
YANG -
ACTIVE -
/ HEAT -
POSITIVE -
HA (SUN) -
/ PRANA -
RIGHT NOSTRIL -

MANIPURA          ACT

RAM

NAVAL CHAKRA

**IDA NADI**
- PARASYMPATHETIC
- INTROVERSION
- FEMININE
- YIN  \
- INACTIVE
- COOLNESS
- NEGATIVE
- THA (MOON)
- MIND  \
- LEFT NOSTRIL

SWATISTHANA          FEEL

VAM

SACRAL CHAKRA

MOOLADHARA          MATTER

LAM

ROOT CHAKRA

KUNDALINI - SHAKTI

## 1.Root Chakra - (Mooladhara)

*Location* - at the centre of the root of the torso, in a slightly different place for men and women - for men, its centre is the perineum, for women it is the top of the cervix
*Visualisation* - a dark red, brown, earthy-coloured lotus with four petals
*Physical* - connected to bowel, buttocks, legs and feet
*Life* - basic human needs, food, shelter, clothing, family, money
*Element* - Earth
*Mantra* - LAM
*Sense* - Smell

## 2. Sacral Chakra - (Swatisthana)

*Location* - at the sacrum, slightly back from alignment to the others
*Visualisation* - an orange lotus with six petals
*Physical* - connected to intestines, lower back, reproductive organs, urinary system
*Life* - human wants and desires, emotions and sexuality
*Element* - Water
*Mantra* - VAM
*Sense* - Taste

## 3. Navel/Solar Plexus Chakra - Manipura

*Location* - centred at the navel
*Visualisation* - a yellow lotus with ten petals
*Physical* - connected to stomach, liver, gall bladder, pancreas
*Life* - personal power, confidence, self-worth, ego, action, reaction
*Element* - Fire
*Mantra* - RAM
*Sense* - Sight

## 4. Heart Chakra - (Anahata)

*Location* - the centre of the chest
*Visualisation* - a green lotus with twelve petals
*Physical* - connected to heart, lungs, circulation, shoulders, upper spine, arms and hands
*Life* - unconditional love, compassion, giving and receiving, expansion, spiritual growth
*Element* - Air
*Mantra* - YAM
*Sense* – Touch

## 5. Throat Chakra - (Vishuddhi)

*Location* - the throat
*Visualisation* - a turquoise blue lotus with sixteen petals
*Physical* - connected to throat, neck, teeth, jaw, mouth, immunity
*Life* - communication and purification
*Element* - Space
*Mantra* - HAM
*Sense* - Hearing


## 6. Third Eye - (Ajna)

*Location* - between the eyebrows at the centre of the head
*Visualisation* - an indigo lotus with two petals
*Physical* - connected to pituitary gland (hormones of stress, reproduction, digestion), nose, left eye, nervous system
*Life* - balance, inner wisdom, insight, intuition, non-reaction
*Element* - Light
*Mantra* - OM
*Sense* - Mind


## 7. Crown - (Sahasrara)

*Location* - the top of the head
*Visualisation* - a purple or white thousand-petaled lotus
*Physical* - connected to pineal gland (thirst, hunger and sexual desire), right eye
*Life* - bliss, enlightenment, the destination when all of the other chakras are perfectly aligned
*Element* - Infinity
*Mantra* - SoHam
*Sense* - Soul


*"Emotion always has its roots in the unconscious and manifests itself in the body."*
~ *Irene Claremont de Castillejo*

## Chakras and Overeating

Now let's take a closer look:

### 1. Roots of Overeating - Mooladhara

The desire to eat comes from a basic ancient instinct within our limbic brain, our unconscious mind and our Root Chakra, which all work together so that generations of knowledge before us will ensure that we continue to survive. When this chakra is working in balance, we are able to eat just what we need. There is no need to panic. Even when we are hungry, we know that more food will be along soon. When the Root is out of balance, we live in fear or worry of lack, not always food. It can be lack of money, security, shelter or family. Overeating is a common consequence as we try to fill the lack of one basic need with another i.e. food. Constipation and other bowel issues are also common as we are energetically 'holding on' to matter out of fear of losing it.

### 2. Emotions of Overeating - Swadisthana

At the Sacrum, we are processing our feelings, our desires and our wants. The centres of the Root and Sacral chakras are quite close together and I often wonder whether this may be why we feel we need something when in fact we actually just want it! We don't need chocolate; we just want it. The same goes for a new dress, a handbag, the latest phone, slimmer thighs, bigger breasts, holidays, pets, cars, etc. There is nothing wrong with wanting things. But we do have to understand that getting what we want will not make us happy unless it is a necessary part of health or happiness. The delight we get from having our external desires satisfied is temporary. To believe that any of our wants will make us happy is an illusion and will only bring more desire. This desire, when out of control, causes stress. We mistake happiness for external things when happiness is a state of being that happens from the inside. We can relate this so easily to food. We can convince ourselves that we need more carbs, more protein, sugar or coffee, or to finish our super-size meal. But it is a desire, not a need, and is likely to be one from which the joy is very short-lived. It is an illusion.
When this chakra is out of balance, the emotions are unstable. The overeater will want to try to comfort them with food. Being the water element, we need to drink lots of pure water to 'cool' down the emotions and obsessive desires.

### 3. The Power and the Ego - Manipura

When it comes down to emotions, it's the ego that feels threatened, our individual body, mind and soul that sees us as separate from everything else. People talk about enlightenment, awakening, finding inner peace and bliss. This happens when we realise that we are not separate from each other, but one vibrational force as humans, animals, plants, even stones. We are all connected by our source. We have personal power, but it can only be charged up by the love and support of others. When this chakra is out of balance, we can be in either extreme – powerless or overpowering. In balance we are confident yet humble, empowered yet caring. This chakra is a huge one for overeaters, as in the midst of emotions they are powerless over food. It comes from a lack of self-esteem, self-confidence and self-worth. It is therefore those very traits that need to be worked on. This chakra is in the stomach area, and beyond satiating hunger, it is the lack of power, confidence and self-esteem that we are feeding when we overeat. The element here is fire. The yogis call the fire of digestion 'agni'. When we do overeat, we will often suffer acidity, ulcers and IBS which is excess fire in the digestive system. In that moment, we forget that we have all the power we need. We add to it with food, usually highly acidic sugars and starches, and this causes the imbalances to increase.

## 4. The Open Heart Approach - Anahata

It is said that from 2012 we have moved from the age of Pisces (Manipura) to the age of Aquarius (Anahata). Whilst this is not a sudden transition, we are moving into a feminine consciousness of love, compassion and understanding. Whether this is happening in history is actually irrelevant to us. We each of us move up through the chakras in each of our lifetimes, at different paces. It is why even the most unhappiest people seem to find some peace before they die. How and at what rate we move up to bliss is really up to us. The heart is the centre of the chakras and brings together the energies of the first three to allow for transformation and recognition of higher spiritual traits. It is also the transition from the gross chakras to the more subtle.

When we are out of balance here, we are super-sensitive, taking seemingly everything 'to heart'. We feel pain, not just in our own lives but in others around us who are suffering. We are unable to easily accept atrocities that are happening in the world. Overeaters can try to dilute or digest the knotted feeling at the heart centre by eating and drinking. When in this place, we will often eat sweet carbohydrates that slide down easier, because actually we feel crushed in the chest area. Food is eaten to try and soothe the pain. Being the element of air, food is often met with indigestion – burping and flatulence. In balance we are compassionate, but able to maintain our peace and presence. For many women this can be felt around, before and through menopause. It is often confused with the emotions of the sacral chakra but the difference is an overwhelming sense of or need for love and unity of all things. It calls for action, and that action comes with the next chakra, through the voice. In balance, the heart chakra gives self-love, self-care and the ability to listen attentively, respond compassionately and feel the vibrations of others' feelings clearly. Yet there is no adverse reaction.

*"Lend yourself to others, but give yourself to yourself."*
*~ Michel de Montaigne*

## 5. Eating your Words - Vishuddhi

This chakra has two clear functions – communication and purification. When spinning in balance, we are able to communicate effectively and listen attentively. We are also able to perceive deep meaning within communication. The throat chakra is also for purification. We can purify with the breath, and our food and the tonsils play a major part. The intake of food and air has to go through many 'checkpoints' before it can be ingested properly into the body. However, when we are struggling to communicate, this chakra can go out of balance and the immune system can be compromised. The voice and sound in general needs space to manifest itself. The throat is the space element. One-off struggles will usually result in a little throat-clearing or a feeling of a lump in the throat. Long-term communication issues can lead to reduced immunity through stress, a sore throat, a long-term cough, thyroid problems and even cancer. When this chakra is out of sync, we tend not to chew our food properly. Saliva production is slow and we literally find things 'hard to swallow'. Ice cream, chocolate, milkshakes, coffee, alcohol and sweet drinks will be more comforting when we are stressed as a result of communication challenges. We are trying to almost literally eat our words so that they don't come out inappropriately. We may struggle to find a balance between speaking our truth and letting problems go. The next chakra teaches us the balance.

*"Keep your words soft and tender because tomorrow you may have to eat them."*
*~ Unknown*

## 6. Insight and Intuition - Ajna

When the third eye is functioning normally, we are developing deep insight. We realise that the answers to all of our challenges are to be seen and found within. This is where the intuition is developed. This chakra energy moves on such a subtle level and it is constantly trying to balance both the Ida and Pingala nadis. It balances light and heavy, light and dark, yin and yang, male and female, sun and moon – all the opposites you can think of. This is where intuitive eating starts. We are able to go inside and really ascertain what our body needs and make informed choices around food. It doesn't mean we are impeccable in our eating, but that we are allowing, without addiction and understanding fully, the relationship between food and the emotions. We are developing wisdom around food. Overeating happens rarely because the emotions are no longer the drivers. Imagine how often you would eat chocolate (or anything else you like when you are upset about something) if there wasn't an unhelpful emotion involved. Note that this is not a resting place. There are no laurels. You will have moments, times, or even long periods of this wisdom. It is only sustained by practices like those in this book. The freedom you get from the power of this chakra needs regular top-ups to keep it fuelled.


## 7. Crowning Glory - Sahasrara

Some systems say that the Crown chakra isn't really a chakra at all. It is really the result of the balancing and alignment of all of the other chakras. It is often seen as a funnel of light pouring in through the crown. It signifies enlightenment, bliss and pure light. Like many others, the Crown energy is so subtle that words are few in its description. However, here is a wonderful passage from my 'bible' in yoga practice, teaching and even in training other teachers, which I feel says enough:


*"It is the void. Perhaps it should be called the voidless void, the void of totality.*
*It is Brahman. It is everything and nothing.*
*Everything we say about it must be wrong as we would be immediately limiting and categorising it. Even if we say that it is infinite, we are wrong.*
*It transcends all concepts. It is the merging of consciousness and prana.*
*The sahasrara is the culmination of yoga. In fact it is yoga itself….the perfect merging."*
*~Yoga and Kriya, Swami Satyananda Saraswati*

# Exercises

## Bring Your Chakras to Life!

Colour in the Map of the Chakras, earlier in this chapter. This will help you to remember them. Be as creative as you like! The colours and characteristics of each are given after it for guidance.

## Chakra Cleansing

The chakra cleansing can be done as a ritual, daily, weekly or whenever you wish to help to bring the body and mind into balance. Here you will open, cleanse, balance and close the energy centres. There are many ways to balance the chakras. This ritual is a cleansing practice where you focus on each chakra in turn. Energy follows thought. So if your intention is to cleanse and balance, then that is where your energy will go. This is a great ritual to do when you light your candle on your altar each morning. It can take under five minutes when you get used to it. Don't worry if you get it 'wrong'. Your intention is what is important.

It is especially good to do if you have been receiving healing and performing transformational practices, or if your learning has been pushing your soul through some tough lessons. Your energy can sometimes feel depleted. This is a good way to keep your energy stores replenished. Quite often on a spiritual path we can become lethargic, in low mood or even depressed, fearful and tearful, worried and even angry. This is a natural process of release. When it shifts out, it leaves room for new energy – the energy of your self-care and personal power.

This is a suggestion for cleansing the chakras. There are many. As with all traditional practices, there are no rules, only guidelines to help you along the path and receive the best that these methods can offer. As your intuitive power and creativity breaks open, you will know what to do.

Start with the first chakra. Use a minimum of two breaths:

**Inhale** - 'unwind' the chakra with the elemental tool, a rattle, a crystal or your hand anti-clockwise
**Exhale** - either breathing open the lotus (visualising its colour, number of petals etc.) or chanting the Seed Mantra as per the table below
**Inhale** - opening further and breathing in vital force, light and power via the breath into the chakra
**Exhale** - visualise the lotus closing, using the elemental tool or your hand clockwise

Do this for all the first five chakras, up to and including the Throat Chakra

At the **Third Eye** - you can exercise your eyes by rapid blinking, rolling the eyes or doing a couple of rounds of alternate nostril breathing (see Resources for a link to my website) – say seven rounds.

And for the **Crown** - you can massage the top of the head whilst doing the breaths, visualising the breaths opening, cleansing and balancing the lotus with a thousand petals. OM can be used as a Seed Mantra for the Third Eye and the Crown chakras. A headstand or half headstand (feet stay on the floor!) is excellent for this, but only if you have had proper instruction and are aware of contraindications.

# Chakra Mantras

I would like to offer you one more practice and method of working with the chakras that is very simple and effective – the incredible use of sound. These mantras are called seed mantras and are a very powerful way of tuning in with the natural vibration of each chakra and helping it to rebalance if necessary. This can be done at any time. You can chant the mantras out loud, or if you prefer, internally. Either chant the mantra relevant to the physical area of your body that needs healing (where you feel pain) or the aspect of your life that is out of balance.

For example, if you feel that you are not able to communicate very well with someone, you could chant the mantra HAM.

| Chakra | English Name | Seed Mantra | Effect | Emotional Healing Issues with lack of: | Physical Healing |
|--------|-------------|-------------|--------|----------------------------------------|------------------|
| 1st | Base or Root | LAM | Grounding | Basic Human Needs, Food, Water, Sleep, Housing, Money, Family | Bowel, Buttocks, Legs and Feet |
| 2nd | Sacral | VAM | Cleansing/ Cooling | Emotions, Sexuality, Hormones | Intestines, Lower Back, Reproductive Organs, Urinary System |
| 3rd | Navel or Solar Plexus | RAM | Strengthening/ Heating | Personal Power, Ego, Confidence, Attitude | Stomach, Liver, Gall Bladder, Pancreas |
| 4th | Heart | YAM | Acceptance/ Self-Love | Love. Self-Worth. Acceptance, Compassion | Heart, Lungs, Circulation, Shoulders, Upper Spine, Arms and Hands |
| 5th | Throat | HAM | Communication/ Purification | Listening, Speaking, Understanding | Throat, Thyroid, Neck, Teeth, Jaw, Mouth, Immunity |
| 6th | Eyebrow Centre/ 3rd Eye | OM | Insight/ Intuition Clairvoyance | Truth, Knowing Oneself, Recognition, Clarity, Reasoning, Introspection | Pituitary Gland (hormones of stress, reproduction, digestion), Nose, Left Eye, Nervous System |
| 7th | Crown | SO HAM | Inner Peace/Harmony / Bliss | Realisation, Harmony, Union, Illumination, Enlightenment, Wisdom | Pineal Gland (thirst, hunger and sexual desire), Exhaustion, Epilepsy, Right Eye |

Chant it:
- Once repeatedly e.g. ham, ham, ham, etc. **or**
- With OM e.g. om ham, om ham, om ham etc. **or**
- Twice per repetition e.g. ham-ham, ham-ham, ham-ham etc.

Repeat it as many times as you like. 108 is a very powerful number. There are over 72,000 energy channels called nadis in the body. 108 of them are connected with the heart, so you can send healing to each of these with each repetition. The heart is where your compassion for yourself emanates. You can use mala beads for this, or use your fingers to count.


## How these exercises will help you

There are so many benefits to these practices, all of them I have personally experienced. They reduce stress, improve sleep, increase clarity, confidence, creativity and concentration. They calm down reactions of stress in the body, such as asthma, high blood pressure, acidity and other digestive disorders. They strengthen immunity. On a spiritual level, this practice helps us to feel balanced and to understand the subtler aspects of our being. The chakras relate to mind, body and spirit, therefore this practice helps us to strengthen the connection between them all.

Regular chakra cleansing and other cleansing practices in this book such as Sami Chakuay (*Chapter Nine*) and Smudging (*Chapter Twenty-two*) will shift low, heavy and often negative energies, making room for higher, lighter and more positive energies. We will then feel calm, content, blissful and ready to face the world with an authentic smile! This is extremely important also, as we integrate our learnings into our daily home or work life and our relationships with colleagues, family and friends.

This has been a brief introduction to the chakras for the purpose of overcoming emotional overeating. I hope that it serves you for recognising when and where healing is needed. If you want to investigate the MAGIC! of the chakras more, I have included some resources at the end of this book. Look out for other resources in the MAGIC! series too.


*"There are joys which long to be ours. God sends ten thousands truths, which come about us like birds seeking inlet; but we are shut up to them, and so they bring us nothing, but sit and sing awhile upon the roof, and then fly away."*
*~ Henry Ward Beecher*

# A MAGIC! menu for Emergency Emotions

*"It is by presence of mind in untried emergencies that the native metal of man is tested."*
*~ James Russell Lowell*

I have discussed the unconscious mind and its part in overeating a few times in this book. You will be aware that this is where **Discipline** comes in. It is the part of **The 7 Spells of BodyMAGIC!** over which we have the least control. Your **Discipline** comes as you take a breather to do any of the practices below. The result is the **Willpower** that, when away from temptation, is what you really crave. When we master this spell we are truly on the road to recovery.

Think of these like a first aid kit. You wouldn't wait until to cut yourself before you went to the pharmacy and bought some plasters, would you? The prudent thing to do is to have a well-stocked first aid kit in your home, office or suitcase.

You are now going to prepare yourself for the incidental events in life. From now on these events are going to be enjoyed to the fullest. You are going to be conscious, relaxed and totally present with all of your life's food-related events. As emotional overeaters we have often been caught off our guard. We go ahead and indulge, and probably most of the time enjoy it. But it is the next day that we suffer, berate ourselves and think that we should know better.

These tools are like reinforcements to help you in those short moments when you *do* have a choice, when you are making a choice that doesn't serve you or when you have made the choice and feel bad for making it. The emotions can vary from initial anxiety to guilt. It doesn't matter at what stage of the process you decide to use these tools; the long-term benefit will always be there. But with practice it will be earlier and earlier and you'll find yourself giving cravings a kick in the butt!

## Help for Hunger

| 'W' questions |
| --- |
| - why are you hungry? |
| - what can you eat that will suffice now? |
| - will you really keel over if you don't eat in the next hour? |
| - when is your next planned meal or snack? |
| - which mind is overpowering you: your subconscious (habitual patterns), unconscious (fear of starvation) or do you have a conscious and sensible reason for wanting/needing to eat soon? |
| - who is trying to wreck your plans for health and wellness? Is it part of your old self or is someone not supporting you? |

Have a little card or piece of paper in your purse or wallet that has the W questions on it. If you can, escape to the nearest WC or bathroom and take a good look at the list. Breathe deeply as you read through the questions and answer them to yourself.

## Help for Stress

### Flower Remedies

There are several flower essences that help with the emotions that drive us to overeating. Bach have selected three and boxed them as the Emotional Overeating Kit. In stressful times, I used to put a few drops of each into a bottle of water and drink it regularly throughout the day. It sure does help! For really challenging times and strong emotions, I have Rescue Remedy in my bag. There is a link in Resources that will take you to much more information.

### Emotion Elevator

On another little card, write down the unhelpful emotions and their helpful opposites. Use this either before you overeat (here, you're really making progress!), during your overeating or after your overeating. When you feel an overeating drive because of an emotion, refer to the card and work towards the helpful emotion opposite.

| Unhelpful | Helpful |
| --- | --- |
| Anger | Gratitude |
| Cruelty | Compassion |
| Disgust | Admiration |
| Familiarity | Surprise |
| Fear | Hope |
| Greed | Generosity |
| Hate | Love |
| Hurt | Relief |
| Loss | Gain |
| Panic | Knowing |
| Shame | Pride |
| Sorrow | Joy |
| Other | Other |

## Emotional Freedom Technique

Even if you have just overeaten, it's never too late to tap. It's a great emergency treatment for emotional overeating. But do it as soon as you can, for it will move your healing forward that bit closer to where you would prefer it to be.

A summary of the practice and points is here. Please refer to *Chapter Sixteen* for more details.

| The Practice | | The Points | |
|---|---|---|---|
| 1) | Identify Emotion or Behaviour | 1) | Top of the Head |
| 2) | Give it a 1-10 rating (SUD) | 2) | Between the Eyebrows |
| 3) | Set Up Statement x 3, karate chop | 3) | Edge of the Eyebrows |
| 4) | Tapping / Releasing Phase | 4) | Under the Eyes |
| 5) | Deep Breath, Rate SUD again | 5) | Under the Nose |
| 6) | If above 2 go back to 4 | 6) | Top of the Chin |
| 7) | If something more important comes up, go back to 2 | 7) | Chest below the Collarbone |
| | | 8) | Under the Arm(s) |

The Nine Reminders to keep you going. Ask yourself:

1. Have I ever had the opportunity to focus so intently on my emotions related to eating before?
2. How many diets have asked me to get to **Know Myself** or **Know my Worth**? How cool is that?
3. How much money have I actually spent so far on this book, compared with other programmes?
4. When have I ever had the opportunity to find out what really goes on in my mind around food?
5. How hard can it be to see it through? What do I have to lose?
6. How will I ever know if I don't try?
7. Look at my ideals for **health, healing** and **happiness**. They have MAGIC! powers
8. I really can live the rest of my life exactly the way I want to, guaranteed! I have that much personal power now and in the future, if I keep up my practice.
9. I am more likely to regret *not* doing this programme than doing it.

## Journal

When things get really tough, take out your journal. Not your gratitude diary, but the journal you write in most mornings to get stuff off your chest. So what if you've already written three pages already! The paper is a free and available therapist. It may be the last thing you want to do in your moments of meltdown, but what the heck? Just do it anyway. Write down everything you feel, bitch about whatever or whomever you like. This is a detox of your negative thoughts. It is not the same as affirmations. Then, when you feel calmer, keep writing and allow solutions to write themselves on the page. Stick with it until you know what to do or, what not to do to bring yourself back into balance.

**Lion's Breath - Simhasana**

This is a very powerful breathing practice indeed! I love teaching this to my students. They first watch me make a total fool of myself and then they get the chance to work through their own inhibitions and let go of so much ego. Sitting comfortably on the floor…

1. Close your eyes and take a deep, calm breath through the nose
2. As you exhale, lean forward, placing your hands on the floor for support if needed
3. Exhale with a roaring sound (if no-one is going to be a bit worried about you!) sticking your tongue out as far as you can and looking up to the centre of your eyebrows
4. Repeat several times until you feel calmer.

Incidentally, this is a great practice to do when you feel the first signs of a compromised immune system in the back of your throat. On those cold winter days, practice this outside to shift those microbes out of your throat and release unwanted energy.

**OM**

The cosmic sound of OM is a very powerful sound indeed. It is the original sound of the Universe. When we chant this sound, we are reconnecting with the great vibration. Hence the word Uni-Verse. It is grounding, centring and enlightening. It reminds our cells of the connection between all beings, animal, vegetable and mineral. It shifts us from our individual ego and helps us to develop the wisdom of compassion and the peace of letting go.

1. Inhale deeply into your belly
2. Exhale the sound of OM. About half of your breath is the O sound and the remaining half is the mmmm sound. Release it slow and long.
3. Repeat several times.

**Meditation**

So what if you've already meditated once in your day! This is part of your daily practice and will benefit your life now and in the long term. But there will always be troubled days. Why not use meditation as a therapy too! As soon as you can, get some time alone and just sit. If you don't want to close your eyes, find something to stare at for 5-10 minutes. It could be the sea, a rock, a flower, the moon or a star. Great if it is a natural object. If you cannot get outside, how about a crystal or a picture of your spiritual teacher or a symbol? Just stare. Do not intellectualise colours or form, stare blankly. As you do this, so will your mind also become blank. And you will release tension, criticism and emotions that don't serve you.

*"It takes no more time to see the good side of life than it takes to see the bad."*
*~ Jimmy Buffet*

## Chapter Twenty-Five
# Kick Ass in the Kitchen!

I would like to share some ideas about some of my favourite foods and give you a working day and a weekend day menu example to start your creative, as well as your digestive juices flowing. These are the foods that *I* have chosen to include. There are many eating policies and principles. Learn the facts, with research to back it up, and include or eliminate foods that do and don't work for *you*. Always remember that your **health** and your **healing,** as well as your **happiness** are the key ingredients in everything you eat.

I like to keep things simple if possible. If it takes much longer to prepare than to eat, then I'm spending too much time in the kitchen. Whilst I love cooking, the freedom I have from no longer overeating has meant I spend less time thinking, planning, shopping, preparing and cooking food generally. I have more time for other exciting stuff!

A few pieces of kitchen equipment I would not be without:
- [ ] A blender or hand blender for smoothies and pancake mixes
- [ ] A coffee grinder for nuts, seeds and dandelion coffee
- [ ] A sieve for rinsing buckwheat sprouts
- [ ] Jars for making sauerkraut, kimchi and sprouting seeds
- [ ] Good sharp knives, peelers and chopping boards
- [ ] A mandolin; vegetables never looked so professional!
- [ ] A water filter

Also handy but not essential:
- [ ] A slow cooker for soups, casseroles
- [ ] A pressure cooker for beans, lentils and rice when time is short
- [ ] A wok for stir-fries, curries and rice dishes
- [ ] An ice cream maker; when the weather gets hot, there's no need to do without your cooling treat.

Foods that I like to keep stocked up in my cupboards always:
- [ ] Non-glutinous staples for energy; buckwheat, quinoa, millet, rice, amaranth
- [ ] Plant protein; chickpeas, a good variety of lentils, beans, tempeh, tofu
- [ ] Nuts; almonds, walnuts, pecans, hazelnuts
- [ ] Flours for bread and pancakes; buckwheat, rice, gram (chickpea)
- [ ] Seeds; pumpkin, sunflower, flax/linseed, sesame, poppy
- [ ] Eggs
- [ ] Dried foods; tomatoes, dates, goji berries, coconut, seaweed
- [ ] Soya cream; rare occasions, coconut milk
- [ ] Oils; extra-virgin olive, coconut, flax/linseed
- [ ] Spices; cinnamon, paprika, cayenne, turmeric, cumin, coriander, cardamon, ginger
- [ ] Herbs; coriander, dill, rosemary, thyme, parsley, sage, tarragon, basil, oregano, curry leaves

Fresh Essentials (in season) e.g.:

| | | | |
|---|---|---|---|
| Apples or Pears | Garlic | Salad Greens | Squash or Pumpkin |
| Bananas | Lemons and Limes | Broccoli, Cabbage | Bell Peppers |
| Ginger | Cucumber | or Cauliflower | Courgette or |
| Celery | Potatoes inc Sweet | Tomatoes | Aubergine |

## Working Day Menu

**First thing** - boiled water with a squeeze of lemon or ginger tea made the night before

**Breakfast** - *Gluten-free Muesli*. Add any of the following. Good if soaked the night before:
    Flakes - oat, barley, spelt, rye, rice, quinoa
    Hemp or almond milk
    Nuts - almonds, pecans, hazelnuts, brazils
    Pumpkin and sunflower seeds
    Goji berries, apple chunks, raspberries or blueberries
    Chopped dates or prunes
    Desiccated or flaked coconut
    2 tsp of flax, hemp or coconut oil
    Cinnamon, nutmeg

**Mid-Morning** - *Detox Delight Smoothie*. Blend together or otherwise eat the carrot, celery and apple and make tea with the ginger:
    1 apple          1 stick celery
    1 carrot         thumbnail of peeled ginger

**Box Lunch** - *Salad of Many Colours*:
    1 cup buckwheat or quinoa, cooked or sprouted, or cooked brown rice some chopped almonds and/or some ground seeds, finely chopped tomatoes, celery, green or red pepper, red onion, grated carrot and/or beetroot
    Greens - from kale, spinach, lettuce, celery tops, herbs etc.
    Pomegranate or grated apple or orange pieces

    Drizzle over a simple dressing made from:-
    1/4 cup olive oil, 1/4 cup lemon juice, a crushed garlic clove, pinch of cayenne pepper and your favourite fresh herb

**Mid-afternoon** - *Apple or Pear*

**Dinner** - *Love My Lentil Curry*:
*TIP* - cook the lentils first and prepare all the ingredients just before you start to cook.
Cook rice or other accompaniment at the same time.

    1lb of cooked lentils - you can mix types of split lentils (yellow, green, red) or brown or green
    1/2 - 1 tsp of sea or rock salt (according to taste)

    1 tbsp coconut or olive oil - melt in wok or big pan on medium heat, then add
    1 tsp mustard seeds &
    1 tsp cumin seeds - fry until popping then add
    1 fresh chilli (without seeds will give medium heat, with for hotter) &
    2 tsp of freshly grated or finely chopped ginger &
    2 cloves of garlic, crushed or chopped - just 2 minutes more then add
    3/4 teaspoon of turmeric &
    4-8 curry leaves &
    2 large fresh chopped (or blitzed) or tinned tomatoes - simmer for 2 minutes, then add fresh coriander last and to garnish. A squeeze of lemon is delicious and helps release the iron from the lentils.

# Weekend Day Menu

**First thing** - boil a thumbnail-size piece of ginger in 500ml of water, serve with a squeeze of lemon juice and for an immunity boost a teaspoon of good-quality organic honey.

**Breakfast** - *CocoPaps Smoothie* - anti-parasitic, alkalising and excellent for the digestion. Blend the following all together:

        1/3 of a large papaya including the seeds
        350 ml of coconut water
        1 tbsp of desiccated coconut
        1 tbsp of coconut oil
        1-2 tbsp of ground flaxseed
        3 tbsp lemon juice
        1/2 tsp of freshly ground cloves

**Mid-morning Brunch** - *Veggie Skillet* - This is really a leftovers breakfast, but if you are starting from scratch you can use any combination of these and more:

        Aubergine, Onion, Tomatoes, Cooked potatoes/sweet potatoes, Mushrooms, Spinach, Celery, Garlic

Stir fry all you want to include, seasoning well, in a wok with a lid. Once they are warmed through, turn down the heat, crack an egg on top per person and put the lid on. It's ready when the eggs are cooked. You could fry, poach or scramble the eggs separately if you prefer. For a vegan alternative, sprinkle some nuts or seeds into the mix.

**Mid Afternoon** - *Vegan Shepherd's Pie* - a great British favourite - especially in winter:

        3-4 cups brown lentils, boil covered with water for up to 20 mins with
        1 tsp of bouillon or other veg stock &
        2 finely diced carrots
        1 tsp each of parsley, sage, rosemary and thyme
When tender, pour into a casserole dish big enough for the mash topping

Meanwhile boil up:

        4 medium or 3 large white potatoes until tender then add
        4 tbsp of olive oil
        1 tsp of finely chopped fresh or dried parsley
        A pinch of rock salt
        Mash together (adding a little nut or soya milk to get a spreadable consistency) and spoon onto the lentils mix
Top with whatever you like, such as:

        2 tbsp of nutritional yeast and/or
        2 tbsp ground sunflower or pumpkin seeds
        1 sliced tomato, sprinkling of paprika, black pepper and
Bake in a medium oven for 20 minutes to brown off a crust

**Supper** - Celery Soup:

        Half a head of celery including leaves, washed and chopped. Add
        2 medium or 1 very large white potato, scrubbed and diced up well, then rinsed again. Add water to cover (use a big pot)
        1-2 tsp of bouillon, vegetable stock or your favourite herbs, salt and pepper
Cook until potatoes are well cooked. If you like a slightly thicker soup, use a hand blender to blitz just half of the soup, leaving you something to chew on.

## Chapter Twenty-Six

# Health, Healing and Happiness - the Daily Recipe

*"May you live all the days of your life."*
*~ Unknown*

**The BodyMAGIC! approach**

## Recovery from emotional overeating involves an integrated system between body, mind and spirit

## Health

- it's not just changing what and/or how much we are eating – this would be just a *physical* aspect. If weight loss and health could be achieved by these changes alone, this book would not have needed writing, because diets, at least one or more of them, would have worked for me, but they didn't in the long term. Not for me, the emotional overeater.

**BodyMAGIC!** changes the emphasis from diet to optimum **HEALTH**

## Healing

- it is not solely a hypnosis or visualisation of what we would like to look like – that would just be working on the *mental* aspect. Whilst I truly believe that mindful practices have a great deal of success with the emotions involved in overeating, in my experience it takes a lot of time, commitment and dedication for this practice to be effective by itself. Life is short and you have waited long enough! Enthusiasm and patience are part of the journey and all of the practices together will try to develop them.

**BodyMAGIC!**'s mindful practices are geared towards effective **HEALING**

## Happiness

- it is not about foregoing your worldly ways to a greater power than yourself – this would be tackling overeating from solely a *spiritual* aspect. There are devotional practices within this book to help you to 'reconnect' with the essence that you are, with nature. This book is concerned with letting go of beliefs that don't serve you and growing your personal power.

**BodyMAGIC!** focuses its spiritual practices on lasting **HAPPINESS**

## It is a combination of **ALL OF THE ABOVE!**

# Knowing Myself

I have had success with **BodyMAGIC!** because I have woven the practices detailed in this book in a way that has served *me*. Besides following the **7 Spells** (a healthy **Intention, Understanding, Enthusiasm and Commitment**), I have learned how to adapt the emphasis of each of the practices to suit the meanderings of my own, perfectly natural emotions, day to day, even moment to moment. I have learned when to push through the unhelpful reactions of my unconscious mind, allow changes to the habits and patterns of my subconscious mind, and I honour the thoughts of my inner teacher – my conscious mind. This is essential to understanding my emotions and therefore overcoming overeating.

# Knowing My Worth

I have detailed each practice in the relevant chapters to a level that I believe will give you more than enough depth to gain huge benefits. However, I absolutely recognise and respect the different individual being (that is YOU!) doing this work. You may choose to do just some of what is offered here. You may decide to go and learn more about something that resonates really loudly with you. However, in this recipe, I have not given you any quantities. I have suggested a minimum time to be allocated to this practice. If you cannot find this time in your day, then you probably need to look at your self-worth. You have started the process already by reading this book. Don't give up. Because it is not only important for *your* life, but those around you will benefit too. A happy mum, wife, friend, sister, colleague etc. is someone who is great to be around and you will be influencing them too. Quality is what is most important here. Prioritising yourself by allocating time to a practice is the most important aspect of it all. But how much time you allow and what you actually do is up to you – how your body, mind and spirit feel at that time. This is how an **Idea** blossoms into **Success**. You want aspects of all of the spells to propel you! This is just a summary of the ingredients to show you how this MAGIC! tapestry is woven!

**A recipe for BodyMAGIC! using Health, Healing and Happiness**
(guilten-free, high-celebrate, low-fanciful, high-sweetness friendly)

# Ingredients

## for HEALTH
**Physical - what you can see and move; your BODY**
*what you have now, waiting for MAGIC!*

- ☐ A body you love and want to look after
- ☐ A sacred space where you can practice free from draughts and distractions
- ☐ A yoga mat and blanket
- ☐ A cushion, stool or chair in your space for meditation
- ☐ A pad, notebook/diary and/or journal and pens
- ☐ Your altar - with incense, tea-lights, oracle cards, crystals etc.
- ☐ A vision board
- ☐ Up-to-date information and tips about food and nutrition

## for HEALING
**Emotional - what you feel, understand; your MIND**
*your thoughts and practices to make the MAGIC! work*

- ☐ The **7 Spells of BodyMAGIC!**
- ☐ Emotion Elevator
- ☐ The Nine Reminders
- ☐ Mindful Munching
- ☐ The 10 Principal Understandings of BodyMAGIC!
- ☐ Traditional Medicine
- ☐ Emotional Freedom Technique (EFT)
- ☐ The Enneagram
- ☐ Affirmations or Mantras
- ☐ Detoxification of candida overgrowth and/or parasites if necessary
- ☐ Exercises in this book, review, repeat, renew!

## for HAPPINESS
**Spiritual - what you can sense; your SPIRIT/SOUL**
*the MAGIC! ingredient*

- ☐ A desire to connect with Mother Nature
- ☐ A daily ritual/practice
- ☐ A belief in a spiritual guide - some force within you and around you that you can ask for spiritual guidance from - your Higher Self, a deity, angels, a prophet, God, Allah, Jesus, Shiva, Buddha, Rama, Jehovah, the Source, your Divinity, the Universe. The shamans say that this force is known by a thousand names but the essence of that name is the same – a power that is all-knowing, all-loving and offers guidance.

# Method

Mix a little physical, emotional and spiritual in ratios to suit your body, your mood, your motivation, your time, your short-term goals for **health, healing** and **happiness**.

*Morning - 30 minutes or more if you have it:*

1. Connect with your **altar**, by lighting a candle and some incense, and use all of the elements in relation to the chakras to cleanse, prepare and supercharge your energies for your day.

2. **Smudge** yourself and anyone with you. Use the smudging prayer to help direct your attention and focus on what you need for the day. Or as an alternative, you can do Sami Chakuay.

3. **Stretch** and give thanks for the sun's rising and its power to give us health, using the sun salutation or sun breath. Do other stretches as your body needs. Or have a **yoga** practice like the one in *Chapter Eight*.

4. **Meditate** using Anapanasati. Ten minutes is a great start, but as you feel able and have time available, you can extend this. Set a quiet alarm so that you can forget about the time while you practice. Use the practice in *Chapter Five* until you feel ready to go it alone.

5. **Journal** about anything and everything on your mind. You can do this immediately on waking if you prefer. I prefer to meditate first, because that's when my stuff comes up for healing and writing about. I then use the journaling to help me to clear it away before I go about my day.

6. **Oracle** - take a card if you have one, a quotation or affirmation from a book, Facebook, Google or use the Rhyme for Life at the end of this chapter. Write it in your journal and/or on a sticky note, placing it somewhere you can see and remember/recite it throughout the day.

*Lunchtime - minimum 30 minutes*

Take a walk, run, bike ride or swim in nature. Be aware of all of the elements:

**Earth** - the earth you are walking on, the trees and plants growing from it, rocks, stones
**Water** - rain, clouds, dew on the grass, snow on the ground, the sea, a river, lake or pond
**Fire** - the sun, light
**Air** - the wind, breeze, the sound of air rushing past your ears, your breath
**Space** - the space around you and between everything, the sounds in the environment

Repeat a mantra you are working with, before you go back to your afternoon schedule. Do this in the mirror, with meaning.

*Evening - 30 minutes*

1.  Go to a class (yoga, kick-boxing, flower arranging, learning a language - anything that makes your heart sing), or go for a holistic healing or massage treatment if time and finances allow. Or take a bath in salts, or soak and massage your feet. Read some inspiring literature or watch a motivational film. Make time to truly relax and restock your energy.

2.  Write in your gratitude diary. Celebrate the good things from your day. No matter what happened, there is likely to be something small that you can be thankful for. Let go of the negative emotions around your difficulties by visualising sending them down into the ground with your out-breath. These emotions are based on your past conditioning and do not serve you. You are still, and always will be, one awesome and perfect human being!

3.  Set your **Ideas** and **Intentions** for tomorrow. Use the Rhyme of Life below.

4.  Meditate again for a minimum of ten minutes using Anapanasati as you did this morning.

5.  Repeat your affirmation as you stare into your own eyes in a mirror at least three times before you go to bed.


# Eating Practices

- see *Chapter Eleven* for more detailed information.

*As you prepare the food:*
Do this mindfully. Take time to use your senses. Notice the colours, textures, smells. Taste the raw ingredients where appropriate. Notice the sounds as you peel, chop, grate etc.
Try to keep your mind on the process of the food. Have an appreciation of where the food may have come from, imagine where it grew and its path to your kitchen. This love and respect for your food will nurture and nourish your body, your mind and your spirit.

*As you serve the food:*
Present it as if you were setting up an altar, arranging flowers or drawing a picture. This is a simple way of honouring the food as it will honour you.

Don't eat if you feel anger, sadness, fear, hurt or guilt or in the company of anyone else having these emotions.

*As you eat the food:*
Before you eat, say or chant a prayer either out loud or to yourself. A few are given below.
Always sit to eat - this doesn't include your car if you are moving!
Eat without distractions - TV, radio, computers, phones, games
Eat mindfully - use your senses, as above
Notice the sensations of the food in your body, visualise it nourishing every cell
Put down your knife and fork to talk, and wait until your mouth is empty before you speak
Eat slowly - try to chew your food more times than you do now. Some foods, like nuts, seeds, meat, need far more chewing than, say, an omelette

Notice when you no longer feel hunger and start to feel satisfied. Have one more mouthful *if you want to.* Leave what you don't need. Give it to someone else, feed it to animals or give it back to the earth with thanks. Note the size of portion you needed for you to feel satisfied, as a reference for the future.

*"It's still magic even if you know how it's done."*
~ Terry Pratchett

## More on Mornings

I never thought, a few years ago, that I would find time to have even half an hour to myself in the morning. Now I have two hours, at least! I love the mornings! And when I think back to when I used to tell everyone I wasn't a 'morning' person! It changed when I did my first yoga teacher training. I had to get up every single morning before 6 a.m. for almost four weeks. Then I knew that I *could* do mornings. And quite easily, *if* I wanted to.

Mornings are like a rebirth. They are like starting over, and that is why they are so valuable to me. If I leave all of my practices until after breakfast, they are never the same. The possibilities of interruptions, the chance that I may get into my work flow and not want to stop, or the chance to do something unexpected on a whim mean that meditation is practically impossible. Even if I could sit for half an hour and not be disturbed, my mind is having none of it. I am at my best when my practices are in the morning. It's like the old proverb – a stitch in time saves nine. Whatever work I can do on myself early in the morning is a great investment in my whole day. If I connect with myself in these ways, I open up my consciousness to creativity in my work and family. I can feel like everything is a fun experience. I'm not totally rigid. I let go of the emotions as they arise, or I channel them appropriately.

There are some mornings when I don't feel like all of it. I allow myself one morning a week off now if I need it. Sometimes I don't need that either, because I love my practice time! But I regularly go 21 days without a break, because that makes and keeps a habit. Give yourself a month. You have waited long enough for the kind of change that lasts in your **health** and **healing**. You deserve to give it your best shot. And it's a minimum of only 30 minutes, twice per day. If you don't make the lunchtime one, take an extra walk the following morning. Shift these practices around a bit if they don't totally suit your lifestyle. Please try and meditate twice per day, preferably in the same place at the same time. You are feeding your subconscious mind with a new habit. Like the franchise coffee you always used to have on your way to work or with your friends on a Thursday morning, you will miss your meditation when it becomes a habit and you don't get it. This is good!

Also remember that your breakfast is also a practice of its own. Even when you're rushed, you can still be mindfully rushing! Just be aware. Not only is this good for your journey with BodyMAGIC!, you are less likely to forget anything. Eat with consciousness and your body will thank you from the bottom of your bottom!

On those really busy days, when you don't have time for your practice, use a little mindfulness to cover your practice. Here's an example of how I might do this. Even getting up can be a chakra and elemental balancing experience:

1. When you put your feet on the ground and visit the toilet (Earth and Root)
2. When you have a drink of water and splash your face (Water and Sacral)
3. When you switch on the light or open the curtains (Fire and Solar Plexus)
4. Take a deep breath when you step outside or open a window (Air and Heart)
5. Stretch and/or go outside. Be aware of your space and the space around you (Space and Throat)

6. Meditate and/or spend time at your altar, or take a crystal and ask for its help and lessons today (Light and Third Eye)
7. Brush your hair or massage your scalp, being aware of your limitless possibilities (Crown)

*"When you arise in the morning, think of what a precious privilege it is to be alive - to breathe, to think, to enjoy, to love - then make that day count!"*
*~ Steve Maraboli*

## Lunchtime

Your lunchtime will depend on your working life, but try to eat your lunch at the same time every day. It's just another great habit. Your body is less likely to report hunger if it knows it is going to eat at a certain time. Routine is everything with these practices. If you feel hungrier in the mornings, eat more than you think you need for breakfast, or better still, eat your lunch earlier or have a snack mid-morning.

Before or after your lunch, go for a walk in nature. Lift your face to the sun, feel the wind in your hair, feel the ground under your feet. Take off your shoes if you can. If it's warm get some Vitamin D by rolling up your sleeves. This is the happy vitamin, and it's free! If it's raining, connect with the water. Let it wash away any stress or emotions that are not serving you. Ask our Mother Nature for the help she will want to give you. Just ask. Connect with all of the elements. Use them to cleanse and balance your chakras. You can do this while you walk, or sitting with your eyes closed.

Before you resume your work or afternoon activities, visit the bathroom mirror, take a deep breath and repeat your affirmation three times.

## Evening Endings

For some this is the most challenging time for getting into a practice routine. Yet it can be the most rewarding. I personally find that my evening meditation is deeper and less distracted. My to-do list has closed for the day and I am definitely more relaxed in my mind and body. However, it is also a time for families, meals, evening activities and sometimes a lot of noise. So you have to make it work. Just as you allow yourself time for eating to feed your body, so you can find time for meditation and journaling to feed your mind. You will sleep better and wake up more refreshed. It is a minimum of half an hour with your other practices. Once your family and friends get used to it, it will become normal.

*"Magic is believing in yourself, if you can do that, you can make anything happen."*
*~ Johann Wolfgang von Goethe*

## Daily Discipline

People sometimes ask me where the motivation to get up so early comes from. This verse crossed my path around 2006 and it shows it really all starts with going to bed:

### The Day Starts the Night Before

*An early night ensures deep, refreshing sleep.*
*Deep, refreshing sleep ensures one wakes early - rested and revitalised.*
*Waking early - rested and revitalised - ensures time for massage, yoga and meditation.*
*Massage, yoga and meditation ensure the mind and body are awake and alive.*

*Mind and body - fully awake and alive - ensure a happy countenance.*
*A happy countenance ensures a stress-free mind.*
*A stress-free mind creates a positive mind.*
*A stress-free, positive mind imparts love and peace to those around.*

*An atmosphere of love and peace creates a wave of harmony throughout the room.*
*A wave of harmony throughout the room creates a wave of harmony throughout the house.*
*A wave of harmony throughout the house creates a wave of harmony throughout the city.*
*A wave of harmony throughout the city creates a wave of harmony throughout the country.*
*A wave of harmony throughout the country creates a wave of harmony throughout the world.*

*The peace and harmony of every individual in every town, in every city, in every country is in your power and their happiness rests in your arms. If you are fully awake in the present moment, having learnt from and let go of the past, the future will take care of itself. You simply need to bathe in the joy of being fully alive in every present waking moment*
*And the real beauty is - you can start today.*

*~ Danny Cavanagh & Carol Willis*

My mother used to say to me that an hour's sleep before midnight was worth two hours after midnight. I never found out where she learned that, but there could be some truth in it. I try to follow nature with my sleep patterns, as we discussed in *Chapter Nine* - Nature Calls (Natural Sleep, Natural Relaxation). It's all part of nature's healing package. Sleep is like pressing the reset button in so many ways. But especially in the mind. My mum also used to say, "Don't worry, it'll all be OK in the morning", and mostly it was. I like to think that *every* moment is a moment to start afresh. Most of us see a New Year as an opportunity to start anew. Unfortunately, we put such a high expectation on resolutions, like diets, that most of them fail. But to have that opportunity every day is nothing short of magical. The secret is to park yesterday and let it go, take what you learned into today and set your **Ideas** and **Intentions**, just small ones, to move along your journey.

You can do this by writing a small list, such as a sticky note of just four things you'll prioritise today for yourself. You can do it the night before, right after your gratitude diary, or in the morning when you have meditated etc.

This is my rhyme to help you to remember:

### A Rhyme for Life

Something new I want to do
Someone who I want to reach out to
Somewhere free you want to be
Some way real you want to feel

*- Chinmayi Dore*

For example:-
I may want to try a new recipe,
call a friend I have been thinking about for a while,
visit an art exhibition at lunchtime
and feel like I am opening up to new possibilities

Simple but very effective. It's more about the Want To than the Must Do! Try it for a week and notice how you feel. It's about spending time on and with yourself. It's also an extremely important part of your healing and empowerment.

## Chapter Twenty-Seven
# BodyMAGIC! for life

*"The greater danger for most of us is not that our aim is too high and we miss it, but that it is too low and we reach it."*
*~ Michelangelo Buonarrot*

Congratulations! If you have read this book and have spent some time each day with at least some of the practices, I want to thank you from the bottom of my heart for giving this book the time you deserve. The process of adapting life to effect great change is one that takes courage. Change means lots of letting go, and that can be a tough and fearful process. Courage is realising that you deserve to live in freedom from emotional overeating, and taking unwavering, consistent steps towards that freedom. I hope you have found that it's not really been as hard as you once might've thought. I trust that you have noticed certain harmful emotions and behaviours dwindling in their frequency and intensity in your life. There will always be dark days, but I have found that those are the ones with the greatest learnings. Life became unbearable for us because there were too many dark days and we didn't know how to work with them. In dieting, we didn't realise that we were working against them. We didn't know any other way. But all other ways have led us to where we are today.

BodyMAGIC! is for life. This book has just been the beginning of the best and the rest of your life!

## Affirming Improvement

Sometimes we forget how far we have come, how hard things were and how life has improved. You can go back in your journal to see this comparison if you like. Here's another way. I have repeated my words from *Chapter Nineteen* - See it! Say it! Give it! Get it! into affirmations to help you change your mind, when needed. You can add to this list, of course. These words have great power behind them. They will pick you up in troubled times, because you will remember what you are capable of. They are slightly different from other affirmations, as they do touch on the negative aspects of the past. This is so that you can take renewed power from realising your ability to make permanent change. If they resonate with you, write them out in your journal somewhere prominent. These are my gains from following the practices I have shared with you in this book.

I wish you the same success!

*Life in General*
- [ ] my health in mind and body have improved so much
- [ ] I have allowed deep emotional healing to take place and I have real happiness in my life
- [ ] my relationships have shifted and they have become more open and meaningful
- [ ] I am able to see my life and soul's purpose a lot more clearly
- [ ] I have let go of so much fear attached to my future, based on my past
- [ ] the clouds of the past have lifted and I am so joyful, most of the time
- [ ] I have more energy and zest for life
- [ ] I am frowning less and smiling more
- [ ] I am struggling less and thriving more
- [ ] I am sad less and hopeful more

*"The most important thing is to enjoy your life - to be happy - it's all that matters."*
*~ Audrey Hepburn*

*Eating Affirmations*

- ☐ I now find that I am happy to leave food that I don't want
- ☐ I find that I am not thinking about food *all* or even *most* of the time
- ☐ I find that I don't salivate at the thought of chocolate, cakes, ice cream, even XX (your indulgence)!
- ☐ I am able to go for meals and not eat to bursting, and without guilt
- ☐ I am able to watch someone eat a dessert without wanting to try it, because I already had enough
- ☐ I am able to make a loaf of healthy bread/cake/cookies and only have one or two portions of it
- ☐ I am eating more slowly, tasting more and not wishing I could eat it all over again
- ☐ I am not craving simple carbs like sugar when I have low days
- ☐ I have a stock of healthy snacks in the house, most of which I made myself
- ☐ I can make a shopping list, look at recipes, plan meals without having to eat afterwards
- ☐ I know exactly what to eat for health if I am not at home
- ☐ I look forward to spending time with my friends, more than the food I am going to eat
- ☐ I don't panic if I am hungry

## Remember and Review, Recall and Revisit!

I recommend that you read the contents page, at the start of this book, again regularly. It will serve as a memory jogger to help keep you on track. It will help to guide you back to aspects of BodyMAGIC! you don't recall, or haven't integrated into your life. Always remember that life changes so rapidly, so whilst something may have seemed impossible, unreasonable and impractical the first time you read this book, it may be totally suited and indeed useful to your lifestyle a few weeks or months later. In the spirit of "A change is as good as a rest," keep reviewing this list to check your understanding and practice.

*"But remember.*
*Just because you don't believe in something doesn't mean it isn't real."*
*~ Katherine Howe*

# A COLLECTION OF LEARNINGS FROM THIS BOOK AS AN EASY REFERENCE

*Your* Keys to Freedom *in whatever you do in your life:*

**Know Myself**
**Know My Worth**

*First up, let's make no mistake about our findings when it comes to food, diet and living:*

## The 10 Principal Understandings of BodyMAGIC!

*Health*
*Healing*
*Happiness*

1. Improved **health**, an integrated practice of **healing** and finding **happiness** facilitate life-long freedom from emotional overeating.
2. Improved **health** is achieved by reconnecting with Mother Nature through the elements of Earth, Water, Fire, Air, Space. This connection is through eating, drinking, moving, breathing, sleeping and other day-to-day practices in a NATURAL way.
3. Practices of traditional **healing** offer holistic solutions to the challenges of emotional overeating.
4. Real **happiness** is the true meaning of life and can only be found within oneself.
5. Diets, including chemical appetite suppressants, meal replacement plans, fasting and nutritional adjustment methods are not effective in the long term for emotional overeating.
6. Exercise is an important part of the principles of **health, healing** and **happiness**, not a direct method of losing weight.
7. Most emotional overeaters have a food addiction, a diet addiction or an addiction to one food, or a combination of these, which usually results in sub-optimal mental and/or physical health.
8. The basis of addiction is emotional. Therefore, the most important work for this programme is that which focuses on **healing** the emotions of past trauma, being aware of harmful emotions in current day challenges and having tools to manage negative emotions for the future.
9. There are food and drink types that can hinder or help progress, based on current medical research. Therefore, it is necessary to make informed choices about food and drink that is bought, caught, harvested, prepared and eaten. Eliminating or including a food may contribute to **health, healing** and **happiness** but it does not guarantee weight loss.

*Review these spells in any change you make – care for the unconscious mind at step 5!*

## The 7 Spells of BodyMAGIC!

1. **Idea** which becomes **Intention** leads to
2. **Focus** which becomes **Understanding** leads to
3. **Confidence** which becomes **Enthusiasm** leads to
4. **Determination** which becomes **Commitment** leads to
5. **Discipline** which becomes **Willpower** leads to
6. **Self-Knowledge** which becomes **Patience** leads to
7. **Tenacity** which becomes **Success** leads to

Lasting, lifelong **health, healing** and **happiness!**

*Update this or your original one regularly to see how far you have come! Aspire to bliss!*

## The BodyMAGIC! Emotion Elevator

| Unhelpful | Where I see myself at the start of working through BodyMAGIC! (how I feel most of the time). Mark with the date (MM/YY) on the scale between the two polar opposites. | Helpful |
|---|---|---|
| | ⟶ | |
| Anger | | Gratitude |
| Boredom | | Spontaneity |
| Cruelty | | Compassion |
| Disappointment | | Contentment |
| Disgust | | Admiration |
| Doubt | | Faith |
| Fear | | Hope |
| Greed | | Generosity |
| Hate | | Love |
| Hurt | | Relief |
| Loss | | Gain |
| Overwhelm | | Serenity |
| Panic | | Knowing |
| Shame | | Pride |
| Sorrow | (e.g.) 03/18 | Joy |
| Worry | | Peace |

*Fill in the blanks regularly, because change happens fast!*

## Ideals and Intentions

Ideal **Health** –
Ideal **Healing** -
Ideal **Happiness** -

> Make a new vision board at least every year!

*No time to practice? Do this anywhere! A few seconds can change the course of your day!*

## Anapanasati Anytime Meditation

Simply bring your awareness to the tip of your nose and witness the breath moving in and out

# YogaMAGIC! for BodyMAGIC!*

## Asana

Mountain Pose
Half Sun Salutation
Standing Twists
Standing Side Bends
Chair Breathing
Staff Pose
Bird Flying Pose
Child's Pose
Corpse Pose

## Breathing Tips for Asana
1. Always through the nose
2. Never hold your breath
3. Inhale up, exhale down

## Breathing Exercises
1. Conscious Deep Breath (*Chapter 9*)
2. Abdominal Breath (*Chapter 9*)

## Living a Yoga Practice
Yamas and Niyamas

*\*unless specified, all of these practices are in Chapter Eight*

*Choose nature! Get connected however, whenever you can. Nature makes no rules!*

# Back to Nature

## Natural-living Checklist
the food I eat - clean, organic, fresh and whole
the water I drink, filtered, bottled
the air I breathe, fresh air often
the exercise I perform, outside is best
the sleep I have and proper relaxation
the medicine I take - let nature support
the healing I need - consider healing the emotions
the cleaning I do - eco products for you & your family
the beauty I seek - harmful chemicals/animal testing

## Nature-loving Practices
Sami Chakuay - anytime of day
Conscious Deep Breathing
Lunchtime walk - focus on the elements
Gratitude Prayer to Mother Nature
Sound Sleep - Changes and Starts

*"When I look up, there are no limits"*
*~ Chinmayi*

*Nine steps to freedom at mealtimes!*

# Mindful Munching Memorandum

1. *Prepare to impress*
2. *Use your senses*
3. *Sit in super surroundings*
4. *Dodge distractions*
5. *Grace or gratitude*
6. *Shut up and chew!*
7. *Wait for the wash down*
8. *Take a break and contemplate*
9. *Love your leftovers, don't eat them*

*What's the point? Well EFT works on exactly the reason why you are overeating - your emotions!*

# Emotional Freedom Technique

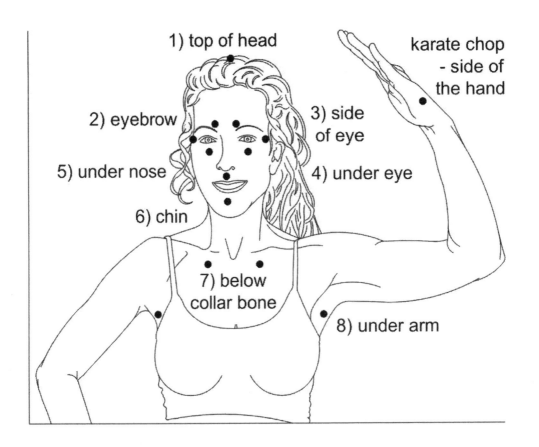

*This amazing shape has taught me so much about myself, my relationships and my world!*

# The Enneagram

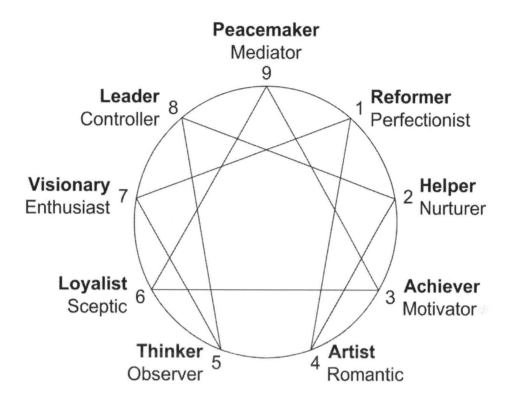

Once you know your type, get an Enneagram Thought for the Day from The Enneagram Institute. It's free and really helps with **Knowing Yourself** and **Knowing Your Worth**

*Short and sweet. Maybe not so much sweet in the future! Choose healthful food over deadly sins!*

# The Seven Seldom Sins

Coffee
Processed foods including unhealthful fats
Alcohol
Sugar, artificial sweeteners and soda
Meat and fish from factories
Dairy
Wheat and gluten

*Get your rituals on with your own personal experience. We were born for ceremony!*

# Rituals

Build an altar and refresh it often, visit it for quiet time at least once a day.
Cleanse your energy field as you would take a shower - smudging is ideal.
Work gratitude into your life wherever possible - it opens up channels to receive what you desire

*Chakras play a huge part in health, healing and happiness. Know them as you know yourself!*

# The Chakras

Connect with your chakras using visualisations (colours, petals etc.) and sound (mantras) and their qualities and energies

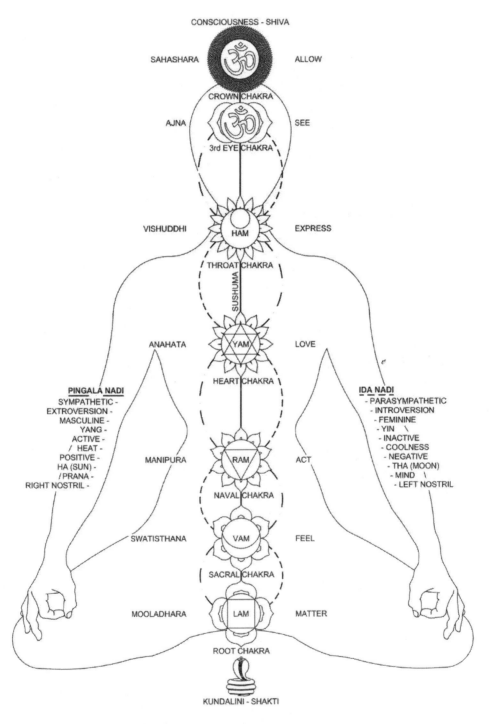

CONSCIOUSNESS - SHIVA

SAHASHARA    ALLOW

CROWN CHAKRA

AJNA    SEE

3rd EYE CHAKRA

VISHUDDHI    HAM    EXPRESS

THROAT CHAKRA

SUSHUMA

ANAHATA    YAM    LOVE

HEART CHAKRA

**PINGALA NADI**
SYMPATHETIC -
EXTROVERSION -
MASCULINE -
YANG -
ACTIVE -
/ HEAT -
POSITIVE -
HA (SUN) -
/ PRANA -
RIGHT NOSTRIL -

MANIPURA    RAM    ACT

NAVAL CHAKRA

**IDA NADI**
- PARASYMPATHETIC
- INTROVERSION
- FEMININE
- YIN \
- INACTIVE
- COOLNESS
- NEGATIVE
- THA (MOON)
- MIND \
- LEFT NOSTRIL

SWATISTHANA    VAM    FEEL

SACRAL CHAKRA

MOOLADHARA    LAM    MATTER

ROOT CHAKRA

KUNDALINI - SHAKTI

*"Without patience, magic would be undiscovered*
*- in rushing everything, we would never hear its whisper inside."*
*~ Tamora Pierce, Sandry's Book*

# Emergency MAGIC!

| Unhelpful | Helpful |
|-----------|---------|
| Anger | Gratitude |
| Cruelty | Compassion |
| Disgust | Admiration |
| Familiarity | Surprise |
| Fear | Hope |
| Greed | Generosity |
| Hate | Love |
| Hurt | Relief |
| Loss | Gain |
| Panic | Knowing |
| Shame | Pride |
| Sorrow | Joy |
| Other | Other |

| "W" questions |
|---------------|
| - why are you hungry? |
| - what can you eat that will suffice now? |
| - will you really keel over if you don't eat in the next hour? |
| - when is your next planned meal or snack? |
| - which mind is overpowering you:- your subconscious (habitual patterns), unconscious (fear of starvation) or do you have a conscious and sensible reason for wanting/needing to eat soon? |
| - who is trying to wreck your plans for health and wellness? Is it part of your old self or is someone not supporting you? |

Refer back to Chapter Twenty-Four for more help and explanations of these tables and other help.

# The Nine Reminders to keep you going!

1.  Have I ever had the opportunity to focus so intently on my emotions related to eating before?
2.  How many diets have asked me to get to **Know Myself** or **Know my Worth**? How cool is that?
3.  How much money have I actually spent so far on this book, compared with other programmes?
4.  When have I ever had the opportunity to find out what really goes on in my mind around food?
5.  How hard can it be to see it through? What do I have to lose?
6.  How will I ever know if I don't try?
7.  Look at my ideals for **health, healing** and **happiness**. They have MAGIC! powers
8.  I really can live the rest of my life exactly the way I want to, guaranteed! I have that much personal power now and in the future if I keep up my practice.
9.  I am more likely to regret *not* doing this programme than doing it.

-  Hit your Journal and write away your worries. Tell it exactly like it is!

- Do some Lion's Breath to release your fiery emotions - RAAAAAAAH!
- Chant OM out loud, under your breath or in your mind, deep breath required, works a treat
- Meditation is great at stopping the unconscious forces that can lead to emotional overeating

There's always a band aid in BodyMAGIC!

Take it in pieces, a little every day, savour and enjoy the moment's MAGIC! like fine chocolate!

# The Daily Recipe

Check your ingredients the night before. Do you need anything to make your perfect Daily Recipe?

## Morning
- 30 to 60-minutes practice

Altar - Smudge - Stretch/Yoga - Meditate (min. 10 minutes) - Journal - Oracle

## Lunchtime
- 30-minutes practice

Walk in Nature - connect with the elements

## Evening
- most evenings, take some other MAGIC! for yourself for 60-90 minutes

Go to a class, have a massage, read a book, take a bath, draw, write or paint, Savasana
- 30-minutes practice

Gratitude diary - Ideas and Intentions - Meditate (min 10 minutes)

### *A Rhyme for Life*
*Something new I want to do*
*Someone who I want to reach out to*
*Somewhere free you want to be*
*Some way real you want to feel*

## Priorities
Do what you feel with the time you have. I suggest that you prioritise meditation if anything, as that is the most important part of your practice. If you don't feel like meditation, there's a good chance that is exactly what you need, because your unconscious mind is fearing the change. It can mean that you are getting close to a shift, so please don't give up!

*'Every saint has a past, and every sinner has a future.'*
*~ Oscar Wilde*

# I Care About What You Think!

Please take a moment to leave a Review on Amazon for this book. You can also leave a review at the end of the videos too if you wish.

Go to your local Amazon (.com, .co.uk, .es, etc), search for Body Magic, select this book, scroll down and you can easily write a review.

Your feedback really helps others decide whether this book is for them. I want to reach lots of people with my message but I want people to understand, from your perspective what the book is really like. The programme will be more effective if it's read by the right people. Then the reviews will get better, so that I sell more books to the people who need it.

## Thank you from my heart!

# What Happens Now?

You have lots of choices and support…

1. Go to **www.bodymagic.website** and sign up for regular blogs, news, practice support and get some free training on Knowing Yourself and Knowing Your Worth immediately.

2. Join **BodyMAGIC! - an End to Emotional Eating** Facebook page where lots of really useful tips, tricks and inspiration are to be found. Find extra information on recipes, natural medicine, yoga, meditation and events. This is also where you will find updates, new research and new approaches to your healing. Ask questions too. The answers will benefit everyone.

3. Join us on **Retreat!** There will be at least one **BodyMAGIC! Retreat** each year. Details are found on www.bodymagic.website. This will accelerate your healing way beyond your expectations.

4. Book a **FREE! 30-minute coaching session** with me. I will help you find solutions to the most challenging aspects of your journey and show you how I can help you personally. Simply go to www.bodymagic.website and a box will pop up like MAGIC!

5. Look out for **online and live events**, webinars, Skype calls, new videos, recordings, classes, workshops and more on the website, in your inbox and on social media.

## *This is only the beginning!*

Here's to your Health, Healing and Happiness now, and in the future!

# References

## *Introduction*

(1) Zhang, Niu, Irene Lo, and Ashutosh Kaul. "Consequences of Rapid Weight Loss - Adipose Tissue and Adipokines in Health and Disease." Humana Press, 2014. 199-216.

## *Chapter Seven* - **Food Facts**

(1) Bleich, Sara N., et al. "Diet-beverage consumption and caloric intake among US adults, overall and by body weight." *American Journal of Public Health* 104.3 (2014): e72-e78.

(2) "Protein and Amino Acid Requirements in Human Nutrition." N.p., 2007. Web. 9 Apr. 2015. 140 <http://whqlibdoc.who.int/trs/WHO_TRS_935_eng.pdf>.

(3) Blakeslee, Sandra. "Complex and Hidden Brain in Gut Makes Stomachaches and Butterflies." *New York Times*. N.p., 23 Jan. 1996. Web. 24 Apr. 2015. <http://www.nytimes.com/1996/01/23/science/complex-and-hidden-brain-in-gut-makes-stomachaches-and-butterflies.html>.

(4) Siri-Tarino, Patty W., et al. "Meta-analysis of prospective cohort studies evaluating the association of saturated fat with cardiovascular disease." *The American Journal of Clinical Nutrition* (2010): ajcn-27725.

(5) Fernandez, Maria Luz. "Dietary cholesterol provided by eggs and plasma lipoproteins in healthy populations." *Current Opinion in Clinical Nutrition & Metabolic Care* 9.1 (2006): 8-12.

(6) Krauss, Ronald M., et al. "Separate effects of reduced carbohydrate intake and weight loss on atherogenic dyslipidemia." *The American Journal of Clinical Nutrition* 83.5 (2006): 1025-1031.

(7) Simopoulos, Artemis P. "The importance of the ratio of omega-6/omega-3 essential fatty acids." *Biomedicine & Pharmacotherapy* 56.8 (2002): 365-379.

(8) Assunçao, Monica L., et al. "Effects of dietary coconut oil on the biochemical and anthropometric profiles of women presenting abdominal obesity." *Lipids* 44.7 (2009): 593-601.

(9) Golomb, Beatrice A., et al. "Trans fat consumption and aggression." *PLOS ONE* 7.3 (2012): e32175.

(10) Stott-Miller, Marni, Marian L. Neuhouser, and Janet L. Stanford. "Consumption of deep-fried foods and risk of prostate cancer." *The Prostate* 73.9 (2013): 960-969.

(11) Ko, Ying-Chin, et al. "Chinese food cooking and lung cancer in women nonsmokers." *American Journal of Epidemiology* 151.2 (2000): 140-147.

(12) Hawkes, Steve, and John Bingham. "Scurvy returns among children with diets 'worse than in the war'." *The Telegraph* 3 July 2013. Web. 9 Apr. 2015. <http://www.telegraph.co.uk/news/health/news/10158690/Scurvy-returns-among-children-with-diets-worse-than-in-the-war.html>.

(13) Smith & Smith. "Middle class children suffering rickets." *The Telegraph* 13 Nov. 2010. Web. 9 Apr. 2015. <http://www.telegraph.co.uk/news/health/news/8128781/Middle-class-children-suffering-rickets.html>.

(14) "Does your child get enough vitamin D?" *Webmd*. Ed. Dr. Rob Hick. Boots, Nov. 2014. Web. 9 Apr. 2015. <http://www.webmd.boots.com/children/guide/child-vitamin-d>.

(15) Schatzkin, Arthur, et al. "Lack of effect of a low-fat, high-fiber diet on the recurrence of colorectal adenomas." *New England Journal of Medicine* 342.16 (2000): 1149-1155.

(16) Ho, Kok-Sun, et al. "Stopping or reducing dietary fiber intake reduces constipation and its associated symptoms." *World Journal of Gastroenterology* 18.33 (2012): 4593.

(17) Suez, Jotham, et al. "Artificial Sweeteners Induce Glucose Intolerance by Altering the Gut Microbiota." *Obstetrical & Gynecological Survey* 70.1 (2015): 31-32.

### Chapter Nine

(1) Mendes, Elizabeth. "Americans Spend $151 a Week on Food; the High-Income, $180." *GALLUP*. N.p., Aug. 2012. Web. 9 Apr. 2015. <http://www.gallup.com/poll/156416/americans-spend-151-week-food-high-income-180.aspx>.

(2) Rao, Mayuree, et al. "Do healthier foods and diet patterns cost more than less healthy options? A systematic review and meta-analysis." *BMJ* 3.12 (2013): e004277.

(3) Matheny, Keith. "Study: Diabetes drug affecting fish in Lake Michigan." *Detroit Free Press* 15 Jan. 2015. Web. 9 Apr. 2015. <http://www.freep.com/story/news/local/michigan/2015/01/13/metformin-diabetes-drug-pollution-lake-michigan/21734507/>.

(4) "Gym Membership Statistics." *Statistic Brain*. N.p., 13 July 2013. Web. 9 Apr. 2015. <http://www.statisticbrain.com/gym-membership-statistics/>.

(5) "Nearly half of adults feel stressed every day or every few days." *Mental Health Foundation*. Ed. Andrew McCulloch. N.p., 8 Jan. 2013. Web. 9 Apr. 2015. <http://www.mentalhealth.org.uk/our-news/news-archive/2013-news-archive/130108-stress/>.

(6) Cappuccio, Francesco P., et al. "Meta-analysis of short sleep duration and obesity in children and adults." *Sleep* 31.5 (2008): 619.

(7) Barat, Ishay, Frederik Andreasen, and Else Marie Skjøde Damsgaard. "The consumption of drugs by 75-year-old individuals living in their own homes." *European Journal of Clinical Pharmacology* 56.6-7 (2000): 501-509.

(8) "How Toxic Are Your Household Cleaning Supplies?" *Appetite for Change*. N.p., n.d. Web. 9 Apr. 2015. <https://www.organicconsumers.org/news/how-toxic-are-your-household-cleaning-supplies>.

(9) Russell, June. "Chemical Sensitivities and Perfume." *June Russell's Health Facts*. N.p., 28 Apr. 2003. Web. 9 Apr. 2015. <http://www.jrussellshealth.org/chemsensperf.html>.

(10) Halken, Melanie. *Forbes*. N.p., 3 Dec. 2012. Web. 9 Apr. 2015. <http://www.forbes.com/sites/melaniehaiken/2012/03/12/dangerous-beauty-top-5-contaminated-beauty-products/2/>.

## Chapter Ten

(1) Nordqvist, Christian. *MNT Knowledge Center.* N.p., Mar. 2009. Web. 9 Apr. 2015. <http://www.medicalnewstoday.com/info/addiction/>.

*(2)* de Matos Feijó, Fernanda, et al. "Saccharin and aspartame, compared with sucrose, induce greater weight gain in adult Wistar rats, at similar total caloric intake levels." *Appetite* 60 (2013): 203-207.


## Chapter Twelve

(1) Freston, Kathy. "13 Breathtaking Effects of Cutting Back on Meat." *AlterNet.* N.p., 21 Apr. 2009. Web. 9 Apr. 2015. <http://www.alternet.org/story/137737/13_breathtaking_effects_of_cutting_back_on_meat>.

(2) Chibuzor, Michael. "Top Weight Loss Pills for Women That Work." *Fitness Expert Awards.* N.p., 3 Sept. 2014. Web. 9 Apr. 2015. <http://fitnessexpertawards.com/weight-loss-pills-for-women-that-work/>.

(3) Atallah, Renée, et al. "Long-Term Effects of 4 Popular Diets on Weight Loss and Cardiovascular Risk Factors - a Systematic Review of Randomized Controlled Trials." *Circulation: Cardiovascular Quality and Outcomes* 7.6 (2014): 815-827.

(4) Fao, W. F. P. "IFAD (2012) The State of Food Insecurity in the World 2012: Economic growth is necessary but not sufficient to accelerate reduction of hunger and malnutrition." FAO, Rome (2014).

(5) Gimenez, Eric H. "We Already Grow Enough Food for 10 Billion People -- and Still Can't End Hunger." *Huffpost Taste.* N.p., 5 Feb. 2012. Web. 9 Apr. 2015. <http://www.huffingtonpost.com/eric-holt-gimenez/world-hunger_b_1463429.html>.

(6) Guisinger PhD, Shan. "Dangers of Dieting a Body Adapted to Famine." *F.E.A.S.T.* N.p., Mar. 2012. Web. 9 Apr. 2015. <http://temp.feast-ed.org/Resources/ArticlesforFEAST/DangersofDietingaBodyAdaptedtoFamine.aspx>.


## Chapter Thirteen

(1) Collis, Helen. "Stress and anxiety are the most common reasons for sick leave - and men are more likely to be off longer than women." *MailOnline.* N.p., 27 June 2013. Web. 9 Apr. 2015. <http://www.dailymail.co.uk/health/article-2349574/Stress-anxiety-common-reasons-sick-leave--men-likely-longer-women.html>.

(2) Keller, Abiola, et al. "Does the perception that stress affects health matter? The association with health and mortality." *Health Psychology* 31.5 (2012): 677.


## Chapter Fourteen

(1) Nilsson, Robert. "Pictures of the brain's activity during Yoga Nidra." *Bindu Magazine.* N.p., 27 July 201313. Web. 9 Apr. 2015. <http://www.yogameditation.com/Articles/Issues-of-Bindu/Bindu-11/Pictures-of-the-brain-s-activity-during-Yoga-Nidra>.

### Chapter Sixteen

(1) Church, Dawson. "Clinical EFT as an evidence-based practice for the treatment of psychological and physiological conditions." *Psychology* 4.08 (2013): 645.

(2) Ortner, Nick. "Chronic stress is killing you! (And how EFT can change the whole story)." *The Tapping Solution*. N.p., n.d. Web. 9 Apr. 2015. <http://www.thetappingsolution.com/blog/chronic-stress-killing-eft-can-change-whole-story/>.


### Chapter Seventeen

(1) "Health, Addictions and Type." *The Enneagram Institute*. N.p., n.d. Web. 9 Apr. 2015. <http://www.enneagraminstitute.com/addictivepersonality.asp#.VSbmy0ZYKnd>.


### Chapter Eighteen

(1) Perlmutter, David. *Grain brain: the surprising truth about wheat, carbs, and sugar - your brain's silent killers.* N.p. Yellow Kite, 2014.

(2) Lipman, Dr. Frank. "No More MSG: The Food Additive You Should Learn Live Without." *Dr. Frank Lipman - THE VOICE OF SUSTAINABLE WELLNESS*. N.p., Mar. 2012. Web. 10 Apr. 2015. <http://www.drfranklipman.com/no-more-msg-the-dangerous-food-additive-you-must-live-without/>.

(3) Adams, Mike, narr. "Blueberries faked in cereals, muffins." Health Ranger, 2011. Web. 10 Apr. 2015. <http://tv.naturalnews.com/v.asp?v=7EC06D27B1A945BE85E7DA8483025962>.

(4) Wild, Sarah, et al. "Global prevalence of diabetes estimates for the year 2000 and projections for 2030." *Diabetes Care* 27.5 (2004): 1047-1053.

(5) "American Diabetes Association Releases New Research Estimating Annual Cost of Diabetes at $245 billion - See more at: http://www.diabetes.org/newsroom/press-releases/2013/annual-costs-of-diabetes-2013." *American Diabetes Association*. N.p., Mar. 2013. Web. 10 Apr. 2015. <http://www.diabetes.org/newsroom/press-releases/2013/annual-costs-of-diabetes-2013.html>.

(6) Mercola, Dr. Joseph. "Why Coke Is a Joke - New Ad Campaign Defends Aspartame." *Mercola.com*. N.p., 28 Aug. 2013. Web. 10 Apr. 2015. <http://articles.mercola.com/sites/articles/archive/2013/08/28/soda-aspartame.aspx>.

(7) Mercola, Dr. Joseph. "This Sweetener Is Far Worse Than High Fructose Corn Syrup." *http://www.huffingtonpost.com*. N.p., 15 June 2010. Web. 10 Apr. 2015. <http://www.huffingtonpost.com/dr-mercola/agave-this-sweetener-is-f_b_537936.html>.

(8) Leech, Joe. "Truvia: Good or Bad." Authority Nutrition. N.p., n.d. Web. 28 Apr. 2015. <http://authoritynutrition.com/truvia-good-or-bad/>.

(9) "Air pollution from farming: preventing and minimising." *www.gov.uk*. N.p., Aug. 2012. Web. 10 Apr. 2015. <https://www.gov.uk/reducing-air-pollution-on-farms>.

(10)"Pollution from Giant Livestock Farms Threatens Public Health." *www.nrdc.org*. N.p., Feb. 2013. Web. 10 Apr. 2015. <http://www.nrdc.org/water/pollution/nspills.asp>.

(11)"Meat and the Environment." *www.thenazareneway.com*. The Nazarene Way of Essenic Studies, n.d. Web. 10 Apr. 2015. <http://www.thenazareneway.com/vegetarian/meat_and_the_environment.htm>.

(12) Ferlay, J., et al. "Cancer incidence and mortality patterns in Europe: estimates for 40 countries in 2012." *European Journal of Cancer* 49.6 (2013): 1374-1403.

(13) Hicks, Cherrill. "Give up dairy products to beat cancer." *The Telegraph* June 2014. Web. 10 Apr. 2015. <http://www.telegraph.co.uk/foodanddrink/healthyeating/10868428/Give-up-dairy-products-to-beat-cancer.html>.

(14) Wark, Chris. *www.chrisbeatcancer.com*. N.p., n.d. Web. 10 Apr. 2015. <http://www.chrisbeatcancer.com/>.

### Chapter Twenty

(1) Mercola, Dr. Joseph. ""Could Candida Be Sabotaging Your Health?" *www.mercola.com*. N.p., n.d. Web. 10 Apr. 2015. <http://mercola.fileburst.com/PDF/Candida-Special-Report.pdf>.

(2) Doheny, Kathleen. "Drugs in Our Drinking Water?" *www.webmd.com*. Ed. Louisa Chang MD. N.p., Mar. 2008. Web. 10 Apr. 2015. <http://www.webmd.com/a-to-z-guides/features/drugs-in-our-drinking-water>.

# About the Author

Chinmayi Dore was born in Northampton and grew up in Rugby, UK. She left a banking career in 2007, at the age of 41 to pursue a desire to help others - physically, mentally and spiritually, committing herself to an intense period of learning and retraining in yoga and holistic therapies.

She had appreciated the benefits yoga and traditional medicine can bring to modern life for many years before deciding to learn how to pass them on to others. Whilst now a practising therapist, yoga, meditation and shamanistic teacher, she believes that continuous learning is essential in this ever-changing world and necessary as the whole planet becomes more aware of what holistic, complementary medicine has to offer.

Chinmayi successfully completed 200 hours of yoga teacher training with the Yoga Alliance at the Yandara Yoga Institute in Mexico and 500 hours with the Yoga Alliance at the Anand Prakash Ashram near Rishikesh in India. On her graduation in India, she was given her spiritual name - Chinmayi (meaning 'bestower of bliss'), by her lifetime teacher Yogrishi Vishvketu. She has travelled extensively through India practising with many different teachers and styles wanting to bring a little more of the spiritual and scientific essences of the practice back to the West through her classes and training. She continues to do this with her online offering - YogaMAGIC!

Her trip to Peru in 2011 introduced her to shamanic healing where she realised that the philosophies and principles of shamanism and yoga could actually sit very well together. Hence her teaching of Shamanic Yoga began. Chinmayi occasionally runs Shamanic Yoga workshops and teacher training courses. She continued her studies with the Shamanka School of Shamanism where a 2-year course of learning and practice afforded a Master Practitioner Certificate. Chinmayi is a Yoga Alliance experienced yoga teacher (EYT500). In addition, she holds a recognised Anatomy and Physiology qualification (level 3-distinction) with ITEC.

Chinmayi is also qualified to diploma/practitioner level for the following complementary therapies:-

Nutritional Guidance, Holistic Massage, Aromatherapy, Indian Head Massage, Thai massage, Reiki I, II and Masters, Hot Stone Therapy, Reflexology, Seated Acupressure Massage, Natural Facelift Massage, Advanced Massage Diploma, Deep Tissue Massage, Ear Candling, Hot Stone Reflexology, Manual Lymphatic Drainage Massage, Emotional Freedom Technique (EFT or Tapping).

Chinmayi now lives in the mountains of Granada in Spain with her husband Myron, where they occasionally run courses, workshops and retreats in many of the techniques for which Chinmayi is qualified. Visit www.chinmayimagic.com for updates and more information.

# Resources

### *Chapter Three* - Journaling for Joy

*The Artist's Way* - Julia Cameron – ISBN-13: 978-0330343589
Julia has also written a workbook, a starter kit and other books around creativity.

### *Chapter Four* - MeditationMAGIC!

**The Yoga Sutras** - recommended texts:

*The Yoga Sutras of Patanjali* - Sri Swami Satchidananda – ISBN-13: 978-1938477072
*Four Chapters on Freedom* - Swami Satyananda Saraswati – ISBN-13: 978-8185787183

**Meditation CDs**
*MeditationMAGIC! - The Collection* can be ordered from www.chinmayimagic.com.

**YouTube**
*MeditationMAGIC! - Exercises for sitting magically - Part 1*
   https://www.youtube.com/watch?v=FR9wV9cL1bY

*MeditationMAGIC! - Poses for sitting magically - Part 2*
   https://www.youtube.com/watch?v=Ux55QZimFnk

### *Chapter Five* - Support or Solitude?

Overeaters Anonymous 12-step recovery program - http://www.oa.org

### *Chapter Seven* - Food Facts

**Nutrition Knowledge**

*The Optimum Nutrition Bible* - Patrick Holford – ISBN-13: 978-0749925529

*Crazy Sexy Diet: Eat Your Veggies, Ignite Your Spark, And Live Like You Mean It!* - Kris Carr - ISBN-13: 978-1599218014

*Hungry for Change: Ditch the Diets, Conquer the Cravings, and Eat Your Way to Lifelong Health* - James Colquhoun - ISBN-13: 978-0062220868

'Eat Fat to Lose Fat' - Dr. Mary Enig and Sally Fallon at http://www.eatfatlosefat.com/index.php have some interesting facts about coconut oil.

'Nuts and your heart: Eating nuts for heart health' - Mayo Clinic http://www.mayoclinic.org/diseases-conditions/heart-disease/in-depth/nuts/art-20046635

*The Straight Dope on Cholesterol* - Dr. Peter Attia https://www.youtube.com/watch?v=dAWdHYSrh7M

'How too much omega-6 and not enough omega-3 is making us sick' - http://chriskresser.com/how-too-much-omega-6-and-not-enough-omega-3-is-making-us-sick

Vitamins and Minerals - http://www.cabrillo.edu/~sreddy/DH162B/Chapter%2012%20-%20Pharm.pdf

*Vitamins & Minerals - an Overview* - Nancy O'Sullivan - https://www.youtube.com/watch?v=DJ_NN2WdJBc#t=341

*Dark Deception* - Dr. Joseph Mercola - www.mercola.com

Minerals Chart - Dr. Decuypere  http://www.health-alternatives.com/minerals-nutrition-chart.html

'Better Together - combining nutrients for health' - Mathew Kadey https://experiencelife.com/article/better-together/

'What Is So Menacing About Fiber?' - Dr. Konstantin Monastyrsky - https://www.youtube.com/watch?v=WQaBG1q2oEl#t=66


**N-eat Nineteen**

*An Apple a Day - Union of Concerned Scientists* - https://www.youtube.com/watch?v=4Fxm3h8l90l

Apple - more at - http://www.besthealthmag.ca/best-eats/nutrition/15-health-benefits-of-eating-apples#ilvEU8gBmrVpvxUA.97

Lemon - more at - http://www.lifehack.org/articles/lifestyle/11-benefits-lemon-water-you-didnt-know-about.html

Berries - more at - http://www.everydayhealth.com/diet-nutrition-pictures/amazing-health-benefits-of-berries.aspx#10

Papaya - parasite cleanse - http://superfoodprofiles.com/papaya-seeds-parasites

Coconut - health benefits - http://authoritynutrition.com/top-10-evidence-based-health-benefits-of-coconut-oil/

Greens - chlorophyll - http://raw-food-diet-inspiration.com/chlorophyll-benefit.html/

Celery - http://www.whfoods.com/genpage.php?tname=foodspice&dbid=14#healthbenefits

Potatoes - http://www.medicalnewstoday.com/articles/280579.php

Buckwheat - http://www.whfoods.com/genpage.php?tname=foodspice&dbid=11

Quinoa - http://www.mindbodygreen.com/0-4994/7-Benefits-of-Quinoa-The-Supergrain-of-the-Future.html

Lentils - http://www.care2.com/greenliving/9-reasons-to-love-lentils-the-mightly-little-powerfood.html/3

Seeds - http://www.cookinglight.com/eating-smart/nutrition-101/seed-nutrition

Nuts - http://www.bbcgoodfood.com/howto/guide/health-benefits-nuts

Eggs - http://www.care2.com/causes/how-to-be-an-ethical-egg-eater.html

Cinnamon - http://cinnamonvogue.com/cinnamoncommonuses.html

Garlic - http://www.garlic-central.com/garlic-101.html

Ginger - http://foodmatters.tv/articles-1/10-healing-benefits-of-ginger

Turmeric - http://umm.edu/health/medical/altmed/herb/turmeric

Seaweed - http://www.justseaweed.com/sea-veg


## Vegetarianism and Protein Needs

The Vegetarian Guide - www.michaelbluejay.com/veg - why, myths, health, environment, facts and figures and a very useful tool for estimating how much protein you need.

*Perfectly Contented Meat-Eater's Guide to Vegetarianism* - Mark Warren Reinhardt. A light-hearted look at vegetarianism for the meat-eater - ISBN-13: 978-0826410825


## *Chapter Eight -* YogaMAGIC!

For the FREE video for the yoga sequence in this chapter go to Yoga Magic Book Instruction. Enter password BeginYogin which includes instruction on all of the practice recommended:

Tadasana, Sun Breath, Standing Twisting, Standing Side Bending, Chair Breathing, Staff Pose and Corpse Pose

For the additional FREE video, an hour-long beginner's class. Go to BodyMAGIC! Yoga.


## *Chapter Nine -* Nature Calls

### Natural Food
'Harmful Chemicals in the Meat you Eat'
http://www.streetdirectory.com/food_editorials/cooking/meat_recipes/harmful_chemicals_in_the_meat_you_eat.html

### Natural Exercise
Sustrans (Sustainable Transport) - http://www.sustrans.org.uk

### Natural energy
Connecting with and cleansing your energy field. Look out for these Instructional videos coming soon!

Chinmayi's YouTube Channel
ShamanicMAGIC! - Sami Chakuay
PranayamaMAGIC! - The Yogic Breath
PranayamaMAGIC! - The Lion's Breath
PranayamaMAGIC! - Conscious Deep Breathing
PranayamaMAGIC! - Abdominal Breathing

## Natural Water

'Looking after Water in your Home' -
https://dl.dropboxusercontent.com/u/299993612/Publications/Reports/Customers/lookingafterwater.pdf

'Why I Oppose Fluoridation of Public Drinking Water' - Anne Marie Helmenstine, PhD.
http://chemistry.about.com/od/chemistryarticles/a/aa090704a.htm

## Natural Healing

Facebook page - **Food Facts and Fallacies, Myths and Magic** has regular posts of useful information about the magical properties of food.

'Eat Your Medicine: Food as Pharmacology' - Dr. Mark Hyman http://drhyman.com/blog/2011/10/14/eat-your-medicine-food-as-pharmacology/

'23 People That Lived to 100 Spill Their Secrets of Longevity'
http://modernhealthmonk.com/23-secrets-of-longevity/

## Natural Cleaning

Wholefoods, cleaning products, essential oils, and personal hygiene resources:

https://www.buywholefoodsonline.co.uk- delivers worldwide
http://www.ecostoreusa.com - for USA readers

'Toxic Chemicals and Household Cleaners' - http://www.health-report.co.uk/toxic_household_chemicals.htm

'Homemade and Natural Cleaning Products' - Sarah Aguirre
- http://housekeeping.about.com/od/environment/a/Homemade-And-Natural-Cleaning-Products.htm

List of the More Widely Known Dangerous Ingredients in Body & Food Products - Pure Zing -
http://www.purezing.com/living/toxins/living_toxins_dangerousingredients.html

## Natural Base Preparations and Essential Oils (some organic):

USA - Uncle Harry's Natural Products - http://www.uncleharrys.com/
UK - Oils4Life Aromatherapy - http://www.oils4life.co.uk

## Organic Ready-Made Preparations:

UK - Holland and Barratt - Dr. Organic range - http://www.hollandandbarrett.com
UK - Green People - products for the whole family including vegan - http://www.greenpeople.co.uk

## *Chapter Eleven -* Intuitive Eating and Mindful Munching

### Food Mantras/Blessings

| | |
|---|---|
| *Brahma Panam, Brahma Havir* | The act of offering is Brahman. |
| *Brahma Agnau* | The offering itself is Brahman. |
| *Brahma Hutam* | The offering is done by Brahman in the |
| *Brahmeva Tena Gantavyam* | sacred fire which is Brahman. |
| *Brahma Karma Samadhi Na* | He alone attains Brahman, who, in all |
| *OM Shanti, Shanti, Shanti* | actions, is fully absorbed in Brahman. |

*"For each new morning with its light, for rest and shelter of the night, for health and food, for love and friends, for everything Thy goodness sends"*
*~ Ralph Waldo Emerson*

### *Chapter Fifteen* - Traditional Medicine

I have hundreds of books on different therapies. I have chosen one from many very useful books on each subject. Please explore further if you feel a leaning towards one or more of the therapies covered.

**General**
*Mind Over Medicine* - Lissa Rankin – ISBN-13: 978-1848509603

www.naturalnews.com - Natural Cures for Common Diseases and Development

www.chrisbeatcancer.com/ - when Chris Wark was diagnosed with stage 3 colon cancer at age 26, doctors told him that he was going to need nine to twelve months of chemotherapy following surgery. He found his health again and has an interesting theory about why we get cancer.

**Yoga Therapy**
*Yoga as Medicine: The Yogic Prescription for Health and Healing* - Timothy McCall - ISBN-13: 978-0553384062

**Aromatherapy**
*The Fragrant Pharmacy* - Valerie Ann Worwood - ISBN-13: 978-0553403978

### *Chapter Eighteen* - The Seven Seldom Sins

*Grain Brain* - Dr. David Perlmutter - ISBN-13: 978-1444971907

### *Chapter Twenty* - Gremlins in Your Gut

Shankhaprakshalana - ChinmayiMAGIC! - http://www.relaxologies.co.uk/shankhaprakshalana.html

'Could Candida be Sabotaging your Health?' - Dr. Mercola (free report)
http://www.mercola.com/downloads/bonus/candida-yeast/default.htm

'The Yeast Connection' - Dr. Crook
http://www.yeastconnection.com/yeast.html#questionaire
and book *The Yeast Connection*.

'How to Use Papaya Seeds for Parasites'
http://superfoodprofiles.com/papaya-seeds-parasites

### *Chapter Twenty-Three* - Energy and the Chakras

A really useful resource is a book and meditation CD in the back of Doreen Virtue's *Chakra Clearing: Awakening Your Spiritual Power to Know and Heal* - ISBN-13: 978-1561705665

*The Hidden Messages in Water* - Masaru Emoto - ISBN-13: 978-1416522195

*Anatomy of the Spirit: The Seven Stages of Power and Healing* - Caroline Myss – ISBN-13: 978-0553505276

If you want to deepen these practices further and explore this subject more - *The Chakras in Shamanic Practice: Eight Stages of Healing and Transformation* - Susan J. Wright is a really deep insight into how working with the chakras can make huge transformations in one's life, with practical exercises and tasks for you to work with.

### *Chapter Twenty-Four* - Emergency MAGIC!

Information on Bach Emotional Overeating Kit - flower essences for overeating
http://www.bachfloweressences.co.uk/categories/Bach-Emotional-Eating-Kit/